D1125115

ENCYCLOPEDIA
OF
COUNSELING
MASTER REVIEW AND
TUTORIAL

Howard Rosenthal, Ed.D.

ACCELERATED DEVELOPMENT
A member of the Taylor & Francis Group

ENCYCLOPEDIA OF COUNSELING
Master Review and Tutorial

Technical Development: Tanya Benn
                         Cynthia Long
                         Marguerite Mader
                         Shaeney Pigman
                         Sheila Sheward

Library of Congress Cataloging-in-Publication Data

Rosenthal, Howard, 1952-
    Encyclopedia of counseling : master review and tutorial / Howard
Rosenthal.
        p. cm.
    Includes bibliographical references and index.
    ISBN 1-55959-041-6
    1. Counseling--Examinations, questions, etc. 2. Counseling-
-Examinations--Study guides. I. Title
BF637.C6R6734   1993   93-2805
158'.3'076--dc20   CIP

LCN: 93-2805

ISBN: 1-55959-041-6

Order additional copies from

ACCELERATED/DEVELOPMENT
A member of the Taylor & Francis Group
7625 Empire Drive
Florence, KY 41042
1-800-634-7064

ACKNOWLEDGEMENTS

It's here! The ultimate weapon against test anxiety—a user-friendly study guide that has no archetype. The ideas, information, and the style are my own, though it would be impossible to complete a complex work such as this on a solo basis. I would therefore be remiss, if I did not acknowledge the tremendous assistance afforded by others.

First, hats off to my wife, Patricia, for her continued support. After all, trying to navigate through a house inundated with behavioral science books piled knee high isn't exactly most people's idea of a good time!

Next, I must mention the hard work and superb editing suggestions of Jennifer Grotpeter, Michael Slavkin, Michael Heil, S. Amelia Goodwin, Melanie Franklin, and Robin Simons. And my brother, Wayne Rosenthal, who fancies the challenge of a complex statistical problem.

Then, of course, there's Carolyn Duncan, who literally put her reputation (as well as her professional career) on the line by being the first person to test the merits of this book on an actual state licensing exam. She passed, I might add, and with more than flying colors.

Peggy Grotpeter's countless hours of diligent work stand out second to none and resulted in the finest, most comprehensive and easy-to-use study guide index available.

Special thanks go to Dr. Arthur C. Myers for his assistance in the area of psychological testing.

Last, credit certainly goes out to Dr. Joseph Hollis and his fine staff at Accelerated Development Publishers, who continue to set the pace for materials in the field of counseling psychology.

PREFACE

The question is often asked of me, What does the successful counselor know that the unsuccessful practitioner doesn't? The answer is, **Plenty!** Here is a book which can teach you, **Plenty!**

Using a generous supply of 900 questions, teamed up with highly detailed answers, this one of a kind tutorial text reads like a novel, but imparts information like a post-graduate seminar.

I personally don't believe that education in the social sciences needs to be dry, dull, or boring, and this book goes on to prove it.

Who can benefit from this book? Perhaps a better question would be, Who couldn't benefit from this book?

Initially, my intent was merely to create the ultimate study guide for counselors preparing for state licensure or national board certification exams. But as I shared portions of my manuscript with students and professionals I realized that this book was going well beyond the scope of any ordinary study guide.

When I completed the manuscript, it was after all, in reality, an intricate string of carefully worded questions and answers linked to form an *Encyclopedia of Counseling.* In this book you will discover a veritable gold mine of information. Here you will find a reference that covers it all from A, as in "alloplastic," to Z, as in the "Zeigarnik effect." If a concept or theorist in any way, shape, or form pertains to counseling or psychotherapy, there's one heck of a good chance that you'll find it within these pages. But don't take my word for it; simply flip through the pages and convince yourself.

Feedback further emphasized the encyclopedic nature of this work. Psychologists and social workers who perused the manuscript insisted that my materials were useful in terms of helping them prepare for licensure.

Mental health educators suggested that my book would be the perfect adjunct text for their classes.

A psychiatric nurse told me my information, "filled the gaps" in her education. And a graduate student wanted to know where my book was when she had to struggle through her research methodology course!

A group therapist working in a residential setting said the book gave her a myriad of creative ideas for curbing burnout and pumping new life into her group therapy sessions.

Simply put, if you are a student, a teacher, an interventionist in search of licensure or certification, or a therapeutic practitioner in the field of mental health, then this book will make you a better, more knowledgeable professional.

WHY THIS BOOK SUCCESSFULLY PREPARES YOU FOR STATE LICENSING, CERTIFICATION, COURSE WORK, OR SUCCESSFUL COUNSELING

- Tutorial format contains 900 questions and answers to expand your knowledge.

- Plenty of repetition promotes learning even if you have been out of school for an extended period of time.

- Key concepts are explained in several different ways.

- Covers all major areas commonly found on counselor state licensing and certification exams . . . highly recommended for oral and written boards.

- Chocked full of memory devices and special hints for tackling tough exam questions you won't find elsewhere.

- Pictorial representations of key concepts help reduce study time.

- Easy to use index conveniently lists topics by question number.

- Lively, folksy, conversational style promotes confidence, reduces test anxiety and actually makes studying enjoyable.

- Text is specifically designed for the busy professional or student who must make maximum use of study time.

- The perfect companion to Accelerated Development's "Studying for Licensure" audio study guide program and other fine references.

So, need I ask . . .

WHO ELSE WANTS TO SAY, "I PASSED!"

TABLE OF CONTENTS

ACKNOWLEDGEMENTS iii

PREFACE v

LIST OF FIGURES xi

1   STUDY GUIDES: MY OWN HUMBLE BEGINNINGS 1

   Audio Doctor to the Rescue *5*
   Why this New Breed of Encyclopedia Can Benefit
      All Mental Health Professionals *9*

2   HOW TO END EXAM WORRIES 11

   What Makes this Master Review and Tutorial
      Different? *13*
   How to Improve Your Memory in One Evening......................*15*
   A Passing Look at Questions and Answers
      with Some Good News for Perfectionists *17*

3   HUMAN GROWTH AND DEVELOPMENT 33

4   SOCIAL AND CULTURAL FOUNDATIONS 85

5   HELPING RELATIONSHIPS 137

6   THEORIES OF COUNSELING 189

7   GROUPS 241

8   LIFE-STYLE AND CAREER DEVELOPMENT 293

9   APPRAISAL 341

10   RESEARCH AND EVALUATION **385**

11   PROFESSIONAL ORIENTATION **445**

12   GRAPHICAL REPRESENTATIONS **501**

13   RESOURCES **509**

    Statistical Tests Used in Counseling Research *510*
    Parametric Tests *510*
    Nonparametric Tests *511*
    Major Psychoeducational Diagnostic Tools *512*
    Sources for Obtaining Ethical Guidelines *517*

INDEX **519**

ABOUT THE AUTHOR **539**

LIST OF FIGURES

12.1 Bell-shaped curve and related
statistical information 502

12.2 Bimodal curve 503

12.3 Flatter curve 503

12.4 Leptokurtic distribution 504

12.5 Positively skewed distribution 504

12.6 Negatively skewed distribution 505

12.7 Bar graph or histogram 505

12.8 Double-barred histogram 506

12.9 Scattergram of a perfect linear
positive correlation 506

12.10 Scattergram of a perfect linear
negative correlation 507

12.11 Scattergram showing a lack of relationship 507

12.12 Holland's hexagon model 508

12.13 Schematic of Berne's transactional analysis..................508

CHAPTER 1

STUDY GUIDES: MY OWN HUMBLE BEGINNINGS

It sounded like a barking dog, only a heck of a lot louder, though I certainly knew they didn't allow animals in the halls. After all, this was an institution for higher learning.

As I rounded the corner I was no longer perplexed. The ruckus emanated from one Dr. Jack Furbis, head of the illustrious history department. He was red as a beet, perhaps even a tad purple as I watched him read a fellow student the riot act. As he displayed his true colors I could see why the greater part of the student body referred to him as Dr. Vegetable Head.

"Listen to me; those study guides are worthless . . . and . . . and, they are cheating. Yes, they're trash, pure trash mister. If I had my way it would be illegal for the bookstore to sell that junk."

Two things ran through my mind. The first was that I thanked my lucky stars that I didn't have Doc Vegetable Head for a course. The second was that my curiosity about these so-called study guides was piqued. I wanted to find out just exactly what those devilish treatises contained.

The woman who ran the bookstore knew exactly where I could find the works responsible for Doc Furbis's elevated blood pressure. They were conveniently located in the section designated "Study Guides."

Seemingly, these purveyors of grade cards made in heaven covered every conceivable subject. Some analyzed short stories and novels. Others explained how to pass the GRE (Graduate Record Examination) or a civil service test to secure employment at the post office. Another described how to pass an exam in order to receive advance placement in college biology.

All I could say to myself was: "Thanks for the find, Dr. Furbis. These study guides are terrific." I walked away with no less than four on that prophetic day—one for statistics, one for American History, and a couple of others pertaining to psychology and sociology.

For the next 18 years I doubt whether I came within shouting distance of a bonafide study guide; but then it happened. As part of my work in supervising some students for state counselor licensure I felt that in addition to providing guidance on their cases it was my moral duty as their so-called licensing supervisor to help them prepare for the written exam that would be staring them square in the face when they finished their 3000 hours of supervision with yours truly.

To be sure the rumors were already starting to fly, and believe me, they were anything but pleasant.

"It's a bear . . . I've never seen anything like it . . . the hardest test I ever took in my life."

"We never covered any of that stuff in my counseling courses, that's for sure."

"Honestly, I never heard of half the terms on the test; I have no idea how I passed it."

One counselor who was treating clients with anxiety disorders told me she was beginning to experience panic attacks herself and was having nightmares based on rumors and the anticipation of actually having to take the monster; excuse me, I mean the test!

The test responsible for the horrendous intimidation was the NCE aka the National Counselor Examination which was and is the test used to evaluate counselors for the status of NCC, or National Certified Counselor. The National Counselor Examination (NCE) and the National Certified Counselor (NCC) were creations of the National Board for Certified Counselors (NBCC). One thing you discover in a hurry when you investigate counselor licensure and certification requirements is that the field is inundated with alphabet soup acronyms.

The interesting thing is that it is unethical for persons who have taken the exam to reveal any of the questions on the test. The way I figure it, the NBCC can breathe easy knowing that, at least in my case, the individuals I conversed with were so intimidated by the exam that it could have been written in a foreign language. In case I haven't made my point, allow me to be a bit more explicit: The examinees I spoke with were so threatened by the test that they couldn't even verbalize what they found so difficult; hence, they were in no danger whatsoever of revealing anything concrete! So much for the issue of test ethics violations.

Frankly, I was perplexed by the whole issue. For starters, I recalled that, much to my chagrin, I personally had taken the test. You see, when licensing came to my state, Missouri, I was grandfathered-in based on the fact that I had NCC status. I found out via the counselor licensing board that Missouri, like so many other states, did not have a licensing test and thus was using the NCE. I even discovered that in Missouri the examinee could kill two birds with one stone, if you will, by scoring high enough to secure NCC as well as state licensure. In other words, since the test was the NCE used to determine NCC status, you also could snare NCC.

My memory of the test was hardly a catastrophic one. Though I could remember truly struggling with a number of the questions, I was not mortified by them. True, I had several advantages. One was that I was doing some supervision of helpers and college teaching at the time. This might have meant that I was more familiar with a number of principles than your average everyday counselor on the street, agency or private practice. Another issue was that the test was supposedly evolving, which was most likely a very diplomatic way of saying that it was getting more difficult with each update or version! Moreover, the required score to put a license number after your John Hancock was creeping up. Thus, the bottom line was that although my experience with the test had not been a negative one, I realized that times change and I needed to dip into my resources for a little accurate empathy to help those who would need to tangle with the NCE or one of its derivatives. I say one of its derivatives inasmuch as many states are using the NCE as a licensing instrument. Those states that are not doing so will still look to the NCE for guidance. Therefore, even if your state does not use the NCE per se, there is a very good chance that your exam would be very similar to say the least.

Armed with this information I concluded that the answer to my supervisees' dilemma was just a bookstore away. I imagined that I'd zip over to the nearest bookseller, peruse the Study Guide section, and return with a text on the National Counselor Examination. I even rationalized that on the one in a million chance that Dr. Furbis was taking in the bestsellers list that day, he still wouldn't recognize me behind the extra dark sunglasses I made a point of wearing.

I had it all figured out. It was going to be easy—except for one minor snafu I hadn't counted on; namely, that the store didn't carry a book intended for LPC or NCC study. I was shocked. Since my glorious college days it seemed that the authors of these study guides had added nearly every title under the sun *except a book to help with counselor licensure and certification.* I was sure there was a mistake, yet the woman at the checkout counter assured me her faithful computer indicated that the store did not carry such a work. In disbelief I hit every major, minor, college, and university bookstore in our town (and believe me, there were plenty of them) without a success. I even offered to let them order it from out of town ("I don't mind the six-week wait," I told them) but was informed that I couldn't purchase a book that didn't exist. Tired and weary from having book dealers' doors slammed in my face I assumed a depressed posture and headed home empty-handed. I got in my car, fired it up, put the car in gear, and popped a tape in my cassette deck . . . yes I popped a tape in my cassette deck and a giant light labelled "insight" lit up in my head.

AUDIO DOCTOR
TO THE RESCUE

It has been said that genius is often right in front of your nose, but in this case it was tugging at my ear lobes. A number of years earlier when I had to tangle with oral and written boards for my doctorate I had recorded what I felt was key information onto cassette tapes. These cassettes then turned my home stereo, portable cassette player, boombox, and walkman into veritable teaching machines. Best of all, I used the tape player in my car in order to convert boring traffic jams into worthwhile learning experiences. To be sure, I was the only road warrior travelling Highway 40 west who was using stalled tractor trailer trucks as an excuse to learn that negative reinforcement was not the same thing as punishment.

A bit eccentric, perhaps, but I breezed through my orals and writtens. I thus geared up to produce some cassette tapes for my students. Yet there was one little problem—I had no idea what was on the test!

Since I was a National Certified Counselor myself, I picked up the phone and called NBCC to see if they could point me in the right direction. Sure enough, they did. Within minutes after terminating my telephone conversation I was ordering a copy of *HOW TO PREPARE: YOUR GUIDE TO THE NATIONAL COUNSELOR EXAMINATION.* Though this 30-page booklet, published in 1988 by NCC, explicitly states that the guide is not intended to enhance your performance on the exam, I would advise anyone taking the test to secure a copy. The booklet gives vital information regarding the nature and format of the exam. There is also an 80-question practice test replete with answers.

In my case, the work clarified the eight basic areas of the exam (more on that later) and gave me a fine bibliography that the authors refer to as "potential references."

I then returned to my local college bookstores (still hiding behind my extra dark shades, of course!) and began buying up every brand of study guide available in order to help students prepare for the GRE (Graduate Record Examination) in psychology. Using somewhat superficial logic, I assumed that there would be at least a moderate amount of overlap between the two disciplines (i.e., counseling and psychology). Sure the NCE was the big leagues, the test intended for those who already possessed a master's or a doctorate. Nevertheless, I hypothesized that many principles of behavior were relevant at all levels of education, though the post graduate version might be a tad more precise or complex than the explanation given to students who had only completed a bachelor's degree.

As I perused these guides there was something else I was trying to master, and that was the thinking process of the experts who put these type of tests together (the idea being that I could ultimately think like these folks). Needless to say, once I could ultimatley think like them I could make some very good educated guesses about what questions my supervisees might have to reckon with come NCE time.

As I studied the guides, I began to actually feel that I was beginning to think like these authors. It then occurred to me that perhaps something else was transpiring. That "something else" was that the repetitive nature of the questions which appeared in study guides a, b, and c were not necessarily indicative of the authors' respective cognitions. I began to see instead that the tendency for certain issues to appear again and again was most likely an indication that these were key points in the mind of almost any behavioral science scholar.

Thus, armed to the teeth with an arsenal of GRE study guides, NCE recommended textbooks, and a stack of books that represented my own 12-year stint in college, I headed for my trusty tape recorder.

Again, I took to the streets as I cruised over the highways and byways of America's heartland listening to myself babble on hour after hour. A trip to the office was no longer a trip to the office. Instead it became a lecture in Albert Ellis' Rational-Emotive Therapy, Jung's Analytic Psychology, or a few hints on distinguishing the statistical mean from the median or perhaps the mode.

While I was supporting my tape addiction, some of my students had enrolled in courses given by companies who marketed programs which were specifically intended to help students prepare for licensing or certification exams. From everything I heard and saw (i.e., the materials) the programs were doing a fine job. My only concerns were (a) the programs had pretty stiff price tags (e.g., one student I knew attended one which cost over $500) and (b) many of them required the future licensed counselor to travel to the city where the seminar was being held. The combined cost of the bill plus travel, plus room and board, added up to a fairly sizable chunk of change, not to mention the inconvenience. I spoke with a number of busy professionals who said they just couldn't fit such programs into their schedules. Others didn't want to break into their piggy banks.

I therefore continued to fine-tune my tapes, analyzing feedback I received from a number of individuals. My final product consisted of nearly nine hours of material. Four of the tapes consisted of vital information and lecture material geared specifically toward the eight areas of the exam. Two of the tapes contained an innovative 225 question review which was like a practice test. I say innovative because I used the questions to convey information. For example, I might say, "Perls is the father of Gestalt Therapy. Who is the father of the Person-Centered Approach?" Moreover, on most of the questions I chose to expand on the answer, thus providing the listener with information which could conceivably help the person answer a number of other questions on the actual exam.

Accelerated Development Publishers in Muncie, Indiana decided to market the finished product. Today the program can be purchased in part (i.e., the 275 Review Questions or the Vital Information lectures) or as a complete package at a very reasonable price. If you are interested in securing a copy—and by all means you should be—you can call Accelerated Development toll free at 1-800-222-1166.

Mission accomplished . . . well not quite. You see, about the same time my tapes went to the publisher my friendly college bookstore called to report that a miracle had taken place: They had several new books specifically intended to help counselors prepare for state licensing and certification exams.

I have little doubt that I was the first on my block to own and read these books. Quite frankly, I felt the books were well-written and very helpful.

Why this book then, you may ask? It's an excellent question, indeed. The first and foremost reason is that the above-referenced works as well as the preparation booklet by NBCC do not include explanations of the answers. Thus, the reader of such works may well pick the correct answer to a test question but may have answered it correctly for the wrong reason. This reminds me of something I once heard a prolific self-help writer comment on during a lecture. He stated that people would write him and tell him that they were helped tremendously by using the principles he outlined in his books. Unfortunately, when they went on to explain, it was obvious they were not following the advice set forth in his books, and they certainly weren't practicing anything that remotely resembled his self-improvement theories!

You've probably heard the story about the chemistry professor. First he puts a worm in a beaker of water and allows it to swim around. Next he places the worm in a beaker of alcohol and it disintegrates. The professor then turns to the class and asks the students to describe what they learned. "It's obvious," responds a student, "if you drink a lot of alcohol you'll never get worms."

And so I became a man with a mission—a mission to write a worm-free study guide. Now let's see what's in it for bookworms like yourself.

WHY THIS NEW BREED OF ENCYCLOPEDIA CAN BENEFIT ALL MENTAL HEALTH PROFESSIONALS

Now I must be honest with you and share the fact that there was another impetus for this book. From all reports, the tapes were a success. I began receiving calls and letters from across the country praising the merits of my audio study program. Many of the tape users began asking the same question, namely: "How can I get a copy of your book to go along with the tapes?"

Unfortunately, I had to tell them that there was no book. Listeners liked my folksy, conversational, and sometimes humorous tutorial teaching style on the tapes, and now they wanted to see it in print.

I knew the tape users were telling me the truth about the style. I had previously used this style successfully in an earlier book *(Not With My Life I Don't: Preventing Your Suicide and That of Others*, Accelerated Development Publishers, 1988).

As I began the monumental task of putting together this text, I kept adding more and more critical information until it became obvious that this work would go well beyond the boundaries of an ordinary study guide. I ultimately created a master review and tutorial, an *Encyclopedia of Counseling* if you will.

Certainly this book still will serve as a superb guide for counselors (or study groups) seeking state licensing or national board certification, but it certainly is not limited to this purpose.

As this text now stands, it also will assist psychologists, psychiatrists, social workers, crisis workers, pastoral counselors, psychiatric nurses, educators, guidance personnel, and any other mental health professional preparing for course work, oral or written boards, or licensing and certification.

It makes an ideal text to supplement advanced human services classes, graduate seminars, and practicum or internship experiences.

Moreover, you will discover that it neatly summarizes an amazing amount of key material. Hence, you'll find that it is the perfect refresher course if you have been out of school for an extended period of time.

Simply put: You don't need to be studying for licensure or certification to benefit from this book. **Here is a book that belongs on the shelf of every serious mental health professional's personal library.** Nevertheless, if you are worried about taking a test or exam of any sort, you can secure support merely by turning the page.

CHAPTER 2

HOW TO END
EXAM WORRIES

"I'm not a happy camper," remarked Jeff Nelson, a 43-year-old clinical director for a not-for-profit counseling center.

In an attempt to display my best accurate empathy I nodded affirmatively and reached over the counter and pulled a red gum ball from the gum ball machine. "Come on, have one, the red ones are the best, honest. These are the same ones we give the kids under ten and they swear by the red ones. Some say they're better than counseling, even play therapy, for curing depression."

"No thanks, I'm trying to quit. Besides, I'm hooked on the sugarless stuff now. Anyway, I was fine until I got sand kicked in my face."

"Sand," I said furrowing my brow. "You mean sand as in beaches, sand traps on golf courses and that sort of thing?"

"Oh I'm sure you've heard this one before. I'm sitting on the beach, minding my own business when this big, beefy type kicks sand in my face. He's big and hairy and goes by the name of NCE."

"And let me guess," I replied sarcastically, "the dude packs about 200 CACREP content area questions to help balloon up his deltoids and to peak his biceps up to the size of Mount Rushmore."

"Ah, so you know this guy. And um, you've heard this tale of woe before."

"Yes, of course, I've heard it . . . it's the Charles Atlas parable. But this is the counseling version where the bully wears his NCE/CACREP trunks . . . Look let's get to the point since you're not my client and I'm not getting paid to listen to this saga. How many points did you flunk the licensure test by?"

"One."

"You flunked the test by one point?"

"One measly point."

"How much did you study?"

"Hey, come on now. You know I got my doctorate from a powerful program. And I know all that stuff."

"Oh really. Who is the father of guidance?"

"Well um, it's Freud, I guess. Isn't it?"

"Sorry Charlie . . . I mean Jeff. Can you tell me the difference between a type I and a type II statistical error?"

"Say, I said I knew the material; I didn't say I was a statistical genius or anything."

"Yeah, I agree you needn't be a statistical genius to pass the state licensing exam, but you need to know that an ANOVA isn't a constellation of stars. Explain the alloplastic-autoplastic dilemma in cross-cultural counseling."

"Explain who?"

"Jeff look, I'm your friend, right? And you want me to be honest with you, right? Well, Jeff, you didn't study, and to be brutally frank you didn't deserve to pass the licensing exam. In fact, it's hard to believe you scored as high as you did. Did you get some extra points for spelling your name correctly or something?"

"I really didn't think I had to study. I thought I knew the material."

"Oh, you weren't alone, I heard that 39 out of 88 people who took the test with you failed."

"So let's cut the small talk, I'll take a set of your study guide tapes and um a couple of those gum balls . . . red, of course . . . hey you're not really going to use this dialogue in your new study guide book, are you?"

Yes Jeff, I decided to use the dialogue. The salient point is that most people who wish to snare LPC/NCC credentials will need to study for the test. It's nice to have a degree from an Ivy League school but it's no guarantee you will pass the NCE. I decided to include this story because it is not atypical—Jeff is not the only examinee who hypothesized that he knew the material.

When I talk with counselors who have signed up to take the NCE (or for that matter any other exam), I can't help thinking about the old adage that asserts that a little knowledge is a dangerous thing. Sure you've heard of Pavlov and maybe you even remember that his name is associated with classical conditioning. But can you discern a conditioned stimulus from an unconditioned response? And yes, you know what a counseling experiment is but can you ferret out the DV from the IV? Of course, you'll need to recall what DV and IV stand for. I could go on but I think the point is obvious: A little bit of knowledge is a dangerous thing because it may give you false confidence ergo you won't study ergo you may not pass your exam.

WHAT MAKES THIS MASTER REVIEW AND TUTORIAL DIFFERENT?

The answer: a lot of things. For one thing, it will give you 900 questions to grapple with. Unlike traditional study guides, however, many of the questions are "ringers" in the sense that they are purposely loaded with valuable information to help you successfully answer other questions on an exam. So, just as an example, I might say, "William Glasser is the father of Reality Therapy. Who is the father of Gestalt Therapy?" Thus, the questions themselves impart key information. Often, this will be information that will help you answer future questions that are a tad more difficult. This means that the most effective method of using this study guide is to begin with question number one and work through all of the questions in order without skipping any.

As you can see this is a lot different than many study guides. Many will begin with a practice test so you can assess your level of knowledge. This study guide is a new breed. It decidedly does not include a practice pretest or post-test. Instead, each question is intended to teach you key points and hence is a learning experience.

And as a bonus there is a wealth of repetition when explaining critical information. UNLIKE MANY SOURCES THIS TEXT WILL OFTEN NOT LIMIT ITSELF TO ONE DESCRIPTION. OFTEN FIVE OR SIX DIFFERENT DEFINITIONS OR EXPLANATIONS WILL BE PROVIDED IN REGARD TO "MUST KNOW" CONCEPTS. I'd rather have you accuse me of being redundant than miss a question due to a lack of understanding. If you use this book and/or my tapes and get sick of me telling you this or that, then you can safely assume that now you really know the material.

Now here is a factor I cannot overstate. To get the most out of this study guide you absolutely, positively must read the answers to each question. Here again, this could differ from other study guides you have utilized. I intentionally expand on many of the answers so that the information could conceivably help you answer several actual questions on an actual exam. When it is appropriate (and not obvious) I shall explain why the other three choices are incorrect and go on to explicate their relevance (or lack of it!) to the question at hand. Moreover, I have gone out of my way to make the material interesting by adding a little levity and even outright humor whenever possible. I'll tell you a little secret I learned from lecturing to over 80,000 people now on the topic of mental health—it's not what you say that grabs the audience, but rather the way you say it. In this book I have pulled out all the stops and used my vast lecturing experience to insure that you won't be recommending this book to your clients as sleep therapy!

You have my word as a gentleman, a scholar, and a fellow counselor that I have done everything in my power to keep the answers lively and chocked full of relevant information (a mighty difficult task, indeed). So just in case you still aren't certain you understand let me state forthrightly that you must read each and every answer if you want the maximum benefit from this study guide (yes, even when you answered the question correctly). I personally don't believe that counseling or counselor education needs to be dry, dull, or boring and the material herein reflects this position.

HOW TO IMPROVE YOUR MEMORY IN ONE EVENING

Another unique factor in this study guide is the use of mnemonic or so-called memory devices. For some people, some of the time, memory devices can make a remarkable difference. In fact, I have discovered that very often memory devices are so powerful that an individual can literally be taught to remember something in seconds which he or she has struggled with for years. Skeptical? Fine, then consider this example from my own life. For years, I couldn't remember whether the word that meant letterhead was stationery or stationary. Imagine the embarrassment of being armed to the teeth with 12 years of post high-school education, four college degrees and a full-fledged doctorate and yet my memos to my secretaries invariably used the word letterhead for fear I would use the wrong version of stationery. Incidentally, repeatedly looking the word up in the dictionary did not seem to help the situation. Then I discovered this highly effective, yet incredibly simple memory trick. The word is spelled with the suffix "ery" when referring to a letterhead and "ary" when describing a motionless or fixed state. The word letter (as in letterhead) has an "e" and so does stationery when it is used to describe writing materials. Hence, when you want stationery to mean a letterhead you use the version spelled "ery" since letter is spelled with an "e."

The trick is simply to associate the difficult-to-recall principle with something (or somethings) that you can easily recall. At times these associations may be very serious ones and at other times it may be easier to use one that seems foolish. The secret is to play around with associations to discover which ones work best for you.

Try this one on for size. Whose picture is on a five-dollar bill? If you know, that's wonderful; you certainly don't need a mnemonic device. If you don't know, why not consider this: A Lincoln is a large car and will hold approximately five people. I doubt whether you will ever forget it again. Each time I pull a five-spot out of my pocket now I mentally see those five people seated comfortably in a Lincoln. A Lincoln would hold more than one person (imagine a one-dollar bill), but it certainly would be mighty tough to squeeze 10 or 20 persons into the vehicle (imagine a 10- or 20-dollar bill).

Now let me zero in on an example from our own field. For a number of years now I've been mentioning Ivan Pavlov's famous classical conditioning experiment in the classes I teach. The problem is that come test time the material seems very complex. The students can't seem to remember whether the UCS is the bell, the meat, the dog's nickname or perhaps the name of the dog's ex-wife. (So what else is new, right?) Maybe some unusually honest reader can remember struggling with UCS, CS, CR, and UCR questions in the past, or worse yet is dreading the possibility that one could actually make its way into an oral or written board, or god forbid, the NCE. Well relax, I've got a few tricks up my sleeve and apparently they work.

You see the last several times I covered this material in my class I included a memory device. I told the class to remember that in the US we eat a lot of meat. Why? Because in Pavlov's landmark experiment the US, or UCS as it is sometimes written, is the meat.

Corny? You bet it is. Childish? Perhaps. But I must inform you that nobody—that means zip, zero, not a soul—has missed the UCS question since I've been teaching this memory association! This study guide, unlike any before it, includes a veritable treasure chest of memory goodies. When I created my audio study guide tapes I included some choice memory devices, however, this book will introduce you to an even greater number.

You'll discover two really neat things as you read my memory devices. The first is that even if you forget the memory device, you will usually remember the principle you wish to recall. You could forget that a Lincoln is a large car which holds approximately five people, yet you will in all probability remember that a five-dollar bill sports a shot of Lincoln's mug. The second factor you might notice is that you feel that my memory suggestion is too stupid, too complex, too irrelevant, or ironically, just too confusing to remember! Nevertheless, I'm willing to bet that very often my suggestion which is inappropriate for you will give you an idea for a memory device which does indeed make sense to you.

Now let us take a passing look at some questions and answers.

A PASSING LOOK AT
QUESTIONS AND ANSWERS
WITH SOME GOOD NEWS
FOR PERFECTIONISTS

QUESTION: Frankly I could care less about counselor licensing, cerification, or the NCE. I'm a clinical psychology major taking an advanced graduate course in psychotherapeutic strategies. Can your 900 questions and answers help me?

ANSWER: This may come as a shock to you, but I've dicovered that Freud, Jung, Wolpe, Rogers, Glasser, and nearly anyone else's theory you could possibly name remains the same whether you learn it in the school of counseling, psychology, psychiatry, social work, or education. Onward!

QUESTION: Well, I am concerned about snaring my counselor's license. What can I expect when I finally meet the National Counselor Exam face to face?

ANSWER: The National Counselor Exam is composed of 200 questions. In order to answer each question you will be given four alternative responses. Your task will be to pick the best possible response.

QUESTION: Is there ever more than one correct answer?

ANSWER: No. You will simply take a number two pencil and blacken the alternative of your choice (i.e., a,b,c, or d) on the answer sheet.

QUESTION: Is there a penalty for guessing?

ANSWER: No.

QUESTION: I can't wait another minute. What's the good news for perfectionists?

ANSWER: All right, as I said earlier, the test consists of 200 generic counseling questions. There are eight content areas and each is composed of 25 questions. The good news for perfectionists is that you will only be scored on 20 questions in every content area. Each category has five items that are being field-tested to ascertain their appropriateness for future use.

QUESTION: Now wait a minute. Let me get this straight. Are you saying that I don't need a perfect score on the test to get a perfect score?

ANSWER: That's right! You will be scored on just 20 items in each of eight sections, thus a perfect score is 20x8 or 160. Again, 40 items (i.e., five items in each of the eight sections) are simply put there for field-testing.

QUESTION: Terrific! How will I know which items are being field-tested?

ANSWER: Simply put, you won't. You should therefore do your best on all of the 200 items. The good news, nevertheless, is that as a perfectionist you can keep in mind that you could conceivably miss 40 items on the exam and still receive a perfect score. Well, are you breathing any easier now?

QUESTION: What are the eight areas covered on the exam?

ANSWER: Human Growth and Development; Social and Cultural Foundations; Helping Relationships; Groups; Lifestyle and Career Development; Appraisal; Research and Evaluation; and Professional Orientation. Note: Additional research into the tasks performed by professional counselors could result in new areas or a different number of areas. Hence, professional counselors should always contact NBCC or their state licensing bureau before sitting for the exam.

QUESTION: Let's say I take the exam and flunk it. Won't I be taking the same test if I take the exam the next time it is given?

ANSWER: Wishful thinking, but the answer is an unequivocal "no." A new form or version of the test will be given. And oh yes, do something about that attitude problem of yours!

QUESTION: I want to be licensed as a clinical psychologist. Will I need to pass the National Counselor Examination?

ANSWER: No. In order to obtain psychology licensure in any state in the U.S. or province in Canada, you will need to pass the Examination for Professional Practice in Psychology (or the EPPP, for short). This 200-question, multiple-choice test was developed by the Association of State and Provincial Psychology Boards (ASPPB), and it is scored and standardized by the Professional Examination Service (PES). Like the NCE, there is no penalty for guessing, and each question has only one correct answer. In some states, the candidate must also sit for an oral, written, or supplementary jurisprudence examination. Areas covered on the EPPP include: Problem Definition and Diagnosis; Design, Implementation and Assessment of Intervention; Research and Measurement; Professional, Ethical, and Legal Issues; and Applications to Social Systems. It is critical for you to remember that some exam areas are emphasized more than others. The EPPP is administered twice a year (generally in October and April), and you should be aware of the fact that passing scores vary according to state or province. The test purportedly gets more difficult with each administration. This book does not cover all the topics tested on the EPPP such as psychopharmacology, physiological psychology, abnormal psychology, or industrial-organizational psychology. Moreover, this text focuses on ACA, ASGW, and NBCC ethics. Your exam will require a knowledge of ethical guidelines set forth by the American Psychological Association. My advice: study this book, contact your state licensing bureau, and call the ASPPB at (205) 832-4580 for their booklet concerning the exam format.

QUESTION: Can you comment briefly on social work licensing?

ANSWER: Certainly. Social workers will need to contend with the examinations established by the American Association of State Social Work Boards (AASSWB). Like the NCE and the EPPP, the AASSWB is a multiple-choice test. You will be given 3 1/2 hours to complete the 170 items, though only 150 are used in the scoring process. There are four credentialing categories of the AASSWB designated as Basic, Intermediate, Advanced, and Clinical. Your state licensing bureau will help you determine which version you will need to take. Currently each test consists of 11 areas. These areas vary based on the test. Some examples are Human Development and Behavior; Effects of Culture, Race, Ethnicity, Sexual Orientation, and Gender;

Assessment in Social Work Practice; Social Work Practice with Individuals, Couples, Families, Groups, and Communities; Interpersonal Communication; Professional Social Worker/Client Relationship; Professional Values and Ethics; Supervision in Social Work; Practice Evaluation and the Utilization of Research; Politics and Procedures Governing Service Delivery; and Social Work Administration. The emphasis on each of the 11 areas is not equal and depends on which examination you are taking. Take the "Social Work Practice with Individuals, Couples, Families, Groups, and Communities" category as an example. It constitutes 29% of the basic examination, but 32% of the intermediate and advanced versions. To find out the precise percentages used in the exam you will be taking, I suggest you contact your social work state licensing board to secure a copy of the *AASSWB Candidate Handbook*. Also, find out if your state requires supplementary testing requirements. One other tip: Since social work licensing requirements are different throughout the country, you should contact the National Association of Social Workers (NASW) at (202) 408-8600 and request a copy of their booklet entitled *State Comparison of Laws Regulating Social Work* if you plan to practice in areas outside your own state.

QUESTION: Any suggestions for an acute case of test anxiety?

ANSWER: Yes, take these 900 questions and call me in the morning. Seriously, you can begin by studying the review questions and answers in this book. Exposure to a fearful stimuli often lessens its impact. Generally, the more you study and the more you know, the more confident you will become. Remember that confidence is the sworn enemy of test anxiety.

QUESTION: What if I review all 900 questions and still suffer from test anxiety; then what?

ANSWER: Think about it for a moment. What would you suggest to a client? You would probably prescribe relaxation training, systematic desensitization, biofeedback, or perhaps hypnosis. As a counselor why not try using relaxation techniques, self-systematic desensitization, or even self-hypnosis on yourself. And if all of the aforementioned strategies fail, try seeing another counselor for help. Intervention in this area is generally extremely effective. As a professional counselor myself I can tell you that I've helped numerous individuals who were plagued with test terror. A counselor also can help you investigate other reasons for your difficulty such as a dire fear of failure, an aversion to success, or a high tendency to be self-critical.

QUESTION: Say I answer four questions in a row with a "c." Should I shy away from answering the next question with a "c" even if I firmly believe that "c" is the correct answer? In other words, how many a's, b's, c's or d's in a row is too many?

ANSWER: A fine question, indeed. The answer is that one question on the real test, as well as my test herein, is not related to the next question. Thus, you should not waste one iota of your time worrying about how many a's, b's, c's, or d's you have marked.

QUESTION: Just what does constitute a passing score on the NCE?

ANSWER: As of this writing, NBCC cutoff scores fall around the 60% figure which means that you would need to answer approximately 95 out of the 160 questions correctly. State licensing boards often use different cut-off scores, and thus you must call your state licensing board for further information.

QUESTION: Is this study guide affiliated with NBCC in any manner?

ANSWER: No. As of this writing NBCC is not affiliated with any programs which purport to enhance NCE performance.

QUESTION: I am scared to death of timed tests and I've heard I will be taking a timed exam. Is there anything you can tell me to keep me from catastrophizing over this?

ANSWER: Well a course of rational-emotive therapy might be helpful but let's start with something a little simpler first. On the NCE, for example, you will have four hours to complete the exam or 1.2 minutes per question. Nearly everybody who takes the test finishes in less than four hours. My advice to you is *relax, read each question carefully, and take your time . . . time is not an issue to be overly concerned about when you are taking most comprehensive exams.* Most persons will discover that they have enough time to check over responses to make certain that a careless error has not been made.

QUESTION: Will I be allowed to smoke during the National Counselor Examination?

ANSWER: Generally no. Perhaps this would be a good time to sell your stock in the tobacco companies and give up cancer sticks.

QUESTION: After glancing at your study guide and the sample questions in the NBCC Guide it seems that some of the questions actually have more than one correct answer. For example, I saw a question in which I felt that choices "a" and "b" were both appropriate responses. What gives?

ANSWER: This is what is known in the trade as a "best answer" question. Thus, although several answers may seem correct, your job is to ferret out the finest or the so-called best response. Moreover, I cannot stress too strongly that you should read each question very carefully. Words like "always," "never," and "most," can change the meaning of a question. Pay special attention to such words which are used to qualify the precise nature of the question. Also be prepared to tackle "negative" or so-called "reverse type" questions. Questions of this ilk will emphasize that you mark the response which is the only one which is incorrect. For example: All of the following are behavior therapy techniques except . . . or, Transference is not . . .

QUESTION: I've heard that some questions on the NCE and other major behavioral science exams are based on "analogy questions." Can you clarify this strategy?

ANSWER: Certainly. If you crack your trusty dictionary you will discover that the word analogy basically refers to the similarities between things which are otherwise different. An analogy can be used to explain something by comparing it to something different, yet similar. It's actually a lot simpler than you might think. Take this example. Binet is to IQ as _____ is to psychoanalysis. Your answer choices are: a. Glasser, b. Rogers, c. Berne and d. Freud. The answer in this case would be "d." The logic here is that Binet is considered a pioneer in the formation of the IQ test. The only pioneer in the psychoanalytic movement listed in the answers is Freud. If it's still a tad foggy in your mind don't lose any sleep over it. This guide is literally inundated with analogy type questions so that you will not have surprises whatsoever come test time.

QUESTION: Do you absolutely, positively guarantee you'll cover every single possible question that I'll tangle with on the NCE or other major examinations? After all, 900 questions is a lot of questions!

ANSWER: I absolutely, positively can guarantee you that I will NOT COVER EVERY POSSIBLE QUESTION THAT YOU WILL HAVE TO TANGLE WITH ON THE NCE. No ethical person or company marketing a book, tape, or study program would ever make such an outlandish promise. The idea here is to make you familiar with the major concepts and principles and theorists in the eight major content areas. I have no idea exactly what questions you will see on the test. In fact, the chances of you seeing a question on an exam which is identical (i.e., word for word) to my questions is highly unlikely. If you do take an exam and see a question identical to mine, then it's probably your lucky day. You'll no doubt pass the test and I'd suggest you head out to buy a lottery ticket after completion of the exam! THE QUESTIONS IN THIS STUDY GUIDE CAN BE THOUGHT OF AS A TRIGGERING DEVICE TO HELP YOU REVIEW AND EXPAND YOUR KNOWLEDGE IN A GIVEN AREA. THEY ARE NOT INTENDED TO BE THE QUESTIONS YOU WILL SEE ON THE EXAM.

QUESTION: Okay, I can see why your questions would not be identical to those utilized on various versions of the NCE. Is it safe to say that your questions are very similar to those I will encounter on quizzes, classroom tests, or the NCE?

ANSWER: Well yes and no. Please allow me to explain. In many cases, yes my questions and answer choices will probably be strikingly similar to the types of questions you will find on your state licensing or certification exam. In other cases this will not be true inasmuch as many of my questions and their respective answer choices are intended to convey pertinent information. Many, if not most of my questions, are intended to teach you key material—material that will help you take the sting out of some of the tough questions you could encounter on counseling examinations. Let me make it perfectly clear, however, that on the real test the questions are decidedly not worded to teach you key information. On the real exam, for example, you probably will not find a question such as: The mean is the arithmetic average. Which statement best describes the mode? In this study guide, nevertheless, questions like this are commonplace. Moreover, on many of the questions I have even picked the incorrect answers for the purpose of teaching you something. Again, the major purpose of this guide is to help you learn.

QUESTION: What would you say about an individual who answers the 900 questions but fails to read the answers?

ANSWER: I guess I'd have to say the person had a self-defeating personality. I can in no way overemphasize that you absolutely must read each and every answer if you want to get the most out of this program of study. The answers clearly give vital, additional information that you will not learn merely by reading the question (yes, even if you answered the question correctly). Have I made myself clear?

QUESTION: You really seem to push those so-called memory devices of yours. Isn't that, well . . . a bit gimmicky? I mean isn't rote memory fairly useless if you don't really comprehend the material?

ANSWER: Yes, finally we agree on something. I am totally against you using memory devices—or any learning strategy for that matter—if you do not use them to understand the principles. Even my African Grey Parrot can listen to a phrase out of a graduate text in counseling and repeat it back from rote memory. (Well, perhaps I'm exaggerating just a bit, but at least he's trying.) On the other hand, you must be able to remember a principle to explain its usefulness in the field of counseling. Hence, I have provided the reader with a wealth of memory devices as well as a lot of repetition. In reference to your position that the memory techniques are gimmicky I'd advise you to reserve judgment until you have personally given them a whirl. Remember that in everyday life, science is often described as what works! You must be able to recall a principle to understand it.

QUESTION: Is it all right to skip questions or entire sections?

ANSWER: I certainly would not advise it for counselors seeking LPC/NCC credentials. You see this book is designed so that the information you learn from any given question will help you answer later questions. The knowledge in this guide is cumulative. Thus, for best results, answer the questions in numerical sequence. If, however, you are merely using this text to brush up for a lesser exam or perhaps to study for a pop quiz, you might wish to concentrate on a relevant section or utilize the index, which conveniently lists key topics by question number.

QUESTION: After glancing at your questions I can honestly say that many of them seem very incredibly simple while others look extremely difficult. Is this a typical response?

ANSWER: Congratulations, you're normal. That's precisely what most people studying for the exam would say.

QUESTION: I'd like to pick your brain for a moment. After you decided what was critical material for a question did you consult an authoritative source to help you construct the best possible questions and answers?

ANSWER: One source . . . one source . . . surely you jest? Numerous times during the preparation of this guide I couldn't walk across the room to my computer and continue keyboarding without tripping over a two-foot pile of behavioral science literature. Many times, I consulted 10 or 12 reference books before constructing a single question. My goal was to find a simple explanation you could understand. I used dictionaries, journals, references, study guides, newsletters, and textbooks from the fields of counseling, psychology, psychiatry, social work, mathematics, education, and sociology to name a few. I then became eclectic and used the best of every source, not to mention my own knowledge and creative teaching skills, to create a synthesis that would make the material easy to assimilate. And by all means, when you don't comprehend an answer or a principle look it up in another source. A study guide is never intended to be your sole source of information.

QUESTION: I consider myself an auditory learner and have gained a wealth of material by listening to your exam review tapes. Can you give me a good reason to wade through your 900 questions and answers in this book?

ANSWER: Certainly. No matter how strongly you protest to your state licensing board or NBCC that you are an auditory learner you will still be tangling with the NCE via pencil and paper. This book gives you 900 chances to prepare for the task that awaits you.

QUESTION: Any advice for those of us who must experience an oral exam?

ANSWER: First, remember that one word answers are a no-no. You must impress upon your board of examiners that you understand the material. I'd also be prepared to argue against a given theoretical position. If, for example, you are asked to explicate on the merits of behaviorism, I'd be prepared to find fault with behaviorism and point out the merits of an opposing view such as psychoanalysis. Currently, about a dozen states utilize a procedure which involves an oral exam for persons seeking licensure. And needless to say, if you are working on your doctorate you generally will need to pass your oral boards before you can write a dissertation.

QUESTION: Do all states have counselor licensing?

ANSWER: No. But before you pack your bags and move, keep in mind that more and more states are indeed passing some form of counselor credentialing legislation. As of this writing, 38 states plus the District of Columbia have credentialing legislation. Again, most states (currently 26) rely on the NBCC test (the NCE), but several states will accept the Academy of Clinical Mental Health Counselors (ACMHC) Exam. Thus, if you already have Certified Clinical Mental Health Counselor status, contact your state licensing board.* Two states have drafted their own exams, while several others will accept the exam of the Commission on Rehabilitation Counselor Certification (CRCC).

*Beginning July 1, 1993, the Certified Clinical Mental Health Counselor (CCMHC) credential will be administered by NBCC and thus will be considered an NBCC specialty.

QUESTION: How many state credentialed counselors are in the U.S., and do these counselors need continuing education units to retain their status?

ANSWER: In the U.S. nearly 50,000 are state credentialed counselors. Most—but not all—states have a continuing education requirement. Here again, the requirement varies from state to state. Counselors with NBCC status must complete 100 contact hours of continuing education within five years or take the NCE again to remain certified. Nearly 18,000 counselors currently have NBCC certification.

QUESTION: Will your questions always fall in the same content area as they would on an actual exam?

ANSWER: Surprisingly enough, no! Here's why. In this book the questions are presented in a given order so the material will flow smoothly for learning purposes. Thus, a question on an actual exam could appear under the "Groups" section, while in this guide a similar question might appear under "Helping Relationships." If you know the material, it won't matter in which content area it appears.

QUESTION: Speaking of the "Helping Relationships" section, I notice you supply the reader with an awesome 200 questions and answers rather than the generous number of 100 supplied for each of the other seven sections. Do you consider this the most important section?

ANSWER: No. This format did, however, allow me to provide you with a brief cook's tour of the major principles related to the most popular schools of counseling. I have no doubt that on another exam many of these principles could appear in other sections. Thus, the salient point is that you should not skip any section of this guide.

QUESTION: What should I do the night before the big exam?

ANSWER: Take in a show, have a nice dinner, take a leisurely drive in the country, or anything else you enjoy. Get a good night's sleep, but whatever you decide to do, don't cram. Study for a reasonable period of time during each study session and always do it well in advance of the exam . . . and well in advance does not mean the night before the test!

QUESTION: Your practice questions often present the reader with answers which encompass the answers presented by two choices (e.g., choice "d" says a and c). Is this format used on the NCE at this time?

ANSWER: The current *NCE Preparation Guide* does not indicate the use of this format; nevertheless, I incorporated it into this book as I felt it served as an excellent learning tool. Whether you like it or not, I think you'll have to admit that the format forces you to read every choice carefully, and that's a habit I definitely want you to acquire.

QUESTION: Any last words of wisdom?

ANSWER: Yes, if this book saves you one measly point on the exam, then it was worth my while writing it and your time wading through the 900 questions and answers. So . . . I'll be certain to include LPC, NCC after your name the next time I write you!

CHAPTER 3

HUMAN GROWTH AND DEVELOPMENT

1. Freud's stages are psychosexual while Erik Erikson's stages are

    a. psychometric.
    b. psychodiagnostic.
    c. psychopharmacological.
    d. psychosocial.

Let's begin with an easy one. Only one choice fits the bill here. The Freudian stages (oral, anal, phallic, latency and genital) emphasize sexuality. Erik Erikson's eight stages (e.g., trust vs. mistrust or integrity vs. despair) focus on social relationships and thus are described as psychosocial. To mention the other answer choices is to dispose of them. Psychometric simply refers to mental testing or measurement. Psychodiagnostic pertains to the study of personality through interpretation of behavior or nonverbal cues. In counseling, per se, it also can mean that the counselor uses the aforementioned factors and/or tests to label the client in a diagnostic category. Psychopharmacology studies the effects that drugs have on psychological functions. **(d)**

2. In Freudian theory instincts are emphasized. Erik Erikson is an ego psychologist. Ego psychologists

    a. emphasize id processes.
    b. refute the concept of the superego.
    c. believe in man's powers of reasoning to control behavior.
    d. are sometimes known as radical behaviorists.

To say that the id is the bad boy of Freudian theory is to put it mildly! The id is the seat of sex and aggression. It is not rational or logical, and it is void of time orientation. The id is chaotic and concerned only with the body, not with the outside world. Freud emphasized the importance of the id while Erikson stressed ego functions. The ego is logical, rational and utilizes the power of reasoning and control. Simply put, ego psychologists, unlike the strict Freudians, accent the ego and the power of control. The term superego in choice "b" refers to the moralistic and idealistic portion of the personality. The behaviorists, mentioned in choice "d," do not believe in concepts like the id, the ego, and the superego. In fact, radical behaviorists do not believe in mental constructs such as "the mind" nor do they believe in consciousness. The behaviorist generally feels if it can't be measured then it doesn't exist. **(c)**

3. The only psychoanalyst who created a developmental theory which encompasses the entire life span was

    a. Erik Erikson.
    b. Milton H. Erickson.
    c. A.A. Brill.
    d. Jean Piaget.

In Freudian theory, the final stage (i.e., the genital stage) begins at age 12 and is said to continue throughout one's life span. Many scholars do not feel that Freud's theory truly covers the entire life span. They find it difficult to believe that a crisis at age 12 remains the central issue until senility sets in! Erikson, another psychoanalyst and a disciple of Freud's, however, created a theory with eight stages in which each stage represents a psychosocial crisis or a turning point. Since the final stage does not even begin until age 60 most personality theorists believe that his theory actually covers the entire life of an individual. As for the other choices, Brill is analytic and will be discussed in the section on career theory. Milton H. Erickson, not to be confused with Erik Erikson, has a "c" in his name and is generally associated with brief psychotherapy and innovative techniques in hypnosis. Piaget is the leading name in the cognitive development in children. **(a)**

4. The statement, "the ego is dependent on the id," would most likely reflect the work of

    a.   Erik Erikson.
    b.   Sigmund Freud.
    c.   Jay Haley.
    d.   Arnold Lazarus.

In Freudian theory the id is also called the pleasure principle and houses the animalistic instincts. The ego, which is known as the reality principle, is pressured by the id to succumb to pleasure or gratification regardless of consequences. Erikson, an ego psychologist, would not emphasize the role of the id, but rather the power of control or the ego. Jay Haley is known for his work in strategic and problem solving therapy often utilizing the technique of paradox. He claims to have acquired a wealth of information by studying the work of Milton H. Erickson mentioned in the previous question. Arnold Lazarus is considered a pioneer in the behavior therapy movement, especially the use of systematic desensitization, a technique which helps clients cope with phobias. Today his name is associated with multimodal therapy. **(b)**

5. Jean Piaget's theory has four stages. The correct order from stage one to stage four is

    a.   formal operations, concrete operations, pre-operations, sensorimotor.

    b.   formal operations, preoperations, concrete operations, sensorimotor.

    c.   sensorimotor, preoperations, concrete operations, formal operations.

    d.   concrete operations, sensorimotor, preoperations, formal operations.

Time for your first memory device. It would make sense that Piaget's first stage emphasizes the senses and the child's motoric skills, hence the name sensorimotor stage. I can remember the last stage by reminding myself that people seem to be more formal as they get older. The final stage is of course formal operations. As for the other two stages, the stage with "pre" (i.e., preoperations) must come before the remaining stage which is concrete operations. Do not automatically assume that my memory devices will be the best ones for you. Instead, experiment with different ideas. The memory strategies presented here are simply ones which my students and I have found helpful. **(c)**

6. Some behavioral scientists have been critical of Piaget's developmental research inasmuch as

    a.   he utilized the t-test too frequently.

    b.   he failed to check for type I or alpha errors.

    c.   he worked primarily with minority children.

    d.   his findings were often derived from observing his own children.

Piaget was trained as a biologist and then worked with Alfred Binet in France. Binet created the first intelligence test. Piaget's research methods, though very innovative, could be classified as informal ones. He sometimes utilized games and interviews. Who were his subjects? Well, often they were Lucienne, Laurent, and Jaqueline: his children. Some researchers have been critical of his methods. Answer choice "a" is incorrect as a t-test is a statistical test used in formal experiments to determine whether there is a significant difference between two groups. The "t" in t-test should be written with a lower case "t" and is technically utilized to ascertain if the means of the groups are significantly different from each other. When using the t-test the groups must be normally distributed. Some books will refer to the t-test as the Student's t. Choice "b" will be discussed in much greater detail in the section on research and evaluation. This choice is incorrect inasmuch as Piaget generally did not rely on statistical experiments that would be impacted by type I or alpha errors. **(d)**

7. A tall skinny pitcher of water is emptied into a small squatty pitcher. A child indicates that she feels the small pitcher has less water. The child has not yet mastered

    a.   symbolic schema.
    b.   conservation.
    c.   androgynous psychosocial issues.
    d.   trust versus mistrust.

This is a must know principle for any major test in counseling! In Piaget's theory the term conservation refers to the notion that a substance's weight, mass, and volume remain the same even if it changes shape. According to Piaget the child masters conservation and the concept of reversibility during the concrete operations stage (ages seven to 11 years). Now here is a super memory device. Both conservation and the ability to count mentally (i.e., without matching something up to something else physically) both occur in the concrete operational thought stage. Fortunately, conservation, counting, and concrete operations all start with a "c." How convenient! And you thought memorizing these principles was going to be difficult. The other answer choices are ridiculous and that's putting it mildly. In Piaget's theory symbolic schema is a cognitive structure that grows with life experience.

A schema is merely a system which permits the child to test out things in the physical world. Choice "c," androgynous, is a term which implies that humans have characteristics of both sexes. (The Greek word andros means man while the Greek word for woman is gyne.) And, of course, by now you know that trust vs. mistrust is Erikson's first psychosocial stage. **(b)**

8. In Piagetian literature, conservation would most likely refer to

    a.   volume or mass.
    b.   defenses of the ego.
    c.   the sensorimotor intelligence stage.
    d.   a specific psychosexual stage of life.

If you missed this question go back to square one! The answer given for number 7 clearly explains this principle. Again, a child who has not mastered conservation does not think in a very flexible manner. A child, for example, is shown a pie cut into two pieces. Next, the same pie is cut into ten pieces. If the child has not mastered conservation he or she will say that the pie that is now cut into ten pieces is bigger than when it was cut into just two pieces. You can't fool a child who has mastered conservation, however. This child will know that the pie has not changed in volume and mass. In general, the statistical research of David Elkind supports Piaget's notions regarding conservation. Piaget and Elkind report that mass is the first and most easily understood concept. The mastery of weight is next, and finally the notion of volume can be comprehended. (A good memory device might be MV, such as in most valuable player. The "M," or mass, will come first and the "V," or volume, will be the final letter. The "W," or weight, can be squeezed in-between.) **(a)**

9. A child masters conservation in the Piagetian stage known as

    a.   formal operations—12 years and older.
    b.   concrete operations—ages 7 to 11.
    c.   preoperations—ages 2 to 7.
    d.   sensorimotor intelligence—birth to 2 years.

Remember your memory device: conservation begins with a "c" and so does concrete operations. The other three stages proposed by Jean Piaget do not begin with a "c." **(b)**

10. _____ expanded on Piaget's conceptualization of moral development.

    a.   Erik Erikson
    b.   Freud
    c.   Lawrence Kohlberg
    d.   John B. Watson

Kohlberg is perhaps the leading theorist in moral development. Kohlberg, Erikson, and Maslow's theories are said to be epigenetic in nature. Epigenetic is a biological term borrowed from embryology. This principle states that each stage emerges from the one before it. The process follows a given order and is systematic. John B. Watson, mentioned in choice "d," is the father of American behaviorism and coined the term "behaviorism" in 1912. **(c)**

11. According to Piaget, a child masters the concept of reversibility in the third stage known as concrete operations or concrete operational thought. This notion suggests

    a.   that heavier objects are more difficult for a child to lift.
    b.   the child is ambidextrous.
    c.   the child is more cognizant of mass than weight.
    d.   one can undo an action, hence an object can return to its initial shape.

Choice "d" is the definition of reversibility. The word ambidextrous, utilized in choice "b," refers to an individual's ability to use both hands equally well to perform tasks. **(d)**

12. During a thunderstorm, a six-year-old child in Piaget's stage of preoperational thought (stage 2) says, "The rain is following me." This is an example of

    a.   egocentrism.
    b.   conservation.
    c.   centration.
    d.   abstract thought.

Expect to see a question on the test like this one and you can't go wrong. This is the typical or prototype question you will come across in order to ascertain whether you are familiar with the Piagetian concept of egocentrism. By egocentrism, Piaget was not really implying the child is self-centered. Instead, egocentrism conveys the fact that the child cannot view the world from the vantage point of someone else. Choice "d" mentions abstract thought which does not occur until Piaget's final or fourth stage known as formal operations. **(a)**

13. Lawrence Kohlberg suggested

    a.   a single level of morality.
    b.   two levels of morality.
    c.   three levels of morality.
    d.   preoperational thought as the basis for all morality.

Kohlberg's theory has three levels of moral development: Preconventional, Conventional, and the Postconventional level which is referred to in some texts as the Personal Integrity or Morality of Self-Accepted Principles level. Each level can be broken down further into two stages. **(c)**

14. The Heinz story is to Kohlberg's theory as

     a.   a brick is to a house.
     b.   Freud is to Jung.
     c.   the Menninger Clinic is to biofeedback.
     d.   a typing test is to the level of typing skill mastered.

This is your first chance to wrestle with an analogy type question. The Heinz Story is one method used by Kohlberg to assess the level and stage of moral development in an individual. The story goes like this:

> A woman in Europe was dying of cancer. Only one drug (a form of radium) could save her. It was discovered by a local druggist. The druggist was charging $2,000, which was ten times his cost to make the drug. The woman's husband, Heinz, could not raise the money and even if he borrowed from his friends, he could only come up with approximately half of the sum. He asked the druggist to reduce the price or let him pay the bill later since his wife was dying but the druggist said, "No." The husband was thus desperate and broke into the store to steal the drug. Should the husband have done that? Why?

The individual's reason for the decision (rather than the decision itself) allowed Kohlberg to evaluate the person's stage of moral development. In short, the reasoning utilized to solve a moral dilemma such as the Heinz story, could be used to assess moral development. Kohlberg's stages and levels are said to apply to all persons and not merely to those living in the U.S. Thus, it is evident that the Heinz Story is most like choice "d," a typing test. C.G. Jung mentioned in choice "b" is the father of analytic psychology. Freud is the father of psychoanalysis. And lastly, the Menninger Clinic in Kansas is a traditional psychoanalytic foothold as well as the cite of landmark work in the area of biofeedback which is a technique utilized to help individuals learn to control bodily processes more effectively. And, oh yes, before you go out and have a good cry, let me emphasize that the story of Heinz is fictional and simply used as a research tool.   **(d)**

15. The term "identity crisis" comes from the work of

    a.   Kohlberg.
    b.   Erikson.
    c.   Adler.
    d.   Jung.

Erikson felt that in an attempt to find out who they really are adolescents will experiment with various roles. Choice "c" refers to another name you should know, Alfred Adler, the founder of individual psychology, which stresses the inferiority complex.   **(b)**

16. Kohlberg's three levels of morality are

    a.   preconventional, conventional, postconventional.
    b.   formal, pre-formal, self-accepted.
    c.   self-accepted, other directed, authority directed.
    d.   preconventional, formal, authority directed.

In the preconventional level the child responds to consequences. In this stage reward and punishment greatly influence the behavior. In the conventional level the individual wants to meet the standards of the family, society, and even the nation. Kohlberg felt that many people never reach the final level of postconventional or self-accepted morality. A person who reaches this level is concerned with universal, ethical principles of justice, dignity, and equality of human rights. Kohlberg's research indicated that under 40% of his middle-class urban males had reached the postconventional level. Ghandi, Socrates, and Martin Luther King Jr. have been cited as examples of individuals who have reached this level, in which the common good of society is a key issue.   **(a)**

17. Trust versus mistrust is

    a.   an Adlerian notion of morality.
    b.   Erik Erikson's first stage of psychosocial development.
    c.   essentially equivalent to Piaget's concept of egocentrism.
    d.   the basis of morality according to Kohlberg.

Erikson proposed eight stages and this is the first. This stage corresponds to Freud's initial oral-sensory stage (birth to approximately 1 year). Each of Erikson's stages is described using bipolar or opposing tendencies. Although Piaget and Erikson are the most prominent stage theorists, you should also become familiar with the work of Harry Stack Sullivan who postulated the stages of infancy, childhood, the juvenile era, preadolescence, early adolescence, and late adolescence. Sullivan's theory, known as the psychiatry of interpersonal relations, is similar to Erikson's theory in that biological determination is seen as less important than interpersonal issues and the sociocultural demands of society. **(b)**

18. A person who has successfully mastered Erikson's first seven stages would be ready to enter Erikson's final or eighth stage

    a.   generativity versus stagnation.
    b.   initiative versus guilt.
    c.   identity crisis of the later years.
    d.   integrity versus despair.

Each stage is seen as a psychosocial crisis or a turning point. Erikson did not imply that the person either totally succeeds or fails. Instead, he says that the individual leans toward a given alternative (e.g., integrity or despair). The final stage begins at about age 60. An individual who has successfully mastered all the stages feels a

sense of integrity in the sense that his or her life has
been worthwhile. **(d)**

19. In Kohlberg's first or preconventional level, the individual's
moral behavior is guided by

   a. psychosexual urges.
   b. consequences.
   c. periodic fugue states.
   d. counterconditioning.

In the consequences stage (called premoral) an M&M
or a slap on the behind is more important than societal
expectations and the law. In choice "c" the term fugue
state refers to an individual who experiences memory
loss (amnesia) and leaves home often to change his or
her job and identity. What does this have to do with
answering the question regarding Kohlberg, you ask?
Nothing, that's decidedly why it's the wrong answer!
In choice "d" you are confronted with the word
counterconditioning. This is a behavioristic technique
in which the goal is to weaken or eliminate a learned
response by pairing it with a stronger or desirable response.
Systematic desensitization is a good example, but more
on that later. **(b)**

20. Kohlberg's second level of morality is known as
conventional morality. This level is characterized by

   a. psychosexual urges.
   b. a desire to live up to society's expectations.
   c. a desire to conform.
   d. b and c.

At the conventional level the individual wishes to conform
to the roles in society so that authority and social order
can prevail. Kohlberg felt that attempts to upgrade the
morals of our youth have failed and he has referred
to some character building education programs as "Mickey
Mouse stuff!" **(d)**

21. Kohlberg's highest level of morality is termed post-conventional morality. Here the individual

    a.   must truly contend with psychosexual urges.
    b.   has the so-called "good boy/good girl" orientation.
    c.   has self-imposed morals and ethics.
    d.   a and b.

Only one answer is correct here folks. Choice "a" reflects the Freudian theory, while choice "b" is stage three of Kohlberg's theory, which occurs at the conventional level. In the "good boy/good girl orientation" the person is concerned with approbation and the ability to please others to achieve recognition. **(c)**

22. According to Kohlberg, level three, which is postconventional or self-accepted moral principles,

    a.   refers to the Naive Hedonism stage.
    b.   operates on the premise that rewards guide morals.
    c.   a and b.
    d.   is the highest level of morality, however, some people never reach this level.

Hedonism mentioned in choice "a" occurs in stage two of the preconventional level. Here the child says to himself, "If I'm nice others will be nice to me and I'll get what I want." Choice "b" actually refers to the first stage of the preconventional level which is the punishment versus obedience orientation. **(d)**

23. Both Piaget and Kohlberg

    a.   believed in sequential development which moves from a lower to a higher stage.
    b.   were strict neo-Freudians.
    c.   emphasized organ inferiority.
    d.   a, b, and c.

Piaget and Kohlberg both relied on stages to explain structural development. In choice "c" the concept of organ inferiority is mentioned. This term is primarily associated with the work of Alfred Adler who created individual psychology. **(a)**

24. Freud and Erikson

    a. could be classified as behaviorists.
    b. could be classified as maturationists.
    c. agreed that developmental stages are psychosexual.
    d. were prime movers in the biofeedback movement.

In the behavioral sciences, the concept of the maturation hypothesis (also known as the maturation theory) suggests that behavior is guided exclusively via hereditary factors, but that certain behaviors will not manifest themselves until the necessary stimuli is present in the environment. In addition, the theory suggests that the individual's neural development must be at a certain level of maturity for the behavior to unfold. A counselor who believes in this concept strives to unleash inborn abilities, instincts, and drives. The client's childhood and the past are seen as important therapeutic topics. **(b)**

25. John Bowlby's name is most closely associated with

    a. morality.
    b. developmental stage theories.
    c. bonding and attachment.
    d. the unconscious mind.

Bowlby's name starts with a "b" as does the word "bonding." Aren't memory devices wonderful? John Bowlby saw bonding and attachment as having survival value or what is often called adaptive significance. Bowlby insisted that in order to lead a normal social life the child must bond with an adult before the age of three. If the bond is severed at an early age, it is known as "object loss," and this is said to be the breeding ground for abnormal behavior or what is often called psychopathology. Mahler calls the child's absolute dependence on the female caretaker "symbiosis." Difficulties in the symbiotic relationship can result in adult psychosis. **(c)**

26. In which Eriksonian stage does the mid-life crisis occur?

    a.   generativity versus stagnation
    b.   integrity versus despair
    c.   a and b
    d.   Erikson's stages do not address mid-life issues

Most theorists believe that the mid-life crisis occurs between ages 35 and 45 when the individual realizes his or her life is half over. Persons often need to face the fact that they have not achieved their goals or aspirations. Incidentally, the word generativity refers to the ability to be productive and happy by looking outside one's self and being concerned with other people. Some exams may refer to this stage as "generativity versus self-absorption." Daniel Levinson, who wrote *Seasons of a Man's Life*, viewed the mid-life crisis as somewhat positive, pointing out that men who do not face it may indeed stagnate or become stale during their fifties. In other words, avoiding or bypassing the crisis can lead to lack of vitality in later years. **(a)**

27. The researcher who is well known for his work with maternal deprivation and isolation in rhesus monkeys is

    a.   Harry Harlow.
    b.   John Bowlby.
    c.   Lawrence Kohlberg.
    d.   all of the above.

Harlow's work is now well-known in the social sciences. Harlow believed that attachment was an innate tendency and not one which is learned. Monkeys placed in isolation developed autistic abnormal behavior. When these monkeys were placed in cages with normally reared monkeys some remission of the dysfunctional behavior was noted.

Evidence that this is true in man comes from the work of Renee Spitz, who noted that children reared in impersonal institutions (and hence experienced maternal deprivation between the sixth and eighth month) cried more, experienced difficulty sleeping, and had more health-related difficulties. Spitz called this "anaclitic depression." These infants would ultimately experience great difficulty forming close relationships. **(a)**

28. The statement: "Males are better than females when performing mathematical calculations" is

    a.   false.
    b.   true due to a genetic flaw commonly found in women.
    c.   true only in middle-aged men.
    d.   true according to research by Maccoby and Jacklin.

Maccoby and Jacklin reviewed the literature and found very few differences that could be attributed to genetics and biological factors. The superiority of males in the area of mathematics was not significant until high school or perhaps college. Girls who excelled in science and math often identified with their fathers and were encouraged to value initiative and were given independence. Thus, the major impetus for sex role differences may come from child-rearing patterns rather than bodily chemistry. **(d)**

29. The Eriksonian stage that focuses heavily on sharing your life with another person is

    a.   actually the major theme in all of Erikson's eight stages.
    b.   generativity vs. stagnation—ages 35 to 60.
    c.   intimacy vs. isolation—ages 23 to 34.
    d.   a critical factor Erikson fails to mention.

If you didn't know the answer did you guess? Yes, of course I'm being serious. Remember no penalty is assessed for guessing on the NCE. An educated guess based on the fact that intimacy implies sharing one's life would have landed you a correct answer here. Counselors need to be aware that an individual who fails to do well in this stage may conclude that he or she can depend on no one but self. **(c)**

30. We often refer to individuals as conformists. Which of these individuals would most likely conform to his or her peers?

    a.   a 19-year-old male college student.
    b.   a 23-year-old male drummer in a rock band.
    c.   a 57-year-old female stockbroker.
    d.   a 13-year-old male middle school student.

Conformity seems to peak in the early teens. **(d)**

31. In Harry Harlow's experiments with baby monkeys

    a.   a wire mother was favored by most young monkeys over a terry cloth version.
    b.   the baby monkey was more likely to cling to a terry cloth mother surrogate than a wire surrogate mother.
    c.   female monkeys had a tendency to drink large quantities of alcohol.
    d.   male monkeys had a tendency to drink large quantities of alcohol.

Infant monkeys preferred the terry cloth mothers to wire mothers even though the wire mothers were equipped to dispense milk. Harlow concluded "contact comfort" is important in the development of the infant's attachment to his or her mother. A 165-day experiment revealed that the monkeys were spending an average of one and a half hours per day with the wire mother and 16 hours with the terry cloth mother. Bowlby, mentioned previously, would say that in humans the parents act as a "releaser stimulus" to elicit relief from hunger and tension through holding. **(b)**

32. Freud postulated psychosexual stages

    a. id, ego, and superego.
    b. oral, anal, phallic, latency, and genital.
    c. eros, thanatos, regression, and superego.
    d. manifest, latent, oral, and phallic.

Choice "a" depicts Freud's structural theory of the mind as being composed of the id, the ego, and the superego. In choice "c" the word eros refers to the Freudian concept of the life instinct while thanatos refers to the self-destructive death instinct. Analysis is just brimming with verbiage borrowed from Greek mythology. The term regression is used to describe clients who return to an earlier stage of development. In choice "d" you should familiarize yourself with the terms manifest and latent which in psychoanalysis refer to the nature of a dream. Manifest content describes the dream material as it is presented to the dreamer. Latent content (which is seen as far more important by the Freudians) refers to the hidden meaning of the dream. **(b)**

33. In adolescence

    a. females commit suicide more than males.
    b. suicide is a concern but statistically very rare.
    c. the teens who talk about suicide are not serious.
    d. males commit suicide more than females, but females attempt suicide more often.

This answer would apply not just to adolescence but to nearly all age brackets. One theory is that males are more successful in killing themselves because they use firearms whereas females rely on less lethal methods. Choice "b" is false inasmuch as suicide is generally the eighth leading cause of death in this country as well as the second or third leading killer of teens each year. And as far as choice "c" is concerned, a counselor should always take it seriously when a client of any age threatens suicide. The truth is that the vast majority of those who have killed themselves have communicated the intent to do so in some manner. So take clients' suicide threats seriously. Have I made myself clear?   **(d)**

34. In the general population

    a.   the suicide rate is 2/100,000.
    b.   suicide is one of the top ten causes of death.
    c.   suicide rates tend to up with age.
    d.   b and c.

Official statistics indicate about 30,000 suicides each year in the U.S. Suicidologists (and yes there is such a word!) believe that the actual number may be closer to 75,000 due to complications in accurately coding the cases. Choice "a" reflects the approximate suicide rate in black females. The overall suicide rate in the U.S. in any given year is about 12/100,000. Interestingly enough, personality measures such as the MMPI and the Rorschach are not good predictors of suicide or for that matter of suicide attempts. In essence, test profiles of suicidal individuals generally are not distinguishable from those persons who are not suicidal.   **(d)**

35. The fear of death

    a.   is greatest during middle age.
    b.   is an almost exclusively male phenomenon.
    c.   is the number one psychiatric problem in the geriatric years.
    d.   surprisingly enough occurs in the teen years.

In Erikson's stages the individual would accept the finality of life better during the final stage than in the middle age years.   **(a)**

36. In Freudian theory, attachment is a major factor

    a.   in the preconscious mind.
    b.   in the mind of the child in latency.
    c.   which evolves primarily during the oral stage.
    d.   a and b.

This would make sense from a logical standpoint because the oral stage is the first Freudian psychosexual stage and occurs while the child is still an infant (i.e., the stage goes from birth to one year). As mentioned earlier, attachments in human as well as animal studies indicate that the bonding process takes place early in life. **(c)**

37. When comparing girls to boys, it could be noted that

    a.   girls grow up to smile more.
    b.   girls are using more feeling words by age two.
    c.   girls are better able to read people without verbal cues at any age.
    d.   all of the above.

Boys on the other hand are more physically active and aggressive probably due to androgen hormones. Boys also seem to possess better visual-perceptual skills. **(d)**

38. The Freudian developmental stage which "least" emphasizes sexuality is

    a.   oral.
    b.   anal.
    c.   phallic.
    d.   latency.

Here's an easy one. Remember how I mentioned in question 32 that latent refers to the hidden meaning of the dream? Well in the developmental stages the sexual drive seems hidden (or at least not very prominent) during latency. Sexual interests are replaced by social interests like sports, learning, and hobbies. Now this is very important: Latency is the only Freudian developmental stage which

is not primarily psychosexual in nature. It occurs roughly
between ages six and 12.   **(d)**

39. In terms of parenting young children

    a.   boys are punished more than girls.
    b.   girls are punished more than boys.
    c.   boys and girls are treated in a similar fashion.
    d.   boys show more caregiver behavior.

Hint: Before you sit for the NCE or written or oral boards,
take a moment to review the major theories and research
related to child rearing. Stanley Coopersmith, for example,
found that child-rearing methods seem to have a
tremendous impact on self-esteem. A study he conducted
indicated that, surprisingly enough, children with high
self-esteem were punished just as often as kids with
low self-esteem. The children with high self-esteem,
however, were provided with a clear understanding of
what was morally right and wrong. This was not usually
the case in children with low self-esteem. The children
with high self-esteem actually had more rules than the
kids with low self-esteem. When the child with high
self-esteem was punished the emphasis was on the
behavior being bad and not the child. Parents of children
with high self-esteem were more democratic in the sense
that they would listen to the child's arguments and then
explain the purpose of the rules. The Coopersmith study
utilized middle-class boys, ages ten to 12. Choice "d"
stands incorrect since girls routinely display more caregiver
behavior.   **(a)**

40. When developmental theorists speak of nature or nurture
    they really mean

    a.   how much heredity or environment interact to
         influence development.
    b.   the focus is skewed in favor of biological
         attributes.
    c.   a and b.
    d.   a theory proposed by Skinner's colleagues.

In this question the word "nature" refers to heredity and genetic make-up, while "nurture" refers to the environment. The age-old argument is whether heredity or environment has the greatest impact on the person's development. Today theorists shy away from an extremist position and admit that both factors play a major role. Just for the record, choice "d" mentions B.F. Skinner who was the prime mover in the behavioristic psychology movement. Behaviorists, like Skinner, tend to emphasize the power of environment.   **(a)**

41. Stage theorists assume

    a. qualitative changes between stages occur.
    b. differences surely exist but usually can't be measured.
    c. that humanistic psychology is the only model which truly supports the stage viewpoint.
    d. b and c.

Choice "b" is incorrect inasmuch as differences can often be measured. Just ask any behaviorist! Choice "c" makes no sense because analysts (who are not considered humanistic) such as Freud and Erikson have supported the stage theory viewpoint.   **(a)**

42. Development

    a. begins at birth.
    b. begins during the first trimester of pregnancy.
    c. is a continuous process which begins at conception.
    d. a and c.

Developmental psychologists are fond of looking at prenatal influences (i.e., smoking or alcohol consumption) that affect the fetus before birth.   **(c)**

43. Development is cephalocaudal, which means

   a.   foot to head.
   b.   head to foot.
   c.   limbs receive the highest level of nourishment.
   d.   b and c.

The head of the fetus develops earlier than the legs. Cephalocaudal simply refers to bodily proportions between the head and tail. **(b)**

44. Heredity

   a.   assumes the normal person has 23 pairs of chromosomes.
   b.   assumes that heredity characteristics are transmitted by chromosomes.
   c.   assumes genes composed of DNA hold a genetic code.
   d.   all of the above

Here is a vest pocket definition of heredity. You should also be familiar with the term "heritability" which is the portion of a trait which can be explained via genetic factors. **(d)**

45. Piaget's final stage is known as the formal operational stage. In this stage

   a.   abstract thinking emerges.
   b.   problems can be solved using deduction.
   c.   a and b.
   d.   the child has mastered abstract thinking but still feels helpless.

Again, unfortunately Piaget felt a large number of individuals never really reach this stage; hence, the difficulty of subjects like algebra, physics, and geometry. Another characteristic of the formal operations stage is that the child can think in terms of multiple hypotheses. If you ask a child to answer a question such as, "Why did someone shoot the president?", a child who has mastered formal operations (approximately age 11 and beyond) will give several hypotheses while a child in the previous stages would most likely be satisfied with one explanation. For exam purposes remember that abstract concepts of time (e.g., What was life like 500 years ago?) or distance (e.g., How far is 600 miles?) can only be comprehended via abstract thinking which occurs in this stage. Answer "d" is incorrect inasmuch as Piaget felt that when the child finally reached the final stage he or she would be ready for adulthood and would not experience childlike feelings of helplessness. **(c)**

46. Kohlberg lists _____ stages of moral development which fall into _____ levels.

    a.   6,3
    b.   6,6
    c.   3,6
    d.   3,3

Preconventional Level with Stage 1, Punishment/Obedience Orientation, and Stage 2, Naive Hedonism (also called instrumental or egotistic) Orientation. The entire first level is sometimes called the "premoral level." Conventional Level with Stage 3, Good boy/Good Girl Orientation, and Stage 4, Authority, Law and Order Orientation. This entire level is often known as "morality of conventional rules and conformity." Postconventional Level with Stage 5, Democratically Accepted Law or "Social Contract" and Stage 6, Principles of Self-Conscience and Universal Ethics. The last level is sometimes termed the "morality of self-accepted principles level." **(a)**

47. A person who lives by his or her individual conscience and universal ethical principles

    a.   has reached the highest stage of moral development.
    b.   is in the preconventional level.
    c.   is in the postconventional level of self-accepted moral principles.
    d.   a and c.

Still confused? Review answer given for question 46. **(d)**

48. Freud's Oedipus Complex

    a.   is the stage in which fantasies of sexual relations with the opposite sex parent occurs.

    b.   occurs during the phallic stage.

    c.   a and b.

    d.   is a concept Freud ultimately eliminated from his theory.

The Oedipus Complex is the most controversial part of Freud's theory and choices "a" and "b" roughly describe it. The Oedipus Complex is said to occur between ages three and five. Looking for a good memory device? Well here it is. The Oedipus Complex occurs during the phallic stage and both words conveniently contain the letter "p." Some tests may actually refer to this stage as the phallic-oedipal stage. **(c)**

49. In girls the Oedipus Complex may be referred to as

    a.   systematic desensitization.

    b.   covert desensitization.

    c.   in vivo desensitization.

    d.   the Electra Complex.

In the Oedipus Complex in boys and the Electra Complex in girls, the child fantasizes about sexual relations with the parent of the opposite sex. This creates tension since this is generally not possible. The child hence is said to have a fantasy in which he or she wishes to kill the parent of the opposite sex. (Here Freud relied on the Greek tragedy by Sophocles in which, Oedipus, the protagonist, unknowingly killed his father and married his mother.) Freud went on to hypothesize that eventually the child identifies with the parent of the same sex. This leads to internalization of parental values and thus the conscience or superego is born. As for choices "a," "b," and "c," they are all behavioral terms and hence incorrect. The term covert in choice "b" refers to any psychological process which cannot be directly observed while in choice "c" I introduce you to in vivo which means the client is exposed to an actual situation which might prove frightful or difficult. The word desensitization refers to behavior therapy techniques that help to ameliorate anxiety reactions. **(d)**

50. The correct order of the Freudian psychosexual stages is
   a. oral, anal, phallic, latency, and genital.
   b. oral, anal, genital, phallic, and latency.
   c. oral, phallic, latency, genital, and anal.
   d. phallic, genital, latency, oral, and anal.

Freud is the father of psychoanalysis which is the most comprehensive theory of personality and therapy ever devised. **(a)**

51. Gibson researched the matter of depth perception in children by utilizing

   a. Piaget's concept of conservation.
   b. Erik Erikson's trust versus mistrust paradigm.
   c. Piaget's formal operations.
   d. a visual cliff.

It seems no child development book is complete without a picture of an infant crawling toward an experimenter on a visual cliff. The visual cliff is a device which utilizes a glass sheet which simulates a drop-off. Interestingly enough, infants will not attempt to cross the drop-off thus indicating that depth perception in humans is inherent (i.e., an inborn or so-called innate trait). By approximately eight months of age the child begins to show stranger anxiety, meaning that he or she can discriminate a familiar person from a person who is unknown. **(d)**

52. Theorists who believe that development merely consists of quantitative changes are referred to as

    a.   organismic theorists.
    b.   statistical developmentalists.
    c.   empiricists.
    d.   all of the above.

Empiricism grew out of the philosophy of John Locke in the 1600's and is sometimes referred to as associationism. According to this theory scientists can learn only from objective facts. Empiricism comes from the Greek word meaning experience. This philosophy adheres to the principle that experience is the source for acquiring knowledge. Remember that empiricism is often said to be the forerunner of behaviorism and you could pick up a point on the test you'll be taking. Choice "a" mentions the organismic viewpoint that is slanted toward qualitative rather than quantitative factors that can be measured empirically. Strictly speaking, organismic psychologists do not believe in a mind-body distinction. Since empiricists believe developmental changes can be measured and the organicists feel that change can be internal, the two views are sometimes said to be opposing viewpoints. **(c)**

53. An empiricist view of development would be

    a.   psychometric.
    b.   behavioristic.
    c.   against the use of formal statistical testing.
    d.   a and c.

Here again, the empiricist view is behavioristic. Using a little logic you can see that answer "c" is false inasmuch as some behaviorists have literally gone on record as saying, if you can't measure it then it doesn't exist! In case I still haven't made myself clear, behavioristic empiricist researchers value statistical studies and emphasize the role of the environment. Organismic

supporters feel the individual's actions are more important
than the environment in terms of one's development.   **(b)**

54. In the famous experiment by Harlow, frightened monkeys
    raised via cloth and wire mothers

    a.   showed marked borderline personality traits.
    b.   surprisingly enough became quite friendly.
    c.   demonstrated a distinct lack of emotion.
    d.   ran over and clung to the cloth and wire
         surrogate mothers.

    When given the choice of two cloth-covered mothers—
    one who provided milk and one that did not—the infant
    monkeys chose the one that gave milk. In a later
    experiment Harlow and a colleague discovered that a
    warm mother and a mother who rocked were superior
    to a cool mother or a mother who did not rock.   **(d)**

55. A theorist who views developmental changes as quantitative
    is said to be an empiricist. The antithesis of this position
    holds that developmental strides are qualitative. What
    is the name given to this position?

    a.   behaviorism
    b.   organicism
    c.   statistical developmentalism
    d.   all of the above

    The term organismic also has been used to describe
    Gestalt psychologists such as Kurt Goldstein who
    emphasize a holistic model.   **(b)**

56. In Piaget's developmental theory, reflexes play the greatest
    role in the

    a.   sensorimotor stage.
    b.   formal operational stage.
    c.   preoperational stage.
    d.   acquisition of conservation.

It would make sense that the child would use reflexes in the first stage which is termed sensorimotor intelligence. Piaget has said that the term "practical intelligence" captures the gist of this stage. Piaget emphasized the concept of "object permanence" here. A child who is beyond approximately eight months of age will search for an object that is no longer in sight (e.g., hidden behind a parent's back or under a blanket). The child learns that objects have an existence even when the child is not interacting with them. **(a)**

57. A mother hides a toy behind her back and a young child does not believe the toy exists anymore. The child has not mastered

    a.   object permanence.
    b.   reflexive response.
    c.   representational thought.
    d.   a and c.

The child who has not mastered object permanence is still a victim of "out of sight, out of mind." The child, needless to say, needs representational thought to master object permanence which also is called object constancy. During this initial stage the child learns the concept of time (i.e., that one event takes place before or after another) and causality (e.g., that a hand can move an object). **(d)**

58. The schema of permanency and constancy of objects occurs in the

    a.   sensorimotor stage—birth to 2 yrs.
    b.   preoperational stage—2 to 7 yrs.
    c.   concrete operational stage—7 to 12 yrs.
    d.   formal operational stage—12 years and beyond.

If you missed this question take a break; you've probably been studying too long! After a little rest and relaxation review questions 56 and 57. Incidentally, around the second month of age the child begins to smile in response to a face or a mask that resembles a face. **(a)**

59. John Bowlby has asserted that

     a.   attachment is not instinctual.
     b.   attachment is best explained via Skinnerian principle.
     c.   a and b.
     d.   conduct disorders and other forms of psychopathology can result from inadequate attachment and bonding in early childhood.

Remember, Bowlby starts with a "b" and so does bonding. Bowlby, a British psychoanalyst, felt that mothers should be the primary caretakers, while the father's role is to support the mother emotionally rather than nurturing the child himself. Although this view was well accepted when it was proposed in the early 1950s, most counselors probably would not agree with it today. **(d)**

60. The Harlow experiments utilizing monkeys demonstrated that animals placed in isolation during the first few months of birth

     a.   still developed in a normal fashion.
     b.   still related very well with animals reared normally.
     c.   appeared to be abnormal and autistic.
     d.   were fixated in concrete operational thought patterns.

The word autistic means extremely withdrawn and isolated. **(c)**

61. According to the Freudians, if a child is severely traumatized, he or she may _____ a given psychosexual stage.

     a.   skip
     b.   become fixated at
     c.   ignore
     d.   a and c

Here is a must-know term for any major exam. In psychoanalytic theory the word fixation implies that the individual is unable to go from one developmental stage to the next. The person literally becomes stuck (or fixated) in a stage where he or she feels safe. Therefore, when life becomes too traumatic, emotional development can come to a screeching halt though physical and cognitive processes may continue at a normal pace. **(b)**

62. An expert who has reviewed the literature on TV and violence would conclude that

    a. watching violence tends to make children more aggressive.
    b. watching violence tends to make children less aggressive.
    c. in reality TV has no impact on a child's behavior.
    d. what adults see as violent, children perceive as caring.

Experiments have demonstrated that even nursery school age children display more violence after observing it. Other researchers emphasize that the more we see, hear, and read about violence, the less it bothers us; ergo, we behave in a more violent manner. **(a)**

63. A counselor who utilizes the term "instinctual" technically means

    a. behavior results from unconscious aggression.
    b. women will show the behavior to a higher degree than men.
    c. a and b.
    d. behavior that manifests itself in all normal members of a given species.

Instincts are innate behaviors that do not need to be practiced or learned. Instincts are unlearned behavioral responses. **(d)**

64. The word "ethology," which is often associated with the work of Konrad Lorenz, refers to

   a.   Piaget's famous case study methodology.
   b.   the study of animal behavior in their natural environment.
   c.   studies on monkeys raised in Skinnerian air cribs.
   d.   all of the above.

The study of ethology was developed by European zoologists who tried to explain behavior using Darwinian theory. Today, when counselors refer to ethology, it concerns field research utilizing animals (e.g., birds or fish). The term "comparative psychology" refers to laboratory research using animals and attempts to generalize the findings to humans. Konrad Lorenz is best known for his work on the process of "imprinting." Imprinting is an instinct in ducklings and other animals in which the infant instinctively follows the first moving object it encounters, which is usually the mother. Lorenz used himself as the first moving object, and the newborns followed him around instead of the real mother! This illustrates the principle of "critical periods," which states that certain behaviors must be learned at an early time in the animal's development. Otherwise, the behaviors will never be learned at all. Just for the record, choice "c" mentions Burrhus Fredrick Skinner's air crib which was a relatively bacteria free, covered crib that Skinner relied on to help raise his daughter! Skinner is famous for his operant conditioning model. It will be examined in greater depth in future questions.   **(b)**

65. A child who focuses exclusively on a clown's red nose but ignores his or her other features would be illustrating the Piagetian concept of

   a.   egocentrism.
   b.   centration.
   c.   formal abstract reasoning.
   d.   deductive processes.

Centration occurs in the preoperational stage and is characterized by focusing on a key feature of a given object while not noticing the rest of it. Egocentrism in choice "a" refers to the preoperational child's inability to see the world from anyone else's vantage point. Piaget and Inhelder showed children a model mountain from all sides. The children then sat in front of the model and were asked to pick a picture that best described what the experimenter was seeing. The experimenter was sitting in a different location. Children continually picked pictures of their own view. The abstract reasoning in choice "c" takes place in the final formal operational stage. Deductive thinking processes in choice "d" allow an individual to apply general reasoning to specific situations. **(b)**

66. Piaget felt

    a.   homework depresses the elementary child's IQ.
    b.   strongly that the implementation of Glasser's concepts in Schools Without Failure should be made mandatory in all elementary settings.
    c.   that teachers should lecture a minimum of four hours daily.
    d.   teachers should lecture less, as children in concrete operations learn best via their own actions and experimentation.

"D" is the only correct answer inasmuch as Piaget felt that before the final stage (i.e., formal operations which begins at age 11 or 12) a child learns best from his or her own actions, not lectures, and his or her interactions and communications with peers rather than adults. Piaget, nevertheless, was quick to point out that he did not consider himself an educator but rather a genetic epistemologist. Epistemology is a branch of philosophy that attempts to examine how we know what we know. William Glasser in choice "b" is the father of reality therapy. **(d)**

67. Piaget's preoperational stage

    a.   is the final stage which includes abstract reasoning.
    b.   includes mastering conservation.
    c.   includes the acquisition of symbolic schema.
    d.   all of the above.

Symbolic mental processes allow language and symbolism in play to occur. A milk carton can easily become a spaceship or a pie plate can become the steering wheel of an automobile. The preoperational stage occurs from age two to seven. If you erroneously felt any of the other choices were correct review all the previous questions related to Piagetian theory. **(c)**

68. Sigmund Freud and Erik Erikson agreed that

    a.   each developmental stage needed to be resolved before an individual could move on to the next stage.
    b.   developmental stages are primarily psychosexual.
    c.   developmental stages are primarily psychosocial.
    d.   a person can proceed to a higher stage even if a lower stage is unsolved.

Freud felt the stages were psychosexual and his disciple Erikson felt they were psychosocial yet both agreed that individuals must resolve one stage before forging on to the next. Other well-known figures in developmental processes include Havinghurst, who proposed developmental tasks for children (developing conscience, morality, and a scale of values or learning to get along with age mates), and Loevinger, who focused on ego development via seven stages and two transitions with her highest level "integrated" (being similar to Maslow's self-actualized individual or Kohlberg's self-accepted universal principles stage). **(a)**

69. The tendency for adult females in the U.S. to wear high heels is best explained by

    a.   the principle of negative reinforcement.
    b.   sex role socialization.
    c.   Konrad Lorenz's studies on imprinting.
    d.   ethological data.

In the past the belief was that the differences between men and women were the result of biological factors. However, most counselors today feel that the child "learns" gender identity and male/female roles. Sandra Bem has spoken out against gender stereotyping (e.g., a woman's place is in the home), and feels when males and females are not guided by traditional sex roles individuals can be more androgynous and hence more productive. Choice "a," negative reinforcement, is a behavioristic term. Negative reinforcement occurs when the removal of a stimulus increases the probability that an antecedent behavior will occur. Never forget: All reinforcers—positive and negative—increase the probability that a behavior will occur. In positive reinforcement the addition of a stimulus strengthens or increases a behavior. If you still don't understand, relax, there's plenty more in the "Helping Relationships" section of this guide. **(b)**

70. The sequence of object loss, which goes from protest to despair to detachment, best describes the work of

    a.   Freud.
    b.   Adler on birth order.
    c.   Erikson.
    d.   Bowlby.

In psychoanalysis the term "object" describes the target of one's love. Bowlby felt that if the child was unable to bond with an adult by age three he or she would be incapable of having normal social relationships as an adult. **(d)**

71. A counselor who is seeing a 15-year-old boy who is not doing well in public speaking class would need to keep in mind that

    a.   in general, boys have better verbal skills than girls.

    b.   in general, girls possess better verbal skills than boys.

    c.   in general, boys possess better visual perceptual skills and are more active and aggressive than girls.

    d.   b and c.

"D" is the correct response, since choices "b" and "c" are both accurate according to research of Maccoby and Jacklin. Although I previously stated that most sex role differences are the result of learning, not biological factors, the tendency for boys to be more aggressive is probably one of the behavioral differences which can be attributed to androgen hormone. Actually, this is a very tricky question indeed. Assuming you could separate fact from male/female fiction you still might have marked choice "b" feeling that choice "c" was irrelevant in terms of counseling the client. My feeling is that "c" nevertheless is relevant since you might wish to emphasize positive qualities that the client possesses. Thus, if you marked choice "b," give yourself a grade of A-, or convince yourself that I'm just plain wrong. After all, that's what makes baseball games, political elections, oral and written boards, or even licensing and certification exams. Of course, since you're dealing with your perfectionism in a rational manner, it really won't matter now, will it?　　**(d)**

72. Two brothers begin screaming at each other during a family counseling session. The term that best describes the phenomenon is

    a.   the primal scene.

    b.   preconscious psychic processes.

    c.   sibling rivalry.

    d.   BASIC-ID.

In counseling, sibling rivalry refers to competition between siblings (i.e., a brother and a brother, a brother and a sister, or a sister and a sister). The "primal scene" noted in choice "a" is a psychoanalytic concept that suggests that a young child witnesses his parents having sexual intercourse or is seduced by a parent. The incident, whether real or imagined, is said to provide impetus for later neuroses. Choice "b" is also an analytic term and is known as the "foreconscious" in some textbooks. The preconscious mind is deeper than the conscious but not as deep as the unconscious. Preconscious material is not conscious but can be recalled without the use of special psychoanalytic techniques. This will be examined in more detail in the "Helping Relationship" section. The final choice, BASIC-ID, is an acronym posited via behaviorist Arnold Lazarus who feels his approach to counseling is multimodal, relying on a variety of therapeutic techniques. BASIC-ID stands for: Behavior, Affective Responses, Sensations, Imagery, Cognitions, Interpersonal Relationships, and Drugs.   **(c)**

73. A preschool child's concept of causality is said to be animistic. This means the child attributes human characteristics to inanimate objects. Thus, the child may fantasize that an automobile or a rock is talking to him. This concept is best related to

    a.   Carl Jung's concepts of anima, animus.
    b.   Freud's wish fulfillment.
    c.   Piaget's preoperational period age 2 to 7 years.
    d.   ego identity.

Animism occurs when a child acts as if nonliving objects have lifelike abilities and tendencies. Choice "a" mentions two concepts of the Swiss psychiatrist C.G. Jung, the father of analytic psychology. The anima represents the female characteristics of the personality while the animus represents the male characteristics. (Two super memory devices are that men generally have muscles [ani"mus"] and ma means mother who is female [ani"ma"].) Jung calls the anima and the animus "archetypes" which are inherited unconscious factors. Choice "b" wish fulfillment is a Freudian notion that dreams and slips of the tongue are actually wish fulfillments. The term ego identity, used in choice "d," is most often associated with Erikson's fifth stage: identity versus role confusion. When an adolescent is able to integrate all his or her previous roles into a single self-concept the person has achieved ego identity. An inability to accomplish this task results in role confusion, which is known as an identity crisis.   **(c)**

74. Erikson's thoughts on personality development have influenced counselors more than any other neo-Freudians. His concept of ego identity refers to

   a.   the ego striving to produce a unique, autonomous self.
   b.   his belief that the ego is not content with the mere assimilation of parental values.
   c.   a and b.
   d.   none of the above.

Erikson believes the individual is the one who has to make something of his or her life. A person is not merely the values of others he or she admires.   **(c)**

75. An individual is told the Heinz story and responds with, "If I stole the drug, I'd lose respect for myself, as I would not be living up to my own standards of honesty." This individual

   a.   would be in Kohlberg's conventional stage.
   b.   would be functioning in Kohlberg's post-conventional or highest level.
   c.   would be an anal character.
   d.   would be orally fixated.

In the highest level the person strives to live up to his or her own conscience. Surprisingly enough, if the person responded to the Heinz Story by stealing the drug the individual's answer could still be indicative of post-conventional morality! Remember that the level and stage assessment are not based on whether the individual decides to steal the drug or not. Instead, the determination is based on the logic or the rationale for the decision. A person, for example, who says, "If I don't steal the drug and my wife dies, I'll always know I didn't live up to my own conscience, even though others and the law wouldn't blame me," is still practicing postconventional thought. An anal character (choice "c") is said to be extremely stingy, orderly, and compulsive. The oral character (choice "d") is said to be dependent if he was allowed to suck too much or aggressive if he was not allowed to suck enough. When a person is fixated in a Freudian developmental stage he will try to satisfy motives from that particular stage. **(b)**

76. According to the Yale research by Daniel J. Levinson,

   a. Erikson's Generativity vs. Stagnation stage simply doesn't exist.
   b. 80% of the men in the study experienced moderate to severe mid-life crises.
   c. an "age 30 crisis" occurs in men when they feel it will soon be too late to make later changes.
   d. b and c.

Levinson and his colleagues were surprised to discover adult developmental transitions in white-collar and blue-collar men seemed to be relatively universal. Sheehy has pointed out that both men and women tend to experience typical crises, or so-called "passages," and each passage can be utilized to reach one's potential. **(d)**

77. Erikson's middle age stage (ages 35-60) is known as Generativity versus Stagnation. Generativity refers to

a. ability to do creative work or raise a family.
b. the opposite of stagnation.
c. the productive ability to create a career, family, and leisure time.
d. all of the above.

Choice "d" gives you a thumbnail sketch of Erikson's seventh or second-to-last stage. A person who does not master this stage well becomes self-centered, hence, you also will see the stage termed "Generativity versus Self-Absorption." A nice memory device here is that "generativity" sounds like "generation" and a successful individual in this stage plans for the next generation. Havinghurst, mentioned earlier, would refer to this stage as the middle adult years (he also mentions young adult and old adult periods). Havinghurst feels that the middle adult should achieve civic responsibility, maintain a home, guide adolescents, develop leisure, adjust to bodily changes, and learn to relate to a spouse. Good advice, but if it seems a little dated it is; 1952 vintage. The 1950's were the golden years for developmental psychology. **(d)**

78. A person who can look back on his or her life with few regrets feels

    a. the burden of senile psychosis.
    b. ego-integrity in the Integrity versus Despair stage.
    c. despair which is the sense that they have wasted life's precious opportunities.
    d. the burden of generalized anxiety as described in the DSM.

According to Erikson, successful resolution of this stage results in the belief that one's life served a purpose. Choice "a" introduces the term "senile psychosis," which is decidedly incorrect but a relevant term nevertheless. The word psychosis refers to a break from reality which can include hallucinations, delusions and thought disorders. In senile psychosis this condition is brought on via old age. At times, the term will be used in a looser sense to imply a loss of memory. Choice "d" throws out two other "must-know," new terms. In counseling, anxiety (or generalized anxiety) refers to fear, dread, or apprehension without being able to pinpoint the exact reason for the feeling. Anxiety is in contrast to a phobia in which the client can pinpoint the cause or source of fear (e.g., riding a elevator). The letters DSM stand for the *Diagnostic and Statistical Manual of Mental Disorders*, produced by the American Psychiatric Association. This is a manual used to classify and label mental disorders so that all mental health practitioners will mean roughly the same thing (symptomatology etc.) when they classify a client. The branch of medicine which concerns itself with the classification of disease is known as "nosology." Thus counselors use the DSM as their primary nosological guide. **(b)**

79. Sensorimotor is to Piaget; as Oral is to Freud; as _____ is to Erikson.

    a.   Integrity versus Despair
    b.   Kohlberg
    c.   Trust versus Mistrust
    d.   morality

This is the analogy question mentioned earlier, and identifying the correct answer is actually quite simple. The question matches Piaget's name to his first stage (i.e., sensorimotor) and Freud's name to his first stage (i.e., oral) thus you will match Erikson's name to his first stage which is trust versus mistrust. **(c)**

80. Which theorist was most concerned with maternal deprivation?

    a.   A. Lazarus
    b.   H. Harlow
    c.   J. Wolpe
    d.   A. Ellis

Harry Harlow was born in 1905 and died in 1981. He is best known for his work with rhesus monkeys at the University of Wisconsin. Choice "c" mentions Joseph Wolpe who pioneered the technique of systematic desensitization, a behavioristic technique used to ameliorate phobic reactions. Albert Ellis (Choice "d") is a New York clinical psychologist who developed a form of treatment known as Rational-Emotive Psychotherapy which teaches clients to think in a more scientific and logical manner. Ellis was originally trained as an analyst and is a very prolific writer. **(b)**

81. When development comes to a halt, counselors say that the client

    a.   has learned helplessness syndrome.
    b.   suffers from a phobia.
    c.   suffers from fixation.
    d.   is displaying the risky shift phenomenon.

This is primarily an analytic concept. Freud felt that frustration and anxiety are normal when passing through a developmental stage, but when they become too powerful emotional growth will literally stop and the person becomes stuck (fixated) in the current stage. Learned helplessness in choice "a" connotes a pattern in which a person is exposed to situations in which he or she is truly powerless to change and then begins to believe he or she has no control over the environment. Such a person can become easily depressed. This concept is generally associated with the work of Martin E.P. Seligman who experimentally induced learned helplessness in dogs via giving them electric shocks while placed in a harness. These dogs—unlike untrained dogs—did not even try to escape the painful shocks when the harnesses were removed. Choice "b" is phobia, which is a known fear, such as a fear of furry animals or flying in an airplane. In counseling, a phobia is often distinguished from anxiety. In an anxiety reaction, the client is unaware of the source of the fear. The final choice, risky shift phenomenon, describes the fact that a group decision is typically more liberal than the average decision of an individual group member prior to participation in the group. Simply put, the individual's initial stance will generally be more conservative than the group's decision. **(c)**

82. Kohlberg proposed three levels of morality. Freud, on the other hand, felt morality developed from the

    a. superego.
    b. ego.
    c. id.
    d. eros.

Eric Berne, the father of Transactional Analysis, put Freudian lingo in everyday language and spoke of the parent ego state which is roughly equivalent to the super-ego. The parent ego state is filled with the shoulds, oughts, and musts which often guide our morality. **(a)**

83. Which theorist would be most likely to say that aggression is an inborn tendency?

    a. Carl Rogers
    b. B.F. Skinner
    c. Frank Parsons, the Father of Guidance
    d. Konrad Lorenz

Bad news folks: Konrad Lorenz compared us to the wolf or the baboon and claimed that we are naturally aggressive. According to Lorenz, aggressiveness is part of our evolution and was necessary for survival. The solution? Well, according to Lorenz, we should utilize catharsis and get our anger out, using methods such as competitive sports. Choices "a" and "c" cite two of the most influential names in the history of counseling. Carl Ransom Rogers created nondirective counseling, later called client-centered counseling, and more recently, person-centered counseling. Frank Parsons, has been called the father of guidance. In the early 1900s Parsons set up centers to help individuals in search of work. **(d)**

84. The statement, "Bad behavior is punished, good behavior is not," is most closely associated with

    a.   Kohlberg's premoral stage at the preconventional level.
    b.   Kohlberg's conventional level.
    c.   the work of Carl Jung.
    d.   Piaget's autonomous stage, which begins at about age 8.

In the initial stage morality is guided by a fear of punishment. Choice "d" is concerned with the Piagetian conceptualization of moral development. Piaget suggested two major stages: the heteronomous stage, and the autonomous stage which begins at approximately age 8. Heteronomous morality occurs between ages 4 and 7 as the child views rules as absolutes that result in punishment. Autonomous morality is characterized by the child's perception that rules are relative and can be altered or changed. **(a)**

85. A critical period

    a.   makes imprinting possible.
    b.   emphasizes manifest dream content.
    c.   signifies a special time when a behavior must be learned or the behavior won't be learned at all.
    d.   a and c.

A critical period is a time when an organism is susceptible to a specific developmental process. A critical period marks the importance of heredity and environment on development. In humans, for example, language acquisition is thought to begin at around age 2 and ends at about age 14. **(d)**

86. Imprinting is an instinct in which a newborn will follow a moving object. The primary work in this area was done by

    a.   Erik Erikson.
    b.   Milton H. Erickson.
    c.   Konrad Lorenz.
    d.   Harry Harlow.

Some behavioral scientists refer to instinctual behavior as "species-specific," meaning that the behavioral trait occurs in every member of the species. The behavior is unlearned and universal.   **(c)**

87. Marital satisfaction

    a.   is usually highest when a child is old enough to leave home.
    b.   often decreases with parenthood and is lowest prior to a child leaving home.
    c.   correlates high with performance IQ.
    d.   is highest among couples who have seven or more college educated children.

Despite a divorce rate of nearly 50% in the U.S., most Americans still desire to marry.   **(b)**

88. Maslow, a humanistic psychologist, is famous for his "hierarchy of needs" which postulates

    a.   lower order physiological and safety needs and higher order needs, such as self-actualization.
    b.   that psychopathology rests within the id.
    c.   that unconscious drives control self-actualization.
    d.   that stimulus-response psychology dictates behavioral attributes.

Answers "b," "c," and "d" are necessarily incorrect inasmuch as Abraham Maslow rejected both analytic psychology and behaviorism as he felt they dehumanized men and women. Maslow's theory has been dubbed as "humanistic psychology," or "third force" psychology. Maslow felt the person first needs to satisfy immediate or basic needs such as food and water. Next safety and security must be dealt with. Next a need for love, affection, and belonging emerges. The highest level is termed self-actualization, meaning the person becomes all he or she can be. A word to the wise: some tests may refer to higher order needs (i.e., any need which is not physiological) as "metaneeds." **(a)**

89. To research the dilemma of self-actualization, Maslow

    a.   used ducklings as did Konrad Lorenz.
    b.   psychoanalyzed over 400 neurotics.
    c.   worked exclusively with schizophrenics in residential settings.
    d.   interviewed the best people he could find who escaped "the psychology of the average."

You didn't mark choice "a" . . . did you? Imagine trying to learn about self-actualization from studying baby ducklings! No Maslow didn't utilize ducklings, nor did he turn to persons with severe psychological problems. Maslow said if you research the "psychopathology of the average" you will have a sick theory of human behavior! The answer: work with those who have transcended the so-called average or normal existence. **(d)**

90. Piaget is

    a.   a maturationist.
    b.   a behaviorist.
    c.   a structuralist who believes stage changes are qualitative.
    d.   cognitive-behavioral.

According to the structuralist viewpoint, each stage is a way of making sense out of the world. Choice "d," cognitive-behavioral, generally applies to counselors who emphasize thought processes in terms of their impact on emotions as well as behavioristic strategies (e.g., reinforcement or homework assignments). **(c)**

91. _____ factors cause Down's Syndrome which produces mental retardation.

    a.   Environmental
    b.   Genetic
    c.   Chemical dependency
    d.   Unconscious

Persons with Down's syndrome have a rather flat face, a thick tongue, and slanted eyes. Down's syndrome, which is the result of a chromosomal abnormality, causes brain damage which results in an IQ of 50 or less (100 is normal). Down's syndrome also has been called "mongolism" which was inspired by the slanted almost Asiatic eyes. Other genetic or hereditary conditions include: Phenylketonuria (PKU) which is an amino acid metabolic difficulty that causes retardation unless the baby is placed on a special diet; Klinefelter's syndrome, in which a male shows no masculinity at puberty; and Turner's syndrome, where a female has no gonads or sex hormones. **(b)**

92. Piaget referred to the act of taking in new information as assimilation. This results in accommodation, which is a modification of the child's cognitive structures (schemas) to deal with the new information. In Piagetian nomenclature, the balance between assimilation and accommodation is called

    a.   counterbalancing.
    b.   equilibration.
    c.   balance theory.
    d.   ABA design.

Choice "a" refers to an experimental process in which a researcher varies the order of conditions to eliminate irrelevant variables. Choice "c," balance theory, suggests that individuals avoid inconsistent or incompatible beliefs. In other words, people prefer consistent beliefs. This is sometimes known as the tendency to maintain "cognitive consistency." ABA design, noted in choice "d," is experimental and research lingo. The A stands for the baseline, which is the behavior before an experimental or treatment procedure is introduced. B is the treatment. After the treatment is implemented the occurrence of A (the behavior in question) is measured to see if a change is evident. **(b)**

93. There are behavioral, structural, and maturational theories of development. The maturational viewpoint utilizes the plant growth analogy in which the mind is seen as being driven by instincts while the environment provides nourishment thus placing limits on development. Counselors who are maturationists

   a.   conduct therapy in the here and now.
   b.   focus primarily on nonverbal behavior.
   c.   believe group work is most effective.
   d.   allow clients to work through early conflicts.

Counselors of this persuasion allow the client to work through the old painful material. Theoretically, the counselor acts almost like a perfect nonjudgmental parent. And thus the client can explore the situation in a safe, therapeutic relationship. Psychoanalysts and psychodynamic therapists fall into this category. **(d)**

94. Ritualistic behaviors, which are common to all members of a species, are known as

   a.   hysteria.
   b.   pica.
   c.   fixed-action patterns elicited by sign stimuli.
   d.   dysfunctional repetition.

Theoretically, a fixed-action pattern (abbreviated FAP) will result whenever a releaser in the environment is present. The action, or sequence of behavior, will not vary. In choice "a" the word hysteria is presented. Hysteria is said to occur when an individual displays an organic symptom (e.g., blindness, paralysis, or deafness), yet no physiological causes are evident. Choice "b," pica, is a condition in which a person wishes to eat items that are not food (i.e., the item has no nutritional value) such as consuming a pencil or perhaps a watch band. Just in case you're wondering, fast-food consumption is not considered a sign of pica in our society . . . yet! **(c)**

95. Robert Kegan speaks of a "holding environment" in counseling in which

    a. the client is urged to relive a traumatic experience in an encounter group.
    b. biofeedback training is highly recommended.
    c. the client can make meaning in the face of a crisis and can find new direction.
    d. the activity of meaning making is discouraged.

Choice "d" is necessarily incorrect inasmuch as Kegan encourages "meaning making." Kegan suggests six stages of life span development: incorporative, impulsive, imperial, interpersonal, institutional, and interindividual. **(c)**

96. Most experts in the field of counseling agree that

    a. no one theory completely explains developmental processes; thus, counselors ought to be familiar with all the major theories.
    b. Eriksonian theory should be used by counselors practicing virtually any modality.
    c. a counselor who incorporates Piaget's stages into his or her thinking would not necessarily need a knowledge regarding rival therapeutic viewpoints.
    d. a realistic counselor needs to pick one developmental theory in the same manner he or she picks a psychotherapeutic persuasion.

Since each theorist's work has a slant to it (e.g., Freud—psychosexual factors; Kohlberg—moral factors; Piaget—intellectual/cognitive factors, etc.), a well-rounded counselor will necessarily need a basic knowledge of all the popular theories. **(a)**

97. Equilibration is

     a.   a term which emphasizes the equality between the sexes.
     b.   performed via the id according to the Freudians.
     c.   a synonym for concrete operational thought.
     d.   the balance between what one takes in (assimilation) and that which is changed (accommodation).

In case you haven't caught on I'm banking on the fact that repetition can do wonders for your exam review. So one more time, just for the record: equilibration (or equilibrium) occurs when the child achieves a balance. When new information is presented, which the child's current cognitive structures known as "schemas" cannot process, a condition referred to as "disequilibrium" sets in. The child therefore changes the schemas to accommodate the novel information, and equilibration or equilibrium is mastered. **(d)**

98. A counselor is working with a family who just lost everything in a fire. The counselor will ideally focus on

     a.   Maslow's higher order needs such as self-actualization.
     b.   building accurate empathy of family members.
     c.   Maslow's lower order needs such as physiological and safety needs.
     d.   the identified patient.

Maslow, a pioneer in third force or humanistic psychology, suggested the following hierarchy: survival needs, security, safety, love, self-esteem, and self-actualization. The assumption is that lower order needs must be fulfilled before the individual can be concerned with higher order needs.   **(c)**

99. The anal retentive personality is

    a.   charitable.
    b.   stingy.
    c.   kind.
    d.   thinks very little about money matters.

To put it bluntly, the anal retentive character is said to be cheap!   **(b)**

100. From a Freudian perspective, a client who has a problem with alcoholism and excessive smoking would be

    a.   considered an oral character.
    b.   considered an anal character.
    c.   considered a genital character.
    d.   fixated at the latency stage.

Here is where good old common sense comes in handy. The oral region of the body (i.e., the mouth) would be the portion of the body most closely related to smoking and alcoholism.   **(a)**

SOCIAL AND CULTURAL FOUNDATIONS

101. Counseling a client from a different social and/or cultural background is known as

    a.   cross-cultural counseling.
    b.   multicultural counseling.
    c.   intercultural counseling.
    d.   all of the above.

Choices "a," "b," and "c" are roughly synonymous and hence mean approximately the same thing when you encounter them in the literature. The ACA division that deals explicitly with this topic is the Association for Multicultural Counseling and Development (AMCD). **(d)**

102. Culture refers to

    a.   customs shared by a group which distinguish it from other groups.
    b.   values shared by a group.
    c.   attitudes and beliefs which characterize members of a group.
    d.   all of the above.

The sum of choices "a," "b," and "c" add up to a wonderful little definition of culture. One's culture can really be delineated by those customs which set him or her apart from another culture. Immigrants or persons who must live in a culture which is different from their native culture often experience "culture conflict." By definition culture conflict manifests itself whenever a person experiences conflicting thoughts, feelings, or behaviors due to divided cultural loyalty (i.e., loyalty to two or more cultures). Culture conflict also can describe the difficulties which arise when persons of different cultures live in the same geographical area. How will you know which definition of cultural conflict applies to a test question? Well, the only good answer is that you must read every question very carefully in order to ferret out the context of the question.   **(d)**

103. Multicultural counselors often work with persons who are culturally different. This means the client

   a.   is culturally biased.
   b.   suffers from the diagnosis of cultural relativity.
   c.   belongs to a different culture than the helper.
   d.   presents problems which deal only with culturally charged issues.

Here is a very important distinction. Multicultural counselors work with the entire range of human difficulties just like other counselors. Yes, multicultural counselors do indeed deal frequently with cultural issues and therefore choices "a" and "b" could be true, but they are decidedly not the best answers. Choice "d" is easy enough to eliminate if you read it carefully and noted the word "only." Let's zero in for a moment on the term noted in choice "b," "cultural relativity," also described as "cultural relativism" on some exams. Cultural relativity connotes that a behavior cannot be assessed as good or bad except within the context of a given culture. The behavior must be evaluated relative to the culture. In the U.S., for example, teen pregnancy prior to marriage is considered a negative behavior and viewed as a difficulty.

In other parts of the world premarital pregnancy may be seen as something which is positive as it establishes the woman's fertility. Such a woman may even be described as more "marriageable." THE MULTICULTURAL COUNSELOR MUST ASSESS THE CLIENT'S BEHAVIOR BASED ON THE CLIENT'S OWN CULTURE—NOT MERELY ON THE COUNSELOR'S CULTURE. THE MEANING AND/ OR DESIRABILITY OF A GIVEN BEHAVIOR, TRAIT, OR ACT IS BASED ON THE CULTURE. It is said that effective counselors must transcend the "culture bound values" barrier in which the counselor is "bound" to his or her own values and tries to impose them on clients.   **(c)**

104. In order to diagnose clients from a different culture

   a.   the counselor ideally will need some information regarding the specifics of the culture.
   b.   the counselor will find the DSM useless.
   c.   the counselor will find the ICD diagnosis useless.
   d.   NBCC ethics prohibit the use of DSM diagnosis when counseling clients from another culture.

Some of the literature in this area distinguishes "material culture" (e.g., books, paintings, homes, and tools) from what is termed "nonmaterial culture" (e.g., customs, values, humor, social ideas or traditions). Some exams will refer to material culture items as "artifacts." In any case, the current trend in counseling suggests that the counselor must understand cultural factors. This trend is known as "cultural awareness" and it is contrasted by a position of "cultural tunnel vision." A good cross-cultural counselor will not impose his or her values on a client from a different cultural perspective. Another cultural term you may see on an exam is "culture-epoch theory" which suggests that all cultures—like children— pass through the same stages of development in terms of evolving and maturing. In regard to choice "d," Section B, paragraph 13 of the NBCC code of ethics stipulates that counselors must incorporate "culturally relevant techniques into their practice" and should acquire "sensitivity to client populations served." The appropriateness of a given DSM diagnosis is not specifically addressed.   **(a)**

105. In the U.S., each socioeconomic group represents

    a.   a separate race.
    b.   a separate culture.
    c.   the silent middle class.
    d.   a separate national culture.

Choice "a," race, refers to the identification of individuals via distinct physical or bodily (somatic) characteristics such as skin color or facial features. The assumption is thus made that a given racial group can be distinguished from others by virtue of their looks. Many social scientists have questioned whether race is indeed a valid term since it is sometimes questionable as to what constitutes a given race. Choice "d," national culture, is a term used to describe the cultural patterns common to a given country. Nevertheless, keep in mind that in reality there is the "ideal culture," which is the way individuals are supposed to behave, as well as the "real culture," which encompasses all behaviors within the culture, even those which are illicit or frowned upon. When a group of persons vehemently oppose the values of the culture they are said to be members of a "counterculture."   **(b)**

106. Which therapist was not instrumental in the early years of the social psychology movement?

    a.   Freud
    b.   Durkheim
    c.   McDougall
    d.   Berne

Eric Berne, the father of Transactional Analysis (choice "d") is the only answer which makes sense here. Here's why. Freud (choice "a") is known for his influential 1921 book, *Group Psychology and the Analysis of the Ego*, which suggested that the group was held together by a bond between the leader and the group members that was seen as somewhat analogous to a hypnotist and his or her subject. A bit far-fetched according to some, but clearly indicative of Freud's fascination with the power of hypnosis. The Frenchman, Emile Durkeim (choice "b") is considered one of the founders of modern sociology. His principles were first outlined in his 1895 work, *Rules of Sociological Method*. He is also well-known for his research into suicide which culminated in another literary work, *Suicide*, two years later. Durkheim is said to have taken group phenomena beyond the armchair speculation stage into formal research. William McDougall (choice "c") is the father of "hormic psychology," a Darwinian viewpoint which suggested that individuals in or out of groups are driven by innate, inherited tendencies. Although this approach began to lose ground after the behaviorist movement picked up steam, McDougall is well-remembered for his 1908 landmark work, *Introduction to Social Psychology*. **(d)**

107. _____ and _____ would say that regardless of culture, humans have an instinct to fight.

    a.   Maslow; Rogers
    b.   Ellis; Harper
    c.   Freud; Lorenz
    d.   Glasser; Rogers

Freud believed that man was basically driven by the instincts of sex and aggression. Lorenz—partially basing his theory on the fact that certain tropical fish will attack an alternate target even when the actual target of aggression is removed—is another believer in the so-called "innate aggression theory." I find this logic a tad fishy when applied to the genus homo sapiens. P.S. McDougall, mentioned in the previous question, could also join the ranks of Freud and Lorenz as an "instinct theorist." **(c)**

108. _____ believe that aggression is learned. Thus, a child who witnesses aggressive behavior in adults may imitate the aggressive behavior.

a. Instinct theorists
b. Innate aggression theorists
c. Social learning theorists
d. Followers of Erik Erikson

If you marked choices "a" or "b" then it's crystal clear that you are not reading the answers carefully enough. Review the last question. The social learning theory contradicts the "innate/instinct aggression theory" by emphasizing the environment rather than genetics or inborn tendencies. This model is generally associated with the work of Bandura and his associates who noted that children who viewed live or filmed aggression imitated the behavior. The phenomenon is greatest when the adult is admired, powerful, or well-liked. Hmmm. I wonder how many television personalities, rock stars, and sports figures are keeping abreast of the findings in social psychology? **(c)**

109. The APGA, which became the AACD until 1992 and is now ACA, contributed to the growth of cross-cultural counseling by

a. the 1972 formation of the Association for Non-White Concerns in Personnel and Guidance.
b. the 1972 ethic which made it unethical to see culturally different clients without three hours of relevant graduate work in this area.
c. the 1972 ethic which required a 3,000 hour practicum in order to work with culturally different clients.
d. urging nonwhites to take graduate counseling courses.

The civil rights movement was instrumental in terms of setting the stage for minority concerns. **(a)**

110. As a bonafide subspecialty, multicultural counseling

    a.   recognizes culture as the primary consept.
    b.   recognizes that ethnicity influences counseling.
    c.   recognizes that socioeconomic factors and race influence counseling.
    d.   all of the above.

Multicultural counseling is currently considered the fastest growing subspecialty in the field. **(d)**

111. The three factors which enhance interpersonal attraction are

    a.   assertiveness, anxiety, ego strength.
    b.   close proximity, physical attraction, similar beliefs.
    c.   culture, race, assertiveness.
    d.   ego strength, anxiety, race.

Proxemics, or the study of proximity, relates to personal space and territoriality. Festinger discovered that friendship and attraction were highest for apartment dwellers living next door to each other. The attraction waned even among people living two or three doors away. Although we like attractive people, the research shows that we generally end up with mates who are on our own level of attractiveness. Studies have literally shown that voters prefer attractive candidates though they are unaware of their bias. I often do a mini-experiment in my classes in which I pass out a picture of a very attractive individual and one who is very plain. I then ask the class to rate both individuals in regard to IQ and salary. True to the research, my class generally gives the good looking individual an inflated IQ and salary. Studies also indicate that attractive people fare better in legal altercations (yes, even when they have committed a crime). Moreover, they are more likely to receive help during a time of need, and they are better able to sway the opinions of an audience. Compliments, or what some of the literature refers to as "rewardingness" (a genuine caring), could also be added to the list of factors which helps to intensify attraction. **(b)**

112. Cross-cultural counseling

    a.   is the oldest subspecialty in the profession.
    b.   is one of the newest subspecialties in the profession.
    c.   degree programs are plentiful.
    d.   is very narrow in scope.

Although Frank Parsons, the father of guidance, acknowledged the significance of culture, it did not really begin to emerge as a true accepted subspecialty until the 1970s. Perhaps the newness of the movement accounts for the inaccuracy of choice "c." And of course, choice "d" could not possibly be correct since a model which encompasses the study of culture around the world is necessarily global in scope. (A person's perception of his or her relationship to the world as a whole is often termed a "world view.") **(b)**

113. _____ helped to abet the multicultural movement.

    a.   Berne's landmark work in TA
    b.   The fact that Lazarus was not a native American
    c.   The fact that Freud was not born in America
    d.   The 1954 Supreme Court decision to outlaw public school segregation

Counseling between Whites and Blacks became much more common. **(d)**

114. _____ helped to abet the intercultural counseling movement.

    a.   Jensen's views on IQ testing
    b.   The civil rights movement.
    c.   Jung's feeling that all men and women from all cultures possess a collective unconscious
    d.   The *Tarasoff* Duty

First remember that intercultural counseling means the same thing as multicultural counseling. Review the answer to 109 if this question presented any difficulty. Jensen, choice "a," tried to prove that Blacks had lower IQ's due to genetic factors while the Tarasoff case mentioned in choice "d" resulted in the counselor's duty to warn an intended victim who might be the target of danger or violence. **(b)**

115. When a counselor speaks of a probable outcome in a case, he or she is technically referring to

    a.   the prognosis.
    b.   the diagnosis.
    c.   the intervention.
    d.   attending behavior.

Prognosis refers to the probability that one can recover from a condition. When dictating on cases the counselor would do well to discuss the length of treatment and the status expected at the end of treatment. **(a)**

116. When a counselor speaks of what he or she believes to be needed to transpire from a psychotherapeutic standpoint, he or she technically is referring to

    a.   recommendations.
    b.   the diagnosis.
    c.   the prognosis.
    d.   the notion of transference.

One difficulty with formal diagnosis (i.e., using the Diagnostic and Statistical Manual of the American Psychiatric Association) is that a given diagnosis does not imply or recommend a given treatment process. The DSM will not say, for example, treat a major depression with reality therapy, or an adjustment disorder with mixed emotional features using a client-centered approach. **(a)**

117. Some research suggests that very poor economic conditions correlate very highly with

    a.   passivity.
    b.   nonassertive behavior.
    c.   a and b.
    d.   aggression.

This is not a new phenomenon. Research indicates that in the late 1800s and the first 30 years of the 1900s lynchings in the South increased as cotton prices dropped! **(d)**

118. A wealth of research demonstrates that

    a.   surprisingly enough, Blacks generally request Asian counselors.
    b.   surprisingly enough, Asians generally request Black counselors.
    c.   in most instances, clients prefer a counselor of the same race and a similar cultural background.
    d.   in most instances, clients prefer a counselor of the same race, yet a different culture.

In multicultural counseling, "likes attract." Social psychologists who have studied attraction tell us that similarity increases attraction. The phrase "in most instances" was intentional. Research demonstrates if the other person is a member of a different nationality, race, or culture but is perceived as "similar" (i.e., more like you than someone of the same race and culture), then you still will be more attracted to the individual perceived as "similar" despite race or cultural barriers. **(c)**

119. The frustration-aggression theory is associated with

    a.   Ellis.
    b.   Freud and Jung.
    c.   Miller and Berne.
    d.   Dollard and Miller.

Frustration occurs when an individual is blocked so that he or she cannot reach an intended goal (or the goal is removed). The Dollard/Miller hypothesis asserts that frustration leads to aggression. Albert Ellis, (note choice "a") the father of rational-emotive psychotherapy, felt that unfortunately many clients do indeed believe that frustration causes aggression. Ellis felt this transpires due to the client's irrational thought process (i.e., actually believing it is true) rather than some automatic response pattern. Zimbardo believed that when individuals lose their identity (sometimes called "deindividuation") they are likely to become aggressive and/or violent. Berkowitz discovered that the presence of weapons raises the level of violence as well as the probability that it will occur. Counselors need to keep this in mind when dealing with suicidal and homicidal clients (e.g., an individual is more likely to turn his or her aggression against self if he or she owns a gun; firearms constitute the number one method of committing suicide in our country). **(d)**

120. A popular balance theory in social psychology is _____ cognitive dissonance theory.

    a.   Dollard and Miller's
    b.   Crites and Roe's
    c.   Festinger's
    d.   Holland and Super's

Choices "b" and "d" are names primarily associated with the career counseling movement. The concept of balance theory suggests that people strive for consistency/balance in terms of their belief systems. Simply put, individuals attempt to reduce or eliminate inconsistent or incompatible actions and beliefs. A state of incompatibility is known as "dissonance," which literally means discord. Leon Festinger in 1957 suggested that individuals are motivated to reduce the tension and discomfort, thus putting an end to the dissonance. A statement like, "I'd rather smoke three packs of cigarettes a day and enjoy myself than quit and live an extra year or two," would be an example of cognitive dissonance in action. The person in this example has "changed the balance" by making his or her thinking consistent. Dissonance is often reduced using denial. Thus the individual who says, "Sure I smoke, but the research which suggests it is harmful is not accurate," is also practicing cognitive dissonance, since he or she is using a form of denial. **(c)**

121. Culture is really a set of rules, procedures, ideas, and values shared by members of a society. Culture is said to be normative. This implies that

    a. one culture will have norms which differ only slightly from another.
    b. culture excludes customs.
    c. culture provides individuals with standards of conduct.
    d. culture is never socially learned.

Cultures often differ markedly from each other, and most experts would agree that the customs are nearly always learned and shared with members of the society. **(c)**

122. A statistical norm measures actual conduct while a cultural norm

    a. describes how people are supposed to act.
    b. has little to do with expectations.
    c. is irrelevant when counseling a client.
    d. all of the above.

Choice "b" is the direct antithesis of the correct alternative choice "a." Some multicultural practioners suggest that culture is really a system of norms. Here is an important distinction: A statistical norm measures actual conduct, while a cultural norm describes the expectations of how one should act. **(a)**

123. Mores are beliefs

    a.   regarding the rightness or wrongness of behavior.
    b.   which should be the central focus in multicultural counseling.
    c.   that are conscious decisions made by persons in power.
    d.   that are identical with the folkways in the culture.

Mores—the plural of mos which is rarely used in the literature—develop as a given group decides what is good and bad for the welfare of the people. People are generally punished for violating the mores. On an exam you may be asked to distinguish "folkways" (see choice "d") from mores. Folkways, like mores, describe correct, normal, or habitual behavior. The difference is that breaking a folkway generally results in embarrassment while breaking a more causes harm to others or threatens the existence of the group. If, for example, you are an American and you drink a large bowl of soup directly from a soup bowl rather than using a spoon, then you have violated an American folkway. Your behavior won't really win you friends or positively influence people, but you won't be asked to spend time in a maximum security correction facility either. If, on the other hand, you kill three people and rob a bank, you have violated mores and your behavior could indeed result in serious punishment. Some of the literature does not attempt to describe mores as a separate entity but rather as a type of folkway and thus choice "d" isn't really that far off the mark. If you're looking for a simple memory device, why not try the fact that "mores" begins with an "m" as does the word "morals." Mores are behaviors that are based on morals. If you drink your soup out of a large bowl or pot, you may be in violation of an American folkway or in dire need of a course in etiquette, though I doubt whether your friends will classify you as immoral! **(a)**

124. _____ was the first pioneer to focus heavily on sociocultural issues.

    a.   Erikson
    b.   Adler—the Father of Individual Psychology—
    c.   Maultsby—the Father of RBT—
    d.   Frank Parsons—the Father of guidance—

Frank Parsons and his associates are considered the first social reformers concerned with guidance in the U.S. **(d)**

125. A counselor who is part of a research study will be counseling clients at the polar regions and then at a point near the equator. Her primary concern will be

    a.   universal culture.
    b.   national culture.
    c.   ecological culture.
    d.   b and c.

Clemmont Vontress suggested that multicultural counselors would do well to remember that we are all part of a universal culture (choice "a"). We all have similar or universal needs (e.g., the hierarchy proposed by Maslow) and requirements for food, water, air, and sleep regardless of our cultural affiliation. Vontress noted that universal culture can be distinguished from national, regional, racio-ethnic, and ecological culture. Ecological culture implies that cultural norms are often the result of practical and survival behaviors related to the climate or the resources in a given physical or geological environment. Eating, drinking, clothing, and shelter behaviors would clearly be different in the polar regions than in the equator, dessert region, or New York city. From a personal standpoint the counselor's primary concern would probably be the ecological culture, albeit choice "b" (national culture) would no doubt run a close second. **(d)**

126. Biological similarities and sameness is indicated by

    a. ecological culture.
    b. mores.
    c. regional and national culture.
    d. universal culture.

Perhaps it is safe to say that biologically we are all more alike than different. The adept cross-cultural counselor will always keep in mind that he or she—like the client—is a product of universal culture. **(d)**

127. Early vocalization in infants

    a. is more complex in Black babies.
    b. is more complex in Caucasian babies.
    c. is nearly identical in all cultures around the globe.
    d. is the finest indicator of elementary school performance.

From one side of the globe to the other, the initial sounds made by babies are very similar. The cultural environment then strengthens certain verbalizations via the process of reinforcement. The first word usually is spoken after approximately one year of life. The child may use one or two word phrases (e.g., "me eat" or "I Betty") initially. These are known as "holophrases." Initially, the child's language is egocentric. By the fourth year most children can construct simple sentences. Children in middle-class homes usually have richer language patterns than those of lower socioeconomic homes. Lack of environmental stimulation (referred to as an "unstimulating" environment on some exams) does indeed hinder vocalization development. **(c)**

128. In the 1920s, Bogardus developed a social distance scale which evaluated

    a.   socioeconomic trends.
    b.   how an individual felt toward other ethnic groups.
    c.   disadvantaged youth.
    d.   language barriers between Blacks and Asians.

"Ethnic" can be defined as that which pertains to a racial, national, religious, or cultural group. Measurement of attitudinal attributes began in the 1920s. The Bogardus data were indicative of negative attitudes toward a number of groups including Blacks, Jews, Mexicans, and Turks. A replication of the study in 1947 revealed that the negative attitudes still prevailed. **(b)**

129. According to the foot-in-the-door obedience to authority phenomenon, a counselor who needs to make a home visit to a resistant client's home

    a.   should conduct the interview from the porch.
    b.   should double-bind the client.
    c.   should ask to come in the home.
    d.   should exude accurate empathy, but never ask to enter the home.

Choices "a," b," and "d" could be utilized; nonetheless, they do not describe the "foot-in-the-door" obedience phenomenon. The phenomenon asserts that when a person agrees to a less repugnant request, then he or she will be more likely to comply with a request which is even more distasteful. Thus, a counselor who first asks to come in the house and receives an answer of "yes," can then, for example, ask for medical information related to a possible case of child abuse. Social science researchers report that trivial commitments lead to a so-called "momentum of compliance." The notion is generally related to a 1966 study by Freedman and Fraser in which housewives who were first asked to sign a safe driving petition were more apt to comply with the request to put a large "Drive Carefully" sign on their front lawns.

The moral of the experiment is to always ask for a small favor and you'll have a better chance of getting a person to say "yes" when you ask for a bigger favor. Could a memory device which takes advantage of the fact that Freedman and Fraser start with an "f" like the word "foot" help you to remember the researchers whose often quoted studies support this principle? **(c)**

130. Most countries have an official language, a stated viewpoint, and a central government. This is reflected mainly by

    a.   national culture.
    b.   human culture.
    c.   regional culture.
    d.   ecological culture.

Hint: Although choice "b" is not the correct answer don't let it throw you if your exam refers to "universal culture" as "human culture." The above statement best describes national culture. Big business and high-tech media are lessening the gap between national cultures. In this day and age an individual living on the opposite pole of the earth could be wearing the same prestigious pair of designer jeans as you. Thus, some experts have suggested that traditional cultures will eventually be supplanted by a "unified world culture" or a "unified global culture." As of late, the term "third cultures" has been used to describe financial markets, international law, and other elements which transcend national culture. **(a)**

131. Whereas a culture is defined primarily via norms and values, a society differs from a culture in that a society

    a.   is defined as a set of mores.
    b.   has a distinct lack of norms.
    c.   is a self-perpetuating independent group who occupies a definitive territory.
    d.   none of the above.

The boundaries of a culture and a society are not the same. Cultures operate within societies; however, all members of a given society may not share the same culture. **(c)**

132. Ethnocentrism

    a.   uses one's own culture as a yardstick to measure all others.
    b.   means race.
    c.   is a genetic term.
    d.   all of the above.

Statements like "superior race," "savages," "backward people," or "the chosen few" capture the essence of the concept of ethnocentrism. In short, all societies are ethnocentric in the sense that they use their own view as a standard of reference and view themselves as superior. **(a)**

133. All of these statements are ethnocentric except

    a.   you can't trust anyone over the age of 40.
    b.   Americans are generous.
    c.   Blue-collar workers are mean and selfish.
    d.   The Gross National Product in the U.S. exceeds the figure in Mexico.

Ethnocentrism is based on opinion while choice "d" is fact. Ethnocentrism was clearly expressed in the World War II joke which suggested that Hitler couldn't build a race of supermen because superman could only be an American. **(d)**

134. Ethnocentrism

    a.   is not universal.
    b.   promotes a sense of patriotism and national sovereignty.
    c.   promotes stability and pride, yet danger in the nuclear age.
    d.   b and c.

According to researchers Levine and Campbell you can scratch off choice "a" as ethnocentrism is truly a universal phenomenon in which the ethnic group tries to prove they are superior. Our government (as well as others) engage in choice "b" (a form of ethnocentrism) deliberately. Choice "c" reminds us of the ultimate danger in trying to prove sovereignty in an atomic age. **(d)**

135. Regardless of culture, the popular individual

    a.   has good social skills.
    b.   values race over ethnicity.
    c.   dresses in the latest styles.
    d.   never possesses a modal personality.

My best guess would be that most of you correctly chose the best alternative (choice "a") based on common sense. So save your money on clothes (choice "c") and fine tune your social skills! The only thing which might have made the question difficult was the introduction of the term "modal personality" in choice "d." The term—derived from the statistical concept of the mode, which is used to describe the score which occurs most frequently— refers to a composite personality which is the most typical profile of a given group of people. A modal personality is the personality which is characteristic of the group in question. **(a)**

136. Social exchange theory postulates that

    a.   a relationship will endure if both parties are assertive.
    b.   a relationship will endure if the rewards are greater than the costs.
    c.   a relationship will endure if both parties are sexually attracted to each other.
    d.   men work harder to keep a relationship strong.

Social exchange theory assumes that rewards are things or factors we like, while costs are things we dislike. The theory assumes that a positive relationship is characterized by "profit." Reward minus cost equals profit. Some counselors are understandably turned off by this "vest pocket definition of relationships" based on behavioral psychology and economic theory. A client who says to a family member, "As long as I pay the bills, you'll do your chores," is basing a relationship on rewards and costs. An alternative explanation of relationships is provided by the "complementarity theory" which states that a relationship becomes stronger as two people's personality needs mesh. The word complementary indicates that one personality can make up what is lacking or missing in the other personality. For example, according to this theory, a dominant man and a non-dominant woman would have a fine chance of relating well toward each other. **(b)**

137. Balance theory postulates

    a.   a move from cognitive consistency to inconsistency.
    b.   a move from cognitive inconsistency to consistency.
    c.   a tendency to achieve a balanced cognitive state.
    d.   b and c.

Here's a mini-review: Inconsistent thoughts are often called "dissonance." Most counselors agree that disonnance is a distasteful state of mind which the individual will attempt to change. **(d)**

138. Most individuals believe that people whom they perceive as attractive

     a.   are nonassertive.
     b.   are aggressive.
     c.   have other positive traits.
     d.   are socially adept but not very intelligent.

This can cause the professional counselor difficulty if he or she tends to minimize a client's problems merely because he or she is good-looking. For example, a thought such as, "With looks like that she is no doubt the life of the party," demonstrates how the counselor erroneously assumes that a woman who is good-looking will have good social skills and feel comfortable at a social gathering. Clients—like books—cannot be judged by their covers, yet this tendency is quite common. **(c)**

139. A counselor who works primarily with a geriatric population needs to be aware that

     a.   Black counselees make the best clients.
     b.   American Indians do not believe in cognitive interventions.
     c.   surprisingly enough, attractiveness is a fine predictor of retirement adjustment.
     d.   surprisingly enough, financial security and health are the best predictors of retirement adjustment.

Yes, an old adage which suggests that money can help buy (or at least abet) happiness might just have a grain of truth. Here's why. According to the U.S. Bureau of Census, in 1988 one out of every eight Americans over 65 had an income below the poverty level! The prevailing feeling, is that counselors of the future will be increasingly forced to deal with an older population as the U.S. population in general ages (the so-called "Age Wave"). In 1900 only four percent of the U.S. population were over 65; as of this writing the total is over 12% and growing. If I were you, another question I'd expect to see on my exam would relate to myths which impact upon counselors working with the aged. Two of the most popular myths are that (a) intelligence declines in old age (in reality only eight percent of the aged are truly senile) and (b) the elderly are incapable of sex. In regard to the former, some exam questions could disagree with this generalization slightly, as the theory of "terminal drop" postulates that a decrease in intellectual functioning does occur, but even according to this theory, it only occurs during the final five years of life. Counseling older adults will become more common in the future; the human life expectancy has doubled since the turn of the century. **(d)**

140. Most experts would agree that a cross-cultural counselor's diagnosis

    a.   must be performed without regard to cultural issues.
    b.   must be done within a cultural context.
    c.   a and b.
    d.   none of the above.

The "cultural approach to normality" suggests that the behavior of the majority of the people defines what is considered "normal." An important point to note, however, is that deviant behavior, such as in the case of a very powerful leader or a genius, may be lauded. **(b)**

141. A counselor who is seeing a client from a different culture would most likely expect _____ social conformity than he or she would from a client from his or her own culture.

    a.   more
    b.   less
    c.   the same
    d.   more realistic

We demand more rigid standards from our own culture. **(b)**

142. In terms of diagnosis,

    a.   a client's behavior could be sane and appropriate in one culture, yet disturbed and bizarre in another.

    b.   culture is irrelevant in children under 14.

    c.   culture is an issue with males, but not with females.

    d.   culture is an issue with females, but not with males.

Again, the concept of "cultural relativism" implies that one's behavior can only be evaluated in relation to the culture. Behavioral scientists have thus attempted to create "cultural free" diagnostic instruments but as of this date none have been totally effective. **(a)**

143. In the U.S., a frequent practice is to see a perfect stranger for therapy.

    a.   This trend seems to be true in any area of the world.

    b.   This is true for LPCs but not true for MSW therapists.

    c.   This is true for LPCs and MSWs but not clinical psychologists.

    d.   However, in other cultures it would not be the norm to see a stranger and receive pay for help.

In E. Fuller Torrey's thought provoking book, *The Mind Game: Witch Doctors and Psychiatrists,* he explains that in Nigeria, helpers have accepted a female client as a wife in lieu of a fee! He also notes that in other cultures a therapist cannot accept a fee unless the treatment is successful. **(d)**

144. According to the cognitive dissonance theory of Leon Festinger, a man who buys a $20,000 platinum watch would most likely

    a.   feel intense guilt.
    b.   read test reports after the purchase to justify his behavior.
    c.   harbor severe hatred regarding his mother.
    d.   harbor severe hatred regarding his father.

Although all the choices are plausible, choice "b" best expresses the tendency to justify behavior to create a state of "consonance" (a fancy word for harmony) between attitudes and behavior. Hence, if a test report states that the watch is a good buy, the belief and the behavior are consistent. In case you haven't picked it up yet, I'm betting you'll see at least one question regarding cognitive dissonance on your exam.　　　　**(b)**

145. A woman who is being robbed

    a.   would probably get the most assistance in a crowd with a large number of bystanders.
    b.   would find that the number of people who would respond to her distress actually decreases as the number of bystanders increases.
    c.   would never have a bystander try to help her.
    d.   none of the above.

Here is a principle which is often quoted: The number of people who will help a victim in distress decreases, and the time it will take to intervene increases, as the number of bystanders increases. Helping an individual in distress is generally called "altruism" in the literature. This same principle could conceivably apply in a psychological sense when you are working with groups and a client is the victim of scapegoating.　　　　**(b)**

146. A counselor reading this book says, "I could care less about passing the NCE or licensing exam." This

    a.   is displacement.
    b.   is an attempt to reduce dissonance via consistent cognitions.
    c.   is an attempt to reduce dissonance by denial, thus minimizing tension.
    d.   is projection.

Choices "a" and "d" are ego defense mechanisms. This topic is covered in the Helping Relationships section of this book. Choice "b" is incorrect since reading this book to pass the exam and not caring about passing are "inconsistent." **(c)**

147. The statement, "Even though my car is old and doesn't run well, it sure keeps my insurance payments low,"

    a.   is displacement.
    b.   is an attempt to reduce dissonance via consistent cognitions.
    c.   is projection.
    d.   would never reduce dissonance in an individual.

This also could be described as the "sweet lemon" variety of rationalization (see the Helping Relationships section of this book). **(b)**

148. In the case of the individual who purchased the $20,000 watch, cognitive dissonance theory postulates that

    a.   he or she might ignore positive information regarding other models and secure a lot of information regarding the $20,000 platinum model.
    b.   he or she might sell the $20,000 watch immediately following the purchase.
    c.   he or she might focus heavily on negative information regarding rival models.
    d.   a and c.

This is a tough question since the alternatives are a bit complex. Remember: cognitive dissonance theory predicts that the person will look for things which are consistent with his or her behavior. Is choice "a" consistent? Of course. Yet choice "c" is also possible since the individual could ignore positive attributes of the competition (i.e., choice "a") or maximize their negative features (i.e., choice "c"). Counselors should keep in mind that consistency is considered a desirable personality trait in most cultures. **(d)**

149. In the U.S., middle- and upper-class citizens seem to want a counselor who

    a.   will give them "a good talking to."
    b.   gives a specific and steady stream of advice.
    c.   helps them work it out on their own.
    d.   is highly authoritarian and autocratic.

The theory here is that middle- and upper-class citizens are taught that independence is a virtue. The person would not want to be dependent on a therapist, parents, etc. as is implied in choices "a," "b," and "d." **(c)**

150. In a traditional culture which places a high premium on authority figures,

    a.   passivity on the part of the counselor would be viewed in a negative manner.
    b.   a client would be disappointed if he or she did not receive advice.
    c.   assigning homework and teaching on the part of the counselor would be appropriate.
    d.   all of the above.

An active-directive model works best with persons who respond well to an authority figure. **(d)**

151. Cognitive dissonance research deals mainly with

    a.   attraction.
    b.   cognition and attitude formation.
    c.   cognitions and emotion.
    d.   none of the above.

The notion is that the discrepancies or inconsistencies that create tension are caused by cognitions and attitudes. **(b)**

152. Parents who do not tolerate or use aggression when raising children produce

    a.   less aggressive children.
    b.   more aggressive children.
    c.   passive-aggressive children.
    d.   passive-dependent children.

Children who are abused by their parents are more likely to be abusers when they have children of their own.   **(a)**

153. Overall, Rogerian person-centered counseling

    a.   is rarely utilized in cross-cultural counseling.
    b.   is too nondirective for intercultural counseling.
    c.   a and b
    d.   has been used more than other models to help promote understanding between cultures and races.

In the 1970's Rogers conducted workshops to enhance cross-cultural communication. People from all over the world participated. Person-centered techniques are popular in Japan. Person-centered therapy is nonjudgemental and thus is considered a superb modality for multicultural/ racial usage. The exception (mentioned earlier) could occur when counseling an ethnic or racial group that demands structure and/or authority from a helper. Lower-class clients generally view the helper as an advice giver. Estimates indicate that approximately 50% of all ethnic-minority clients quit counseling after the first session feeling they will not secure what they want from the helper.   **(d)**

154. In intercultural counseling the term therapeutic surrender means

    a.   nothing—it is not a valid term.

    b.   most therapists will give up in 16 sessions or less if progress is not evident.

    c.   the client psychologically surrenders himself or herself to a counselor from a different culture and becomes open with feelings and thoughts.

    d.   the therapist assumes a passive therapeutic stance.

Therapeutic surrender occurs when a client is able to trust the counselor and self-discloses. Contrary to choice "a" the term is used frequently in intercultural counseling. **(c)**

155. The literature suggests these factors as helpful in promoting therapeutic surrender:

    a.   an analysis of cognitive dissonance.

    b.   rapport, trust, listening, conquering client resistance, and self-disclosure.

    c.   paradoxing the client.

    d.   analyzing flight-to-health variables.

Choice "d" is an analytic concept which asserts that the client has improved too rapidly and the real difficulty (i.e., unconscious conflicts) has not been resolved. A similar term, "flight from reality," is used when the client resorts to psychosis (i.e., losing touch with reality) to avoid dealing with current life difficulties. **(b)**

156. In terms of trust and therapeutic surrender,

    a.   it is easier to trust people from your own culture.

    b.   lower-class people often don't trust others from a higher social class.

    c.   lower-class clients may feel that they will end up as losers dealing with a counselor from a higher social class.

    d.   all of the above.

Language barriers, on the part of the client or the counselor, intensify the difficulty of therapeutic surrender. One good technique is to steer clear of slang or fancy therapeutic jargon and try to speak in a clear, concise, and direct manner. **(d)**

157. A(n) _____ client would most likely have the most difficulty with self-disclosure when speaking to a Caucasian counselor.

    a.   middle-class Caucasian female
    b.   upper-class Black female
    c.   lower-class Black male
    d.   upper-class Caucasian male

Males in general have difficulty expressing feelings. Black males are especially hesitant about revealing themselves to Caucasians. **(c)**

158. According to assimilation-contrast theory, a client will perceive a counselor's statement, which is somewhat like his or her own, as even more similar (i.e., an assimilation error). He or she would perceive any dissimilar attitudes as

    a.   even more dissimilar (i.e., a contrast error).
    b.   standardization.
    c.   similar to his or her own.
    d.   paraphrasing.

In any case, if a counselor is highly regarded and trustworthy, his or her statements will be better accepted than if the helper has poor credibility. **(a)**

159. When counseling a client from a different culture, a common error is made when negative transference

    a.   is interpreted as positive transference.
    b.   is interpreted as therapeutic resistance.
    c.   a and b.
    d.   none of the above.

Since transference relates to incidents which occurred prior to treatment, such issues must be distinguished from the current helping relationship. **(b)**

160. Counselors who have good listening skills

    a. facilitate therapeutic surrender.
    b. hinder therapeutic surrender.
    c. often ignore the importance of therapeutic surrender.
    d. are too nondirective to promote therapeutic surrender.

Good listening facilitates any type of helping. **(a)**

161. Counselors can more easily advise

    a. clients from their own culture.
    b. clients from a different culture.
    c. clients of a different race.
    d. clients utilizing ethnocentric statements.

To persuade someone is easiest when he or she has similar views, ideas, and background. It is entirely possible that a client of a different culture has been taught not to trust persons with the counselor's cultural background. **(a)**

162. To empathize is easiest with

    a. a client who is similar to you.
    b. a client who is dissimilar to you.
    c. lower-class Hispanic clients.
    d. upper-class Asian male clients.

See the last answer . . . ditto! **(a)**

163. In cross-cultural counseling, structuring is very important. This concept asserts that counseling is most effective

    a.   when structured exercises are utilized.
    b.   when a counselor takes an active-directive stance.
    c.   when nondirective procedures are emphasized.
    d.   when the nature and structure of the counseling situation is described during the initial session.

Structure has a number of meanings in the field of professional counseling (see the Groups section of this book for additional meanings). In the context of multicultural counseling, structure indicates the counselor will explain the role of the helper as well as the role of the helpee. This helps ward off embarrassment and further enhances the effectiveness of the counseling process. The greater the social/cultural gap, the more important the need for structuring. Despite the merits of the Rogerian model, some would claim that it falls short of the ideal paradigm when a high degree of structure is the treatment of choice. As mentioned earlier, clients from other cultures can harbor gross misconceptions of what represents the helping process. **(d)**

164. A client from another culture will

    a.   talk to the counselor the same as he or she would to a peer.
    b.   speak to the counselor differently than he or she would one of his or her own background.
    c.   generally use slang on purpose to confuse the counselor.
    d.   generally play dumb to receive the counselor's sympathy.

Often individuals are courteous and polite with those who are of the same cultural origin, but are suspicious and don't trust outsiders. **(b)**

165. A Black client tells a White counselor that things are "bad" though she literally means something is good. The counselor's misunderstanding could best be described as a

    a.   cognitive error.
    b.   cognitive dissonance error.
    c.   connotative error.
    d.   confounding variable.

According to Atkinson, Morten, and Sue the three major barriers to intercultural counseling are culture bound values (mentioned earlier), class bound values, and language differences. Connotation applies to the emotional content of a word which is different than the true or dictionary definition. The tendency for words to convey different connotations is often referred to as a "semantic differential." Choice "d," a confounding variable, is an extraneous variable which is not purposely introduced by an experimenter conducting research. This difficulty is inherent in correlational data.   **(c)**

166. A monolingual U.S. counselor

    a.   speaks only English.
    b.   speaks English and Spanish.
    c.   works as a counseling interpreter.
    d.   fits the definition of bilingual.

Mono literally means "one" or "single." Persons who are bilingual (i.e., an individual who speaks two languages) can be employed as interpreters to facilitate efficacious intervention. In order to reduce the difficulty introduced by "semantic differential" and "connotative errors"— mentioned in the answer to the previous question—the bilingual individual would ideally be bi-cultural (i.e., have familiarity with the culture of the counselor and the client).   **(a)**

167. _____ was a prime factor in the history of intercultural counseling.

    a. Frankl's experience in a concentration camp
    b. Perl's use of the German concept of Gestalt
    c. Freud's visits to the U.S.
    d. The 1954 Supreme Court decision, Brown vs. the Board of Education, which outlawed public school segregation

Choice "a" Frankl is the father of logotherapy, an existential form of treatment which stresses "healing through meaning." Choice "b" mentions Fritz Perls the father of Gestalt Therapy which attempts to ameliorate a mind/body split supposedly responsible for emotional distress. Gestalt is a German word which roughly means the "whole" form, figure, or configuration. The final alternative is correct. Desegregation created culturally different populations for school counselors. **(d)**

168. Multicultural counseling promotes

    a. eclecticism.
    b. rigidity.
    c. psychodynamic models.
    d. neurolinguistic programming.

Most experts would insist that choice "a" is best inasmuch as intercultural counselors need to be flexible. An "eclectic" position (i.e., selecting treatment intervention strategies from diverse counseling models) would generally come closest to meeting this requirement. **(a)**

169. Cross-cultural counselors often adhere to the emic viewpoint. The word "emic"

    a. is associated with the Supreme Court decision of 1954 outlawing segregation.
    b. suggests that all clients are alike regardless of culture.
    c. is associated with RBT.
    d. is an anthropological term based on the word "emigration."

J.G. Draguns suggested the emic-etic distinction in cross-cultural counseling. The emic viewpoint emphasizes that each client is an individual with individual differences, while the etic view adheres to the theory that humans are humans—regardless of background and culture. Thus, the same theories and techniques can be applied to any client the counselor helps. Hence, a counselor who values the "emic" view will try to help clients by understanding the client's specific culture, while the "etic" counselor emphasizes the sameness among clients that literally transcends cultural boundaries. The "etic" counselor would not alter his or her technique when working with a client from a different culture or a minority group. DISTINCTIONS SUCH AS ETIC/EMIC ARE OFTEN EASIEST TO REMEMBER IF YOU RELY ON A MEMORY DEVICE. CAN YOU COME UP WITH ONE?   **(d)**

170. A practicum supervisor who says to his or her supervisee, "You can deal with your Asiatic clients the same as you deal with anybody else," is espousing the

     a.   emic viewpoint.
     b.   alloplastic viewpoint.
     c.   etic viewpoint.
     d.   autoplastic viewpoint.

Here's help for those of you who came up empty-handed in terms of snaring a suitable memory device (and hence may have struggled with the question). I like to remember that "etic," which sports a "t," and sounds remarkably similar to "etiquette," is similar in the sense that when practicing etiquette we practice good manners with all individuals whether they are Black, White, Asian, etc. Likewise, counselors who espouse the etic viewpoint, will use the SAME STRATEGIES AND TECHNIQUES ON VIRTUALLY ANY CLIENT. In this case, for example, the Asiatic client will be treated no differently than an American, an Indian American, a French Canadian, or for that matter anybody else. Actually the etic distinction also reminds me of the educational concept of "mainstreaming" which asserts that all children—even those with disabilities and handicaps—can benefit from placement in a regular classroom. But just when you thought the coast was clear you were confronted with another distinction or dilemma (see choices "b" and "d") for the multicultural helper. **(c)**

171. The statement, "All humans, from all cultures, all races, and all nations, are more alike than different," is based on the

    a. emic viewpoint.
    b. alloplastic viewpoint.
    c. etic viewpoint.
    d. autoplastic viewpoint.

    If you chose an alternative other than "c," then you need to reread answers to questions 169 and 170. **(c)**

172. A counselor is confronted with his or her first American Indian client. After the initial session, the counselor secures several books which delineate the cultural aspects of American Indian life. This counselor most likely believes in the

    a. emic viewpoint.
    b. alloplastic viewpoint.
    c. etic viewpoint.
    d. autoplastic viewpoint.

    The "emic" view holds that an approach which is cultural specific is generally the most effective. **(a)**

173. An Asian counselor says to a Black client, "If you're unhappy with the system, get out there and rebel. You can change the system." This is the _____ viewpoint for coping with the environment.

    a. emic viewpoint
    b. alloplastic viewpoint
    c. etic viewpoint
    d. autoplastic viewpoint

This question is testing your knowledge of the autoplastic/alloplastic dilemma in intercultural helping. The "autoplastic" view asserts that change comes from within, while the "alloplastic" conceptualization is that the client can cope best by changing or altering external factors in the environment (as alluded to in this question). Memory devices, anyone? **(b)**

174. A young Hispanic male is obviously the victim of discrimination. His counselor remarks, "I hear what you are saying and I will help you change your thinking so this will not have such a profound impact on you." In this case the counselor had suggested

    a.   an alloplastic method of coping.
    b.   an autoplastic method of coping.
    c.   the emic-etic distinction.
    d.   the emic viewpoint.

Try this memory device on for size. The word "auto" generally refers to changing the "self." Consider the technique of "auto-suggestion" or "auto-hypnosis." Or how about the act of writing an "autobiography?" In each of the aforementioned cases, the person works to create the project, solve the difficulty, or, simply put, change the self. In the "autoplastic" approach the counselor helps the client change himself or herself (as in this question). And what if you think of a more elegant memory device . . . then I say "go for it!" . . . It will come in mighty handy on the test date! **(b)**

175. Black ghetto clients are generally

    a.   very open and honest with their feelings.
    b.   the most amenable group in regard to psychotherapeutic intervention.
    c.   a and b.
    d.   not very open with their feelings.

They are often taught not to trust the establishment. A lack of trust usually results in a lack of openness and self-disclosure. **(d)**

176. Positive transference is to love; as negative transference is to hostility; as ambivalent transference is to

    a.   anger.
    b.   hate.
    c.   uncertainty.
    d.   admiration.

Ambivalent transference occurs when the client rapidly shifts his or her emotional attitude toward the counselor based on learning and experiences related to authority figures from the past. The "Helping Relationship" section of this book goes into more depth regarding the notion of transference. **(c)**

177. The word "personalism" in the context of multicultural counseling means

    a.   all people must adjust to environmental and geological demands.
    b.   the counselor must adjust to the client's cultural mores.
    c.   a counselor who personalizes the treatment is most effective.
    d.   biologically speaking there is no reason why humans must adjust to environmental demands.

Culture must mold itself such that individuals can best thrive and survive in a given environment. Personalism implies that the counselor will make the best progress if he or she sees the client primarily as a person who has learned a set of survival skills rather than a diseased patient. Fierce environmental conditions such as living in a desert or a poverty stricken neighborhood, cause individuals to cooperate with each other more and stick together as a group. This, nevertheless, can cause problems for the counselor who has never lived in a ghetto or a desert and hence is seen as an outsider. The "person," who has lived in the ghetto or the desert will want to check out the counselor's authenticity as a "person," and a counselor who keeps his or her "professional distance" runs the risk of being seen as superficial. A comment such as, "You don't care about me, you just care about your paycheck (or "the agency," or "the court," or "your stupid report," etc.) is indicative that the multicultural counselor is being perceived as remote and not very personal. This could create problems for the counselor since (a) in the U.S. "professionalism" is stressed more than "personalism" in the sense that a good counselor is not "supposed" to get very close to clients and if (b) the counselor has not necessarily grown up in a culture that stresses such a high level of interpersonal cooperation. **(a)**

178. A client whose counselor pushes the alloplastic viewpoint may believe his counselor is simply

     a.   too Rogerian.
     b.   attacking the system.
     c.   too Freudian.
     d.   too cognitive.

The salient point here is that generally, a synthesis, rather than a pure alloplastic or autoplastic position, will be the most effective. **(b)**

179. Good cross-cultural counselors are

     a.   flexible.
     b.   rigid.
     c.   utilizing TA and/or Reality Therapy in nearly every case.
     d.   generally behavioristic.

Although choices "c" and "d" are not the best choices, a case could certainly be made for using these modalities in an intercultural helping relationship. TA, Reality Therapy, and behavioral interventions all stress "contracting." The process of contracting has its merits in cross-cultural situations since it keeps the counselor from shoving a dose of his or her own cultural values down the client's throat (i.e., the client has input before signing or agreeing with the contract). Furthermore, TA has been praised for illuminating cultural and ethnic injunctions. On the other hand, TA lingo is often complex for a client with a different background. Quite unlike behaviorism, Gestalt is a superb modality for cultures that need to liberate their feelings. In addition, it is helpful when working with a population which emphasizes nonverbal communication. The danger in utilizing Gestalt comes from pushing techniques (i.e., trying to insist upon them before clients are ready for them) that emphasize feelings on a cultural or ethnic group which views the expression of feelings as a sign of weakness. Practitioners are warned that behaviorism (choice "d") is not a panacea in multicultural work inasmuch as some cultures do not value assertiveness. EVERY BRAND OF THERAPY HAS ITS MERITS AND ITS DISADVAN-TAGES; IT IS THEREFORE BEST IF THE MULTICULTURAL COUNSELOR REMAINS FLEXIBLE.   **(a)**

180. A client remarks, "Hey, I'm Black and I can't hide it." This is illustrative of the fact that

    a.   race is not the same as ethnicity.
    b.   Blacks struggle when expressing feelings.
    c.   a connotative impediment exists.
    d.   severe ambivalent transference exists.

This question attempts to see whether you can discern race from ethnicity. The assumption here is that you can see racial differences since they are the result of genetics. If a client really made this type of statement, the counselor might wish to deal directly with the racial issue. The counselor could inquire, "In what way do you feel that the fact that I'm White and you're Black will affect the counseling process?" Jones and Seagall suggested that such a question should be asked no later than the second session. Choice "d" would not be totally outlandish, however, the question does not provide enough information to make it the best choice.   **(a)**

181. Experts in the field of multicultural counseling feel that the counselor's training

    a.   must come from an APA approved graduate program.
    b.   must come from a CACREP approved graduate program.
    c.   should be broad and interdisciplinary.
    d.   need not include RET.

Choice "d," RET or Rational-Emotive Therapy, certainly can be helpful when counseling clients from another culture since it does not stress mental illness. The perception of the RET practitioner as a "teacher" makes the process of helping more palatable to some populations. Choice "c" is the best answer. An adept multicultural helper ideally would study topics which go beyond traditional counseling theory. Some educators have even suggested that an exchange program in which counselors study in foreign universities could be beneficial. **(c)**

182. Doing cross-cultural counseling

    a.   makes counselors increasingly aware of cultural differences.
    b.   allows counselors to see that culture is merely a matter of semantics.
    c.   is different since clients are more likely to return for help after the first session.
    d.   allows counselors to ignore the concept of pluralism.

Choice "c" is incorrect. Preliminary studies indicate that clients from other cultures do not use counseling as often as they could. Moreover, the dropout rate is premature, perhaps 20% higher after the initial session than relationships which are not intercultural. The concept of "pluralism" literally means that an individual exists in more than one category. A condition known as "separatism" exists when a group of people totally withdraw from the political majority. Pluralism presents a less extreme option. Cultural pluralism occurs when persons of a cultural heritage retain their traditions and differences, yet cooperate in regard to social, political and economic matters. In counseling per se, the term suggests that certain categories of individuals (e.g., women, older adults, minorities, alternative cultures, or the handicapped) often need special services. An Asian American, for example, could feel torn between adhering to Asiatic culture while trying to become more Americanized. THE COUNSELOR MUST SHOW RESPECT FOR THESE INDIVIDUALS IN ORDER TO DO EFFECTIVE TREATMENT; HENCE, THE NOTION OF PLURALISM CANNOT BE IGNORED.   **(a)**

183. F.H. Allport created the concept of social facilitation. According to this theory an individual who is given the task of memorizing a list of numbers will

    a.   perform better if he or she is alone.
    b.   perform better if he or she is part of a group.
    c.   perform better if he or she has undergone psychotherapy.
    d.   perform better if he or she is an auditory learner.

This is indeed an interesting phenomenon. The presence of other persons (e.g., coworkers, athletes, students, etc.) improves an individual's performance even when there is no verbal interaction!   **(b)**

184. In social psychology, the sleeper effect asserts that

    a.   sleep learning facilitates social skills.
    b.   after a period of time, one forgets the communicator but remembers the message.
    c.   after a period of time, one remembers the communicator but forgets the message.
    d.   REM sleep facilitates insight.

Perhaps more importantly, the so-called sleeper effect asserts that when you are attempting to change someone's opinion the change may not occur immediately after the verbal exchange. In other words, when a counselor provides guidance to a client a delay may occur before the client accepts the message. The communication may have more impact after some time has passed. **(b)**

185. In 1908, two books, one by _____ and one by _____, helped to introduce social psychology in America.

    a.   Moreno; Yalom
    b.   Holland; Roe
    c.   Barber; Salter
    d.   McDougall; Ross

William McDougall wrote *Introduction to Social Psychology* which expounded on his "hormic psychology" position that individual as well as group behavior is the result of inherited tendencies to seek goals. Ross authored *Social Psychology.* Other famous names noted in the alternatives include Jacob Moreno, who pioneered psychodrama and coined the term "group therapy"; Irving Yalom, an existentialist, well-known for his strides in group work; John Holland, who stressed that a person's occupational environment should be congruent with his or her personality type; Anne Roe, who postulated that jobs can compensate for unmet childhood needs; T.X. Barber, who espoused a cognitive theory of hypnotism; and Andrew Salter, a pioneer in the behavior therapy, hypnosis, and autohypnosis movements. **(d)**

186. _____ is associated with obedience and authority.

    a.   Stanley Milgram
    b.   Arthur Janov
    c.   A.T. Beck
    d.   Robert Harper

In one of the most shocking and frightening investigations of all time, Milgram discovered that people who were told to give others powerful electric shocks did so on command. Subjects were told that they were to punish a learner strapped to an electric chair when he gave an incorrect answer. Out of 40 experimental subjects only 14 refused to go to the highest level of shock (i.e., in excess of 435 volts)! And get this . . . in some of the experiments the persons administering the shocks (which unbeknownst to them were unreal) were actually given a 45-volt shock themselves so they could feel the intensity of this punishment. So much for accurate empathy! Even when the subjects heard the person receiving the shocks screaming they often continued to raise the level of voltage when told to do so. This principle is often used to explain "obedience to authority" in social situations such as Salem witch hunts or Nazi war crimes. Fortunately, follow-up research indicated that most of the individuals who participated in the Milgram experiment did not feel they were harmed by the experience.   **(a)**

187. Milgram discovered that normal people would administer seemingly fatal electric shocks to others when instructions to do so were given by a person perceived as

    a.   a peer.
    b.   an equal.
    c.   an individual from another culture.
    d.   an authority figure.

Prior to the experiment, psychiatrists predicted that only one percent would administer the highest level of shock. In reality, 62% dished out "fatal shock punishment" in response to an incorrect answer. If the experimental authority figure was in the room, the tendency to obey was higher than if he or she was not physically present. In a related study by Bickman, individuals told to give a dime or a paper bag to a stranger did so twice as often when the person giving the orders was dressed as a guard rather than a peer.   **(d)**

188. The tendency to affiliate with others

    a.   is highest in the middle child.
    b.   is highest in dysthymics.
    c.   is highest in firstborns and only children.
    d.   is based on hormonal output.

Choice "b" refers to a diagnostic category from the DSM-III-R. Dysthymia—which might also be called "neurotic depression" or "depressive neurosis" on your exam—is a longstanding depressed mood which exists for at least a year in children and adolescents or two years in adults. In the behavioral sciences the word "affiliation" refers to the need one has to associate with others. Choice "c" correctly reflects the landmark research of Stanley Schachter which concluded that the need to affiliate decreases for later-born children.   **(c)**

189. A client tells his counselor that he has a choice of entering one of two prestigious Ph.D. counseling programs. Kurt Lewin would call this an

    a.   approach-avoidance conflict.
    b.   approach-approach conflict.
    c.   avoidance-avoidance conflict.
    d.   avoidance vector.

Choices "a," "b," and "c" indicate the three basic categories of conflict which result in frustration. In the "approach-approach" format (suggested in this question) the individual is presented with two equally attractive options simultaneously. Of the three types, counselors believe that the "approach-approach" is the easiest to help clients cope with since in most cases (unlike the situation presented in this question) the client can attempt both options: first one, then the other. Moreover, approach-approach conflicts typically instill less anxiety than the other two types.   **(b)**

190. When a person has two negative alternatives, it is called an

    a.   approach-approach conflict.
    b.   approach vector.
    c.   avoidance-avoidance conflict.
    d.   avoidance cohesiveness.

When a client says, "I don't know whether to pay the hefty fine or go to jail," he is struggling with an "avoidance-avoidance" conflict in which both choices are undesirable to say the least. Clients in this position often daydream, flee from the situation, or regress instead of confronting the choices. The client also may waver or vacillate when he or she comes close to making a choice.　**(c)**

191. A male client tells his counselor that he is attracted to a gorgeous woman who is violent and chemically dependent. This creates an

    a.   approach-avoidance conflict.
    b.   avoidance-avoidance conflict.
    c.   avoidance of life space.
    d.   approach affiliation.

The "approach-avoidance" conflict presents a positive factor (a terrific-looking woman) with a negative factor (she is a substance abuser prone to violent behavior) at the same time. Most counselors would agree this is the toughest type of conflict for the client to tackle as it generates the highest level of frustration.　**(a)**

192. According to Osgood's Congruity theory, a client will accept suggestions more readily if

    a.   the client likes the counselor.
    b.   the client dislikes the counselor.
    c.   the client distrusts the counselor.
    d.   the counselor is in a higher economic bracket.

Here again, the tendency is based on "balance theory." If you like your counselor, your tendency to accept a suggestion would be balanced (i.e., consistent with your opinion). If you did not like or trust the counselor, then accepting his or her suggestions would produce an imbalance (i.e., an inconsistent attitude).   **(a)**

193. Osgood and Tannenbaum's Congruity theory predicts

   a. attitudes that change the most are initially less extreme.
   b. if you believe in something strongly, your attitude is less likely to change than if you have moderate feelings about it.
   c. the closer your attitude is to neutral, the more it will change.
   d. all of the above.

Thus, a person from a minority, a different ethnic group, a different culture, or even an individual of the same culture who vehemently opposes therapy and counseling will be a tough individual to engage in the treatment process.   **(d)**

194. A classic experiment in social psychology was conducted by Sherif et al. at the boys' summer camp near Robber's Cave, Oklahoma. The important finding in this study was that

   a. most people cooperate in a social setting.
   b. competition plays a small role in most of our lives.
   c. a and b.
   d. a cooperative goal can bring two hostile groups together thus reducing competition and enhancing cooperation.

Sometimes loosely called the "Robber's Cave experiment," this study set up two distinct groups which were hostile toward each other. The study concluded that the most effective way to reduce hostility between groups was to give them an alternative goal which required a joint effort and could not be accomplished by a single group.   **(d)**

195. Sex role stereotyping would imply that

    a.   a counselor would only consider traditional feminine careers for his female client.

    b.   a male counselor would rate a female client's emotional status differently than he would a male client's.

    c.   female clients are treated the same as male clients.

    d.   choices a and b.

According to studies, counselors are prejudice toward women. Prejudice means that we are negative or have a rigid inflexible attitude toward a given group of people and can often act on our unfavorable thoughts. Moreover, the prejudice individual often "prejudges" others without substantial evidence. Choices "a" and "b" are illustrative of stereotyping in which the counselor has generalized feelings about a given group (in this case women). Unfortunately, research would suggest that the response in choice "a" might well be a typical one. In a 1973 study by Schlossberg and Pietrofesa, counselor trainees were instructed to help a female counselee choose between an engineering or a teaching career. All the counselor trainees tried to steer her clear of engineering, typically a masculine career. As for choice "b," I can only say "ditto." A 1970 study by Broverman, Broverman, Clarkson, Rosenkrantz, and Vogel found that all the therapists who filled out a questionnaire used a different standard of mental health when rating men than they used for women. Women and other minorities are sometimes said to be victims of a "caste system." The term "caste system" implies that there are fixed layers of superiority and inferiority which you are born into and thus cannot escape. Exam hint: My guess is that in the coming years women's issues, older adults, single parent families, blended families, bereavement, and gay concerns will be important topics on the Social and Cultural Foundations area on your exam. PLEASE MAKE IT A PRIORITY TO KEEP UP WITH THE LITERATURE IN THESE KEY AREAS. THIS GUIDE IS NOT INTENDED TO DO JUSTICE TO THESE TOPICS.   **(d)**

196. The statement, "Whites are better than Blacks," illustrates

    a.   a weakening of the caste system in the U.S.
    b.   racism.
    c.   sexism.
    d.   codependency.

Choice "a" is definitely wrong since the view that Whites are better than Blacks is indicative of a caste system mentality (see the answer to the previous question). Choice "d" codependency is a term which grew mainly out of the chemical dependency movement. The word has various definitions though it mainly refers to an individual who is emotionally involved with a chemically dependent person (perhaps even members of his or her family) and/or is addicted to a relationship with another person or drugs. "Racism," the correct answer, occurs when an assumption is made that some races are better than others. Hence, the race which feels superior can deny the other race rights and respect. "Sexism" is an analogous term. In sexism, one sex assumes that the other is inherently inferior.   **(b)**

197. In terms of research related to affiliation

    a.   misery loves miserable company.
    b.   firstborns are more likely to affiliate than other children born later.
    c.   people affiliate in an attempt to lower fear.
    d.   all of the above.

Often the statement is made that misery loves more than company; it loves miserable company. Stanley Schachter set up an experiment in which subjects were informed that they were going to receive a very painful electrical shock (high anxiety) or a very weak one which would merely tingle. The subjects were told that they could wait alone for ten minutes before receiving the shock or wait with others participating in the study. Of those subjects who were told they would receive a mere "tingle" only 1/3 chose to wait with others, while over 62% of the high anxiety group decided to do so. Follow-up research seems to indicate that a person with high anxiety will not choose to be with others unless the other individuals are in a similar situation. Sarnoff and Zimbardo discovered in a 1961 study that males placed in extremely embarrassing situations in which they would need to act like infants were much less willing to affiliate with others going through the same thing. One interpretation would be that individuals are more comfortable sharing real fear than anxiety which could result in embarrassment or shame. This research is somewhat similar to Leon Festinger's "Theory of Social Comparison" which postulates that people have a need to compare themselves with others to assess their own abilities and options. The theory further asserts that we will compare ourselves to others who are basically similar to us. IMPORTANT REMINDER: RESEARCHERS IN THE FIELD OF COUNSELING ARE SOMEWHAT CRITICAL OF MOST PSYCHOSOCIAL EXPERIMENTS SINCE THE EXPERIMENTAL SITUATIONS ARE OFTEN ARTIFICIAL AND THE STUDIES LACK EXTERNAL VALIDITY WHICH IS THE ABILITY TO HELP UNDERSTAND BEHAVIOR OUTSIDE THE EXPERIMENTAL SETTING.   **(d)**

198. Six persons attend a counseling group. After the group, five members praise the merits of a group activity assigned by the group leader. The sixth person, who has heard the opinion of the other five people, felt the activity was useless and boring. According to studies on social behavior, the sixth individual would most likely tell the other five that

a. he totally disagreed with their assessment.
b. he too felt the group activity was very helpful.
c. he really wasn't certain how he felt about the activity.
d. a and c.

Experiments by Solomon Asch and Muzafer Sherif would predict that the person would most likely "sell out" and agree with the other five. In one study Asch discovered that approximately 35% of the persons tested in a perceptual activity gave an answer which was clearly incorrect in order to conform!!! Social researchers consistently have discovered that people will conform to an obviously incorrect unanimous decision 1/3 of the time. Moreover, studies indicate that as few as three other people can abet conformity in a social setting. Who conforms the most? The answer includes individuals who are authoritarian and thus are heavily influenced by authority figures, people who are external approval seekers, and persons who feel that outside external factors control them.   **(b)**

199. The client who would most likely engage in introspection would be a

a. 19-year-old Hispanic mother on welfare with two children.
b. 49-year-old Caucasian homeless male.
c. 40-year-old divorced Caucasian female who is out of work and has three children.
d. 52-year-old single Black male school administrator.

The key to this question is to focus on social class rather than acculturation, minority status, or sex. Clients in higher social classes have more time to "look within themselves" (introspect) since they need not dwell as much on external survival needs.   **(d)**

200. A Japanese client who was reluctant to look you in the eye during her counseling session would most likely be displaying

    a.   severe negative transference.
    b.   positive transference.
    c.   normal behavior within the context of her culture.
    d.   ambivalent transference.

Here is where a knowledge of culture would come in handy. Asians are often brought up with the belief that it is a sign of respect to avoid eye contact with an authority figure. In addition, it is considered proper to talk no more than is necessary, which of course is not congruent with the way most native Americans think. Moreover, many Asiatic clients have been taught that it is shameful to brag or to express one's own desires, ambitions, or strong feelings. This background could well present a roadblock for a counselor operating under a paradigm that stresses abreaction. Some Asians have been brought up to believe that all problems are solved only within the privacy of family meetings. If mental illness does exist, it is considered a genetic flaw and a family secret. Hence, Asians place a very high premium on self-control, which is an issue that can be examined in counseling. Thus, Sue & Sue suggested that Asian-Americans respond best to brief therapy that is directive and structured with specific problem-solving goals. Often our somewhat scientific approaches to counseling really reflect what the American society views as real or scientific. Hispanic Americans (meaning of Spanish origin and sometimes referred to as "Latinos" in some of the literature) often value folk healing which is very spiritual, such as going into a trancelike state and talking with God. **(c)**

CHAPTER **5**

HELPING RELATIONSHIPS

201. Sigmund Freud is the father of psychoanalysis which is both a form of treatment and a very comprehensive personality theory. _____ and _____, who originally worked with Freud, created individual psychology and analytic psychology respectively.

    a.   Carl Jung; Alfred Adler
    b.   Alfred Adler; Carl Jung
    c.   Joseph Breuer; A.A. Brill
    d.   Alfred Adler; Rollo May

Alfred Adler was the father of individual psychology while Carl Gustov Jung (correctly pronounced Yung) founded analytic psychology. But a word of caution is in order here: read all test questions carefully. Since the question utilizes the word "respectively" Adler's name (i.e., individual psychology) must come before Jung's name (i.e., analytic psychology) hence choice "a" is false. The question itself also emphasizes the key point that psychoanalysis is both a form of therapy as well as a theory of personality. Joseph Breuer was a Viennese neurologist who taught Freud the value of the talking cure, which is also termed catharsis. Brill's name is usually associated with the impact that Freudian theory has on career choice while Rollo May was a prime mover in the existential counseling movement. **(b)**

202. Eric Berne's Transactional Analysis (TA) posits three ego states: the child, the adult, and the parent. These roughly correspond to Freud's structural theory which includes

    a.   oral, anal, phallic.
    b.   unconscious, preconscious, and conscious.
    c.   a and b.
    d.   id, ego, and superego.

I must emphasize that neither Freud nor Berne characterized these ego states as biological entities. That is to say, a neurologist could not open up an individual's brain and map out the id or dissect the parent ego state. Instead, the id, ego, superego, and the child, adult, and parent are hypothetical constructs used to explain the function of the personality. In Freudian theory, as well as in TA, experts in the field often refer to the aforementioned entities as the "structural theory." You will recall that the entities in choice "a" (oral, anal, and phallic) are the names of Freud's first three psychosexual stages. The unconscious, preconscious, and conscious noted in choice "b" relates to Freud's topographic notion that the mind has depth like an iceberg. The word topography means mapping, in this case that the Freudians have mapped the mind.   **(d)**

203. In transactional analysis, the _____ is the conscience, or ego state concerned with moral behavior while in Freudian theory it is the _____.

    a.   adult; unconscious
    b.   parent; ego
    c.   parent; superego
    d.   parent; id

Hint: Read test questions of this ilk very carefully. If I had a dollar for every instance that a counselor read conscience as conscious (or vice versa) I'd surely have a larger bank balance!!! Don't be a victim—read the question carefully. Eric Berne's transactional analysis utilizes popular terminology. The parent ego state has been likened to Freud's superego. If a child has nurturing caretakers, he or she is said to develop "nurturing parent" qualities such as being nonjudgmental and sympathetic to others. The parent ego state, however, may be filled with prejudicial and critical messages. Persons who fall into this category will tend to be intimidating, bossy, or know-it-alls. An individual whose caretaker left or died at an early age might be plagued with what TA refers to as the "incomplete parent." This person could expect others to parent him or her throughout life, or might use the lack of parenting as an excuse for poor behavior. ("Of course, I can't keep a job; I never had a mother to teach me how." TA calls this the game of "Wooden Leg.") **(c)**

204. Freud felt that successful resolution of the Oedipus complex led to the development of the superego. This is accomplished by

    a.   identification with the aggressor, the parent of the same sex.
    b.   analysis during the childhood years.
    c.   identification with the parent of the opposite sex, the aggressor.
    d.   transference.

Oedipus means "swollen feet" and comes from the Greek tragedy by Sophocles. In the story Oedipus is unaware that he has killed his father and married his mother. According to Freudian theory the child's libido or sex energy is directed toward the parent of the opposite sex. The child, nevertheless, realizes that retaliation would result if he (or she in the case of the Electra Complex) would act on these impulses. The child thus strives for identification with the parent of the same sex to achieve vicarious sexual satisfaction. Now I must be honest and remind you that many behavioral scientists find this notion a bit far fetched. The word transference in choice "d" is also a psychoanalytic concept. Transference implies that the client displaces emotion felt toward a parent onto the analyst, counselor, or therapist. **(a)**

205. Freudians refer to the ego as

    a.   the executive administrator of the personality and the reality principle.
    b.   the guardian angel of the mind.
    c.   the pleasure principle.
    d.   the seat of libido.

Some scholars refer to the ego as the "executive administrator" since it governs or acts as a police officer to control the impulses from the id (instincts) and the superego (the conscience). The ego is a mediator. The ego is also called the reality principle. Choices "d" as well as "c" describe the id. And just in case you chose choice "b" I can only say "the guardian angel of the mind" . . . get serious, I just made it up!   **(a)**

206. Freud's theory speaks of Eros and Thanatos. A client who threatens a self-destructive act is being ruled primarily by

    a.   Eros.
    b.   Eros and the id.
    c.   Thanatos.
    d.   both Eros and Thanatos.

Is it Greek or is it Freudian theory? You decide. Eros is the Greek god of the love of life. To the Freudians this meant self-preservation. Thanatos, is the Greek word for death. Later Freudian writings use the word to describe a death wish or what is sometimes called the death instinct.   **(c)**

207. The id is present at birth and never matures. It operates mainly out of awareness to satisfy instinctual needs according to the

a.   reality principle.
b.   notion of transference.
c.   Eros principle.
d.   pleasure principle.

The id is the pleasure principle. The ego is the reality principle and the superego is the ego ideal.   **(d)**

208. If you think of the mind as a seesaw, then the fulcrum or balancing apparatus would be the

a.   id, which has no concept of rationality or time.
b.   ego.
c.   superego, which judges behavior as right or wrong.
d.   BASIC-ID.

If you missed this one, review the answer to question 205. Educators often utilize the seesaw or fulcrum analogy when explaining the relationship of the id, ego, and superego.   **(b)**

209. A therapist who says to a patient, "Say whatever comes to mind," is practicing

a.   directive counseling.
b.   TA.
c.   paraphrasing.
d.   free association.

Free association is literally defined as instructing the client to say whatever comes to mind. This is more or less the antithesis of directive approaches (choice "a") in which the client is asked to discuss certain material. Paraphrasing (choice "c") results whenever a counselor restates a client's message in the counselor's own words.   **(d)**

210. The superego contains the ego ideal. The superego strives for_____, rather than _____ like the id.

a.   perfection; pleasure
b.   pleasure; perfection
c.   morals; ethics
d.   logic; reality

The superego is more concerned with ideal than what is real. The superego is composed of values, morals, and ideals of parents, caretakers, and society. And oh yes, as for choice "c," the id ethical . . . with the possible exception of handling biological needs like hunger and thirst . . . never! The id is chaotic and has no sense of time.   **(a)**

211. All of these theorists could be associated with the analytic movement except

a.   Freud.
b.   Jung.
c.   Adler.
d.   Wolpe.

Read this question very carefully. This is the so-called reverse or negative type question, and questions of this ilk do appear on the NCE and other major exams. Questions of this nature ask you to ferret out the "incorrect" rather than the "correct" response. In this case, all of the choices except "d" name therapists in the psychoanalytic movement. Joseph Wolpe developed a paradigm known as "systematic desensitization" which is useful when trying to weaken (i.e., desensitize) a client's response to an anxiety producing stimuli.   **(d)**

212. Most scholars would assert that Freud's 1900 work entitled *The Interpretation of Dreams* was his most influential work. Dreams have

a.   manifest and latent content.
b.   preconscious and unconscious factors.
c.   id and ego.
d.   superego and id.

For Freud, the dream was the royal road to the unconscious mind. According to Freud, the dream is composed of a surface meaning which is the manifest content, and then hidden meaning or so-called latent content. In therapy, dream work consists of deciphering the hidden meaning of the dream (e.g., symbolism) so the individual can be aware of unconscious motives, impulses, desires, and conflicts.   **(a)**

213. When a client projects feelings toward the therapist which he or she originally had toward a significant other, it is called

    a.   free association.
    b.   insight.
    c.   transference.
    d.   resistance.

Some counselors feel that transference is actually a form of projection, displacement, and repetition in which the client treats the counselor in the same manner as he or she would an authority figure from the past (e.g., a mother, a father, a caretaker, or significant other). Just for review purposes choice "a," free association, is an analytic technique in which the client is instructed to say whatever comes to mind. Choice "b," insight, refers to the process of making a client aware of something which was previously unknown. This increases self-knowledge. Insight is often described as a novel sudden understanding of a problem. Choice "d" is resistance. Psychoanalysts believe that a client who is resistant will be reluctant to bring unconscious ideas into the conscious mind. Non-analytic counselors generally utilize the term in a looser context and use the word to describe clients who are fighting the helping process in any manner. **(c)**

214. Which case is not associated with the psychodynamic movement?

a. Little Hans
b. Little Albert
c. Anna O.
d. Schreber

Little Albert was a famous case associated with the work of John Broadus Watson who pioneered American Behaviorism. In 1920, John Watson and Rosalie Rayner conditioned an eleven-year-old boy named Albert to be afraid of furry objects. First Albert was exposed to a white rat. Initially the child was not afraid of the rat; however, Watson and Rayner would strike a steel bar which created a loud noise whenever the child would get near the animal. This created a conditioned (i.e., learned) fear in the child. This experiment has been used to demonstrate the behavioristic concept that fears are learned rather than the analytic concept that they are somehow the result of an unconscious process. Incidentally, rumor has it that Albert was never cured of his experimentally induced affliction. Horrors! Choices "a," "c," and "d" refer to landmark psychoanalytic cases which are often cited in the literature. The 1880's case of Anna O. (actually a client named Berta Pappenheim) was considered the first psychoanalytic patient. Anna O. was a patient of Freud's colleague Joseph Breuer. She suffered from symptoms without an organic basis which was termed hysteria. In hypnosis she would remember painful events which she was unable to recall while awake. Talking about these traumatic events brought about relief and this became the talking cure or catharsis. Although Freud became disenchanted with hypnosis, his association with Breuer led him to his basic premise of psychoanalysis which was that techniques which could produce cathartic material were highly therapeutic. The case of Little Hans is often used to contrast behavior therapy (Little Albert) with psychoanalysis. It reflects the data in Freud's 1909 paper, "An Analysis of a Phobia in a Five-Year-Old Boy," in which this child's fear of going into the streets and perhaps even having a horse bite him were explained using psychoanalytic constructs such as the Oedipus Complex and castration anxiety. Thus, Little Hans reflects psychoanalytic explanations of behavior, while Little Albert is indicative of the behavioristic paradigm. Daniel Paul Schreber has been called the "most frequently quoted case in modern psychiatry." In 1903 Schreber—after spending nine years in a mental hospital—wrote *Memoirs of a Mental Patient*. His family was rather wealthy and bought almost every copy in circulation. Nevertheless, Freud got his hands on one and in 1911 published *Psychoanalytical Notes upon an Autobiographical Account of a Case of Paranoia*. Schreber's major delusion was that he would be transformed into a woman, become God's mate and produce a healthier race. Freud felt that Schreber might have been struggling with unconscious issues of homosexuality. **(b)**

215. In contrast with classical psychoanalysis, psychodynamic counseling or therapy

    a.   utilizes fewer sessions per week.
    b.   does not utilize the couch.
    c.   is performed face to face.
    d.   all of the above.

Classical psychoanalysis is quite lengthy—three to five sessions per week for several years is not unusual—not to mention expensive. A complete analysis could cost well over $100,000 in some parts of the nation. Psychodynamic therapy and counseling makes use of analytic principles (e.g., the unconscious mind) but relies on less sessions per week to make it a bit more practical. Psychodynamic therapists generally dispense of the couch and sit face to face as in other forms of counseling and therapy. Freud once commented in regard to the merits of the couch that he could not stand to be stared at for many hours during the day. Moreover, he felt the couch could enhance the free association process. **(d)**

216. Talking about difficulties to purge emotions and feelings is a curative process known as

a.	catharsis and/or abreaction.
b.	resistance.
c.	accurate empathy.
d.	reflection of emotional content.

Hard-core analysts often prefer the word abreaction over the nontechnical term catharsis. Other writers use the word catharsis to connote mild purging of emotion, and abreaction when the repressed emotional outburst is very powerful and violent. Freud and Breuer initially used the term to describe highly charged repressed emotions which were released during the hypnotic process. When all is said and done, most exams will do as I have done here and use the terms in a synonymous fashion. Choice "c" accurate empathy means that the counselor can truly understand what the client is feeling or experiencing. Reflection of emotional content (Choice "d") is accomplished when the counselor restates the client's verbalization in such a manner that the client becomes more aware of his or her emotions. Choices "c" and "d" are emphasized very heavily in the non-directive (later called client-centered and then person-centered) approach to counseling.	**(a)**

217.	Id, ego, superego is to structural theory as _____ is to topographical theory.

	a.	child, adult, parent
	b.	abreaction, catharsis, introspection
	c.	ego ideal
	d.	unconscious, preconscious, conscious

First, let me explain why choice "a" is incorrect. Id, ego, and superego refer to Freud's structural theory of the personality while child, adult, and parent is the structural model proposed by Eric Berne, father of Transactional Analysis. The question, nevertheless, does not ask you to compare the id, ego, and superego to another structural theory; it asks you to compare it to the components in the topographical theory. Remember, the one where the mind is seen as an iceberg? The term "introspection" introduced in choice "b" describes any process in which the client attempts to describe his or her own internal thoughts, feelings, and ideas. **(d)**

218. The most controversial aspect of Freud's theory is

    a.   catharsis.
    b.   the interpretation of dreams.
    c.   the notion of the preconscious mind.
    d.   the Oedipus complex.

This is known as the Electra Complex when it occurs in females. Also be aware that the most important concept in Freud's theory is the unconscious mind. **(d)**

219. Evidence for the unconscious mind comes from all of these except _____.

    a.   hypnosis.
    b.   slips of the tongue and humor.
    c.   dreams.
    d.   subjective units of distress scale.

Subjective units of distress scale or SUDS is a concept used in forming a hierarchy to perform systematic desensitization; a behavior therapy technique for curbing phobic reactions, anxiety, and avoidance responses to innocuous situations. The SUDS is created via the process of introspection by rating the anxiety associated with the situation. Generally, the scale most counselors use is 0 to 100 with 100 being the most threatening situation. The counselor can ask a client to rate imagined situations on the subjective units of disturbance scale so that a treatment hierarchy can be formulated. Just for the record, slips of the tongue (Choice "b"), or what Freud called "the psychopathology of everyday life," will be technically referred to as "parapraxis" on some exams. **(d)**

220. In a counseling session, a counselor asked a patient to recall what transpired three months ago to trigger her depression. There was silence for about two and one-half minutes. The client then began to remember. This exchange most likely illustrates the function of the

    a.   preconscious mind.
    b.   ego ideal.
    c.   conscious mind.
    d.   unconscious mind.

The rationale here is simple enough. The conscious mind is aware of the immediate environment. The preconscious mind is capable of bringing ideas, images, and thoughts into awareness with minimal difficulty (e.g., in this question the memory of what transpired several months ago to trigger the client's depression). The unconscious, on the other hand, is composed of material which is normally unknown to the client. Thus, if the hypothetical client in this question had said, "Isn't that strange I can't remember what happened to trigger the depression," the correct answer would be choice "d" the unconscious mind (assuming, of course, the memory loss was not due to biological factors). And—strictly for the sake of repetition—the ego ideal of the superego is the perfect self or ideal self that the person judges himself or herself against. **(a)**

221. Unconscious processes which serve to minimize anxiety and protect the self from severe id or superego demands are called

    a.   slips of the tongue.
    b.   ego defense mechanisms.
    c.   id defense processes.
    d.   latent dream material.

The id strives for immediate satisfaction while the superego is ready and willing to punish the ego via guilt if the id is allowed to act on such impulses. This creates tension and a certain degree of pressure within the personality.

The ego controls the tension and relieves anxiety utilizing "ego defense mechanisms." Simply put, ego defense mechanisms are unconscious strategies which distort reality and are based on self-deception to protect our self-image. Although this concept has its roots in Freud's psychoanalysis, counselors of most persuasions now agree that defense mechanisms are relevant when studying the personality. Counselors who are not psychoanalytic, nevertheless, may not agree with the theoretical conceptualization that such behavior is the result of id, ego, and superego processes.   **(b)**

222. Most therapists agree that ego defense mechanisms deny or distort reality. Rationalization, compensation, repression, projection, reaction formation, identification, introjection, denial, and displacement are ego defense mechanisms. According to the Freudians, the most important defense mechanism is

    a.   repression.
    b.   reaction formation.
    c.   denial.
    d.   sublimation.

Freud saw defense mechanisms as an unconscious method one uses to protect himself or herself from anxiety. The Freudians feel that repression is the kingpin or granddaddy of ego defense mechanisms. A child who is sexually abused, for example, may repress (i.e., truly forget) the incident. In later life, the repression that served to protect the person and "helped her through the distasteful incident at the time" can cause emotional problems. Psychoanalytically trained counselors thus attempt to help the client recall the repressed memory and make it conscious so it can be dealt with. This is called insight and is often curative. Choice "b," reaction formation, occurs when a person can't accept a given impulse and thus behaves in the opposite manner. Choice "c," denial, is similar to repression except that it is a conscious act. An individual who says, "I refuse to think about it," is displaying denial. Sublimation in choice "d" is present when a person acts out an unconscious impulse in a socially acceptable way. Hence, a very aggressive individual might pursue a career in boxing, wrestling, or football. **(a)**

223. Suppression differs from repression in that

   a. suppression is stronger.
   b. repression only occurs in children.
   c. repression is automatic or involuntary.
   d. all of the above.

If you missed this one, review question 222. Some exams refer to suppression as denial. **(c)**

224. An aggressive male who becomes a professional boxer because he is sadistic is displaying

   a. suppression.
   b. rationalization.
   c. sublimation.
   d. displacement.

Again, if you missed this question review the question and answer for 222. A rationalization (choice "b") is simply an intellectual excuse to minimize hurt feelings. A student who says, "Hey, I'm glad I didn't get good grades, only nerds get good grades," is practicing classical rationalization. The person who rationalizes will tend to interpret his thoughts and feelings in a positive or favorable manner. The final choice, displacement—also a defense mechanism—occurs when an impulse is unleashed at a safe target. The prototype example (which you could easily come across on a host of mental health exams) would be the man who is furious with his boss but is afraid to show it and so he comes home and kicks the family dog. Hopefully, the family dog will have good enough sense to kick him back! **(c)**

225. An advertising psychologist secretly imbeds the word "SEX" into newspaper ads intended to advertise his center's chemical dependency program. This is the practice of

    a.   sublimation.
    b.   repression.
    c.   introjection.
    d.   none of the above.

Okay, fess up; did you choose "a"? I'll bet you're not the only one! Let me say this in a way so hopefully you'll never miss this type of tricky question again: Sublimation is not the same as subliminal. Sublimation is a defense mechanism, while subliminal perception supposedly occurs when you perceive something unconsciously and thus it has an impact on your behavior. I say "supposedly" because the American Psychological Association (APA) has taken the position that subliminal perception is not effective. The opposite stance has been taken by Wilson Bryan Key who has written books such as *Subliminal Seduction* and *Media Sexploitation* in which he points out how advertisers and others have relied on this technique. So, a word to the wise: Read each exam question carefully. Here you will note that the question is describing a subliminal, yet the word "subliminal" is not an answer choice making choice "d" the only correct answer. Choice "c," introjection, takes place when a child accepts a parent, caretaker, or significant other's values as his own. In the case of this defense mechanism, a sexually abused child might attempt to sexually abuse other children. **(d)**

226. A man receives a nickel an hour pay raise. He was expecting a one dollar per hour raise. He is furious but nonassertive. He thus smiles and thanks his boss. That night he yells at his wife for no apparent reason. This is an example of

    a.   displacement.
    b.   denial.
    c.   identification.
    d.   a Type II error.

Here the man yells at his wife instead of kicking the family dog. This is displacement par excellence. Identification (choice "c") is also a defense mechanism which results when a person identifies with a cause or a successful person with the unconscious hope that he or she will be perceived as successful or worthwhile. Finally, a Type II or so-called beta error is a statistical term which means that a researcher has accepted a null hypothesis (i.e., that there is no difference between an experimental group and a group not receiving any experimental treatment) when it is false. Plenty more questions of this sort when you reach the sections on statistics and research methodology. **(a)**

227. A student tells a college counselor that he is not upset by a grade of "F" in physical education which marred his 4th year perfect 4.0 average, inasmuch as "straight A students are eggheads." This demonstrates

    a. introjection.
    b. reaction formation.
    c. sour grapes rationalization.
    d. sweet lemon rationalization.

Remember the fable in which the fox couldn't secure the grapes so he said they were probably sour anyway? Well here's the human equivalent affectionately known as the sour grapes variety of rationalization. "I didn't really want it anyway," is the way this one is usually expressed. Choice "d" depicts the "sweet lemon" variety of rationalization. Here the person tells you how wonderful a distasteful set of circumstances really is. Thus, in rationalization the person either underrates a reward (sour grapes) or overrates a reward (sweet lemon) to protect the self from a bruised ego. **(c)**

228. A master's level counselor lands an entry level counseling job in an agency in a warm climate. Her office is not air conditioned, but the counselor insists she likes this because sweating really helps to keep her weight in check. This illuminates

a. sour grapes rationalization.
b. sweet lemon rationalization.
c. repression.
d. sublimation.

Review the previous question if you missed this. And here's a wonderful memory device. In our society we overrate the value of (or at least overeat) sweets in our diet. In the sweet lemon variety of rationalization the person overrates the situation. In this question the counselor is essentially saying, "Oh, gee, I just love to sweat, it keeps the water weight off of me and keeps my weight down." Right; and lemons taste sweet . . . dream on! **(b)**

229. A teenager who had his heart set on winning a tennis match broke his arm in an auto accident. He sends in an entry form to play in the competition which begins just days after the accident. His behavior is influenced by

    a. denial.
    b. displacement of anger.
    c. sublimation.
    d. organ inferiority.

This is classic denial. The tennis player is failing to face reality. Organ inferiority (choice "d") is usually associated with the work of Alfred Adler who pioneered a theory known as "individual psychology." **(a)**

230. _____ is like looking in a mirror but thinking you are looking out a window.

    a. Repression
    b. Sour grapes rationalization
    c. Projection
    d. Denial

Simply put, the person who engages in projection attributes unacceptable qualities of his or her own to others. **(c)**

231. Mark is obsessed with stamping out pornography. He is unconsciously involved in this cause so that he can view the material. This is

    a.   reaction formation.
    b.   introjection.
    c.   projection.
    d.   rationalization.

In reaction formation the person acts the opposite of the way he or she actually feels. An adult living with a very elderly parent, for example, may spend all his or her time caring for the parent when in reality, the individual unconsciously would like to see the elderly person die. **(a)**

232. Ted has always felt inferior intellectually. He currently works out at the gym at least four hours daily and is taking massive doses of dangerous steroids to build his muscles. The ego defense mechanism in action here is

    a.   reaction formation.
    b.   compensation.
    c.   projection.
    d.   rationalization.

Compensation is evident when an individual attempts to develop or overdevelop a positive trait to make up for a limitation (i.e., a perceived inferiority). The person secretly hopes that others will focus on the positives rather than the negative factors. **(b)**

233. Jane feels very inferior. She is now president of the board at a shelter for the homeless. She seems to be obsessed with her work for the agency and spends every spare minute trying to help the cause. When asked to introduce herself in virtually any social situation, Jane invariably responds with, "I'm the president of the board for the homeless shelter." Jane is engaging in

a. projection.
b. displacement.
c. introjection.
d. identification.

If this is unclear review the explanation under question 226. **(d)**

234. A client who has incorporated his father's values into his thought patterns is a product of

a. introjection.
b. repression.
c. rationalization.
d. displacement.

Yes, by the time you're finished wrestling with this set of questions you will definitely know your defense mechanisms! Sometimes introjection causes the person to accept an aggressor's values. A prisoner of war might incorporate the value system of the enemy after a period of time. **(a)**

235. The client's tendency to inhibit or fight against the therapeutic process is known as

a. resistance.
b. sublimation.
c. projection.
d. individuation.

A client who refuses to follow a counselor's directives such as a homework assignment or completing a battery of tests would be a typical example of resistance or what counselors call the "resistant client." **(a)**

236. Freud has been called the most significant theorist in the entire history of psychology. His greatest contribution was his conceptualization of the unconscious mind. Critics, however, contend that

a. he was too concerned with the totem and the taboo.
b. he failed to emphasize sex.
c. his theory is difficult to test from a scientific standpoint.
d. he was pro female.

How can concepts like the id, ego, or unconscious conflicts be directly measured? The answer is, that for the most part, they can't. This has been a major criticism of Freud's theory. Choice "a" alludes to Freud's writings on the totem (an object that represents a family or group), the taboo, and the dread of incest. Freud felt that even primitive peoples feared incestuous relationships. The dread of incest is not instilled merely via modern societal sanctions.   **(c)**

237. The purpose of interpretation in counseling is to

a. help the therapist appear genuine.
b. make the clients aware of their unconscious processes.
c. make clients aware of nonverbal behaviors.
d. help clients understand feelings and behaviors related to childhood.

This is the kind of question that separates the men from the boys and the women from the girls. It is what is known as a "best answer" type of question. Although choices "c" and "d" are not necessarily incorrect, choice "b" is a textbook definition of interpretation.   **(b)**

238. Organ inferiority relates mainly to the work of

a. C.G. Jung's analytical psychology.
b. Alfred Adler's individual psychology.
c. Sigmund Freud's psychoanalytic theory.
d. Josef Breuer's work on hysteria.

The term "individual" stresses the unique qualities we each possess. Individual psychology is keen on analyzing organ inferiority and methods in which the individual attempts to compensate for it. It is interesting to note that Alfred Adler was a very sickly child. Because of rickets (a disease caused by the absence of vitamin D, the so-called sunshine vitamin), Adler could not walk until age four. He was then the victim of pneumonia as well as a series of accidents. Thus, for Adler, the major psychological goal is to escape deep-seated feelings of inferiority. Could Adler's theory reflect his own childhood? You decide. **(b)**

239. When a client becomes aware of a factor in his or her life that was heretofore unknown, counselors refer to it as

    a.   individual psychology.
    b.   confrontation.
    c.   transference neurosis.
    d.   insight.

Insight is the "aha, now I understand," phenomenon. Technically, the term "insight" is equated with the work of the gestalt psychologist Wolfgang Kohler. From 1913 to 1919 Kohler spent time on the island of Tenerife (the largest of the Canary Islands) where he studied chimpanzees and the great apes. In a somewhat landmark experiment one of Kohler's subjects, a rather intelligent chimp named Sultan, needed to secure a dish of food placed outside the cage. The chimp had two sticks but neither would reach the food. Finally, via trial and error, the chimp put the two sticks together to create a longer stick and the problem was suddenly solved (insight took place). In another famous experiment a banana was suspended from the ceiling of the cage, and the chimp needed to stack boxes and stand on them to reach the banana. When the chimp saw the value of using the box or the stick as a tool, Kohler called it an insight experience. His 1925 book *The Mentality of Apes* took the information beyond the Canary Islands to its rightful place in the therapy room. According to some theorists three types of learning exist: reinforcement (operant conditioning), association (classical conditioning), and insight. **(d)**

240. C.G. Jung, the founder of Analytic Psychology, said men operate on logic or the _____ principle, while women are intuitive, operating on the _____ principle.

    a.   eros; thanatos
    b.   logos; eros
    c.   reality; pleasure
    d.   transference; counter transference

Logos implies logic, while eros refers to intuition. Choice "d" uses the terminology, transference and counter transference. In transference, the assumption is that the client will relate to the therapist or counselor as he or she has to significant others. The Freudians are fond of speaking of a "transference neurosis" in which the client is attached to the counselor as if he or she is a substitute parent. Counter transference (also commonly spelled with a hyphen or as one word) is said to be evident when the counselor's strong feelings or attachment to the client are strong enough to hinder the treatment process. **(b)**

241. Jung used drawings balanced around a center point to analyze himself, his clients, and dreams. He called them

    a.   mandalas.
    b.   projective drawings.
    c.   unconscious automatic writing.
    d.   eidetic imagery.

Jung, the father of analytic psychology, borrowed the term mandala from Hindu writings in which the mandala was the symbol of meditation. In Jung's writings the mandala also can stand for a magic protective circle which represents self-unification. A bit mystical, isn't it? Perhaps that is why poets, philosophers, and those with an interest in religion often valued Jung's work more so than did psychiatrists. Choice "d" is a word you will often run across in child psychology and development tests. Eidetic imagery—which usually is gone by the time a child reaches adolescence—is the ability to remember the most minute details of a scene or a picture for an extended period of time. Laypersons will say that such a child has a "photographic memory."   **(a)**

242. _____ emphasized the drive for superiority.

    a.   Jung
    b.   Adler
    c.   Freud
    d.   Freud and Jung

Alfred Adler, the father of Individual Psychology, initially felt that aggressive drives were responsible for most human behaviors. He then altered the theory slightly and said that the major factor was the "will to power." Finally, he concluded that it was the "striving for superiority" or a thirst for perfection that motivated behavior. (Note: The drive for superiority did not imply that the person wanted to dominate others or become a political figure or one of the ruling class.)   **(b)**

243. The statement, "Sibling interaction may have more impact than parent/child interaction" describes

    a.   Sigmund Freud's theory.
    b.   Alfred Adler's theory.
    c.   insight.
    d.   Carl Jung's theory.

Adler, who broke with Freud in 1911, went on to found a number of child-guidance clinics in which he was able to observe children's behavior directly. One criticism of Freud has been that his child development theories were not based on extensive research or observations of children's behavior. **(b)**

244. In contrast with Freud, the neo-Freudians emphasized

    a.   baseline measures.
    b.   social factors.
    c.   unconditional positive regard.
    d.   insight.

This is a must know concept. It is hard to imagine a comprehensive exam which would not touch on this issue. Neo-Freudians such as Alfred Adler, Karen Horney, Erik Erikson, Harry Stack Sullivan, and Erich Fromm stressed the importance of cultural (social) issues and, of course, interpersonal (social) relations. Choice "a" is decidedly incorrect inasmuch as baseline is a behaviorist term. (Remember the behaviorists . . . the rivals of the analysts!) Baseline—sometimes written as two words—indicates the frequency that a behavior is manifested prior to or in the absence of treatment. Unconditional positive regard (Choice "c") is a concept popularized by the late great therapist Carl R. Rogers who felt that the counselor must care for the client even when the counselor is uncomfortable or disagrees with the client's position. In essence, the counselor accepts the client just the way he or she is without any stipulations. **(b)**

245. The terms introversion and extroversion are associated with

    a.   psychoanalysis.
    b.   Freud.
    c.   Adler.
    d.   Jung.

Introversion meant a turning in of the libido. Thus, an introverted individual is his or her own primary source of pleasure. Such a person will generally shy away from social situations if possible. Extroversion, on the other hand, is the tendency to find satisfaction and pleasure in other people. The extrovert seeks external rewards. The introversion-extroversion distinction deals with inward or outward directiveness. Why not try the simplest of memory devices to remember this principle? You can remember that the "in" as in introvert looks "in" or with"in" himself or herself for satisfaction. Of course, an extrovert would be the opposite and look to external factors like social situations. Another idea might be to equate the "e," the first letter in extroversion, with the "e" which is the first letter in external. **(d)**

246. The personality types of the *Myers-Briggs Type Indicator (MBTI)* are associated with the work of

    a.   psychoanalysis.
    b.   Freud.
    c.   Adler.
    d.   Jung.

This test is literally given to several million persons each year! The *Myers-Briggs Type Indicator* is said to be the most widely used measure of personality preferences and dispositions. The measure can be used to assess upper elementary children age 12 and over all the way through adulthood and yields a four-letter code or "type" based on four bipolar scales. The bipolar preference scales are **extroversion/introversion**; **sensing** (i.e., current perception)/**intuition** (i.e., future abstractions and possibilities); **thinking/feeling**; and **judging** (i.e., organizing and controlling the outside world)/**perceiving** (i.e., observing events). **(d)**

247. One of Adler's students, Rudolph Dreikurs

    a.   created the TAT.
    b.   was the first to discuss the use of group therapy in private practice.
    c.   was a noted Freud hater.
    d.   created the hierarchy of needs.

(Dreikurs also introduced Adlerian principles to the treatment of children in the school setting.) The TAT mentioned in choice "a" is a projective test in which the client is shown a series of pictures and asked to tell a story. TAT stands for *Thematic Apperception Test* which was introduced in Henry Murray's 1938 work *Explorations in Personality.* Murray called the study of the personality "personology." As for choice "c" I believe I'd go with Andrew Salter who wrote *The Case Against Psychoanalysis.* Salter did groundbreaking work in behavior therapy which led to the formation of assertiveness training. This information appeared in the 1949 classic *Conditioned Reflex Therapy.* In reference to choice "d" it was Maslow and not Adler who created the hierarchy of needs. **(b)**

248. Adler emphasized that people wish to belong. This is known as

    a.   superiority.
    b.   social connectedness.
    c.   the collective unconscious.
    d.   animus.

The Adlerian theory (choice "b") suggests that we need one another. The collective unconscious in choice "c" is a term coined by C.G. Jung which implies that all humans have "collected" universal inherited unconscious neural patterns. **(b)**

249. Adler was one of the first therapists who relied on paradox. Using this strategy, a client (who was a student in a counselor preparation program) who was afraid to give a presentation in front of his counseling class for fear he might shake and embarrass himself would be instructed to

a. try to exaggerate the behavior and really do a thorough job shaking in front of the class.
b. practice relaxation techniques for 10 to 20 minutes before the speech.
c. practice rational self-talk.
d. practice rational thinking.

Paradoxical techniques also are associated with the work of Victor Frankl who pioneered Logotherapy, a form of existential treatment. Paradoxical strategies often seem to defy logic as the client is instructed to intensify or purposely engage in the maladaptive behavior. Paradoxical interventions are often the direct antithesis of common sense directives such as choice "b." Paradoxical methods have become very popular with family therapists due to the work of Jay Haley and Milton H. Erickson. Currently, this technique is popular with family therapists who believe it reduces a family's resistance to change. Choices "c" and "d" are almost always associated with the so-called cognitive therapies, especially rational-emotive psychotherapy. **(a)**

250. Jung felt that society caused men to deny their feminine side known as _____ and women to deny their masculine side known as _____.

a. Eros; Thanatos
b. animus; anima
c. anima; animus
d. yin; yang

These terms were introduced in the section on human growth and development but just for review purposes and for those who never studied Latin: You can remember that anima is the feminine term as it ends in "ma," and needless to say, it is common to refer to one's mother as "ma." You could also remember animus is the male side of the personality as it ends in "mus" and reminds one of "muscles," which are generally a male attribute. Choice "d" notes the Chinese Taoist philosophy in which the yin is the passive feminine force in the universe, which is contrasted by the yang, the masculine force. **(c)**

251. Jung spoke of a collective unconscious common to all men and women. The material that makes up the collective unconscious, which is passed from generation to generation, is known as

    a.   a hierarchy of needs.
    b.   instinctual.
    c.   paradox.
    d.   archetypes.

Easy to remember if you keep the word archaic in mind. An archetype is actually a primal universal symbol which means the same thing to all men and women (e.g., the cross). Jung perused literature and found that certain archetypes appeared in fables, myths, dreams, and religious writings since the beginning of recorded history. **(d)**

252. Common archetypes include

    a.   the persona—the mask or role we present to others to hide our true self.
    b.   animus, anima, self.
    c.   shadow—the mask behind the persona which contains id-like material, denied yet desired.
    d.   all of the above.

The shadow noted in choice "c" is often called the dark side of the personality, though it is not necessarily negative. Jung noted that the shadow encompasses everything an individual refused to acknowledge. The shadow represents the unconscious opposite of the individual's conscious expression. Hence, a shy retired individual might have recurring dreams that he or she is very outgoing, verbal, and popular. In addition to dreams, the basic nature of the shadow is also evident when an individual engages in projection. The clinical assumption is made that projection will decrease and individuation will increase as therapy renders shadow behaviors conscious. **(d)**

253. A client is demonstrating inconsistent behavior. She is smiling but says that she is very sad about what she did. When her counselor points this out to her, the counselor's verbal response is known as

    a.   active listening.
    b.   confrontation.
    c.   accurate empathy.
    d.   summarization.

Confrontation could also relate solely to verbal behavior. For example, a counselor might confront a client about what he says he is doing in his life versus what he is truly doing. The essence of confrontation is to illuminate discrepancies between the client's and the helper's conceptualization of a given situation. Choice "c," accurate empathy, occurs when a counselor is able to experience the client's point of view in terms of feelings and cognitions. Summarization mentioned in choice "d" transpires whenever a counselor brings together the ideas discussed during a period of dialogue. A counselor might also ask the client to summarize to be certain that he or she has actually grasped the meaning of an exchange. Some counselors believe that summarization should occur at the end of each session or after several sessions. **(b)**

254. During a professional staff meeting, a counselor says he is worried that if techniques are implemented to stop a six-year-old boy from sucking his thumb, then he will begin biting his nails or stuttering. The counselor

    a.   is using the logic set forth in Gestalt Therapy.
    b.   is using RET.
    c.   is most likely a behaviorist concerned with symptom substitution.
    d.   is most likely an analytically trained counselor concerned with symptom substitution.

The answer only can be choice "d" inasmuch as symptom substitution is a psychoanalytic concept. According to the theory, if you merely deal with the symptom, another symptom will manifest itself since the real problem is in the unconscious mind. **(d)**

255. An eclectic counselor

    a.   is analytic.
    b.   is behavioristic.
    c.   attempts to choose the best theoretical approach based on the client's attributes, resources, and situation.
    d.   insists on including all family members in the treatment.

An eclectic counselor uses theories and techniques from several models of intervention, rather than simply relying on one. An eclectic counselor, for example, would not say, "I'm a Rogerian," or "I see myself as a strict behavior therapist." The eclectic counselor uses "the best from every approach." Research indicates that about 50% of all therapists claim to be eclectic, and a number of studies indicate eclecticism is on the rise. **(c)**

256. The word "eclectic" is most closely associated with

    a.   Frederick C. Thorne.
    b.   Freud.
    c.   Piaget.
    d.   Skinner.

It is very important to note that Thorne felt that true eclecticism was much more than "a hodgepodge of facts": it needed to be rigidly scientific. Thorne preferred the term "psychological case handling" rather than "psychotherapy" as he felt the efficacy of psychotherapy had not been scientifically demonstrated. **(a)**

257. A counselor who is obsessed with the fact that a client missed his or her session is the victim of

a.   cognitive dissonance.
b.   transference.
c.   counter transference.
d.   positive transference.

In counter transference the counselor's past is projected onto the client and the helper's objectivity suffers markedly. A counselor who falls in love with a client or feels extreme anger toward a client is generally considered a victim of counter transference. Choice "a," cognitive dissonance, suggests that humans will feel quite uncomfortable if they have two incompatible or inconsistent beliefs and thus the person will be motivated to reduce the dissonance.   **(c)**

258. Life-style and family constellation are emphasized by

a.   Freud.
b.   Jung.
c.   Adler.
d.   Thorne.

Adlerians believe that our life-style is a predictable self-fulfilling prophecy based on our psychological feelings about ourselves. Adler stressed the importance of birth order in the family constellation (e.g., the firstborn could be dethroned by a later child who gets most of the attention; thus the firstborn would be prone to experience feelings of inferiority). Recently, the concept of birth order has been criticized by theorists such as Wayne Dyer, famous for his self-improvement books, such as *Your Erroneous Zones*.   **(c)**

259. A counselor who remarks that firstborn children are usually conservative but display leadership qualities is most likely

a.   a Freudian.
b.   an Adlerian.
c.   a Rogerian.
d.   using a behavioral contract.

You can well imagine why the current family therapy movement has roots in Adlerian theory. **(b)**

260. Existentialism is to Logotherapy as _____ is to behaviorism.

    a.   operants
    b.   associationism
    c.   Skinner
    d.   Socrates

Don't panic . . . this is simply an analogy type question. Let's think this one out together so you can discover how choice "b" checks in as the correct answer. The first word in the question gives us a significant clue. That is to say, "existentialism" is a type of philosophy. Now existentialism (the philosophy) is compared to "Logotherapy," which is a brand of psychotherapy. The question then mentions behaviorism, which is a type of psychology and more loosely defined as a brand of treatment. So, the question tells you that Logotherapy grew out of the philosophy of existentialism and then asks you to fill in the blank with the philosophy which led to the formation of behaviorism. Skinner and his concept of operants are behavioristic to be sure, however, neither is a philosophy. The answer? Well it's associationism which asserts that ideas are held together by associations. Now here's a super hint. Although associationism had it's roots in an essay written by Aristotle on the nature of memory, most exams will list John Locke, David Hume, James Mill, or David Hartley as the pioneers. My guess. Look for the name John Locke come exam time. **(b)**

261. B.F. Skinner's reinforcement theory elaborated on

    a.   Edward Thorndike's law of effect.
    b.   Adler's concept of life-style.
    c.   Logotherapy.
    d.   symptom substitution.

The "law of effect" simply asserts that responses accompanied by satisfaction (i.e., it pleases you) will be repeated while those which produce unpleasantness or discomfort will be stamped out. **(a)**

262. Classical conditioning relates to the work of

    a.   E.G. Williamson.
    b.   B.F. Skinner.
    c.   Frankl.
    d.   Ivan Pavlov.

Interestingly enough Pavlov won a Nobel Prize not for his work in classical conditioning, but for his research on the digestive system. Choice "a," E.G. Williamson, is the father of the so-called Minnesota Viewpoint. Popular some years ago, especially with career counselors, this approach attempts to match the client's traits with a career. A word to the wise: Many exams will bill this as the "trait factor" approach. **(d)**

263. An association that naturally exists, such as an animal salivating when food is presented, is called

    a.   an operant.
    b.   conditioned.
    c.   unconditioned.
    d.   acquisition period.

Let me see if I can make this simple for you so that every time you see some form of the word "conditioned" or "conditioning" you don't feel intimidated. From now on, whenever you see the word conditioned, substitute the word "learned." When you see the word unconditioned substitute the word "unlearned." Now this question becomes a heck of a lot easier, since salivating, is an "unlearned" (same as unconditioned) response. So, for review purposes: conditioned = learned; unconditioned = unlearned. Choice "d," the acquisition period, refers to the time it takes to learn or acquire a given behavior.

If it takes a mentally retarded child two hours to learn to write his name, then two hours would be the acquisition period. **(c)**

264. Skinner's operant conditioning is also referred to as

    a.   instrumental learning.
    b.   classical conditioning.
    c.   cognitive learning.
    d.   learning via insight.

One possible memory device here would be that Skinner's last name has an "i" as does the word "instrumental" whereas the word Pavlov doesn't. **(a)**

265. Respondent behavior refers to

    a.   reflexes.
    b.   operants.
    c.   a type of phobia.
    d.   punishment.

Okay, so you didn't fall in love with my memory device for the last question. Never fear; here's another way to go about it. Pavlov's theory involves mainly "reflexes" such as in the experiment where the dog salivates. The word "reflex" begins with an "r" and so does the word "respondent." The bottom line: Pavlovian conditioning is respondent while Skinner's is instrumental/operant. (P.S. Please don't read this if you get confused easily, but the term "respondent" is generally accredited to Skinner although it applies to the theoretical notions of Pavlovian conditioning.) **(a)**

266. All reinforcers

     a.   are plastic tokens.

     b.   tend to increase the probability that a behavior will occur.

     c.   are secondary.

     d.   do not raise behavior since negative reinforcement lowers behavior.

I can't say this too strongly: All reinforcers—yep, both positive and negative—raise the probability that an antecedent (prior) behavior will occur. In a situation where we have positive reinforcement, something is added following an operant (behavior). Now, this is going to sound a little complicated, but here goes. It is possible to use positive reinforcers to reduce or eliminate an undesirable target behavior. Here's how. Using a procedure known as "differential reinforcement of other behavior" (DRO), the counselor positively reinforces an individual for engaging in a healthy alternative behavior. The assumption is that as the alternative desirable behavior increases via reinforcement, the client will not display the inappropriate target behavior as frequently. In the case of negative reinforcement, something is taken away after the behavior occurs. As for the incorrect choices, a secondary reinforcer is a neutral stimulus, such as a plastic token, which becomes reinforcing by association. Thus, a plastic token could be exchanged for known reinforcers. **(b)**

267. Negative reinforcement often requires the introduction of an aversive (negative) stimulus. It

     a.   is really the same as punishment.

     b.   effectively lowers the frequency of behavior in young children.

     c.   is not the same thing as punishment.

     d.   is a psychodynamic conceptualization.

A comprehensive test that includes questions on behavior modification but does not have a question similar to this one would be about as likely as an orange containing lemon juice. In case my analogy is a bit too sarcastic (or sour) for your taste, the salient point is that you must understand this concept. Negative reinforcement is not punishment. All reinforcers raise or strengthen the probability that a behavior will occur; punishment lowers it. It doesn't take a master's or a doctorate in counseling to grasp the notion that when you were punished as a child the probability of that particular behavior generally decreased for a period of time. I say "for a period of time" since most behavior modifiers feel punishment temporarily suppresses the behavior. This seems to be the case in humans and, according to B.F. Skinner, in rats. This would certainly seem to dethrone choice "b" as the correct response. ADVANCE EXAM REMINDER: Some tests *will discriminate* between positive and negative punishment. Positive punishment is said to occur when something is added after a behavior and the behavior decreases, while negative punishment takes place when a stimulus is removed following the behavior and the response decreases. **(c)**

268. Punishment

    a.   is the same as negative reinforcement.
    b.   is much more effective than reinforcement.
    c.   decreases the probability that a behavior will occur.
    d.   is used extensively in Reality Therapy.

A little review never hurt anybody. To set the record straight, behavior modifiers value reinforcement over punishment. Father of Reality Therapy, William Glasser, M.D., lists 8 steps for effective treatment of which Step 7 admonishes "not to punish." **(c)**

269. In Pavlov's famous experiment using dogs, the bell was the _____, and the meat was the _____.

a. CS, UCS
b. UCS, CS
c. CR, UCS
d. UCS, CR

Ah, remember my memory device from the introduction. It went like this: "In the US we eat a lot of meat." In the Pavlovian experiment the US (which is sometimes written UCS) is the unconditioned (think unlearned) stimulus or the meat. **(a)**

270. The most effective time interval (temporal relation) between the CS and the US

a. is irrelevant—it does not influence the learning process.
b. is 5 seconds.
c. is the .05 level according to social scientists.
d. is .5 or 1/2 of a second.

As the interval exceeds 1/2 second, more trials are needed for effective conditioning. How will you remember that the CS comes before the US? Just remember that "c" comes before "u" in the alphabet. Or better still, common sense would dictate that the reinforcer (the meat/US) would come after the bell (the CS) to reinforce it. Now I'm going to share something with you that will help you on difficult exam questions. When the CS is delayed until the US occurs, the procedure is known as "delay conditioning." If, however, the CS terminates before the occurrence of the US, it is termed "trace conditioning." Here's a slick and easy-to-use memory device. Trace begins with "t" and so does termination. In trace conditioning, the CS will terminate prior to the onset of the US (or UCS as it will be abbreviated on some exams). Hence, if an exam question suggests a time interval of .5 seconds, you would know that the procedure would be classified as trace conditioning. **(d)**

271. Many researchers have tried putting the UCS (i.e., the meat) before the CS (i.e., the bell). This usually results in

a. increased learning.
b. anger on the part of the dog.
c. experimental neurosis.
d. no conditioning.

Whether you put the cart before the horse, "u" before "c" in the alphabet, or the UCS before the CS, it just doesn't work. This is called backward conditioning. Generally backward conditioning is ineffective and doesn't work. Note: The exam you are taking could refer to the typical classical conditioning process where the CS comes before the UCS as "forward conditioning" to distinguish it from "backward conditioning." **(d)**

272. Several graduate students in counseling trained a poodle to salivate using Pavlov's classical conditioning paradigm. One day the department chairman was driving across campus and honked his horn. Much to the chagrin of the students, the poodle elicited a salivation response. What had happened?

a. experimental neurosis had obviously set in.
b. extinction.
c. stimulus generalization or what Pavlov termed irradiation.
d. stimulus discrimination.

Rule #1 for handling those lengthy questions on your exam: ignore all the irrelevant information. Whether it was the department chairman driving across the campus or the dean of students riding his bicycle is about as relevant to answering the question as the price of tea in China! Stimulus generalization, also called second-order conditioning, occurs when a stimulus similar to the CS (the bell) produces the same reaction. Hence, a car horn, a piano key, or a buzzer on a stove timer could conceivably produce the same reaction as the bell. Remember when I mentioned Little Albert's learned fear of white rats? The tendency for him to display fear with other furry white animals is illustrative of the principle of stimulus generalization. **(c)**

273. The department chairman found the poodle's response (see question 272) to his horn humorous. He thus instructed the graduate students to train the dog to salivate only to his car horn and not the original bell. Indeed the graduate students were able to perform this task. The poodle was now demonstrating

    a.   experimental neurosis.
    b.   irradiation.
    c.   pica.
    d.   stimulus discrimination.

Stimulus discrimination is nearly the opposite of stimulus generalization. Here the learning process is "fine tuned," if you will, to respond only to a specific stimulus. In this example, the dog would be taught to salivate only when the department chairman sounds his horn. A piano key, a buzzer on a stove, or the original bell would not elicit (i.e., cause) the reaction. Stimulus discrimination is at times referred to as "stimulus differentiation" in some of the literature. **(d)**

274. The department chair was further amused by the poodle's tendency to be able to discriminate one CS from another (see question 273). He thus told the students to teach the dog to salivate only to the horn on his Ford but not one on a graduate student's Chevrolet truck. In reality, the horns on the two vehicles sounded identical. The training was seemingly unsuccessful inasmuch as the dog merely took to very loud barking. In this case

    a.   experimental neurosis set in.
    b.   irradiation became a reality.
    c.   borderline personality traits no doubt played a role.
    d.   a covert process confounded the experiment.

"Stop it, you're driving this dog crazy," would be the correct response to this question. Pavlov termed this phenomenon "experimental neurosis." When the differentiation process becomes too tough because the stimuli are almost identical, the dog will show signs of emotional disturbance. Reminder: On questions of this nature, some exams will refer to the CS as the NS or "neutral stimulus," and the UCS as the "reinforcing" or "charged stimulus." **(a)**

275. In one experiment, a dog was conditioned to salivate to a bell paired with a fast-food cheeseburger. The researcher then kept ringing the bell without giving the dog the cheeseburger. This is known as

    a. instrumental learning via shaping.
    b. positive reinforcement.
    c. extinction, and the salivation will disappear.
    d. negative reinforcement.

This may be a doggy way to learn about classical Pavlovian respondent conditioning but I believe it is effective. In this case the layperson might say that ringing a bell and not reinforcing the dog with a fast-food cheeseburger is animal cruelty. The professional will see it as extinction. Extinction occurs when the CS is "not" reinforced via the US. Most experts believe that the CR is not eliminated but is suppressed or what is generally called "inhibited." The rationale for this position is that if the animal is given a rest, the CR (i.e., the salivation in this example) will reappear, though it will be weaker. This phenomenon has been called "spontaneous recovery." In Skinnerian or operant conditioning, extinction connotes that reinforcement is withheld and eventually the behavior will be extinguished (eliminated). **(c)**

276. John B. Watson's name is associated with

    a. Little Hans.
    b. Anna O.
    c. Little Albert.
    d. b and c.

The significance of the Little Albert case was that it demonstrated that fears were "learned" and not the result of some unconscious conflict. **(c)**

277. During a family counseling session, a six-year-old girl repeatedly sticks her tongue out at the counselor who is obviously ignoring the behavior. The counselor is practicing

    a.   negative reinforcement.
    b.   chaining.
    c.   reciprocal inhibition.
    d.   extinction.

A word to the wise experimenter or counselor. Some research demonstrates that when using extinction the behavior will get worse before it is eliminated. This tendency technically is called a response burst or an extinction burst. Fortunately, the "burst" or increase in the frequency of behavior is temporary. In plain everyday English then, this counselor can expect the little girl's behavior—in this case sticking out her tongue—to get worse before it gets better. Ignoring a behavior is a common method of extinction. Just for the record, the response burst is generally a major ethical consideration for therapists who are attempting to extinguish self-abusive or self-mutilating behaviors. Choice "b" chaining is also a behavioristic term. A chain is a sequence of behavior in which one response renders a cue that the next response is to occur. When you are writing a sentence and place a period at the end it is a cue that you're next letter will be an uppercase letter. In behavior modification simple behaviors are learned and then "chained" so that a complex behavior can take place. A chain is really just a series of operants joined together by reinforcers. **(d)**

278. In general, behavior modification strategies are based heavily on _____, while behavior therapy emphasizes _____.

a. instrumental conditioning; classical conditioning.
b. Pavlovian principles; Skinnerian principles.
c. Skinnerian principles; Pavlovian principles.
d. a and c.

Technically, behavior modification is Skinnerian (i.e., operant, instrumental), while behavior therapy is Pavlovian (i.e., classical, respondent). **(d)**

279. A behavioristic counselor decides upon aversive conditioning as the treatment of choice for a gentleman who wishes to give up smoking. The counselor begins by taking a baseline. This is accomplished

a. using hypnosis.
b. by charting the occurrence of the behavior prior to any therapeutic intervention.
c. using a biofeedback device.
d. counterconditioning.

The baseline indicates the frequency of the behavior untreated. **(b)**

280. The first studies which demonstrated that animals could indeed be conditioned to control autonomic processes were conducted by

a. E. Thorndike.
b. Joseph Wolpe.
c. Neal Miller.
d. Ivan Pavlov.

In a study that perhaps challenged a 100-year-old psychological doctrine, Miller and Banuazizi showed that by utilizing rewards rats could be trained to alter heart rate and intestinal contractions. Prior to this experiment it was thought that automatic or "autonomic" bodily processes (such as heart rate, intestinal contractions, or blood pressure) could not be controlled. Today, counselors often use the technique of biofeedback to help clients control autonomic responses. Edward Thorndike mentioned in choice "a" postulated the "law of effect" which is also known as "trial and error learning." This theory assumes that satisfying associations related to a given behavior will cause it to be "stamped in," while those associated with annoying consequences are "stamped out." And here is an important point: Practice per se does not insure effective learning. The practice must yield a reward. **(c)**

281. The significance of the Little Albert experiment by John B. Watson and Rosalie Rayner was that

   a.   a phobia could be a learned behavior.
   b.   it provided concrete proof that Skinner's model was correct.
   c.   it provided concrete proof that Pavlov's model was correct.
   d.   none of the above.

The psychoanalytic or Freudian theory espoused the notion that a fear was the result of an unconscious conflict. This is why analytic psychology is often called "depth psychology." Something is assumed to be wrong deep below the level of awareness. **(a)**

282. John B. Watson is to cause as Mary Cover Jones is to

   a.   cure.
   b.   Skinner.
   c.   Piaget.
   d.   Erikson.

John B. Watson demonstrated that a phobic reaction was "learned," while Mary Cover Jones demonstrated that "learning" could serve as a treatment for a phobic reaction. **(a)**

283. In the famous Little Albert experiment, a child was conditioned to fear a harmless white furry animal. Historical accounts indicate that the child also began to fear a Santa Claus mask. This would demonstrate

    a.   panic disorder with agoraphobia.
    b.   stimulus generalization.
    c.   an adjustment reaction.
    d.   stimulus discrimination.

This is simple enough to remember since in stimulus generalization the fear "generalizes." In other words, a Santa Claus mask is white and furry and somewhat similar to a furry white animal, and hence produces the same fearful reaction in the child. **(b)**

284. A counselor who says he practices depth psychology technically bases his treatment on

    a.   Pavlov's dogs.
    b.   Mary Cover Jones.
    c.   John B. Watson.
    d.   Freud's topographic hypothesis.

The process of elimination can work wonders here. Even if you couldn't distinguish Freud's topographic theory from a hole in the ground you would answer this question by eliminating choices "a," "b," and "c" based on the fact that Pavlov, Jones, and Watson were pioneers in the behaviorist movement. **(d)**

285. When a counselor refers to a counseling paradigm, she really means

    a.   she is nondirective.
    b.   she is very directive.
    c.   a treatment model.
    d.   she is not a depth psychologist.

You must be familiar with the word "paradigm" which is utilized excessively in this field. A paradigm is a "model." Choice "a" is used to describe a counselor who allows the client to explore thoughts and feelings with a minimum of direction. This approach, which was initially popularized via the work of Carl R. Rogers, is also called the "client-centered" or the "person-centered" approach. This is often contrasted with the directive position (choice "b") in which the therapist leads the client to discuss certain topics and provides "direct suggestions" about how the client should think, act, or behave. And here is a wonderful exam tip: Many tests will use the term "active therapy" or "active-directive" therapy to delineate the directive paradigm. **(c)**

286. A man says, "My life has been lousy for the past six months." The counselor replies, "Can you tell me specifically what has made life so bad for the last six months?" The counselor is

    a.   using interpretation.
    b.   using summarization.
    c.   using concreteness.
    d.   using a depth psychology paradigm.

Concreteness is also known as "specificity" in some of the literature. The counselor uses the principle of concreteness in an attempt to eliminate vague language. Choice "a," interpretation, is highly valued in analytic and psychodynamic modalities although it is used in other schools of counseling. Interpretation is said to take place when the counselor uncovers a deeper meaning regarding a client's situation. Most counselor educators believe that the counselor must wait until counselor-client trust is established; otherwise the client is more likely to reject the interpretation. This notion has been called "the timing of interpretation." **(c)**

287. A client who is having panic attacks is told to practice relaxing his jaw muscle for three minutes per day. The counselor here is using

      a.   concreteness.
      b.   a directive.
      c.   interpretation.
      d.   parroting.

When used in the context of counseling, a directive is merely a suggestion. Choice "d" is a no-no in effective counseling. Parroting is a misuse of paraphrasing. In parroting, the counselor restates the client's message back verbatim. The problem? Well, research shows parroting is for the birds! Clients who were the victims of parroting were bored, uncomfortable during the session, and sometimes felt angry toward the counselor. **(b)**

288. _____ is a biofeedback device.

      a.   A bathroom scale
      b.   An AM/FM radio
      c.   A digital clock
      d.   An analyst's couch

A biofeedback device provides you with biological information. A scale and a mirror are two simple examples. In counseling, biofeedback devices are used primarily to teach clients to relax or to control autonomic (i.e., automatic) nervous system functions such as blood pressure, pulse rate, or hand temperature. **(a)**

289. Johnny just loves M & Ms but doesn't do his homework. The school counselor thus instructs Johnny's mom to give the child a bag of M & Ms every night after he finishes his homework. This is an example of

      a.   punishment.
      b.   biofeedback.
      c.   a Pavlovian strategy.
      d.   positive reinforcement.

The idea of any reinforcer (positive or negative) is to increase or strengthen the behavior. In this case something is added to the behavior so it would be "positive reinforcement." **(d)**

290. Genuineness or congruence is really

    a.   identical to concreteness.
    b.   selective empathy.
    c.   the counselor's ability to be himself or herself.
    d.   an archaic Freudian notion.

The counselor who is congruent is real and authentic. This is a counselor who is not playing a role and is not putting up a facade. **(c)**

291. Empathy is

    a.   the ability to understand the client's world and to communicate this to the client.
    b.   Behavioristic.
    c.   a and b.
    d.   the same as sympathy.

Robert Carkhuff is very well-known for his creation of a 5-point scale intended to measure empathy, genuineness, concreteness, and respect. Many counselor educators consider empathy the most important factor in the counseling relationship. When using the Carkhuff scale, a rating of 1 is the poorest while a rating of 5 is the most desirable. A rating of 3 is considered the minimum level of acceptance. Choice "d" is incorrect. Empathy is the ability to experience the client's subjective world. Sympathy is compassion. **(a)**

292. When something is added following an operant, it is known as a _____, and when something is taken away it is called a _____.

a.   negative reinforcer; positive reinforcer
b.   positive reinforcer; negative reinforcer
c.   extinction; shaping
d.   classical conditioning; operant conditioning

If you're getting sick of the word "operant" don't blame me, it's B.F. Skinner's label. Any behavior which is not elicited by an obvious stimulus is an operant. Most behaviors are indeed operants. Skinner differentiated operants from "respondents." A respondent is the consequence of a known stimulus. A dog salivating to food or the pupil in your eye enlarging when you walk into a dark room are examples of respondents. Now you know why Pavlovian conditioning has been called "respondent conditioning."   **(b)**

293. After a dog is conditioned using the well-known experiment of Pavlov's, a light is paired with the bell (the CS). In a short period of time the light alone would elicit the salivation. This is called

a.   extinction.
b.   token reinforcement.
c.   biofeedback.
d.   higher order conditioning.

When a new stimulus is associated or "paired" with the CS and the new stimulus takes on the power of the CS, behaviorists refer to the phenomenon as "higher order conditioning." In this case, the light (which is a neutral stimulus) has taken on the power of the bell. Choice "b" occurs when a token (something which represents a reinforcer) is given after a desirable behavior. The token—which often just looks like a plastic coin—can be exchanged for the primary (i.e., actual) reinforcer. And here's a very helpful hint. Some exams refer to the items or activities which can be purchased with the tokens as "back-up reinforcers."   **(d)**

294. A counselor decides to use biofeedback training to help a client raise the temperature in his right hand to ward off migraines. He would utilize

    a.   a temperature trainer.
    b.   EMG feedback.
    c.   EEG feedback.
    d.   EKG feedback.

Again, a question that separates the men from the boys and the women from the girls. To answer it correctly, you'd need a lucky guess or a smattering of knowledge regarding physiological alphabet soup nomenclature. The Menninger Clinic in Kansas discovered that a very high percentage of individuals could ward off migraine headaches via raising the temperature in their hand. The technique is simply known as biofeedback "temperature training." (Yes, that's right, the most complex sounding choice is not always the correct choice!) In essence, a biofeedback temperature trainer is just an extremely precise high-priced thermometer. As for the wrong answers, EMG means electromyogram and is used to measure muscle tension. A person who is tensing a given muscle group could have an EMG biofeedback device hooked directly to the problem area. The EEG or electroencephalogram is used to monitor brain waves. Counselors sometimes shy away from EEG feedback since it can be confounded by other electrical devices nearby such as an air conditioner or a fluorescent light. EEG training often focuses on the production of alpha waves which is eight to 12 cycles per second. An individual in an alpha state is awake but extremely relaxed. Lastly, EKG or electrocardiogram provides data on the heart. **(a)**

295. A counselor discovered that a client became nervous and often experienced panic attacks when she would tense her frontalis muscle over her eyes. The counselor wanted direct muscle feedback and thus would rely on

a.   the Jacobson relaxation method.
b.   GSR feedback.
c.   EMG feedback.
d.   a simple yet effective mood ring.

No reason for a complex memory device here folks. Why not remember that the "M" in EMG refers to muscle? Edmund Jacobson (Choice "a") was a physiologist who developed a relaxation technique in which muscle groups are alternately tensed and relaxed until the whole body is in a state of relaxation. Due to simplicity and efficacy, the Jacobson Method rapidly became the darling of the behavior therapy movement. Choice "b" is the acronym for galvanic skin response which—although it is a method of biofeedback—provides electrical skin resistance. The role of GSR and emotion is still a bit vague and thus it is not a very popular form of biofeedback treatment. As far as choice "d" is concerned, a tad of common sense should tell you that if a $1.29 mood ring was really effective, no one would ever spend in excess of 70 bucks an hour for biofeedback training!   **(c)**

296. According to the Premack principle, an efficient reinforcer is what the client himself or herself likes to do. Thus, in this procedure

    a.   a lower probability behavior is reinforced by a higher probability behavior.
    b.   a higher probability behavior is reinforced by a lower probability behavior.
    c.   a and b are paradoxically both effective.
    d.   none of the above.

For test purposes be familiar with the acronyms LPB (low probability behavior) and HPB (high probability behavior). The principle asserts that any HPB can be used as a reinforcer for any LPB.   **(a)**

297. A counselor who wanted to teach a client to produce alpha waves for relaxation would utilize

a. EMG feedback.
b. GSR feedback.
c. EEG feedback.
d. EKG feedback.

EEG is used to secure feedback related to brain wave rhythms. **(c)**

298. A reinforcement schedule gives the guidelines or rules for reinforcement. If a reinforcer is given every time a desired response occurs, it is known as

a. an intermittent schedule.
b. an extinction schedule.
c. continuous reinforcement.
d. EMG.

This is easy enough to remember. In continuous reinforcement you "continue" to provide the reinforcement each time the target behavior occurs. Continuous reinforcement is not necessarily the most practical nor the most effective. Most human behaviors are reinforced effectively via the principle of intermittent reinforcement (choice "a"). In this format, the target behavior is reinforced only after the behavior manifests itself several times or for a given time interval. The exam you are taking may refer to intermittent reinforcement as "partial reinforcement," which literally indicates that the behavior is only reinforced a portion of the time. **(c)**

299. The two basic classes of intermittent reinforcement schedules are the _____, based on the number of responses and the _____, based on the time elapsed.

a. ratio; interval
b. interval; ratio
c. continuous; ratio
d. interval; continuous

The two basic classes of intermittent or partial reinforcement are ratio and interval. You can remember that "interval" is based on time rather than the number of responses, since in this society we use the phrase "time interval." (Note: The terms "fixed" and "variable" are often used with ratio and interval. Fixed implies that the reinforcement always takes place after a fixed time or number of responses while variable implies that an average number of responses or time may be used.) **(a)**

300. The most difficult intermittent schedule to extinguish is the

   a. fixed ratio.
   b. fixed interval.
   c. variable interval.
   d. variable ratio.

The memory device I use is VR which reminds me of the Vocational Rehabilitation agency. I remember that this agency is better than an agency going by FI (fixed interval), etc. Perhaps you can think of a memory device based on something personal in your life. Just for the record, choice "b," fixed interval or FI, is the most ineffective of the bunch. **(d)**

CHAPTER 6

THEORIES OF COUNSELING

301. Joseph Wolpe created systematic desensitization, a form of reciprocal inhibition based on counterconditioning. When using his technique the acronym SUDS stands for

    a.   standard units of dysfunction.
    b.   a given hierarchy of dysfunction.
    c.   subjective units of distress scale.
    d.   standard units of dysfunction scale.

The subjective units of distress scale, or SUDS for short, is used to help create choice "b," the anxiety hierarchy. In the SUDS, 0 is used to convey a totally relaxed state, while 100 is the most anxiety producing state a client can imagine. The SUDS helps therapists keep the levels in the hierarchy equidistant from each other. Wolpe's systematic desensitization is a popular treatment of choice for phobias and situations which produce high anxiety. The procedure, nonetheless, is not extremely effective for clients experiencing free-floating anxiety (i.e., a fear not connected to a given stimulus or situation). It is based on Pavlov's classical conditioning paradigm. *Special note is added for readers considering systematic desensitization for the reduction of test anxiety. Please be aware that it is not necessary or desirable to eliminate all anxiety in order to score well on your comprehensive exam. According to the "Yerkes-Dodson Law," a moderate amount of arousal actually improves performance! Thus, mild anxiety often can be a plus, since it keeps arousal at a moderate level. (High arousal is more appropriate for simple tasks rather than complex ones, such as a licensing exam.) So why bring the matter up? First, to show you that a small amount of test anxiety could actually be beneficial, and second, because most major exams for psychology majors will include a question on the "Yerkes-Dodson Law."* **(c)**

302. A stimulus which accompanies a primary reinforcer takes on reinforcement properties of its own. This is known as

   a.   systematic desensitization.
   b.   covert processing.
   c.   secondary reinforcement.
   d.   SUDS.

When a stimulus accompanies a reinforcer it can literally acquire reinforcement properties of its own. When this occurs it is termed as "secondary reinforcement." The classical example is the mother who feeds her baby while talking. In a short period of time the talking becomes a secondary reinforcer and provides some degree of satisfaction for the child. Half of the battle to pass a test on behaviorism is to be familiar with the lingo or what scholars call the "nomenclature" or naming process. Choice "b," covert, is a term which means that the behavior is not observable. In behavior therapy then, a covert process is usually a thought or a visualization which the client imagines. A covert is roughly the opposite of an "overt" which is an observable behavior. Direct treatment of an overt behavior is called "in vivo treatment." **(c)**

303. A teenager in a residential facility has earned enough tokens to buy his favorite brand of candy bar. The candy bar is

   a.   a negative reinforcer.
   b.   a back-up reinforcer.
   c.   an average stimulus.
   d.   a conditioned reinforcer.

Back-up reinforcer is the best answer here since by definition a back-up reinforcer is an item or an activity which can be purchased using tokens. A strict behaviorist would assert that choice "d" is incorrect because back-up reinforcers are often unconditioned. **(b)**

304. An alcoholic is given Antabuse which is a drug that causes nausea when paired with alcohol. This technique is called

    a.   systematic desensitization.
    b.   biofeedback.
    c.   back-up reinforcement.
    d.   aversive conditioning.

The idea here is to pair the alcohol with an aversive, somewhat unpleasant stimulus to reduce the satisfaction of drinking it. Ethical dilemmas are common when using this technique. Some smoking clinics, for example, that used electric shock as a noxious aversive stimuli have been shut down. Imagine a client who comes to the clinic and experiences a heart attack from the treatment process! Techniques like these are known as "in vivo aversive conditioning" since they are not performed in the imagination. **(d)**

305. A counselor decides to treat a client's phobia of flying utilizing Wolpe's technique of systematic desensitization. The first step in the anxiety hierarchy items would be

    a.   imagining that she is calling the airlines for reservations.
    b.   imagining that she is boarding the plane.
    c.   imagining a flight in a DC-9.
    d.   an actual flight in a DC-9.

In systematic desensitization the order of the hierarchy is from least anxiety arousing to the most anxiety evoking items. Behaviorists note that the ideal hierarchy has 10 to 15 evenly spaced items. Therefore, in everyday plain

English, to a person who has a fear of flying, imagining a phone call to secure reservations is certainly less anxiety producing than imagining a flight, boarding a plane, or soaring through the sky in a DC-9. **(a)**

306. A counselor utilizes role-playing combined with a hierarchy of situations in which the client is ordinarily nonassertive. Assertiveness trainers refer to this as

   a.   conscious rehearsal.
   b.   behavioral rehearsal.
   c.   fixed role therapy.
   d.   a and b.

The counselor in this case might also switch roles and model assertive behavior for the client. Choice "c," fixed role therapy, refers to the treatment model created by psychologist George A. Kelly. In this approach the client is given a sketch of a person or a fixed role. He or she is instructed to read the script at least three times a day and to act, think, and verbalize like the person in the script. Kelly's approach is quite systematic and has been called the "psychology of personal constructs" after his work of the same name. **(b)**

307. Systematic desensitization consists of these orderly steps:

   a.   autogenic training, desensitization in the imagination, and construction of the hierarchy.
   b.   relaxation training, construction of anxiety hierarchy, in vivo desensitization, and desensitization in imagination.
   c.   relaxation training, desensitization in imagination, and construction of hierarchy.
   d.   relaxation training, construction of anxiety hierarchy, desensitization in imagination, and in vivo desensitization.

Several important points need to be mentioned here. The first, is that your exam may refer to desensitization in imagination as "interposition." (Interposition is technically a perceptual term which implies that one item conceals or covers another. Thus, in this case, the relaxation obscures the anxiety of the imagined scene in the hierarchy.) The second point is that it is best if hierarchy items are evenly spaced using the SUDS. If items are too far apart, moving up the hierarchy could prove nearly impossible. On the other hand, if items are spaced too close together, then the helping process will be unusually slow . . . and behaviorists place a premium on rapid, efficacious treatment. Lastly, the "in vivo" stage implies that the client will actually expose himself or herself to the scary situations in the hierarchy. Experts believe that "in vivo" experiences should not begin until the client has been desensitized to 75% of the hierarchy items. **(d)**

308. _____ is behavioral sex therapy.

    a.   Classical Vegotherapy
    b.   Orgone box therapy
    c.   Conditioned reflex therapy
    d.   Sensate focus

Sensate focus is a form of behavioral sex therapy developed by William Masters and Virginia Johnson of St. Louis, Missouri. Like Joseph Wolpe's systematic desensitization, this approach relies on counterconditioning. A couple is told to engage in touching and caressing (to lower anxiety levels) on a graduated basis until intercourse is possible. And speaking of sex, choices "a" and "b" illuminate the work of Wilhelm Reich who felt that repeated sexual gratification was necessary for the cure of emotional maladies. An orgone box was a device the client would sit in to increase orgone life energy. Ultimately the FDA outlawed the orgone boxes and Reich died in jail. Today scholars are still arguing whether Reich was a madman or a genius. Conditioned reflex therapy (choice "c"), created by Andrew Salter, set the stage for modern assertiveness training. Some call Salter "the father of behavior therapy." **(d)**

309. A counselor has an obese client imagine that he is terribly sick after eating a high caloric, high fat meal. The client then imagines a pleasant scene in which his eating is desirable. This technique is called

  a. behavioral rehearsal.
  b. in vivo sensitization.
  c. covert sensitization.
  d. in vivo desensitization.

Even if you did not know what any of the choices meant you could still get the question correct! Yes really! You could simply remember that the only answer that mentions the imagination is the one with the word "covert." This would constitute an educated guess. When answering behavior therapy questions, keep in mind that the word desensitization means to make one less sensitive while the word sensitization implies that one is made more sensitive to a stimulus. A counselor who tells an alcoholic to imagine that a drink nauseates him would be relying on "covert sensitization." The client is then instructed to imagine a relief scene such as an enjoyable feeling when the alcohol is removed and replaced with a glass of water. Giving a client Antabuse (mentioned in earlier questions) could be used for "in vivo desensitization." **(c)**

310. One distinction between flooding (also known as "deliberate exposure with response prevention" in recent literature) and Implosive Therapy is that

  a. Implosive Therapy is always conducted in the imagination.
  b. flooding is always conducted in the imagination.
  c. flooding is always safer.
  d. Implosive Therapy is physically more dangerous.

Here's a superb memory device: Implosive Therapy begins with an "i" and so does the word "imagination." Implosive Therapy (the brainchild of T.G. Stampfl) is always conducted using the imagination and sometimes relies on psychoanalytic symbolism. Flooding, which is similar, usually occurs when the client is genuinely exposed to the feared stimulus. Flooding is also called "deliberate exposure with response prevention." Here is how flooding works. Take a man who is afraid of snakes because he feels they will bite him. Using flooding, the client would be exposed to the snake for nearly an hour without the dreaded snake bite. Research has demonstrated that in vivo procedures, like flooding, are extremely effective in cases of agoraphobia (a fear of open places) and obsessive-compulsive disorders (OCD). Flooding and Implosive Therapy do not necessarily utilize relaxation nor do they introduce the fearful stimuli gradually. Both techniques assume that avoiding the fear serves to intensify it and that anticipation of catastrophe (e.g., physical pain or loss of control) initially caused the symptom in question. Caution: Flooding and Implosive Therapy do not work in every case. Cases have been cited in which the prolonged exposure to the feared stimuli actually tended to exacerbate the anxiety!   **(a)**

311. Behavior therapists often shy away from punishment because

    a.   ACA ethics forbid the use of this technique.
    b.   NBCC ethics prohibit the use of operant conditioning.
    c.   extinction works more quickly.
    d.   the effects of punishment are usually temporary and it teaches aggression.

The great behavior modifier B.F. Skinner did not believe punishment was very effective. He felt that after the punishment was administered the behavior would manifest itself once again. Positive measures are seen as more effective than punishment. If punishment is used, remember that it does not cause the person (or other animal for that matter) to unlearn the behavior, and it should be used along with positive reinforcing measures. **(d)**

312. A neophyte counselor discovers that her clients invariably give yes and no answers to her questions. The problem is most likely that

a. the counselor is sympathetic rather than empathetic.
b. the counselor is utilizing too many closed-ended questions.
c. the counselor's timing is poor in terms of interpretation.
d. she is summarizing too early in the counseling process.

A closed-ended question can be answered with "yes" or "no." If a counselor asks, "Is your depression lifting?", the client can easily respond with a yes or a no. Counselors prefer open-ended questions which produce more information. If the aforementioned counselor wanted to rephrase the question in an open-ended manner, she could ask, "Can you tell me about the things in your life you find so depressing?" **(b)**

313. A client remarks that he was just dumped by his girlfriend. The counselor responds, "Oh, you poor dear. It must be terrible! How can you go on living?" This is an example of

a. empathy.
b. accurate empathy.
c. confrontation.
d. sympathy.

This is sympathy, not to mention some of the most horrendous therapy one could imagine! Sympathy often implies pity while accurate empathy is the ability to experience another person's subjective experience. **(d)**

314. A neophyte counselor is afraid he will say the wrong thing. He thus keeps repeating the client's statements verbatim when he responds. This is known as

a. desirable attending behavior.
b. parroting and is not recommended.
c. level 3 on the empathy scale.
d. paradoxical intention.

The client doesn't really need to pay big bucks for this type of help; parroting can be accomplished simply by talking into a tape recorder. If you parrot a client, the response may be something like, "yes, I just said that!" Parroting can cause the client to feel angry and uneasy. In the counseling profession, the term "attending" (choice "a") refers to behaviors on the part of the counselor which indicate that he or she is truly engaged in active listening skills. Examples would be good eye contact or the old stand-by . . . "umhum." Choice "c" is another must know concept for nearly any major counseling test. Robert R. Carkhuff suggests a "scale for measurement" in regard to "empathic understanding in interpersonal processes." In a nutshell it reads like this. Level 1— Not attending or detracting significantly from the client's verbal and behavioral expressions. Level 2—Subtracts noticeable affect from the communication. Level 3—Feelings expressed by the client are basically interchangeable with the client's meaning and affect. Level 4—Counselor adds noticeably to the client's affect. Level 5—Counselor adds significantly to the client's feeling, meaning even in the client's deepest moments. If all of this sounds like a foreign language because you've never heard it before, you can now remove the cotton you placed in your ears during your graduate days, or better still, pick up a copy of Carkhuff's 1969 book *Helping and Human Relations*. **(b)**

315. Viktor Frankl is the father of Logotherapy, which is based on existentialism. Logotherapy means

    a.   healing through meaning.
    b.   healing through the unconscious.
    c.   logic cures.
    d.   all of the above.

Frankl also has been thought of as the father of paradoxical intention. Paradoxical intention is implemented by advising the client to purposely exaggerate a dysfunctional behavior in the imagination. You might find it a bit paradoxical (no pun intended) that a technique which comes from logotherapy—which is clearly a brand of helping based on existential philosophy—is now generally categorized as a behavioristic technique. Recently, counselors have gone beyond the paradoxical imagination and actually prescribe that the client engage in the dysfunctional behavior. (For example, a person with OCD or obsessive-compulsive disorder might be instructed to wash his or her hands 51 times per day instead of the usual 45 times.) **(a)**

316. All of these philosophers are existentialists except

    a.   Plato and Epictetus.
    b.   Sartre, Buber, Binswanger, and Boss.
    c.   Kierkegaard, Nietzsche, and Tillich.
    d.   Heidegger, Dostoevsky, and Jaspers.

Existentialism is considered a humanistic form of helping in which the counselor helps the client discover meaning in his or her life. Existential counseling rejects analysis and behaviorism for being deterministic and reductionistic. The existential viewpoint developed as a reaction to the analytic and behavioral schools and stresses growth and self-actualization. Frankl stressed that individuals have choices in their lives and one cannot blame others or childhood circumstances for a lack of fulfillment. The name Epictetus (in choice "a") is often quoted in regard to Rational-Emotive Therapy, created by New York clinical psychologist Albert Ellis. In the first century A.D., the Stoic philosopher Epictetus said, "Men are disturbed not by things, but of the view which they take of them." This statement captures the major premise of Rational-Emotive Therapy (RET). **(a)**

317. Although behavior therapy purports to be highly scientific, it has been criticized on the grounds that it is reductionistic, simplistic, and does not deal with underlying causes. Existential therapy, on the other hand, has been criticized for

a. being too short-term.
b. overemphasizing techniques.
c. ignoring group strategies.
d. being too vague regarding techniques and procedures.

Existential counseling is more of a philosophy of helping than a grab bag of specific intervention strategies. Critics charge that it is not a systematic approach to treatment. The behaviorists assert that it is abstract and not scientific. The approach rejects traditional diagnosis and assessment procedures. **(d)**

318. Existentialists focus primarily on

a. the teenage years.
b. the client's perception in the here and now.
c. childhood traumas.
d. uplifting childhood memories.

The focus is on what the person can ultimately become. The present and even the future are emphasized. The key to change is seen as self-determination. **(b)**

319. Existential counselors adhere to what Buber called the I-Thou relationship which asserts that

a. the counselor is seen as a highly trained expert with answers.
b. the relationship is vertical.
c. the relationship is horizontal.
d. empathy is not necessary.

A horizontal relationship (e.g., I-Thou) assumes equality between persons. In a vertical relationship the counselor is viewed as an expert. Choice "d" is incorrect as the existentialists stress nonthreatening empathy as necessary for successful therapy. **(c)**

320. Frankl is an existentialist. So are

    a.   Ellis and Perls.
    b.   Perls and Stampfl.
    c.   Yalom and May.
    d.   Janov and Beck.

Rollo May introduced existential therapy in the U.S. Irving Yalom, another existentialist, is noted for his work in group therapy. In his book, *Love's Executioner,* he reveals his approach to treatment with some of his most intriguing clients. Other names that appear in the answer choices to this question include: Fritz Perls, the father of Gestalt Therapy; Albert Ellis who pioneered RET; Arthur Janov, noted for his Primal Scream Therapy; and Aaron T. Beck whose cognitive therapy resembles RET. If the name Stampfl doesn't ring a bell review question 310.   **(c)**

321. Existentialists speak of three worlds, the Umwelt or the _____ world, the Mitwelt or the _____ world, and the Eigenwelt or the _____ world.

    a.   unconscious; preconscious; conscious
    b.   id; ego; superego
    c.   self-identity; relationship; physical
    d.   physical; relationship; identity

Try this if you are searching for a memory device. Mitwelt has the prefix "mi" which sounds like "my" such as in "my wife" or "my brother" or "my son." The "my" shows possessiveness indicative of a "relationship." Eigenwelt sounds suspiciously like the word "identity." By process of elimination you would not need a memory device for the remaining term, Umwelt (the physical and biological system).   **(d)**

322. Frankl's experience in Nazi concentration camps taught him

a. the value of S-R psychological paradigms.
b. that you can't control the environment, but you can control your response.
c. that blaming others can be truly therapeutic.
d. how to blame the environment for our difficulties.

From 1942 to 1945 Frankl was a prisoner in German concentration camps, including Auschwitz and Dachau. Several of his relatives died in the camps. Frankl felt, nonetheless, that suffering would be transformed into achievement and creativity. **(b)**

323. Existential counselors emphasize the clients'

a. free choice, decision, and will.
b. transference.
c. slips of tongue.
d. latent dream symbolism.

Logotherapists often use the term "noogenic neurosis" which is the frustration of the will to meaning. The counselor assists the client to find meaning in life. When exploring the meaning of life some anxiety is normal. Moreover, death is not seen as an evil concept but rather an entity which gives meaning to the process of life. **(a)**

324. Existential theorists speak of phenomenology, which refers to the client's internal personal experience of events and ontology which is

a. mental visualization for the treatment of cancer.
b. the impact of cancer on emotions.
c. a cancerous growth in the brain.
d. the philosophy of being and existing.

The metaphysical study of life experience is called ontology. Please do not confuse this with "oncology" (hinted at in choice "c") which is the medical study of tumors. **(d)**

325. Frankl is to Logotherapy as William Glasser is to

    a.   Rational Therapy.
    b.   Reality Therapy.
    c.   rational-emotive imagery.
    d.   RBT.

Frankl is the father of Logotherapy; Glasser is the father of Reality Therapy. Rational imagery, choice "c," is a technique used by rational-emotive therapists in which the client is to imagine that he or she is in a situation which has traditionally caused emotional disturbance. The client then imagines changing the feelings via rational, logical, scientific thought. Choice "d" refers to Rational Behavior Therapy, created by psychiatrist Maxie Maultsby who studied with Albert Ellis. This approach relies on RET; however, the client performs a written self-analysis. Maultsby claimed the technique is well-suited to problems of substance abuse and is highly recommended as a method of cross-cultural counseling. **(b)**

326. Recently, Reality Therapy has incorporated

    a.   control theory.
    b.   rational imagery.
    c.   TA principles.
    d.   rolfing.

Choice "a" is the principle of BCP in which behavior controls our perception. According to control theory, our behavior is our best attempt to control our world to satisfy our wants and needs. The final choice, rolfing, is not a traditional form of talk therapy but rather a type of deep muscle massage which is assumed to have an impact on the person's emotional state. **(a)**

327. All of these statements regarding Reality Therapy are true except

    a.   the client's childhood is explored.
    b.   excuses are not accepted.
    c.   the unconscious is avoided.
    d.   therapy is concerned primarily with the here and now.

The client's childhood is usually not explored, and if the client brings it up, the reality therapist will often try to emphasize childhood successes feeling that an analysis of the difficulties could actually reinforce maladaptive patterns. Reality Therapy is a present moment form of counseling which focuses on the here and now.   **(a)**

328. A counselor who repeats what a client has stated in the counselor's own words is using

    a.   contracting.
    b.   confrontation.
    c.   paraphrasing.
    d.   parroting.

Communications experts agree that paraphrasing has taken place when a client's thoughts and feelings are restated in the counselor's own words. Contracting (choice "a") with a client in a verbal or written manner is a technique favored by behavior therapists. In reality therapy, a plan is created to help the client master his or her target behaviors.   **(c)**

329. Most experts would agree that _____ is most threatening for clients as well as counselors.

    a.   paraphrasing by the counselor
    b.   open-ended questions
    c.   role rehearsal
    d.   silence

Veteran counselors believe that some of the most valuable verbalizations occur after a period of silence. Silence gives the client time to assimilate the counseling process and is helpful in nondirective therapies as it coaxes the client to direct the session. **(d)**

330. When the past is discussed in Reality Therapy, the focus is on

    a.   failures.
    b.   irrational internal verbalizations.
    c.   transference issues.
    d.   successful behaviors.

Glasser believed that dwelling on past failures can reinforce a negative self-concept or what reality therapists have termed the "failure identity." **(d)**

331. Glasser's position on mental illness is that

    a.   it is best explained by DSM guidelines.
    b.   diagnostic labels give clients permission to act sick or irresponsible.
    c.   it is best explained by ICD categories.
    d.   it is the result of a deep internal conflict.

Reality Therapy has little use for the formal diagnostic process or what is known in clinical circles as "nosology." The DSM (the *Diagnostic and Statistical Manual* of the American Psychiatric Association) and the ICD (the *International Classification of Disease*) provide the guidelines for diagnosis of clients. Glasser rejected this traditional medical model of disease. **(b)**

332. Glasser felt that one needs _____ to act in a responsible manner.

    a.   accurate empathy
    b.   a warm caring mother
    c.   to feel loved and valued
    d.   punishment

Unlike the detached psychoanalyst, the reality therapist literally makes friends with the client. This is the first of eight steps utilized in this model. Step 7 is refusing to use punishment (note choice "d"). **(c)**

333. Glasser's theory was popularized in educational circles after he wrote

    a.   *Control Theory.*
    b.   *The Interpretation of Dreams.*
    c.   *Positive Addiction.*
    d.   *Schools Without Failure.*

He also authored choices "a" and "c" as well as his original 1965 classic, *Reality Therapy,* and an update of the theory in his 1981 book *Stations of the Mind.* His wife Naomi has helped him compile case studies using this approach. Choice "b" has nothing to do with reality therapy but generally is quoted as Freud's most influential work. **(d)**

334. Glasser suggested eight steps in the Reality Therapy process. The final step asserts

    a.   that the client and counselor be persistent and never give up.
    b.   that some problems will not respond to any known plan of action.
    c.   that counselors should contract with the client for no more than five counseling sessions.
    d.   that a client who does not respond to the first seven steps is most likely a borderline personality.

Even when the client wants to give up, the therapist does not. Glasser's theory has been criticized on the basis that it is too simplistic. Unlike most of the other schools of thought discussed in this guide, Reality Therapy has not been included in some texts and dictionaries of psychology. **(a)**

335. According to Glasser, a positive addiction might be

    a.   jogging.
    b.   gambling.
    c.   playing the office football pool.
    d.   playing professional football.

Negative addictions like alcoholism and drug abuse are often mentioned in mental health literature. Glasser stressed that people can be addicted to positive behaviors and this helps to instill self-confidence. A positive addiction must be a noncompetitive activity which can be performed alone for about one hour each day. Moreover, the person can see that performing the activity will lead to improvement. Lastly, the person needs to be capable of performing the activity without becoming self-critical. **(a)**

336. When a counselor reviews what has transpired in past counseling sessions he or she is using

    a.   paraphrasing.
    b.   reflection.
    c.   summarization.
    d.   confrontation.

When a counselor summarizes he or she is bringing together a number of ideas. This summarization also could deal strictly with the material in a single session of counseling. Summarization constitutes a "synthesis" regarding the general tone or feeling of the helping process. Ivey recommends summarization at two or three points during each session and at the close of the session. Summarization is really the ability to condense the material to capture the essence of the therapeutic exchange. **(c)**

337. Glasser felt the responsible person will have a _____ identity.

a. failure
b. success
c. diffused
d. crisis-oriented

The individual who possesses a success identity feels worthy and significant to others. Identity is a person's most important psychological need. A person who is irresponsible, and thus frustrated in an attempt to feel loved and worthwhile, will develop a failure identity and a faulty perception of reality. The client is encouraged to assume responsibility for his or her own happiness (i.e., by learning to fulfill personal needs without depriving others of their need fulfillment). **(b)**

338. William Glasser, M.D., is to Reality Therapy as Albert Ellis, Ph.D., is to

a. Rational-Emotive Therapy (RET).
b. Transactional Analysis (TA).
c. Assertiveness Training (AT).
d. Gestalt Therapy.

Ellis is the father of RET which assumes that the client's emotional disturbance is the result of irrational thoughts and ideas. The cure? A high dose of rational thinking. **(a)**

339. In Albert Ellis' Rational-Emotive Therapy, the client is taught to change cognitions, also known as

a. self-talk.
b. internal verbalizations.
c. impulses.
d. a and b.

The credo here is a simple one: talk sense to yourself. When you change your thinking you can change your life. **(d)**

340. The philosopher most closely related to RET would be

    a.   Buber.
    b.   Epictetus, a stoic philosopher who suggested we feel the way we think.
    c.   Locke.
    d.   Jaspers.

Epictetus said: "People are disturbed not by things, but by the views they take of them." In addition to Epictetus, Ellis also mentioned Alfred Korzybski, the founder of general semantics, and Karen Horney, who first recognized the "tyranny of the shoulds" when reflecting on the creation of Ellis' RET theory. Ellis was quick to quote a statement from *Hamlet:* "There's nothing either good or bad but thinking makes it so." Buber and Jaspers are associated with existential therapy, while Locke's work closely resembled what later came to be known as behaviorism. **(b)**

341. RET suggests the ABC theory of personality in which A is the _____, B is the _____, and C is the _____.

    a.   affect; belief; control
    b.   activating event; belief system; emotional consequence
    c.   affect; behavior; control
    d.   authenticity; belief; emotional consequence

What constitutes an irrational and unhealthy "belief system"? Ex-analyst (please emphasize *ex* inasmuch as Ellis felt that psychoanalysis was slow and often very ineffective) Albert Ellis gave examples: it is absolutely necessary to be loved or approved by every significant person in your life; you must be thoroughly competent in all areas of your life to consider yourself worthwhile; some people are bad and wicked and thus should be punished for their actions; it is awful or catastrophic when things are not the way you want them to be;

unhappiness is caused externally by other things and people; an individual's past determines his or her happiness; it is terrible if a perfect solution to every problem cannot be found; and you need someone stronger than yourself to lean on. **(b)**

342. The ABC theory of personality postulates that intervention occurs at D, _____, and this leads to E, _____.

    a.   the dogmatic attitude; effective behavior.
    b.   direct living; evaluation.
    c.   disputing the irrational behavior at B; a new emotional consequence.
    d.   the emotional disease; a new emotional consequence.

Some of the literature by Ellis refers to E as "an effective new philosophy of life." The theory then, is that you create your own present emotional and behavioral difficulties. And talk about optimistic . . . Ellis believed that no matter how bad life seems, you always—that's right, always—have the power to ameliorate intense feelings of despair, anxiety, and hostility. **(c)**

343. A counselor instructs her client to read a *New Guide to Rational Living* by Albert Ellis and Robert Harper. This is an example of

    a.   bibliotherapy.
    b.   counter transference.
    c.   musturbation.
    d.   concreteness.

Bibliotherapy is the use of books or writings pertaining to self-improvement. *A New Guide To Rational Living*, affectionately called "the Guide" for short, is Ellis' most well-known work. The title of his 1988 work, *How To Stubbornly Refuse To Make Yourself Miserable About Anything Yes Anything*, captures the essence of his theory. To state that Ellis is a prolific writer would be to put it mildly. He has published over 500 papers and written about 50 books! Choice "c" uses the term "musturbation" coined by Ellis. Musturbation occurs when a client uses too many shoulds, oughts and musts in his or her thinking. Some exams may refer to this as "absolutist thinking." **(a)**

344. Shoulds and oughts are _____ according to Ellis.

    a.   musturbations
    b.   masturbations
    c.   awfulizations
    d.   rational

When a preference becomes a dogmatic must or a should then you can bet that the client is in for a case of emotional disturbance. Choice "c" is a word commonly used in RET. Awfulizing or catastrophizing is the act of telling yourself how difficult, terrible, and horrendous a given situation really is. And by the way, if you marked choice "b" better sign up for a sex ed course. Ellis, incidentally, insisted that musturbation is more pernicious than masturbation. **(a)**

345. A client says, "I lost my job and it's the most terrible thing in the world." This client is engaging in

    a.   rational self-talk.
    b.   self-induced empathy.
    c.   cognitive restructuring.
    d.   awfulizing, also known as catastrophizing.

Choice "d" would occur at point B, the belief system, in the ABC model of personality. Choice "c," cognitive restructuring, usually refers to Donald Meichenbaum's approach, which is similar to RET. Restructuring takes place when the client begins thinking in a healthy new way using different internal dialogue. Choice "a" is the most inappropriate answer since Ellis considers awfulizing or terriblizing "irrational" unhealthy behavior. **(d)**

346. Bibliotherapy is a form of

    a.   psychodynamic intervention.
    b.   homework.
    c.   displacement.
    d.   musturbation.

Yes homework, I'm sure the word rings a bell if you think back to graduate school. In the context of counseling, homework takes place whenever the counselor gives the client an assignment which is to be done outside the counseling session. Bibliotherapy is a prime example. Therapies that basically "teach" the client (e.g., RET) are known as "didactic" models of treatment. **(b)**

347. Ellis felt that _____ is at the core of emotional disturbance.

    a.   a trauma before age 5
    b.   a current traumatic activating event
    c.   irrational thinking at point B
    d.   repression of key feelings

Choice "a" is really somewhat humorous in light of the fact that Ellis noted that at a very early age he decided his mother wasn't eligible for any prizes of mental health. While a more analytically inclined therapist might have viewed Ellis' childhood as traumatic, Ellis merely told himself that his mother was a fallible human being and he did not have to be disturbed by her behavior. Ellis believed you can be happy even if you are the survivor of numerous childhood traumas. For test purposes please keep in mind that Ellis, Glasser, and the behaviorists put little stock in the notion of transference. **(c)**

348. Therapeutic cognitive restructuring really refers to

    a.   refuting irrational ideas and replacing them with rational ones.
    b.   keeping a journal of irrational thoughts.
    c.   allowing the client to purge feelings.
    d.   uncovering relevant unconscious material.

This is the process of changing your thoughts ergo your feelings via self-talk, or what Ellis often called internal verbalizations. **(a)**

349. Ellis most likely would not be impressed with a behaviorist's new animal study related to the psychotherapeutic process since

    a.   he does not believe in the scientific method.
    b.   the study would not take transference into account.
    c.   Ellis thoroughly dislikes hypothesis testing.
    d.   only man thinks in declarations (internal sentences that can cause or ward off emotional discord).

As far as choice "a" is concerned it is incorrect inasmuch as Ellis firmly believed that his theory promotes scientific thinking, and lower animals may be incapable of such thought. Ellis described what he called the ABC theory of personality. At point A, there is an activating event; at point B, the person's belief system; and at point C, the emotional consequence. According to Ellis, most therapies can be faulted for not emphasizing irrational beliefs at point B. Such theories wrongly assert that A causes C. **(d)**

350. Internal verbalizations are to RET as _____ is/are to Glasser's Control Theory.

    a.   contracting
    b.   pictures in your mind
    c.   lack of punishment
    d.   a therapeutic plan

A matter of semantics? Perhaps. **(b)**

351. Albert Ellis is to RET as Maxie Maultsby, Jr. is to

    a.   RBT.
    b.   AT.
    c.   TA.
    d.   S-R research.

Maultsby is the father of Rational-Behavior Therapy which is similar to RET but emphasizes a written self-analysis. Maultsby's technique is said to work well for cross-cultural counseling and group therapy. In group work the counselor has a didactic or a teaching role in which participants are taught to apply the techniques to their own life. The leader encourages equal group participation for all members and gives reading assignments (i.e., bibliotherapy) between the sessions. All in all, the leader is highly directive and uses RBT as a model for self-help. Like RET, RBT utilizes rational-emotive imagery on a regular basis. Choice "d" describes an old abbreviation of stimulus-response behavioral psychology. RET and RBT are not fond of this model because it asserts that a stimulus (or what Ellis has basically termed an activating event at point A) causes a response (or what Ellis calls the consequence at point C). The S-R model, according to Ellis, is guilty of leaving out B, the client's belief system. Thus, although Ellis might concede that the S-R paradigm explains rat behavior, it is inadequate when applied to man. The S-R model also has been called the "applied behavior analysis" or "radical behaviorism" by B.F. Skinner. Radical behaviorism makes the assumption that the environment maintains and supports behavior and that only overt behaviors are the subject of treatment. The treatment? You guessed it . . . Skinnerian operant conditioning, of course.   **(a)**

352. Aaron T. Beck, an ex-psychoanalytic therapist who created the Beck Depression Inventory (BDI), developed an approach known as Cognitive Therapy. Although Cognitive Therapy is similar to RET, Beck insisted that

a. dysfunctional ideas are too absolute and broad though not necessarily irrational.
b. the Oedipus Complex is central to the treatment process.
c. Cognitive Therapy is contraindicated in cases of phobia.
d. Cognitive Therapy is contraindicated in cases of anxiety.

Choices "c" and "d" are incorrect. Beck's contention was that depression is the result of a cognitive triad of negative beliefs regarding oneself, one's future, and one's experience. Beck's model has indeed been shown to be applicable in cases of phobia and anxiety. Since Beck disliked the term "irrational ideas," he emphasized "rules" or "formulas of living" which cause unhappiness, and he suggested new rules which the client can test. Note: Some exams use the word "metacognition" to describe an individual's tendency to be aware of his or her own cognitions and/or cognitive abilities. **(a)**

353. The cognitive therapist most closely associated with the concept of stress inoculation is

    a. Albert Ellis.
    b. Donald Meichenbaum.
    c. Maxie Maultsby.
    d. Aaron T. Beck.

Meichenbaum's approach is called "Self-Instructional Therapy." Implementation of his so-called stress-inoculation technique has three basic phases. First the client is involved in an "educational phase." Here the client is taught to monitor the impact of inner dialogue on behavior. Next clients are taught to rehearse new self-talk. This is the "rehearsal phase." Finally, the "application phase" is where new inner dialogue is attempted during actual stress producing situations. Counselor educators often classify approaches which dwell on cognition, while emphasizing behavioral strategies for change (e.g., RET, RBT, Self-Instructional Therapy) as "cognitive-behavioral approaches" to helping. **(b)**

354. Eric Berne created Transactional Analysis or TA. The model was popularized via his popular books *Games People Play* and *What Do You Say After You Say Hello?* TA therapists are most likely to incorporate _____ in the treatment process.

    a.   Meichenbaum's Self-Instructional Therapy
    b.   Reality Therapy
    c.   Gestalt Therapy
    d.   Vegotherapy

Choice "c" may seem to make about as much sense as trying to mix water and oil since TA, from a pure standpoint of classification, is a cognitive approach, while gestalt is experiential. The well-known counselor educator Gerald Corey suggested that this marriage made in therapeutic heaven was actually positive inasmuch as Gestalt Therapy emphasized the affective exploration that was missing from TA, which was too intellectual. In other words, one emphasized what was missing in the other. **(c)**

355. Berne suggested three ego states: the Parent, the Adult, and the Child (P-A-C). The Parent ego state is composed of values internalized from significant others in childhood. TA therapists speak of two functions in the parent ego state, the _____ .

    a.   Nurturing Parent and the Critical Parent
    b.   Critical Parent and the Repressed Parent
    c.   Reactive Parent and the Active Parent
    d.   Passive Parent and the Active Parent

The parent ego state is the synthesis of the messages received from parental figures and significant others, incorporated into the personality. Also known as the "exteropsyche" it bears a very strong resemblance to Freud's superego. When a counselor analyzes out of which ego state a client is primarily operating, it is known as "structural analysis." When a counselor analyzes an ego state within an ego state (e.g., the critical parent or the nurturing parent) it is known as "second order structural analysis." A statement like, "Get some rest honey, you've been studying the NCE material for a long time and you deserve the rest," is an example of the nurturing parent. The nurturing parent is sympathetic, caring and protective. The critical parent, on the other hand might remark, "You should get off your duff and study that NCE material; how in the heck do you plan on passing?" The critical parent is the master of the shoulds, oughts, and musts. On occasion, you will see the parent broken down into another part, the prejudicial parent. The prejudicial parent is opinionated with biases not based on fact. "Women should always wear dresses to work," or "a real man enlists in the marines," would be examples. The death or absence of a parent can result in what TA counselors call an "incomplete parent state." **(a)**

356. The Adult ego state

    a.   contains the "shoulds" and "oughts."
    b.   is the seat of feelings.
    c.   is like Freud's superego.
    d.   processes facts and does not focus on feelings.

The adult corresponds to Freud's ego. It is also known as the "neopsyche." It is rational, logical and does not focus on feelings. Choices "a" and "c" describe the parent ego state. **(d)**

357. The Child ego state is like the little kid within. The child may manifest itself as

    a.   the natural child.
    b.   the adapted child.
    c.   the little professor.
    d.   all of the above.

The child state, sometimes called the "archaeopsyche," resembles Freud's id. The natural child is what the person would be naturally: spontaneous, impulsive, and untrained. The little professor is creative and intuitive. The little professor acts on hunches, often without the necessary information. The adapted child learns how to comply to avoid a parental slap on the hand. Messages we receive from parents to form the ego states are called "injunctions" and cause us to make certain early life decisions. Hence, if an early message was, "I wish you would have never been born," then the decision might be, "If my life gets very stressful, I'll just kill myself." **(d)**

358. TA asserts that healthy communication transactions

    a.   occur where vectors of communication run parallel.

    b.   are known as crossed transactions.

    c.   are always between the Child and Adult Ego States.

    d.   are always empathic.

Choice "a" is a "complementary" transaction in which you get an appropriate, predicted response. The "crossed transaction" (note choice "b") would occur when vectors from a message sent and a message received do not run parallel. (For example, I send a message from my adult to your adult and you respond from your child to my child.) Crossed transactions result in a deadlock of communication and/or a host of hurtful feelings. This principle probably won't be difficult to remember. We generally say it is not a good thing when individuals work at "cross" purposes. In TA a "crossed transaction" is not conducive to healthy communication. Note: See the Graphical Representations section (Chapter 12) of this book. **(a)**

359. TA life positions were made famous by Tom Harris's book, *I'm OK—You're OK.* The title of the book illuminates a healthy life position. The life position tells the counselor how a person goes about receiving strokes or recognition. A person categorized by the position I'm OK—You're Not OK

a.   is generally self-abusive.
b.   blames others for misery.
c.   generally engages in self-mutilation.
d.   is generally suicidal.

Tom Harris suggested four basic life positions. Choices "a," "c," and "d" are indicative of the "I'm Not OK—You're OK" position. A self-abusive person is sometimes known as a "masochistic personality" in the literature. According to Harris the "I'm OK—You're OK" orientation is what successful winners choose. The "I'm OK—You're Not OK" is the position taken by adolescent delinquents and adult criminals. Such persons feel victimized and are often paranoid. In extreme cases this person may see homicidal behavior as an acceptable solution to life's problems. The "I'm Not OK—You're Not OK" is the most pessimistic position. This position could result in schizoid behavior and, in a worse case scenario, the tendency to kill someone else and then take one's own life. **(b)**

360. A man yells at his wife and then slaps her, stating that she does nothing around the house. The woman begins crying and he puts his arm around her to comfort her. He then begins crying and says that he doesn't know how he can continue doing all the housework as it is too difficult. A TA therapist who analyzes the situation using Karpman's triangle would say

    a.   the man is stuck in the I'm Not OK—You're Not OK life position.
    b.   the critical parent is dominating.
    c.   the man is obviously an adult child of an alcoholic.
    d.   the man has moved from the persecutor, to the rescuer, to the victim role.

Karpman suggested that only three roles are necessary for manipulative drama: persecutor, rescuer, and victim. A drama is similar to a TA "game," yet it has a greater number of events and the person switches roles during the course of the interaction. In TA, a game is a transaction with a concealed motive. Games prevent honest intimate discussion, and one player is always left with negative feelings. Games have a predictable outcome as a result of ulterior transactions. An ulterior transaction occurs when a disguised message is sent. **(d)**

361. A TA counselor and a strict behaviorist are both in the same case conference to staff a client. Which technique would the two most likely agree on when formulating a plan of action?

    a.   the empty chair technique
    b.   an ego state analysis
    c.   contracting
    d.   formal assertiveness training

Using choice "a," the empty chair technique, the person imagines that another individual is in a chair in front of him or her, and then the client talks to the person. The technique is popular in TA as well as in the gestalt model. Contracting is the only technique listed that is used readily by TA and behavior therapists. **(c)**

362. A game is composed of transactions which end in a bad feeling for at least one player. Games are said to prevent true intimacy. Which other statement is true of games?

    a.   In a first-degree game someone gets seriously hurt.
    b.   In a first-degree game the harm is minimal, but the level of harm is quite serious in a third-degree game.
    c.   For a game to occur, three people must be involved.
    d.   Games always involve parallel vectors of communication.

It is easy to remember that the higher the number the greater the hurt. For example, a second-degree game is more hurtful than a first-degree. In the first-degree the hurt is innocuous; in the second-degree game the hurt is more serious; while in third-degree games the hurt can be permanent or on occasion deadly. And, oh yes, as far as choice "d" is concerned; some exams will refer to parallel vectors of communication as "complementary transactions." **(b)**

363. Unpleasant feelings after a game are called

    a.   rackets.
    b.   life scripts.
    c.   the little professor.
    d.   an analysis of variance.

When a client manipulates others to experience a childhood feeling, the result is called a "racket." **(Note:** In TA the experience of trying to secure these feelings is known as "collecting trading stamps.") Choice "b" or the life script is a person's ongoing drama which dictates how a person will live his or her life. Claude Steiner has written extensively on scripts. His book, *Scripts People Live*, suggests three basic unhealthy scripts: no love, no mind, and no joy. It is like a theatrical plot based on early parental messages (often called injunctions in TA). Choice "d," abbreviated ANOVA, is a statistical technique used to determine differences between two or more means. Hold your horses, we'll get to statistics soon enough! **(a)**

364. A life script is actually

    a.   an ulterior transaction.
    b.   an ego state.
    c.   a life drama or plot.
    d.   a series of parallel transactions.

The process of ferreting out the client's script is called "script analysis." Steiner, mentioned in the previous answer, analyzes the script of TA pioneer Eric Berne in his book! Ulterior transactions (choice "a") contain hidden transactions as two or more ego states are operating at the same time. For example, a man may say to a woman, "Would you like a ride in my new car?" She says, "Yes, I'd love to." This seems like a healthy (i.e., parallel) transaction from his adult to her adult ego state, and she responds in the same manner. He may, however, have a secret, covert, ulterior message if he is a game player. The ulterior message which goes from his child to hers could be, "Wanna make out in my car?" Her ulterior answer—her child to his child—is, "Sure, I'd love to make out with you."   **(c)**

365. Eric Berne is to TA as Perls is to

        a.   the empty chair technique.
        b.   Gestalt Therapy.
        c.   the underdog.
        d.   the top dog.

Berne is the father of TA, while Frederick S. Perls created Gestalt Therapy. In some books he is called Fritz Perls or "Fritz" for short. All the other concepts apply to Gestalt Therapy. Perls saw the "top dog" as the critical parent portion of the personality which is very authoritarian and quick to use "shoulds" and "oughts." The "underdog" was seen as weak, powerless, passive, and full of excuses. These splits in the personality would wage civil war within the individual. In Gestalt Therapy, the empty chair technique could be employed so the individual could work on these opposing feelings. That is to say, the person could be the top dog in one chair and the underdog in the other.   **(b)**

366. Empathy and counselor effectiveness scales reflect the work of

        a.   Perls and Berne.
        b.   Ellis and Harper.
        c.   Frankl and May.
        d.   Carkhuff and Gazda.

In an attempt to isolate the factors associated with positive therapeutic outcomes, counselor educators generally state that the counselor must possess distinct qualities. In the literature these are known as the "core dimensions." According to research by Truax and Mitchell, an effective counselor is authentic and genuine, not phony; gives positive regard through acceptance; and has accurate empathic understanding. As mentioned earlier, the Carkhuff scale rates the counselor from 1 to 5. The higher the rating the better the counselor is facilitating client growth. Gazda suggested a "Global Scale for Rating Helper Responses." On this scale a 1.0 response does not attend to the client's needs. The counselor may discredit or even scold the client. In case I haven't made myself clear, this is a response which is not helpful in any sense. A 2.0 response, although better than a 1.0, is superficial and deals only partially with surface feelings. The 3.0 response does facilitate growth. Although a 3.0 response is limited primarily to surface feelings, the counselor does not distort the content in his or her reflections. A 4.0 is evident when the counselor goes beyond reflection and deals with underlying feelings and meaning. **(d)**

367. The acronym NLP stands for

    a.   Bandler and Grinder's Neurolinguistic Programming.
    b.   New Language Programs for Computer Therapy.
    c.   New Language Psychotherapy Software.
    d.   Neurological Psychotherapy.

This model (choice "a") makes some incredible claims . . . like the ability to cure a longstanding phobia in less time than it takes to conduct a typical counseling session! Perhaps the two most popular techniques used by NLP practitioners are "reframing" and "anchoring." When using reframing the counselor helps the client to perceive a given situation in a new light so as to produce a new emotional reaction to it (e.g., a glass of water is not half empty; it is really half full). In anchoring, a desirable emotional state is evoked via an outside stimulus such as a touch or a sound or a specific bodily motion. This is similar to classical conditioning or the concept of a posthypnotic suggestion (i.e., a suggestion which works after you leave the hypnotist's office). A client with a phobia of cats, for example, might squeeze his left arm when he came in contact with a cat, and this would bring out an emotion which was not fearful. If you are taking an exam which is slanted toward this model, then you must read *Structure of Magic I* and *Structure of Magic II* by Bandler and Grinder. This approach has been very popular with businessmen (especially sales persons) and emphasizes the importance of eye movements in determining a person's "representational system" for storing information, such as hearing, seeing, or feeling. **(a)**

368. A gestalt therapist is most likely going to deal with a client's projection via

    a.   playing the projection technique.
    b.   the empty chair technique.
    c.   converting questions to statements.
    d.   a behavioral contract.

Choices "a," "b," and "c" are all techniques used frequently in Gestalt Therapy, but remember that you are searching for the best answer. Projection is an ego defense mechanism in which you see something in others that you cannot accept about yourself. Gestalt hits this head-on, and in "playing the projection" the counselor literally asks you to act like this person you dislike. Choice "c" would work thusly. A client might say, "Don't all people in a group feel scared during the initial session of group counseling?" The client is asked to turn the question into an "I statement," in this case, "I feel scared during this initial session of group counseling." In gestalt this is known as "taking responsibility for a feeling or situation." Often, the gestalt counselor literally asks the client to say this. For example, "I feel scared during this initial session of group counseling and I take responsibility for being scared." **(a)**

369. A client says she has a tingling sensation in her hands each time she talks about the probability of marriage. A gestalt therapist would most likely

    a.   ask the client to recount a dream.
    b.   urge the client to engage in thought-stopping.
    c.   prescribe relaxation homework.
    d.   urge the client to stay with the feeling.

Gestalt is concerned primarily with the here and now. When a client tries to avoid a feeling the counselor urges the client to face it or "stay with the feeling" if you will. Perls believed this is necessary for growth. Choice "a," dream work, is an integral part of the gestalt approach to counseling. The client is told to recount the dream "as if it is happening in the present." Everything—yes everything—in the dream is considered a projection of the self. So if the client is being chased by a mean old man in the dream, the client might be asked to "become the mean old man." The gestalt model emphasizes experience rather than interpretation, which makes it especially attractive for group intervention. **(d)**

370. Gestalt therapists sometimes utilize the exaggeration experiment which most closely resembles

    a.   successive approximation.
    b.   paradox as practiced by Frankl, Haley, or Erickson.
    c.   free association.
    d.   paraphrasing with emotional reflection.

As opposed to the other three therapists (in choice "b") Perls emphasized the exaggeration in regard to present moment verbal and nonverbal behavior in the here and now. A gestalt therapist might say, "What is your left hand doing?" (In gestalt, "what" questions are seen as more valuable than "why" questions.) After the client responds, the therapist might add, "Can you exaggerate that movement in your left hand?" Choice "a" is an operant behavior modification term which suggests that a behavior is gradually accomplished by reinforcing "successive steps" until the target behavior is reached. This technique also is known as "shaping" or "shaping using successive approximations." **(b)**

371. A client who is undergoing Gestalt Therapy and states, "It is difficult to get a job in New York City," would be asked by the counselor to

    a.   read the DOT.
    b.   change the verbalization to an "I" statement.
    c.   read the OOH.
    d.   take the *Strong Vocational Interest Inventory.*

A goal of gestalt is to eliminate "it talk" and replace it with "I statements." The other choices all relate to career counseling. The DOT is the *Dictionary Of Occupational Titles* which lists over 20,000 job titles. The OOH stands for the *Occupational Outlook Handbook* published by the Department of Labor. The work attempts to depict projected job trends. The *Strong* is the most popular interest inventory, and it is based on the theory of John Holland. **(b)**

372. Gestalt Therapy incorporates

    a.   psychodrama.
    b.   Cognitive Therapy.
    c.   Conditioned Reflex Therapy.
    d.   Client-Centered Therapy.

Psychodrama incorporates role-playing into the treatment process. Psychodrama was invented by Jacob L. Moreno who first coined the term "group therapy" in 1931. **(a)**

373. According to gestalt therapists, a client who is angry at his wife for leaving him and makes a suicide attempt would be engaging in

    a.   sublimation.
    b.   a panic reaction.
    c.   retroflection.
    d.   repression.

Retroflection is the act of doing to yourself what you really wish to do to someone else. The psychoanalysts often say that the person who wishes to kill self really wants to kill someone else. True? Perhaps. Statistics now indicate that in cases of suicide, 4 out of every 100 begin with the person killing someone else! **(c)**

374. Gestalt means

    a.   a group.
    b.   a form, figure, or configuration unified as a whole.
    c.   a dyad.
    d.   visual acuity.

Although there is no exact English translation, choice "b" roughly describes the nature of the concept. Gestalt also can imply that the integrated whole is greater than the sum of its parts. **(b)**

375. Perls suggested _____, which must be peeled away to reach emotional stability.

    a.   four layers of neurosis
    b.   three layers of neurosis
    c.   two layers of neurosis
    d.   five layers of neurosis

Perls likened the process of therapy to that of peeling an onion. The person has a phony layer, a phobic layer (fear that others will reject his or her uniqueness), an impasse layer (the person feels struck), the implosive layer (willingness to expose the true self), and the explosive layer (person has relief due to authenticity). **(d)**

376. In Gestalt Therapy unexpressed emotions are known as

    a.   unfinished business.
    b.   the emerging gestalt.
    c.   form/figure language.
    d.   the top dog.

Here is a key term in Gestalt Therapy. When an unexpressed feeling of resentment, rage, guilt, anxiety, etc. interferes with present situations and causes difficulties, it is known as "unfinished business." Just in case it comes up on your exam, Perls borrowed the term "gestalt" from the system of psychology proposed by Max Wertheimer of Germany in the 1920's which emphasized that the whole is greater than the sum of the parts. The original gestalt psychologists studied perceptual phenomena (e.g., figure/ground relationships). The three most common principles relating to gestalt psychology are first, "insight learning" (discussed earlier in this book) as discovered by Wolfgang Kohler. Second, Bluma Zeigarnik's well-known "Zeigarnik effect" which suggests that motivated people tend to experience tension due to unfinished tasks, and thus they recall unfinished activities better. Thus, if you sincerely care about the outcome of a task, you will have better recall of that task if it remains incomplete, than if completed. (This certainly is a bit like the concept of "unfinished business" in Gestalt Therapy.) Third, Wertheimer's "phi-phenomenon" wherein the illusion of movement can be achieved via two or more stimuli which are not moving, such as a neon sign which has a moving arrow. **(a)**

377. Gestalt Therapy emphasizes

    a.   cognitive-behavioral issues.
    b.   transference issues.
    c.   traumatic childhood memories.
    d.   awareness in the here and now.

Choice "a" is incorrect. The gestalt mode does not believe that a client can "think" one's self out of unhappiness. The person must experience awareness for growth. **(d)**

378. The gestalt dialogue experiment generally utilizes the concepts of

   a. behavioral self-control.
   b. Control Theory.
   c. top dog, underdog, and the empty chair technique.
   d. the rehearsal experiment.

The exam you are taking could refer to choice "c" as "games of dialogue." In addition to the top dog/underdog split in the personality, empty chair dialogue also could be used for other opposing tendencies such as feminine versus masculine attributes. Gestalt assumes that anxiety is often actually "stage fright." By this the gestalt therapist assumes the client has internally rehearsed a situation and is worried that his or her "performance" will not be up to snuff. This "rehearsal" is said to get in the way of spontaneity and healthy personal experimentation. The rehearsal technique especially lends itself to group work as group members can share their rehearsals with one another and thus awareness of stage fright (e.g., worrying about not saying or doing the right thing), and fear of not being accepted by others can be illuminated. And if you marked choice "b," review the questions on Reality Therapy as Control Theory is associated with this brand of treatment. Control Theory postulates that behavior is really an attempt to control our perceptions. **(c)**

379. Critics assert that Gestalt Therapy

   a. often fails to emphasize the importance of dreams.
   b. ignores nonverbal behavior.
   c. often fails to emphasize cognitive concerns.
   d. does not lend itself readily to group work.

Quite the antithesis of RET and related cognitive therapies, gestalt is considered a bit . . . well . . . anti-intellectual if you will. Perls once asserted that if you lose your mind you can come to your senses! Another charge is that it is too confrontational if practiced in the manner Perls demonstrated. **(c)**

380. Most experts would agree that the peak period of competition between the various schools of counseling and therapy (e.g., Gestalt, Behavioristic, Reality Therapy, etc.) was during

    a.   the late 70s.
    b.   the late 60s.
    c.   the 80s.
    d.   the mid 50s.

In the 1950s counseling—not testing—became the key guidance function. Moreover, the 50s marked a golden age for developmental psychology. In the late 60s the field was literally inundated with competing psychotherapies. In the 70s biofeedback, behavior modification, and crisis hotlines flourished. And in the 80s professionalism (e.g., licensing and improvement in professional organizations) was evident. **(b)**

381. The relationship a client has with a Gestalt therapist would most likely progress _____ than the relationship a client would have with a Rogerian counselor.

    a.   faster
    b.   slower
    c.   at the same pace
    d.   a and b

Because gestalt therapists are generally rather confrontational, theorists assume that the client/counselor relationship will progress at a slower rate. If you marked choice "d" I'd like to suggest that you read the answers more carefully. Answer "d," is a synthesis of choice "a" and "b," and choices "a" and "b" are contradictory! **(b)**

382. The school of counseling created by Carl R. Rogers, Ph.D., has undergone three names changes. Initially it was called _____, then _____, and in 1974 changed to _____.

    a.   nondirective counseling, client-centered therapy, the person-centered approach
    b.   directive, nondirective, client-centered
    c.   person-centered, Rogerian, nondirective
    d.   client-centered, person-centered, nondirective

A word to the wise: expect to see any of these names in regard to questions on Rogers' theory. The initial name, nondirective counseling, was intended to set the approach apart from the directive and analytic models which were popular during the 1940s. In 1951, the process took on its new name, client-centered therapy, which emphasized Rogers' theory of personality and, of course, the fact that the client was not viewed as a "sick patient." In 1974, the approach took on its current name, person-centered, to emphasize the power of the person and Rogers' growing interest in group behavior. **(a)**

383. Rogers' approach is characterized as a(n) _____ approach.

    a.   existential or humanistic
    b.   cognitive
    c.   cognitive behavioral
    d.   neo-dynamic

Some exams will call humanistic psychology "third force psychology" as it was a reaction to behaviorism and psychoanalysis, the two initial forces at the time. In regard to choices "b" and "c," it can be pointed out that cognitive approaches are generally more directive and do not give the client/counselor relationship as much emphasis as the Rogerians. **(a)**

384. Which statement is true of the person-centered approach?

   a.   Reflection is used a lot yet the counselor rarely gives advice.
   b.   Advice is given a lot.
   c.   Reflection is rarely utilized.
   d.   Closed-ended questions keep the sessions moving at a fast pace.

A strict Rogerian would generally not give the client specific techniques for behavioral change or instruct the person "how to think."   **(a)**

385. In the person-centered approach, an effective counselor must possess

   a.   the skill to be confrontational.
   b.   the ability to give advice.
   c.   the ability to do formal psychological testing.
   d.   empathy, congruence, genuineness, and demonstrate unconditional positive regard.

Rogerians speak of "conditions for growth" and a therapeutic atmosphere which produces a "climate for growth." The counselor helps produce the climate via genuineness (or congruence), unconditional positive regard (nonjudgmental acceptance), and empathic understanding. Overall, the research does not support the notion that these factors are necessarily related to positive therapeutic outcomes. Some studies indicate that the client's traits have an even greater impact on the success of psychotherapy.   **(d)**

386. Rogers viewed man as

   a.   basically evil.
   b.   driven by instincts.
   c.   a product of reinforcement.
   d.   positive when he develops in a warm, accepting, trusting environment.

Here is a wonderful little review regarding the manner in which the major modalities of counseling look at mankind. Expect to see several questions of this ilk on any major exam. **(d)**

Rogers (Person-Centered)—Individual is good and moves toward growth and self-actualization.

Berne (Transactional Analysis)—Messages learned about self in childhood determine whether person is good or bad though intervention can change this script.

Freud (Psychoanalysis)—Deterministic; controlled by instincts. Unsocialized, irrational; driven by unconscious forces.

Ellis (Rational-Emotive)—People have cultural/biological propensity to think in a disturbed manner but can be taught to use their capacity to react differently.

Perls (Gestalt)—People are not bad or good. Person has capacity to govern life effectively as "whole." Person is part of environment and must be viewed as such.

Glasser (Reality Therapy)—Individuals strive to meet basic physiological needs and the need to be worthwhile to self and others. Brain as control system tries to meet needs.

Adlerian (Individual Psychology)—Man is basically good.

Jung (Analytic Psychology)—Man strives for individuation or a sense of self-fulfillment.

Skinner (Behavior Modification)—Humans are like other animals. Mechanistic and controlled via environmental stimuli and reinforcement contingencies. Not good or bad. No self-determination or freedom.

Bandura (Neo-behavioristic)—Person produces and is a product of conditioning.

Frankl (Logotherapy)—Existential view is that humans are good, rational, and retain freedom of choice.

Williamson (Trait-factor)—Through education and scientific data, man can become himself. Humans born with potential for good or evil. Others needed to help unleash positive potential. Man mainly rational, not intuitive.

387. A client-centered therapist would

    a.   treat neurotics differently than psychotics.
    b.   treat all diagnostic categories of the DSM using the same principles.
    c.   use more closed-ended questions with adjustment reactions.
    d.   use contracting with clients who are not making progress.

The person-centered model puts little stock in the formal process of diagnosis and psychological assessment. People are people, and when they are labelled they are debased to "patients." Moreover, traditionally, strict adherents to this model do not ask a large number of questions (choice "c"). (Some years ago it was considered a cardinal sin if a graduate student serving a counseling practicum asked a client a question while engaging in the practice of client-centered counseling. Today, the practice of asking clients questions is more common; nevertheless, open-ended questions are highly recommended whenever possible.) Choice "d," contracting, is more popular with behavioristic counselors and "directive" methods rather than "nondirective" strategies. **(b)**

388. Rogers emphasized congruence in the counselor. Congruence occurs when

    a.   external behavior matches an internal response or state.
    b.   the counselor uses silence.
    c.   the counselor reflects emotion.
    d.   the counselor summarizes at the end of the session.

Rogers insists that three key factors are needed for an effective helping climate. The counselor's attitude must include genuineness (also called congruence), unconditional positive regard, and empathic understanding. Congruence is a condition where the counselor is very aware of his or her own feelings and accurately expresses this to the client. Of the three elements Rogers suggested that congruence—which really implies that the counselor is genuine, authentic, and does not put on a professional front—is the most important of the three elements. **(a)**

389. Rogers felt that _____ for client change to occur.

    a.   conditions must vary according to the problem
    b.   three conditions are necessary
    c.   six conditions are necessary
    d.   two conditions are necessary

If you missed this one, take a break. You've been studying too long. When you're refreshed, review the answer to question 388. **(b)**

390. Rogerians insist that an effective therapist needs three personal characteristics:

    a.   willpower, assertiveness, good listening skills.
    b.   willpower, self-control, good listening skills.
    c.   empathic understanding, a knowledge of phrenology, congruence.
    d.   empathic understanding, congruence, unconditional positive regard.

In choice "c," the term "phrenology" refers to an early pseudoscientific psychological doctrine which asserted that one's personality could be determined by the shape and configuration of the skull. **(d)**

391. Critics of the Rogerian approach feel that

    a.   it does not emphasize relationship concerns.
    b.   some degree of directiveness is needed after the initial phase of counseling.
    c.   more confrontation is necessary though Rogers did encourage caring confrontations.
    d.   b and c.

I have heard counselors humorously say that Rogerian counseling is like a joke without a punch line! Many counselors now believe that some degree of directiveness is needed after the relationship is built; otherwise treatment merely goes in circles. Some books and exams refer to the process after the relationship is built as the "action phase" of counseling. J.O. Prochaska is very critical of the research which supposedly indicates the effectiveness of the Rogerian model, as some of the studies lacked a control group, failed to take the placebo effect into account, did not use the best statistical technique, or relied on self-reports of the client. **(d)**

392. Counselors who work as consultants

    a.   generally adhere to Reality Therapy.
    b.   generally adhere to one single theory.
    c.   generally adhere to consultation theory.
    d.   generally do not adhere to one single theory.

Choice "c" is not the best answer inasmuch as no integrated theory of consultation exists at this time. Consultation can target organizational concerns or service delivery. Four major consultation models exist. First, Caplan's mental health consultation in which the consultant does not see the client directly but advises the consultee (i.e., the counselor). This model is interesting because it recommends that the consultant—not the counselor/consultee—be ethically and legally responsible for the client's welfare and treatment. Second, the "behavioral" or "social learning theory model" associated with Bandura, in which the consultant designs behavioral change programs for the consultee to implement. Third, the process consultation model by Schein which is said to be analogous to the "doctor-patient" model. The consultant and consultee work together to come up with a statement of the problem and a solution. The focus is on the agency or organization, not the individual client. Fourth, triadic consultation in which the consultant works with a mediator to provide services to a client. **(d)**

393. Counseling generally occurs in a clinical setting while consultation generally occurs in a _____ setting.

    a.   group
    b.   work
    c.   continuing care
    d.   residential

Here again, the other answer choices are not necessarily incorrect; it is just that this choice is the best answer. Counselors generally focus on a person or a group, while consultants focus more on issues. Another key factor is that in consultation work, empathy—although important—is overshadowed by genuineness and respect. **(b)**

394. Attending behavior that is verbal is also called

    a.   verbal tracking.
    b.   clarifying.
    c.   reflection.
    d.   paraphrasing.

Here is a nice little memory device. The word "attending" is similar to the word "attention." Attending behavior occurs when you give your clients your complete attention. Helpful "nonverbal" behavior would include leaning forward slightly, eye contact, and appropriate facial expression such as smiling. Some exams may speak of task-facilitative behavior versus distractive behavior in regard to the process of attending. When the counselor's thoughts are in relation to the client, this is said to be task-facilitative. When the counselor is thinking about his or her own concerns (e.g., how much money he is making that day or where she will go to lunch), then it is seen as distractive behavior. **(a)**

395. The counselor's social power is related to

    a.   age.
    b.   expertise, attractiveness, and trustworthiness.
    c.   sex.
    d.   degree of directiveness.

Some exams will call social power "social influence." My memory technique here is what I call the "EAT" formula; the "E" is for expertness, the "A" for attractiveness, and the "T" for trustworthiness. The three factors first made an impact on the counseling profession in 1968 when Stanley Strong wrote a landmark article which suggested that counselors perceived as expert, attractive, and trustworthy would not be discredited by the client. Expertness here refers to the manner in which the client perceives the counselor rather than the way the counselor perceives himself or herself. A counselor's self-perception is technically known as "competence." E. Fuller Torrey, author of *The Death Of Psychiatry*, suggested that a wall full of degrees and an impressive office can help to insure that the counselor will be perceived as an expert. Thus, a counselor who is seen as an expert may not actually be competent. Attractiveness implies that positive feelings and thoughts regarding the counselor are helpful. One hypothesis states that if the client and counselor have had similar experiences, the client will view the counselor as attractive. Clients who say, "I like my counselor," are demonstrating that the counselor has been perceived as attractive. The chemical dependency model (CD), in which a recovering addict helps a practicing addict, is based on this principle. In regard to trust, it is felt that a violation of confidentiality will nearly always eliminate this factor. **(b)**

396. Key areas that often cause problems for the counselor's self-image are

    a.   choice of a modality and a learning disability.
    b.   age.
    c.   lack of NCC.
    d.   competence, power, and intimacy.

Competence, power, and intimacy are all factors that impact the counselor's "social influence." Competence reflects a counselor's feelings regarding his or her adequacy. A counselor who feels incompetent could directly or indirectly (e.g., tone of voice or body posture) communicate this to the client. In counseling, power is seen as a positive trait used to enhance the client's growth. Counselors struggling with their own feelings in regard to a lack of power may become rigid, coercive, or even belligerent toward the client. Others may become overly nondirective. A counselor who has personal issues revolving around intimacy also could be extremely nondirective and/or afraid to confront clients for fear of rejection. Clearly, such a counselor stays an arm's length away from clients and could personally benefit from treatment! **(d)**

397. A counselor who is genuine

    a.   does not role-play someone he or she is not so as to be accepted by the client.

    b.   does not change his or her true values from session to session.

    c.   is not empathic.

    d.   a and b.

Gerard Egan stressed that clients are indeed more open and expressive with counselors who seem genuine. Egan is well-known for his books which teach a systematic approach to effective helping (e.g., *The Skilled Helper*). **Note:** Egan has referred to competence in some of his literature as "accomplishment-competence," feeling that an accomplishment (e.g., helping abate a client's depression) can impact upon one's feelings of competence, or the client's perception of the helper's expertise. In other words, the counselor must be able to deliver the goods and truly help the client. **(d)**

398. Ivey has postulated three types of empathy—

    a.   positive, negative regard, cognitive.

    b.   reflective, micro-empathy, forced choice.

    c.   basic, subtractive, and additive.

    d.   micro-empathy, basic, level 8 empathy.

In basic empathy the counselor's response is on the same level as the client's. In the case of subtractive empathy, the counselor's behavior does not completely convey an understanding of what has been communicated. Additive empathy is most desirable since it adds to the client's understanding and awareness. **(c)**

399. _____ and _____ created a program to help counselors learn accurate empathy.

    a.   Truax; Carkhuff
    b.   Rogers; Berenson
    c.   Rogers; Brill
    d.   Carkhuff; Satir

Robert Carkhuff has been quoted time and time again for his statement that, "all helping is for better or worse." Or as he says, "no helpee is left unchanged by any helping interaction." **(a)**

400. The human relations core for effective counseling includes

    a.   power, competence, and trustworthiness
    b.   expertise, attractiveness, and trustworthiness.
    c.   empathy, positive regard (or respect), and genuineness.
    d.   self-image, self-talk, and attending behavior.

Choice "b" (remember?) is the social influence core. The purpose of this question is to make certain you are able to distinguish between the social influence core and the human relations core. **(c)**

CHAPTER 7

GROUPS

401. Prior to the 1960s most counseling took place

      a.   in a group setting.
      b.   with the entire family present.
      c.   in a dyadic relationship.
      d.   in Behavior Therapy clinics.

A dyad is a unit of two functioning as a pair. In this case the counselor and the counselee form the pair. The popularity of family therapy and behavior therapy was not evident in the 1950s. **(c)**

402. A group has

      a.   a membership which can be defined.
      b.   some degree of unity and interaction.
      c.   a shared purpose.
      d.   all of the above.

Put the choices together and you have a fine definition of the word group. A group is really a cluster of people in a recognizable unit. **(d)**

403. The term "group therapy" was coined in 1931 by

    a.   Frank Parsons, the father of guidance.
    b.   Jacob Moreno, the father of psychodrama.
    c.   E.G. Williamson, associated with the Minnesota Viewpoint.
    d.   Fritz Perls, the father of Gestalt.

Ten years before Moreno coined the term "group therapy" he noted that individuals in Vienna involved in theatrical productions without scripts experienced a cathartic reaction which seemed to be curative. In psychodrama the client expresses spontaneous feelings via role-playing. Psychodramatic techniques are appropriate for family therapy as well as group work. **(b)**

404. In the 1940s the two organizations for group therapy that were created were

    a.   NASW and NBCC.
    b.   ASGW and AAS.
    c.   the American Society for Group Psychotherapy and Psychodrama and the American Group Psychotherapy Association.
    d.   AACD and APA.

Choice "b" mentions the ASGW or the Association for Specialists in Group Work. This is the division of ACA that focuses primarily on group intervention. The ASGW journal, *"The Journal for Specialists in Group Work,"* is the publication you will need to keep you updated in this area. Other abbreviations are National Association For Social Work (NASW) and the American Association of Suicidology (AAS). By now you should be familiar with the others. **(c)**

405. Which theorist's work has been classified as a preface to the group movement?

    a.   Freud
    b.   Jung
    c.   Jessie B. Davis
    d.   Adler

Adler was actually engaging in group treatment during the early 1920s at his child guidance facilities located in Vienna. His rationale for group work was simply that " . . . man's problems and conflicts are recognized in their social nature . . . " **(d)**

406. Primary groups are

    a.   preventive and attempt to ward off problems.
    b.   always dyadic in nature.
    c.   generally utilized for long-term psychotherapy.
    d.   always focused on the client's childhood.

Examinations and literature in the area of group processes will often classify groups using a model popularized by community mental health experts such as Gerald Caplan, a pioneer in the crisis intervention movement. The three classifications are primary, secondary, and tertiary. A primary group stresses a healthy life-style or coping strategies which can reduce the occurrence of a given difficulty. A group which teaches birth control to prevent teen pregnancy would be a fine example. In a secondary group a problem or disturbance is present but not usually severe. The secondary group works to reduce the severity or length of a problem and generally includes aspects of prevention. Thus, a group that deals with grief or shyness might fall into this category. The tertiary group usually deals more with individual difficulties that are more serious and longstanding. (The word "tertiary" literally means the third rank.) Choices "c" and "d" would apply mainly to groups categorized as tertiary. **(a)**

407. A group is classified as secondary. This implies that

    a.   it is preventive and attempts to ward off problems.
    b.   a difficulty or disturbance is present.
    c.   two therapists are utilized.
    d.   all of the above.

Choice "a" is not entirely false since a secondary group does have preventive qualities. Nevertheless, this is not the major feature; hence, this is not the best answer. When two therapists are used in a group setting the procedure is known as "coleadership" or "co-facilitation."   **(b)**

408. When comparing a tertiary group with a primary or secondary group

    a.   the tertiary focuses less on individual members.
    b.   the tertiary focuses more on the here and now.
    c.   the tertiary is less likely to deal with severe pathology.
    d.   the tertiary is more likely to deal with severe pathology.

Choice "a" stands incorrect because the tertiary group focuses more on the individual than the primary or secondary group. In reference to choice "b," a counselor dealing with the here and now often relies on the skill of "immediacy." Immediacy takes place (in a group or an individual session) when the counselor explores the client-counselor relationship as it is transpiring right at that moment. Immediacy relates to the counselor's ability to convey what is happening between the counselor and the client.   **(d)**

409. Group norms

    a.   exist only in encounter groups.
    b.   exist only in career counseling groups.
    c.   are not related to group cohesiveness.
    d.   govern acceptable behavior and group rules.

Let's not make this complicated. Norms are explicit and implicit (i.e., not verbalized) rules which tell group members how to behave and how not to behave in a given situation. Group specialists are quick to point out that all groups have norms though often they are not formally presented to group members. Singing loudly while taking the NCE would be violating a norm, although I doubt whether anyone will specifically tell you not to sing at the onset of the exam! Norms actually refer to "expected behaviors." Now of course, norms vary depending upon your role in a group. In an educational class group, for example, the norms for the teacher may indeed be different than for the student. **(d)**

410. Group therapy initially flourished in the U.S. due to

    a.   Freud's lectures in this country.
    b.   a shortage of competent career counselors.
    c.   a shortage of individual therapists during World War II.
    d.   pressure from nondirective therapists.

During World War II many individuals were plagued with severe psychological problems, yet a personnel shortage made it impossible for each and every person to be treated using individual therapy. Moreno had brought the idea of group therapy to the U.S. in 1925, but the supply and demand issues sparked by the war effort were the catalysts which generated this idea whose time had come. **(c)**

411. Group content refers to material discussed in a group setting. Group process refers to

    a.   analysis of the unconscious.
    b.   analysis of the ego.
    c.   the T-group paradigm.
    d.   the manner in which discussions and transactions occur.

Group content refers to what the group is discussing. Group process refers to analyzing the communications or transactions. The process is the way in which the discussion takes place. Choice "c" or T-group merely means "training group." Originally, T-groups were used in industrial and organizational settings to process personnel interaction and improve efficiency. A wealth of work in this area was done by National Training Laboratories (NTL), created by Leland Bradford, Kenneth Benne, and Ronald Lippitt. **(d)**

412. Group cohesiveness refers to

   a. forces which tend to bind group members together.
   b. an analysis of group content.
   c. coleadership.
   d. a style of leadership.

Cohesiveness is a sense of caring for the group and the other group members. The term cohesiveness is associated with Kurt Lewin's "field theory" in which cohesiveness was seen as a binding force among group members. Lewin called the binding force between group members "positive valence." When cohesiveness goes up, absenteeism and other negative factors go down. High cohesiveness leads to high group productivity and commitment. And here's a helpful tidbit of information. Often when a group displays little or no cohesiveness the group will be viewed as "fragmented." Just for review, you will recall that choice "c" (coleadership) is implemented when two persons lead the group. **(a)**

413. Some theorists feel that group therapy differs from group counseling in that

   a. group counseling would be of longer duration.
   b. group therapy would be of longer duration.
   c. group counseling requires far more training.
   d. group therapy addresses a less disturbed population of clients.

George Gazda proposes a typology of three distinctive types of groups: guidance, counseling, and psychotherapy. A guidance group is a primary group in the sense that it is mainly preventive. Listen carefully, however. Some exams and texts no longer use the term guidance group. Instead, you may see the term "affective education group" or "psychological education group." Guidance groups do not deal with remediation of severe psychological pathology. Here is another key point. In individual treatment the words "counseling" and "therapy" are often used interchangeably. However, in the context of group work, therapy is implied when the problem is more severe and more individual work is needed for a longer duration. The psychotherapy group is tertiary and may emphasize the role of the unconscious mind and childhood experiences more than a counseling group. A counseling group would not tend to be psychodynamic and therefore would focus primarily on conscious concerns. A counseling group generally has less structure than a guidance group. In terms of education, the assumption is that the leader of a counseling group needs more training than an individual running a guidance group, while the group therapy leader must have the most training as the group therapist may need to treat people who are not functioning in the range of "normality." **(b)**

414. Most experts would agree that overall

    a. structured exercises are more effective than unstructured techniques.
    b. structured exercises are less effective than unstructured techniques.
    c. all well-trained therapists favor structured exercises over unstructured techniques.
    d. ethical guidelines must forbid unstructured techniques as they can be dangerous to the depressed or anxious client.

A structured group exercise is like an assignment for group members. The leader says, "today we will do so and so . . . " The benefit is that the exercise helps to speed up group interaction and can help focus on a specific issue. Although structured group exercises are very popular and beneficial, they are generally not as effective as unstructured methods. This answer could surprise you if you are new to group work. The well-known existentialist and group theorist Irving Yalom pointed out that structured exercises can create a situation where group stages are passed over. In addition, the exercise itself often serves to purge feelings too rapidly when members are not emotionally equipped to handle this. Also keep in mind that the excessive use of structured exercises can cause the group to lean on or rely too strongly on the leader for support and direction. Perhaps the crowning blow in regard to relying too heavily on structured group exercises came out of an encounter group project by Lieberman, Yalom, and Miles. The project demonstrated that leaders who utilized many structured exercises were more popular than leaders who did not; nevertheless, the outcome for the group participants was lower! Here is an excellent rule of thumb: group exercises must correspond to the level of group development. In a beginning group, for example, exercises which build openness and trust are desirable. In the later stages, the focus of the exercises ideally switches to critical feedback. **(b)**

415. One advantage of group work is that a counselor can see more clients in a given period of time. One disadvantage is that a counselor can be too focused on group processes and

    a.   thus individual issues are not properly examined.
    b.   the group becomes too behavioristic.
    c.   a and b.
    d.   thus the group focuses too much on content.

Choice "a" is especially apt to occur if the leader is process-oriented. (**Remember:** content is the material discussed, while process focuses on the way it is being discussed.) Choice "d" is certainly not the best answer since a leader focusing on content would not be process-oriented. **(a)**

416. According to the risky shift phenomenon, a group decision will

    a.   be less conservative than the average group member's decision, prior to the group discussion.

    b.   be more conservative than the average group member's decision, prior to the group discussion.

    c.   often be aggressive and/or illegal.

    d.   violate the group's confidentiality norms.

Perhaps what I'm about to suggest is a bit scary to think about but bear with me anyway. Think back for a moment to when you were a teenager. (If you can't remember that far back, think of a teenager you are currently familiar with such as a relative or a client.) For the most part, your decisions and behavior were probably fairly rational—conservative if you will. Now think about your behavior when you got together with a bunch of your friends, say for a party or a night out on the town. Wouldn't you have to admit that the group's decisions and behavior were not as conservative as your views prior to the group interaction? In other words, weren't group decisions, well, just a bit more "risky"? If your answer to the aforementioned questions was "yes," then you have the social psychology theory of the "risky shift phenomenon" to explain (not condone!) the behavior of your wild and crazy teen peer group. The risky shift phenomenon dispels the popular notion that groups are very conservative. Some research indicates that the group behavior is not necessarily more risky, but does at least shift more toward the social norm than an individual decision made prior to group participation. **(a)**

417. T-groups often stress ways employees can express themselves in an effective manner. The "T" in T-groups merely stands for

    a.   techniques.

    b.   taxonomy.

    c.   training.

    d.   testing.

The "T" merely stands for "training." It is not unusual for T-groups (i.e., training groups) to be called "laboratory-training groups" or even at times "sensitivity groups." Such a group will focus not on mental health issues but rather on human relations processes between personnel in a business setting. Shared leadership is a common area of concern. Occasionally, a short encounter group or sensitivity group will be termed a "micro-lab." Taxonomy (choice "b") is the science of classification. In the field of counseling, the most common method of determining a client's classification (which is termed a "diagnosis") is to compare the client's symptoms with those listed in the American Psychiatric Association's *Diagnostic and Statistical Manual* or the DSM for short. The DSM is generally used for third-party and insurance payments or research purposes so that mental health professionals will mean the same thing when referring to a client with a given diagnosis. Hint: The exam you will be taking may use the word "nosology" in place of the word "taxonomy." **(c)**

418. A counselor suggests that her client join an assertiveness training group. Most assertiveness training groups are

   a.   unstructured.
   b.   psychodynamic.
   c.   focused heavily on existential concerns.
   d.   highly structured.

Groups that rely on numerous exercises are considered "structured" groups, while those which have few exercises or tasks are often known as "unstructured." Behavioral groups such as an assertiveness training group are generally highly structured. You should be aware that some experts shy away from the term "unstructured" stating that a group cannot "not" possess structure. Such theorists would simply say that a given group has a low degree of structure or "less structure." Nondirective groups, psychodynamic groups (choice "b"), and existential groups (choice "c") generally would lean toward a low degree of structure. Therapies that stress directive techniques and concrete treatment objectives generally have a high degree of structure. Some theorists use the term structured group only when discussing a group which focuses on a specific topic or theme, for example, assertiveness training, stress management, or coping with test anxiety. **(d)**

419. Weight Watchers is a

    a.   T-group.
    b.   self-help group as is A.A.
    c.   therapy group.
    d.   marathon group.

A self-help group (also known as a "support group") is composed of a group of people who are all attempting to cope with a given issue (e.g., alcoholism or weight control). Members have a common goal or problem and learn from each other. The group is not led by a professional though a self-help group may indeed rely on a professional for consultation purposes. And believe me, self-help groups are extremely popular. It is currently estimated that over 500,000 self-help groups exist in the U.S. and serve the needs of approximately 15 million members. Most self-help groups are voluntary. The term "marathon group" introduced in choice "d" is an easy one to remember. A marathon race is a long race, and a marathon group is one long group. A marathon group—somewhat like a marathon race—plays on the theme that after an extended period of time defenses and facades will drop and the person can become honest, genuine, and real. A marathon group may be conducted over a weekend or a period of several days. **(b)**

420. ACA and the ASGW division recommend screening for potential group members

    a.   for all groups.
    b.   only when the group is in a hospital inpatient setting.
    c.   only when the group is composed of minors.
    d.   only if the group deals with chemical dependency.

Screening is easy enough to define. A professional counselor uses a screening process in order to determine who is appropriate and who will not be appropriate for a given group. If a prospective group member is undergoing individual counseling and therapy, the group leader should contact the person performing the individual treatment before making a final decision. **(a)**

421. A counselor is conducting a screening for clients who wish to participate in a counseling group which will meet Tuesday nights at his private practice office. Which client would most likely be the poorest choice for a group member?

    a.   a shy librarian
    b.   an anxious salesman with no group experience
    c.   an extremely hostile and belligerent construction worker
    d.   a student with 16 hours toward her M.Ed. in counseling

Let me help you think this one through. First, the individual's occupation and the time of the group (i.e., Tuesday nights) are irrelevant. The key factor in answering the question is to identify a personality pattern which may not lend itself to group work. Hostile individuals who act out aggressively (choice "c"), persons who are actively suicidal or homicidal, paranoid clients, those who are totally self-centered, or psychotic individuals (psychotic implies that the person is not in touch with reality) are not appropriate for most counseling groups. I have purposely hedged and used the word "most" since there are certainly psychotherapy groups which cater to the aforementioned populations (e.g., a group for hospitalized schizophrenics or a group for suicide attempters). Remember that psychotherapy groups focus more on individual concerns, deal with remediation of more serious pathology, and are of longer duration. Nevertheless, it is still possible that if an individual is too dysfunctional in one of the aforementioned areas, he or she would be inappropriate even for a psychotherapy group and the treatment of choice should be an individual modality. **(c)**

422. A counselor is screening clients for a new group at the college counseling center. Which client would most likely be the poorest choice for a group member?

 a. a first-year student who is suicidal and socio-pathic
 b. a second-year student who stutters
 c. a graduate student with a facial tic
 d. a four-year student with obsessive-compulsive tendencies

If you missed this one then you failed to read the answer from the previous question. I can't stress strongly enough that you will need to understand the practical application of counseling theory—in all eight areas, not just groups—to do well on your exam! Questions of this nature require understanding rather than just rote memory to answer correctly.   **(a)**

423. A screening for group members can be done in a group or privately. Although private screening interviews are not as cost effective or as time efficient, many group leaders feel they are superior inasmuch as private screening sessions

 a. intensify transference.
 b. encourage catharsis.
 c. intensify abreaction.
 d. encourage the counselor/client interaction.

ASGW ethical guidelines recommend a pre-group interview for screening and orientation. The guidelines do not, however, discuss specific selection processes. An individual screening interview allows the client to voice concerns regarding what he or she wants from the group and what procedures will be implemented. The person also can ascertain whether he or she has faith in the leader's ability. Some of the literature emphasizes that screening is a two-way process (i.e., the leader can decide whether the member is appropriate and the member can decide whether the group and the leader are appropriate). Individual screening modalities also can serve to build trust.   **(d)**

424. Most experts in the field of group counseling would agree that the most important trait for group members is the ability

    a.   to open up.
    b.   to listen.
    c.   to trust.
    d.   to convey empathy.

Expert Irving Yalom feels that the main factor in selecting participants for a group is that members can feel cohesive. Research indicates that high denial, low motivation, and low intelligence are associated with premature termination from group therapy.   **(c)**

425. Groups can be open or closed. The two differ in that

    a.   open groups are limited to hospital settings.
    b.   in an open group members can socialize between group meetings.
    c.   closed groups always employ coleaders.
    d.   closed groups allow no new members after the group begins.

You absolutely must be familiar with this important distinction in group work if you want to do well on your exam. A closed group can be likened to a room with a closed door—no new persons can enter. In a closed group the decision is made initially that no new members can join for the life of the group. So, here's a simple little memory device: "closed groups" have "a closed door policy" regarding new members. An open group simply abides by an "open door policy," if you will, by allowing new members to join.   **(d)**

426. One major advantage of a closed group versus an open group is

    a.   cost effectiveness.
    b.   it promotes cohesiveness.
    c.   it lessens counselor burnout.
    d.   it allows the members to meet less frequently.

Generally a closed group will have more cohesiveness or "unity" since the membership is more stable (i.e., new members are not joining), and members get to know each other. Nevertheless, a closed group is not a panacea. Since the closed group does not accept new members after the group is up and running individuals may drop out and this lessens the overall amount of group interaction. In terms of cost effectiveness (choice "a"), the closed group is at a disadvantage. The agency or private practitioner loses revenue when clients leave and are not replaced.   **(b)**

427. One major disadvantage of a closed group versus an open group is that

    a.   if everyone quits, you will be left with no group members.
    b.   closed groups cannot provide depth therapy.
    c.   it promotes paranoid feelings in group members.
    d.   closed groups are much more structured.

It doesn't take a mathematician to discern that if you have six group members and six members quit you are left with no group! In reference to choice "b," there is no evidence to demonstrate that a closed group could not provide excellent in-depth therapy. Since the closed group promotes cohesiveness (yes, I'm repeating myself, but I want to be certain you grasp this concept) and trust (well, that eliminates choice "c" as trust reduces paranoid ideation in many cases) it could be an excellent modality for intensive therapy. And although a closed group could be more structured than an open group, this is not always the case. So much for choice "d."   **(a)**

428. The number of people in an open group is generally

    a.   more stable than in a closed group.
    b.   much smaller after an extended period of time than in a closed group.
    c.   significantly larger than in a closed group.
    d.   more dependent on the group leader's marketing skills than in a closed group.

This is the type of question you might quibble with on an exam; however, it would be mighty difficult to defend any answer except choice "a." Yes, I agree that some of the literature uses the term "stability" to describe the membership in a "closed group." The stability, of course, comes from the policy of not allowing new members. If you read this particular question very, very carefully it speaks of the "number of people in an open group." Remember the hypothetical situation discussed in the last answer. You have a closed group of six members and six members leave the group. You are left with nobody. I'd hardly call that stability, would you? This question is asking you to choose the group strategy, open or closed, which would keep that number of six members stable. In the open group, if six people drop out you could replace them with six new members. I rest my case. Remember that regardless of which exam you must tangle with, a word could be used in a different context than you have encountered in the past. **(a)**

429. One distinct disadvantage of an open group is that

    a.   new members are not accepted after the first meeting.
    b.   the leader does not control the screening process.
    c.   a member who begins after the first meeting has missed information and/or experiences.
    d.   the group is generally too behavioristic for depth therapy to occur.

Open groups have changing membership, and thus different members have been present for different experiences.

Choice "a" is obviously incorrect since new members could indeed enter the group after the first session.   **(c)**

430. When a group member is speaking, it is best to

   a.   try to face the group member.
   b.   not face the group member as this does not appear genuine in a group setting.
   c.   smile while listening.
   d.   suppress genuine emotion.

Choice "a" is often difficult to accomplish as groups are often set up such that members sit in a circular fashion; yet when it is possible, it fosters good "attending behavior" on the part of the group leader. In reference to choice "d," the qualities which enhance individual counseling are also beneficial when doing group work. Genuineness, which is also known as congruence or authenticity, is advisable in all therapeutic settings.   **(a)**

431. A group setting has a flexible seating arrangement in which clients are free to sit wherever they wish. In this setting it is likely that

   a.   a Black client and a White leader would sit close together.
   b.   a White client and a Black leader would sit close together.
   c.   an Oriental client and a Black leader would sit close together.
   d.   an Oriental leader and an Oriental client would sit close together.

Generally persons who are similar will sit next to each other. In this case, choice "d" is the only choice that mentions two persons of the same race. Now I want to introduce you to two important terms which are related to group composition. In a group where the members are very similar or alike the group composition displays what is known as "homogeneity." Weight Watchers would be a case in point. Groups which have "homogeneity" are said to be "homogeneous." Since everybody really has the difficulty or concern (e.g., weight control in this case or alcoholism in A.A.), people often feel a greater degree of "we-ness" or cohesiveness. A "heterogeneous" group or a group which has "heterogeneity" has members who are dissimilar. A general therapy group which has clients with various problems and backgrounds would be an example. (This distinction is easy enough to remember since "heterosexual relationships" are formed via two individuals of a different sex.) The heterogeneous group is more like a microcosm of the social system most of us live in. Moreover, when you combine people you discover that people can learn from each other. **(d)**

432. A group setting has a flexible seating arrangement in which clients are free to sit wherever they wish. In this setting it is likely that

    a.   a male leader in a designer suit and a female client in jeans made into cutoff shorts will sit close together.

    b.   a male leader in a designer suit and a male client in another brand of designer suit will sit close together.

    c.   a female leader in a designer outfit and a male client in a pair of old jeans and an undershirt will sit close together.

    d.   a male leader in a designer suit and a female client in a jogging suit and old tennis shoes with holes in them will sit close together.

Forget the poles of a magnet; in groups "likes" attract. The likelihood is that people who are similar or believe they have "something in common" initially will sit together. **(b)**

433. Which statement made by a doctoral level counselor is illustrative of a leader focused on process rather than product?

a. "Jim seems more relaxed today."
b. "Sally seems a bit self-critical this evening."
c. "I hear a lot of sadness in Betty's voice."
d. "You wince whenever Jane raises her voice."

The counselor's level of education is totally irrelevant. Process focuses on the "process" or manner in which the communication transpires. All of the other choices focus primarily on the analysis of the client's material or what is called "content." **(d)**

434. Which statement made by a group leader in a residential center for adolescents focuses on product rather than process?

a. "Ken has not stolen for a week and thus is eligible for supplementary tokens."
b. "And Karen looks down when Bill discusses relationships."
c. "It sounds like there is a deep sense of hurt . . . "
d. "Oh, so you fold your arms and sort of close up when Carey mentions the angry side of your personality."

Can you guess what is irrelevant in terms of answering this question? **(a)**

435. Groups promote the concept of universality which suggests that

a. we are unique and so are our problems.
b. there is a universal way to solve nearly any difficulty.
c. a and b.
d. we are not the only one in the world with a given problem.

It is therapeutic just to know that you are not the only person in the world who has a given problem! In this respect the group model has an advantage over individual treatment. **(d)**

436. In the late 1930s researchers identified three basic leadership styles:

   a.   directive, nondirective, and semipassive.
   b.   autocratic (authoritarian), democratic, and laissez faire.
   c.   relaxed, anxious, and tense.
   d.   assertive, nonassertive, and aggressive.

The classic study regarding leadership styles was conducted by Lewin, Lippitt, and White in 1939. The importance of the study was that it demonstrated that leadership styles do make a difference. In this famous study, 10- and 11-year-old children met with an adult who behaved in an autocratic (authoritarian), democratic, or laissez faire fashion. The French term "laissez faire" implies that group members can do as they please without leader interference or direction. Children displayed the best behavior when treated in a democratic fashion, while aggressive behavior occurred in response to the other two leadership styles. Generally, the autocratic style proved to be the style members liked least. The study revealed that hostility was 30 times greater in autocratic groups than it was for the other two. This study set the stage for the National Training Laboratories (NTL) mentioned in a previous question. Do not, however, assume that the democratic style is always best. It is not. The autocratic mode seems to be superior when an immediate decision is necessary. When a group has made a decision, and is committed to it, the laissez faire style is usually the leadership model with the most merit. It is interesting to note that although member satisfaction is often highest in response to democratic leadership, this style does not necessarily lend itself to high productivity according to Stogdill who reviewed the major research studies related to this topic. Just for review purposes, choice "d" describes the three communication modes used by assertiveness trainers to determine or discriminate (as it is often called) client response patterns.   **(b)**

437. The autocratic or authoritarian leader may give orders to the group while the laissez faire leader

    a.   assigns a group member as the authoritarian.
    b.   has a hands-off policy and participates very little.
    c.   has the most desirable style of leadership.
    d.   b and c.

If you missed this question please review the previous answer. **(b)**

438. When comparing the autocratic, democratic, and laissez faire styles,

    a.   the autocratic is the most desirable.
    b.   the laissez faire is the most desirable.
    c.   the democratic is the most desirable.
    d.   there is no discernable difference in effectiveness.

Here is every test taker's nightmare. The question is vague. It decidedly does not delineate the specific group situation. Hence, the best way to answer this question is to think in terms of "most situations." Again, the democratic style is not the most effective in every case; however, it probably lends itself to more situations than the other two. **(c)**

439. A group with more than one leader is said to utilize coleaders. Coleadership is desirable because

    a.   the group can go on even if one leader is absent.
    b.   two leaders can focus on group dynamics better than one leader.
    c.   leaders can process their feelings between sessions.
    d.   all of the above.

Coleadership (i.e., the use of two group leaders) has a number of advantages. In addition to those listed in choices "a," "b," and "c," I could add that two leaders can supply more feedback to group members than one leader. They can learn from each other and can model effective communication for the group. **(d)**

440. Coleadership

    a.   reduces burnout.
    b.   increases burnout.
    c.   has no impact on burnout.
    d.   should not be used for open groups.

Noted authors on group practice, Marianne Schneider Corey and her husband Gerald Corey, mention their preference for coleadership but indicate that many leaders do in fact work best on their own. **(a)**

441. Coleadership

    a.   is helpful when one leader is experiencing counter transference.
    b.   exacerbates the harm of counter transference.
    c.   has no impact on the issue of counter transference.
    d.   eliminates all difficulties associated with counter transference.

If you have an issue that is unresolved and it is having a negative impact on your intervention (i.e., counter transference), then your coleader can deal with this particular person and/or issue. **(a)**

442. Coleadership can be a disadvantage when

    a.   leaders are working against each other.
    b.   leaders are intimate with each other.
    c.   leaders question each other's competence.
    d.   all of the above.

It is generally accepted that if there are problems between coleaders it is best if such difficulties are aired in a format that models effective conflict resolution during the session rather than "pretending everything is wonderful." The best advice is to pick your coleader wisely and meet with this person before and after sessions whenever possible. **(d)**

443. Coleaders are apt to work at cross purposes when

    a.   they do not meet between group sessions.
    b.   they do meet between group sessions.
    c.   they are master's level practitioners.
    d.   they are doctoral level practitioners.

Choice "b" is recommended for coleaders, while choices "c" and "d" are irrelevant. **(a)**

444. Gerald Corey, who has written extensively on group therapy, believed _____ is necessary for an effective group leader.

    a.   a master's degree in guidance and counseling
    b.   a doctorate in counselor education
    c.   participation in a therapeutic group and participation in a leader's group (even if the individual is well-educated and is licensed and certified)
    d.   three credit hours in a graduate course in group theory

Sorry folks, but according to some experts a wall filled with degrees, plaques, and certifications is not enough; specific training in group work is necessary in order to become a group leader. A 1985 study by Huhn, Zimpfer, Waltman, and Williamson found that 27% of the 76 programs reviewed offered only one course in group counseling. A training group for future group leaders is one solution to this dilemma. A training group is composed of "leader trainees," and unlike a therapeutic group it is focused on leadership skills. Yalom has gone on record as saying that self-exploration (e.g., personal therapy) is generally necessary for potential group leaders to help them deal with issues which could cause counter transference. **(c)**

445. Most experts would agree that an effective adult counseling group has _____ members.

    a.   9 to 12
    b.   3 to 5
    c.   11 to 16
    d.   5 to 8

An ideal group would have about eight adults. An adolescent group might be slightly smaller, perhaps five or six members. **(d)**

446. Most experts would agree that an effective counseling group for children has

    a.   more members than an adult group.
    b.   less members than an adult group.
    c.   at least two group leaders.
    d.   9 to 12 members.

Three or four children is usually recommended versus about eight people in an adult group. **(b)**

447. Although the length of group counseling sessions will vary, most experts would agree that _____ is plenty of time even when critical issues are being examined.

    a.   3 hours per session
    b.   1 hour per session
    c.   6 hours per session
    d.   2 hours per session

1 1/2 to 2 hours is sufficient for adult group work. Longer groups often abet fatigue in the group members. With children, the group leader should note the members' attention span which is generally shorter than for adults. Since a children's group will have shorter sessions, it is often best to rely on more frequent group sessions.   **(d)**

448. In terms of group risks

> a.   an ethical leader will discuss them during the initial session with a client.
> b.   an ethical leader should never discuss risks with a client.
> c.   research has demonstrated that the less said about them the better the group will interact.
> d.   an ethical leader allows the group to discover risks and work through them at their own pace.

This practice is specified in ASGW's Ethical Guidelines for Group Leaders, rendering choices "b" and "d" as blatant ethical violations.   **(a)**

449. An adept group leader will

> a.   attempt to safeguard clients against risks.
> b.   work to reduce risks and dangers.
> c.   a and b.
> d.   let the group handle the dangers on their own.

Professional counselors should give clients "information" regarding the group so the clients can make "informed" decisions regarding whether or not the group is appropriate (e.g., the purpose of the group, the risks involved, and the leader's qualifications). This practice technically is known as "informed consent," and it is very likely that you will see an exam question related to this issue. Ideally, informed consent occurs during screening before the initial group session, although in the real world this is not always possible. **(c)**

450. A group participant wants to drop out of a group. Since the group is "closed" ASGW ethics state that

  a. the leader must insist that the client stay.
  b. the client must be allowed to withdraw.
  c. the leader should allow other members to put pressure on the participant to stay.
  d. a and c.

In the words of ASGW ethics: "Group leaders shall inform members that participation is voluntary and they may exit the group at any time." Is this guideline realistic? Some experts certainly would question this guideline to say the very least. Consider a client who is "required" by the court to attend your group for the perpetration of sexual abuse. In the literal sense this client is not a "voluntary participant." When a client is required to go to counseling or therapy it is known as "mandatory treatment." **(b)**

451. During the initial session of a group the leader explains that no smoking and no cursing will be permitted. This is known as

  a. setting ground rules.
  b. ambivalent transference.
  c. blocking.
  d. scapegoating.

When ground rules become the standard of behavior then it is known as a "norm." The leader can specify the ground rules early in the group. Examples might be no cussing or hitting another group member. The term "ambivalent transference," choice "b," is a psychoanalytic notion which suggests that a client will treat a therapist with ambivalence, as he or she would any person viewed as an authority figure. **(Note:** Ambivalence implies that the client will experience contradictory emotions such as love and hate alternating from one to the other.) Choice "c," "blocking," is a term often used in group work. Blocking occurs when a leader uses an intervention to stop—or block if you will—a negative or counterproductive behavior which could hurt another member or the group. Choice "d," scapegoating, is precisely the type of behavior a leader would want to block. In scapegoating, members gang up on a single group member. **(a)**

452. Group norms refer to

    a.   a statistically normal group composed of 8 to 12 members.
    b.   a statistically normal group composed of 12 to 14 members.
    c.   a normal group with no cultural differences.
    d.   the range of acceptable behavior within the group.

Norms are the written or unwritten do's and don'ts of the group. **(d)**

453. The study of group operations is often called

    a.   group desensitization.
    b.   the hot seat technique.
    c.   group dynamics.
    d.   structuring the group.

Group dynamics refers to the study of the interrelationships of group members. Group stages, cohesiveness, leadership style, and decision making are prime examples of group dynamics. Any factor that has an impact on the group can be referred to legitimately as a dynamic. The hot seat, choice "b," is a term popularized by Fritz Perls' Gestalt Therapy groups. A person who is the target of the therapist's interventions in the here and now is said to be on the "hot seat." Choice "d," or the structuring of the group, is determined by the presence (or lack of) structured tasks or exercises given to members by the group leader. Important point: Often when an exam uses the term "structured group" (not to be confused with the term "group structure") it connotes a group which focuses on a given theme such as a group for veterans in the Gulf War.   **(c)**

454. The word "dynamic" means the group is

    a.   normal.
    b.   always changing.
    c.   static.
    d.   defined in an operational manner.

Choice "d" is used quite a bit in the social sciences. In order to "operationally define" something you must demonstrate the concrete steps necessary to illuminate the concept. It sounds complex yet it really isn't. To operationally define, say positive reinforcement, you would first note how often a behavior is occurring. Then you might give the client a reward every time he or she performs a desirable behavior, and tabulate the fact that the behavior is occurring more often than before you instituted the procedure. To operationally define the action of writing the letter "t," you could tell the person to first draw a vertical line of one inch and then draw a horizontal line 1/2 inch in length, perpendicular to and 1/3 of an inch from the top of, the vertical line. The idea of the operational definition is that another person can duplicate your actions (i.e., the exact steps) for therapeutic, research, or testing purposes.   **(b)**

455. Experts firmly believe that a common weakness in many groups is

    a.   goal setting.
    b.   using coleaders.
    c.   that the leader uses a democratic style.
    d.   a lack of goal setting.

Often goals are defined yet they are too vague.   **(d)**

456. A group leader who utilizes an abundance of group exercises is

    a.   probably not running an assertiveness training group.
    b.   is running an unstructured group.
    c.   is running a structured group.
    d.   is invariably running a self-help group.

Look closely at choice "a." An assertiveness training group would indeed generally use a lot of structured exercises. Choice "d" is also incorrect since a self-help group would not necessarily utilize a lot of structured exercises.   **(c)**

457. Some theorists object to the word "unstructured" in group work because

    a.   a group cannot not have structure.
    b.   only structured groups are effective.
    c.   unstructured groups are hardly therapeutic.
    d.   unstructured refers only to counseling and not therapy groups.

Some research indicates that structured exercises in the initial stages of the group can facilitate better communication.   **(a)**

458. Some research demonstrates that

    a.   structured exercises early in the group impaired later communication between group members.

    b.   structured exercises with feedback early in the group served to improve communication between group members.

    c.   autocratic or authoritarian leadership styles promote communication best.

    d.   structured exercises are never appropriate.

If you marked choice "c," then stop this very moment and review the answer to question 436. As far as choice "d" goes, beware of any answer which relies on adverbs like "always" or "never." Answers sporting the word "always" are almost always incorrect, and those using "never" are almost never correct! **(b)**

459. In some literature, group cohesiveness is known as

    a.   group unity.
    b.   a sociogram.
    c.   Karpman's triangle.
    d.   the transition stage.

The unity is actually a feeling of belonging, oneness, or togetherness. A sociogram (choice "b") is simply a pictorial account of a group which serves to diagram member interaction. Choice "c," Karpman's drama triangle, is used most often in conjunction with transactional analysis as a teaching device to illuminate the roles of persecutor, rescuer, and victim in interpersonal relationships. The final choice, the transition stage, is the group stage which occurs after the first or so-called initial stage. In the initial stage members get acquainted and learn norms. In the second or transition stage members are often judgmental, resistant, or involved in a struggle for power to establish a hierarchy or "pecking order." **(a)**

460. Group members assume roles within a group. Which of the following is not a group role?

    a.   energizer
    b.   scapegoat
    c.   gatekeeper
    d.   reactive schizophrenia

In counseling the term "reactive" means that a given condition is the result of environmental stress. Hence, reactive schizophrenia, would imply that the person experienced a psychotic episode following a traumatic experience. This would be in contrast to an individual who was seemingly always schizophrenic, and the pathology could not be traced to any given set of circumstances. Choices "a," "b," and "c" are common roles individuals will play in a group setting. The energizer stimulates enthusiasm in the group (e.g., "Come on folks this will be a lot of fun; and besides we'll really learn a lot"). The scapegoat is the person everybody blames. He or she is invariably the target of severe anger and hostility (e.g., "Look Marv, we all agree that if it weren't for you we would have solved the problem two weeks ago"). The gatekeeper tries to make certain that everyone is doing his or her task and is participating. This person may "secretly" or "unconsciously" want to lead the group and could even attempt to establish norms. The danger is that a gatekeeper often does not work on his or her own personal issues (e.g., "From now on I'd like everybody to bring a journal to the group and write down at least one positive thing which happened during the week"). Is that the leader speaking out or the gatekeeper blowing off steam? Only the group members know for sure! **(d)**

461. A group member who insists on asking other members inappropriate questions is known as a Peeping Tom or

    a.   an energizer.
    b.   a scapegoat.
    c.   an interrogator.
    d.   a follower.

The "interrogator" asks a never ending string of questions while the "follower" goes along with the rest of the group. **(c)**

462. The follower goes along with whatever the rest of the group thinks. From a personality standpoint the follower is

    a. aggressive.
    b. assertive.
    c. practicing excitation.
    d. nonassertive.

Choice "c" relates to Andrew Salter's Conditioned Reflex Therapy in which "excitation" or the practice of spontaneously experiencing and expressing true emotions (even negative ones) is seen as necessary in order to attain a state of positive mental health. "Inhibition" or constipation of emotions is seen as the opposite of excitation. Said Salter: "However, in psychotherapy we need have no fear. The diagnosis is always inhibition." **(d)**

463. The _____ may secretly wish that he or she was running the group.

    a. follower
    b. gatekeeper
    c. social isolate
    d. harmonizer

I joke with my students about adding a note to the university course catalog under my group's course which says "only former gatekeepers need to apply." See answer 460 if you fail to see the humor! Choice "d" introduces the harmonizer role. Some books and exams bill this as the "conciliator" or the person who tries to make certain that everything is going smoothly. **(b)**

464. Everybody picks on

    a.   the gatekeeper.
    b.   the harmonizer also known as the conciliator.
    c.   the scapegoat.
    d.   the storyteller.

The storyteller, choice "d," monopolizes a wealth of group time telling endless (often irrelevant) tales. A group leader will sometimes need to help this person get to the point or will need to ask the person precisely how the story is productive in the context of the group setting.   **(c)**

465. A female group member is obviously not participating. A group member playing the _____ is most likely to mention this and urge her to participate.

    a.   gatekeeper
    b.   interrogator
    c.   scapegoat
    d.   storyteller

One popular notion is that these roles relate to the person's pattern of behavior in his or her nuclear family, and if appropriate the group leader can explore this hypothesis. In addition to the popular aforementioned roles, Hartford spoke of an "isolate role." The isolate is ignored by others. Isolates generally feel afraid to reach out or do reach out and are genuinely rejected. For exam purposes keep in mind that the isolate is not the same as the scapegoat. Scapegoats receive attention although it is not by any means overwhelmingly positive. Isolates, on the other hand, receive little or no attention.   **(a)**

466. Cohesiveness or group unity is desirable. It promotes bonding and a sense of "we-ness" between group members. When cohesiveness is strong, nevertheless, it also can be negative as

    a.   it can stunt creativity.
    b.   it can abet conformity.
    c.   a and b.
    d.   it can cause the group to split into factions.

The word "faction" in choice "d" describes a clique or a group of people within a group. You might, for example, have a faction which does not wish to go along with a certain task or group exercise. The sociogram mentioned earlier can help identify group factions. A faction also may be called a "subgroup." **(c)**

467. In a healthy group, members

    a.   assume a role and never change it.
    b.   have no roles.
    c.   are flexible and can change roles.
    d.   spend a great deal of time practicing role reversal.

In order to meet the "changing needs" of the group, members often need to "change roles." Choice "d" or role reversal is a common behavioral role-playing technique. A client who is having difficulty communicating with another person in his or her life role-plays the person with whom he or she is having difficulty. Another group member (or the leader) plays the group member with the problem. This valuable technique gives the group member a new perspective on the situation and allows the person to learn via modelling alternative ways of behaving. **(c)**

468. In a group, task roles

    a.   help solve problems.
    b.   aid in terms of goal setting.
    c.   are seen as positive.
    d.   all of the above.

Here is a key concept. Group specialists classify member roles as: task roles, maintenance roles, and self-serving roles. (On some exams, self-serving roles will be identified as "individual roles.") The distinctions are actually fairly easy to remember. In everyday life when we refer to a "task" we mean a job or something which needs to be accomplished. A task role (e.g., an information giver or a clarifier) simply helps the group carry out a task. A maintenance role (e.g., the follower, mentioned earlier, or an encourager) helps "maintain" or even strengthen group processes. The final category (i.e., the self-serving role) is seen as negative. The person who falls into this category meets his or her own "individual needs" at the expense of the group. A person who downright refuses to participate or a person who criticizes or disagrees with others would be a prime example. **(d)**

469. Maintenance roles, like task roles, are positive since such roles

    a.   help to maintain the group.
    b.   are self-serving.
    c.   help promote autocratic leadership.
    d.   always stress the importance of the here and now.

Remember: maintenance really implies that the role maintains group interaction. Maintenance roles support the group's livelihood and hence are seen as positive. Paul Hersey and Kenneth Blanchard point out that leader activities generally fall into "task actions" and "maintenance actions" (i.e., relationship concerns). Hersey and Blanchard point out that the most effective leadership approach depends on the group situation. The researchers speak of "maturity" in regard to a specific task. If a group member has low maturity—which is really a lack of achievement motivation—then the leader should use "high task" and "low relationship" behaviors. As maturity gets better, a "high task" and "high relationship" paradigm is ideal. And when group members display very high maturity, then a "low task" and "low relationship" leadership format would be desirable. Now listen closely: task action leadership is said to be indicative of one-way communication (i.e., the leader tells the members about a task to accomplish), while relationship behavior is said to be the result of two-way communication (i.e., the leader provides emotional support for members). Hersey and Blanchard suggest that it is not atypical for a member to display maturity on one task and a distinct lack of maturity on the next. Now I want to stress two very important points here. One is that when you see the words "task" and "maintenance" on your exam the concepts could refer to either a group member's role or the leader's behavior. The other concept I want you to be familiar with is that conflict between group members can often be abated by having the leader prescribe a "task" in which all the members must work together in order to accomplish.   **(a)**

470. Self-serving or individual roles are negative inasmuch as

   a.   they promote democratic leadership.
   b.   they work against the group.
   c.   they serve the individual and not the group.
   d.   b and c.

Self-serving or so-called individual roles are counterproductive.   **(d)**

471. Although task roles and maintenance roles are indeed positive the group can suffer if the group is not flexible and remains in one or the other too long since

   a.   an effective group needs some self-serving roles.
   b.   if a group gets stuck in task roles, interaction suffers.
   c.   if a group gets stuck in maintenance roles, little work (or tasks) will be accomplished.
   d.   b and c.

I believe this clarifies the point made earlier that group members will ideally be flexible and able to change roles.   **(d)**

472. Group specialists define role conflict as

      a.   tension between two group members who have assumed different roles.

      b.   a situation in which there is a discrepancy between the way a member is expected to act and the way he or she actually behaves.

      c.   tension between the group leader and a group member.

      d.   members criticizing other members between group sessions.

The word conflict comes from the Latin word "conflictus," which means "striking together with force." Please do not confuse "role conflict" with the group term "conflict of interest" which occurs when a group member maximizes his or her needs and interests at the expense of someone else. **(b)**

473. A major group dynamic is group development. This is usually expressed in terms of

      a.   the number of hours of group conflict.
      b.   theories of group stages.
      c.   the Rosenthal Effect.
      d.   the Hawthorne Effect.

Here is a very helpful hint. Do not—I repeat—do not attempt to memorize every single group stage theory ever invented. First because you have better things to do with your time (I would hope!), and second because there are far too many. Most of the theories are very similar and thus if you know the basic format you will have a very good chance of answering the question correctly. The first stage generally is known simply as the "initial stage." (Now there's one that's so simple you won't need a memory device!) Others have termed this stage as "orientation and exploration," or "preaffiliation" or "forming." The next stage usually is designated as the "transition stage," though you will often see it termed "power and control" or "storming" which logically comes after "forming." The third major stage is the "working stage," "norming stage," "cohesion stage," or "negotiation, intimacy and frame of reference." The final stage is sometimes known as the "separation stage," the "termination stage," or "adjourning." Choices "c" (no relation!) and "d" will be covered in the sections on research.   **(b)**

474. Irving Yalom is a famous existentialist therapist and a pioneer in the group movement. He suggested these four group stages: orientation, conflict, cohesion, and termination. In 1977 Tuckman and Jensen reviewed 25 years of research and came up with five stages: forming, storming, norming, performing, and adjourning. Which stage in Tuckman and Jensen's paradigm is similar to Yalom's orientation stage?

    a.   forming
    b.   storming
    c.   norming
    d.   performing

Okay, you deserved an easy one. Note that different group theories have differences in the number of stages. Your best bet on the exam is to try to note the similarities between the major theories. For example, the initial stage examined in this question (i.e., orientation, forming, preparation, engagement and who knows what some creative theorist will dare call it next!) is focused on the establishment of norms and approach-avoidance behavior of group members. Members will be tentative and size up other members. Members will identify with others based on culture, language, mode of dress, or occupation.   **(a)**

475. The final stage suggested by theories of group stages generally deals with issues of

    a.   group tasks.
    b.   transition.
    c.   power and control.
    d.   separation and termination.

The final stage is said to represent a time of breaking away. Group members can experience loss and need to establish bonds outside of the group setting. The ideal situation would be that termination takes place after the group and its members have reached their goals and have no further unfinished business. Certainly, in reality (such as when a client needs to leave a hospital group as his insurance has run out) this is not always the case. **(d)**

476. The initial group stage has been called forming, orientation, or the preaffiliation stage. This stage is characterized by

   a. avoidance-avoidance conflicts.
   b. a tendency for members to compete with the leader for power.
   c. approach-avoidance behavior.
   d. members working on the interpretation of unconscious behavior.

Yes, I'm being redundant with the words I'm using in my questions and my answers, but this will help you become more accustomed to the lingo of group work. In the first stage people want to be accepted but are scared to participate. Now what about choice "a"? Well, an avoidance-avoidance conflict exists when you have two alternatives which are both unattractive, such as when your boss says you can either take a pay cut or lose your job. The approach-avoidance situation taking place in the initial group stage is a conflict wherein you are attracted and repelled by the same goal. You want to meet group members, but it's scary to think about the fact that you could be rejected. **(c)**

477. A client would generally feel the most suspicious of others in

   a. the final stage of separation or termination.
   b. the intimacy stage.
   c. the forming or so-called exploratory stage.
   d. a group with coleadership.

Safety comes from seeking common ground. That is to say, the new group member seeks out others of similar social status. Like Erikson's first psychosocial stage of development, the initial group stage hosts the "trust versus mistrust" drama. **(c)**

478. Fights between subgroups and members showing rebellion against the leader generally occurs in

    a. the transition stage.
    b. the orientation stage.
    c. the separation stage.
    d. the intimacy stage.

Garland, Jones, and Kolodny appropriately called stage two "power and control." This is the stage in which the fireworks fly as group members verbally attack one another not to mention the group leader. **(a)**

479. A hierarchy or pecking order among members occurs in

    a. the stage of storming, also known as the power and control stage.
    b. the orientation stage.
    c. the separation stage.
    d. the intimacy stage.

Ditto! This is the stage movies are made of. Members rank themselves in terms of status and factions (mentioned earlier). Isolated members who are not protected by the strong subgroup (faction) sometimes drop out. It should come as no surprise that some authors have called this the "high anxiety" or "struggle for control stage." And how is a leader to handle this turmoil? Corey and Corey appropriately suggested that the leader learns to distinguish between a "challenge" and an "attack." Do not assume, said the Coreys, that every confrontation is an attack on your integrity as a leader. Leaders can model responsible assertive confrontation with open and truthful expression. **(a)**

480. A sense of cohesiveness or "we-ness" occurs in

    a.   the initial stage.
    b.   the stage after the transition or conflict stage.
    c.   the final stage.
    d.   most prescreening group interviews.

Yalom simplifies the field with his four-phase theory. Phase three is "cohesion." **(b)**

481. The final group stage is geared toward

    a.   developing intimacy.
    b.   working through power and control issues.
    c.   exploration.
    d.   breaking away.

This phase has been called "consolidation" and occurs after the working stage. The leader helps members make plans for the future. I must point out that group specialists feel that every group does not necessarily pass through every stage (even after an extended period of time) and that there is not always a clear-cut discernable line of demarcation separating one group stage from another. **(d)**

482. A group therapist is constructing a diagram to better understand the dynamics between subgroups and members. This is called

    a.   sculpturing.
    b.   ego state analysis.
    c.   charting a sociogram.
    d.   charting the variance.

The study of measuring person-to-person relationships regarding what members in a group think or feel is known as "sociometry." In essence, sociometry is a quantitative study of relationship concerns in a group. The sociogram, credited to Moreno and Jennings, graphically displays group members affiliations and interactions. Choice "a," or family sculpturing, is a family therapy technique in which the family members are instructed to arrange themselves spatially to create a live representation of family members' bonds, feelings of closeness (or lack of it), and sense of alliances. Choice "b" is a common practice in transactional analysis in which the counselor helps the client discern out of which ego state (i.e., parent, child, or adult) he or she is primarily operating in a given situation. **(c)**

483. A group leader who asks each group member to recapitulate what he or she has learned during a given session is promoting

    a.   summarization.
    b.   clarification.
    c.   blocking.
    d.   linking.

Summarization, which is also appropriate in individual work, is merely the act of bringing together a number of important thoughts, insights, feelings, or transactions. **(a)**

484. A leader who wishes to stop inappropriate discussion should rely on

    a.   summarization.
    b.   clarification.
    c.   blocking.
    d.   linking.

Blocking in groups is very much like blocking a punch in a boxing match. Blocking is used by the leader to stop (or block if you will) a hurtful behavior. Blocking in therapy is often necessary for the protection of group members. Blocking can be used in cases of gossiping or breaking confidentiality. Choice "b," clarification, is another important skill group leaders must possess. A leader uses clarification to ferret out the important points in a client's message. Clarification brings out the gist of a message and illuminates what was really said to lessen any confusion. The final choice, linking, is used to promote cohesion. A link is an attempt to bring together common patterns or themes within the group. **(c)**

485. When a leader attempts to relate one person's predicament to another person's predicament, it is known as

    a.   summarization.
    b.   clarification.
    c.   blocking.
    d.   linking.

When used properly, linking illuminates areas of mutual concern. This often enhances group interaction. **(d)**

486. Strategies that approach the group as a whole are known as

    a.   vertical interventions.
    b.   horizontal interventions.
    c.   crossed transactions.
    d.   parallel transactions.

When working in a group setting, the leader needs to decide whether to work with the group as a whole (called a horizontal intervention) or with individuals within the group (called a vertical intervention—note choice "a"). Of course by now you realize how valuable memory devices are in terms of helping you to remember distinctions. Here's the one I have found valuable in this case. If you picture a group in your mind it appears spread out "horizontally." On the other hand, if you picture yourself doing counseling with an individual in a group, the individual is usually sitting up in a "vertical" position. In the case of the vertical intervention the leader is providing individual counseling in a group work setting. Techniques which focus on group relationships, processes, tasks, and interactions are said to be horizontal intervention strategies. The horizontal approach is often called the "interpersonal" method since it focuses on interactions. The vertical approach has been termed "intrapersonal" leadership. Shapiro, who suggested the intrapersonal-interpersonal leadership distinction, feels that a leader does not really choose one or the other but tends to behave on a continuum in this respect. You would do well to remember that interpersonal leaders favor here and now interventions while intrapersonal leaders are more likely to work on the past, sometimes employing psychodynamic notions. An effective counselor should rely on both types of interventions. If, for example, a leader stresses vertical intrapersonal interventions, members may be hesitant to speak or react in a spontaneous manner. In this case the group member might literally think, "it's not my turn to speak yet; Dr. X is working with Jane now." The other side of the coin, however, is that the horizontal interpersonal leader may lose some power as an expert who can model or reinforce appropriate behavior. **(b)**

487. Strategies that focus on an individual member of the group are known as

    a.   vertical interventions.
    b.   horizontal interventions.
    c.   crossed transactions.
    d.   parallel transactions.

Again, use your memory device. See that individual sitting or standing . . . she's in a vertical position, of course. Choices "c" and "d" relate to transactional analysis. A crossed transaction between two persons' ego states is said to be dysfunctional while a parallel transaction promotes healthy communication. **(a)**

488. A group therapist must make

    a.   fewer decisions than an individual therapist.
    b.   the same number of decisions as an individual therapist.
    c.   modality changes for each group.
    d.   more decisions than an individual therapist.

Thus, most experts would agree that it is more difficult to do productive group work than it is individual work.   **(d)**

489. When a counselor reads the journals in this field it becomes evident that

    a.   group counseling has more research than individual counseling.
    b.   researchers and practitioners are working very closely to provide accurate and effective group strategies.
    c.   a researcher/practitioner split exists in group work.
    d.   no journals focus solely on group work.

Practical research about what exactly works best in a group setting is scarce. Moreover, many studies in the field of group work have not been well controlled. In many studies, the independent variable (i.e., the experimental variable) has not been scientifically defined. Say, for example, the independent variable in a study is a "t-group intervention." This indeed could create a problem since a t-group to leader A might not seem like a t-group to leader B.   **(c)**

490. Experts predict that in the future

    a.   group leaders will be more like life-skills trainers.
    b.   group leaders will become more person-centered.
    c.   group leaders will return to a psychodynamic viewpoint.
    d.   groups will lose their popularity and eventually die out.

The position has been taken that in the past groups have emphasized a narrow focus (e.g., a group for non-assertive bosses), and in the future groups should begin to deal with a broad spectrum of issues or what some call a "comprehensive model" of group work. A comprehensive educational life-skills model could stress preventive mental health skills, hopefully lowering the need for "therapeutic groups." Therefore, ultimately the counselor of the life-skills group would act more like a trainer than a therapist. **(a)**

491. According to researchers groups are effective

   a.   although researchers cannot pinpoint precisely why this is true.
   b.   due to increased transference in group work.
   c.   due to better morale in a group setting.
   d.   due to the emphasis on cognitive restructuring.

Research in the area of group work is sometimes classified as "outcome research" or "process research." Outcome research addresses the question of whether the group was able to reach a given set of goals or simply the desired "outcome." An outcome study attempts to answer the question of whether or not the group was successful (i.e., does the group work). Process research is aimed at the question of "how groups work." Process research asks, "What allows the group to reach a target outcome?" **(a)**

492. A major limitation related to group work is that

   a.   RET cannot be utilized in group therapy.
   b.   it is not really cost effective.
   c.   Gestalt Therapy cannot be used in a group setting.
   d.   a group leader can lose control and members could experience emotional harm.

Let me make certain that the purpose of this question is perfectly clear: You must know the strengths and limitations of group work for almost any comprehensive exam. Choice "d" depicts a major limitation. Other limitations include: (1) that a client may need individual therapy before he or she can benefit from group work; (2) that a client may not be capable of trusting others enough to reveal key material since he or she fears others may find it unacceptable; (3) that the group could become a substitute experience for the real world; (4) that the group counselor may not be as effective with a whole group of people as he or she is with just one person in individual treatment; (5) that some clients may feel pressure to replace their personal norms with those of the group; and (6) that disappointment can set in if the group is not helpful and the person loses faith in treatment without experiencing individual sessions. Group therapy generally is not the treatment of choice when the client is in a state of crisis, needs an interpretation of his or her psychological tests, needs confidentiality for protection (groups are notorious for having more problems with confidentiality than individual treatment), or is phobic in regard to public speaking. Choices "a," "b," and "c" are totally false. **(d)**

493. A major advantage of group work versus individual work is that

    a.   members learn to give help in addition to receiving it.

    b.   the leader has a less complex role.

    c.   the group leader generally possesses more training.

    d.   all of the above.

Other group advantages include that group work allows for "in vivo" interpersonal work; that it is cost effective and allows a trained counselor to help a greater number of people; that it promotes universality; that it can be an effective support system; that members get multiple feedback; and that members can model successful communication and coping skills. And oh yes, although it would be nice if choice "c" were true (since group leaders generally need more training than individual helpers), the truth is that many people are running groups without any training whatsoever in group work. **(a)**

494. Which statement best depicts a major advantage of group work?

    a. Group work usually focuses on the here and now.
    b. Group work is always time limited.
    c. Group work is always superior for career counseling.
    d. The group setting is somewhat analogous to the communication and interaction of everyday life.

Overall, research would support the notion that groups work, and yes, they have advantages. However—and this is one important point folks—there is no body of research which would say that in general group work is superior to other forms of treatment. Please reread the previous sentence . . . yes, it's that important! **(d)**

495. The life-skills model of group work is associated most closely with the work of

    a. Yalom.
    b. Gazda.
    c. Corey and Corey.
    d. Brill.

Gazda's life-skills model rests heavily on preventive mental health and can enhance functioning throughout the life span. Gazda's taxonomy (remember, that's the big word you now know for classification!) includes interpersonal communication and human relations, physical fitness and health maintenance, identity development and purpose in life, and problem solving and decision making. **(b)**

496. In terms of research and the group leader's personality,

    a.   extroverts are the most effective leaders.
    b.   introverts are the most effective leaders.
    c.   qualities such as flexibility, enthusiasm, and common sense may be helpful to a very small degree.
    d.   qualities such as flexibility, enthusiasm, and common sense have a tremendous positive impact.

Unfortunately, overall studies have turned up little in terms of "special characteristics" of group leaders' personalities. So much for the concept of super leaders! **(c)**

497. Coyne suggested that group intervention is intended to

    a.   ferret out unconscious material.
    b.   enhance rational self-talk.
    c.   illuminate dysfunctional nonverbal behavior.
    d.   prevent, to correct, or to enhance behavior.

R.K. Coyne's "group work grid" model includes four intervention levels: individual, interpersonal, organization, and community population. The intervention can be correction oriented or enhancement oriented for either personal or task functions. **(d)**

498. A group leader who wishes to assess the impact of the group ideally would

    a.   hand out a written evaluation form during the final session.
    b.   hold a follow-up session so members can share experiences.
    c.   have an outside "observer" sit in during group sessions and consequently rate the level of behavioral change.
    d.   give each member a pretest and a post-test utilizing a projective measure.

Keep in mind that you are looking for the best answer here. All of the choices are correct; however, choice "c" is superior to the other three. Research in the area of group work has been criticized for not using independent observers. When taking your exam be aware that "member-specific measures" are designed to assess change (or lack of it) in an individual group member. Most member-specific measures, such as a self-rating or (better still) a rating by an outside observer, are not standardized. In contrast to the "member-specific measure," researchers speak of "group-specific measures" which are intended to measure the degree of change (or again, lack of it) in all persons participating in the group. Lastly, the so-called "global measures" such as standardized tests may well assess traits and factors not specifically addressed in the group. For example, giving members of a Weight Watchers group a pre and post MMPI would constitute a global measurement. **(c)**

499. A group leader who is counseling children under 10 years of age could best enhance the treatment process by

    a.   involving parents and asking them for input.
    b.   keeping the parents uninvolved.
    c.   reminding the children to speak softly at all times.
    d.   b and c.

Corey and Corey suggested that parental involvement can reduce resistance and improve cooperation. They also warned counselors not to take sides with a child against a parent or institution. **(a)**

500. When an adolescent complains about his or her parents in the group it is best to

a. jump on the bandwagon and agree with the child.
b. avoid taking sides but help him or her see the parents' point of view via a therapeutic technique such as role-playing.
c. talk only about positive experiences.
d. immediately put the child on the hot seat.

This principle is true for adolescents as well as children under 10. When working with children and adolescents be careful what you say about confidentiality since in the case of child abuse, sexual abuse, neglect, or exploitation, you will be required to break confidentiality. In addition, ethics would dictate that you do likewise if a child is suicidal or plans to seriously harm another individual. Of course, these last two points would apply to all age brackets, in group or individual treatment. **(b)**

CHAPTER **8**

LIFE-STYLE AND
CAREER DEVELOPMENT

501. Life-style and career development have been emphasized

    a.   only since the late 1950s.
    b.   only since the late 1960s.
    c.   only since nondirective counseling became popular.
    d.   since the beginning of the counseling and guidance movement and are still major areas of concern.

The beginning of the guidance movement has often been associated with the work of Frank Parsons (a Cornell graduate who later was Boston's chief law clerk and then the Dean of the Liberal Arts College at Glen Ellyn, Illinois) who started the Boston Vocation Bureau on January 13, 1908 just nine months prior to his death. His landmark work, *Choosing a Vocation*, was published posthumously, thus it is doubtful that he ever knew the true impact he had on the field. Parsons served as the Bureau's director as well as a vocational counselor. The Bureau was set up at the Civic Service House though Parsons also had office hours in branch offices at the YMCA, the Economic Club, and the Women's Educational and Industrial Union. This explains why historians insist that the guidance movement in the U.S. began with vocational guidance. John M. Brewer, a director of the Bureau during WWI and the author of the 1942 work *History of Vocational Guidance,* speculated that as a bachelor Parsons could have been drawn to the Civic Service House in search of friendship. **(d)**

502. Women workers make up nearly

    a.   1/6 of the country's labor force.
    b.   1/10 of the country's labor force.
    c.   1/2 of the country's labor force.
    d.   1/4 of the country's labor force.

In the past 10 years the number of women with full-time jobs in the U.S. has doubled. According to the 1986 figures given via the U.S. Bureau of Labor Statistics nearly one out of two workers is a woman. One notion is that the high divorce rate (which currently impacts nearly one out of two marriages) created the phenomenon of the "displaced homemaker." A displaced homemaker is a woman with children who was a homemaker but is currently in need of work to support her family. Women who have made the transition from homemaker to jobs outside the home could very well be referred to as "reentry women" on your exam. It has been estimated that 75% of all divorces occur in families with children. **(c)**

503. In 1973 Prediger, Roth, and Noeth conducted a nationwide study of career development and its relationship to students. The study, which involved over 28,000 students, revealed that

    a.   a very high proportion of students in high school and at the junior high or middle school level wanted guidance in planning a career.
    b.   students did not want career guidance despite its importance.
    c.   many students were too inflexible to benefit from career guidance.
    d.   high school students wanted career guidance but junior high school or middle school level students did not.

Three-fourths of the eleventh graders wanted help with career planning and the number who wanted help in the eighth grade was nearly as high rendering choice "d" incorrect. MOST STUDIES INDICATE THAT STUDENTS WOULD LIKE MORE HELP IN THE AREA OF CAREER PLANNING. **(a)**

504. A dual career family is one in which both partners have jobs to which they are committed on a somewhat continuous basis. Which statement is true of dual career families?

    a.   Surprisingly enough, dual career families have lower incomes than families in which only one partner works.

    b.   Dual career families have higher incomes than the so-called "traditional family" in which only one partner is working.

    c.   Dual career families have incomes which are almost identical to families with one partner working.

    d.   Surprisingly enough, no research has been conducted on dual career families.

Common sense prevails here as two incomes are indeed usually better than one. **(b)**

505. In the dual career family, partners seem to be more self-sufficient than in the traditional family. In a dual career household, the woman

    a.   generally has children before entering the work force.

    b.   rarely if ever has children.

    c.   is not self-reliant.

    d.   is typically secure in her career before she has children.

Choice "a" is true of the traditional family while choice "d" describes the dual-career family. Choice "c" contradicts research which insists that partners in a dual-career family are more self-sufficient than in the traditional family. **(d)**

506. Studies indicate that

    a.   students receive ample vocational guidance.

    b.   most parents can provide appropriate vocational guidance.

    c.   students want more vocational guidance than they receive.

    d.   career days meet the vocational guidance needs of most students.

If you missed this question please review question 503. **HINT:** SOME EXAMS WILL DISTINGUISH BETWEEN CAREER COUNSELING AND VOCATIONAL GUIDANCE. GUIDANCE IS SEEN AS A DEVELOPMENTAL AND EDUCATIONAL PROCESS WITHIN A SCHOOL SYSTEM WHILE CAREER COUNSELING IS VIEWED AS A THERAPEUTIC SERVICE FOR ADULTS PERFORMED OUTSIDE AN EDUCATIONAL SETTING. SEMANTICS? PERHAPS, BUT YOU MAY NEED IT TO BOOST YOUR EXAM SCORE! **(c)**

507. Statistics reveal that

    a.   more women are working than ever before.

    b.   fewer workers possess a high-school degree than ever before.

    c.   blue-collar jobs are growing faster than white-collar jobs.

    d.   older workers are slower than younger workers and have less skill.

Choice "b" is blatantly false. The number of workers in the labor force with a high-school degree has increased; more than 75% of all workers now sport a high-school diploma. The same could be said of choice "c": blue-collar jobs have not increased as rapidly as white-collar positions. These changes may be based partially on the fact that the U.S. has become a service economy rather than focusing primarily on the production of goods. Some exams—as well as many textbooks—will mention the "changing view of work." This phrase generally indicates that in the past work was seen as drudgery, while today it is seen as a vehicle to express our identity, self-esteem, and status. In the past work was primarily a way to pay the bills. Today, the rewards of a career are often conceptualized as fulfilling emotional needs. This would seem to indicate that people who don't need to work would still continue to do so. Is this really the case? According to a 1978 text on lottery winners by H.R. Kaplan, million dollar winners who quit their jobs felt dissatisfied. (We should all be lucky enough to be included in a study like this!) And did you by any chance mark choice "d"? Well if you did, you need to know that experience impacts job performance more than age does. Some research demonstrates that older workers are actually more adept than younger ones in terms of skill as well as speed! This phenomenon disproved a notion in psychology known as "decrement," which suggested that speed, skills, and retention would decrease as one entered old age.   **(a)**

508. When professional career counselors use the term leisure they technically mean

    a.   the client is having fun at work or away from work.

    b.   the client is relaxing at work or away from work.

    c.   the client is working at less than 100% capacity at work or away from work.

    d.   the time the client has away from work which is not being utilized for obligations.

Leisure time is defined as time away from work in which the individual has the freedom to choose what he or she would like to do. Leisure time is said to be "self-determined." Dual-career families often report a lack

of leisure time which can in turn abet additional stress
for both partners. **(d)**

509. In terms of leisure time and dual career families

    a.   dual career families have more leisure time.
    b.   dual career families have the same amount of
        leisure time as families with one wage earner.
    c.   dual career families have less leisure time.
    d.   dual career families have more weekend leisure
        time.

Both partners in the single career family have more
leisure time. Some books and exams are already using
the term "leisure counseling" which should alert you
to the emphasis which is being placed on this topic.
Fortunately, research shows that in most cases, dual-
career households manage to spend as much time with
their children as households with a single wage earner. **(c)**

510. A client who says, "I feel I cannot really become an
administrator in our agency because I am a woman,"
is showing an example of

    a.   gender bias.
    b.   counselor bias.
    c.   the trait-factor theory.
    d.   developmental theory and career choice.

Here is an agency that makes "biased" employment choices
based on one's "gender." The ideal answer to this dilemma
was set forth in 1964 when Title VII of the Civil Rights
Act (amended in 1972) stated that women would have
equal work opportunities and equal job pay. I purposely
used the word "ideal" inasmuch as some statistics
demonstrated that in 1964 a man was earning a buck
for every 59 cents earned by a woman. Since 1964,
however, there has been little or no change in the gap.
The EEOC is the watchdog for Title VII guidelines that
prohibit discrimination on the basis of color, sex, religion,

race, or national origin. Since 1978, EEOC has enforced "Uniform Guidelines on Employee Selection Procedures." The procedures speak of "adverse impact." A test or selection process is said to have adverse impact if it does not meet the "80% Four-fifths Rule." Here, the hiring rate for minorities is divided by the figure for non-minorities. If the quotient is less than 80% (4/5s), then adverse impact is evident. Thus, a typical exam question might inform you that a firm's selection process is such that 60 of the employees hired are black, while 80 are white. You would then be asked to determine whether the selection process was plagued via adverse impact. Your computation would be: 60/80 = 75%. Since 75% is less than 80%, the process would indeed have an adverse impact. This formula also is used for promotion situations. The fact that minorities ought to be moved "up" more in jobs could be used as a memory device that the minority or subgroup rate is placed "up" or on the top (i.e., the numerator) of the equation. The uniform guidelines also discuss "differential validity." Differential validity is evident when a selection process (e.g., a test) is valid for one group, yet less valid or totally invalid for another group. (Note: This is not the same as "discriminant validity." See question 627 for a discussion of this term.) Tests plagued by differential validity should not be utilized for hiring or promotion purposes. Incidentally, choice "b" or "counselor bias" might be used to describe a counselor who was sympathetic with the agency's position. As for choices "c" and "d" be prepared to see them a lot. The chances are extremely good that you will see a question related to "trait-factor theory" and "developmental theory" on any major exam. The trait-factor theory assumed that via psychological testing one's personality could be matched to an occupation which stressed those particular personality traits. Some industrial psychology exams will speak of "profile matching." In this approach, a job candidate's personality and/or skills profile is matched to that of successful workers. The decision to hire is then based on the closeness or similarity of the match based on a pattern of predictor scores. Choice "d," the developmental approach, views career decisions as longitudinal and reversible. **(a)**

511. One major category of career theory is known as the trait-factor approach which is also called the actuarial or matching approach. This approach

    a.   attempts to match conscious and unconscious work motives.
    b.   attempts to match the worker and the work environment (job factors).
    c.   attempts to match career behavior with attitudes.
    d.   attempts to match cognition with the workload.

Historically speaking, the trait-factor theory is considered the first major theory of career choice. The Parson's work mentioned earlier (i.e., *Choosing a Vocation*) stressed a careful self-analysis conducted "under guidance" and then put down on paper to determine your personal "traits." The traits could then be matched to occupations using advice from individuals who had "made a careful study of men and vocations of the conditions of success." Also familiarize yourself with the name Edmund Griffith Williamson, the chief spokesperson for the so-called "Minnesota Viewpoint," which expanded upon Parson's model to create a theory of counseling which transcended vocational issues. Choice "a" would be indicative of a psychoanalytic theory of career counseling. **(b)**

512. The trait-factor or matching approach is associated with

    a.   Parsons and Williamson.
    b.   Roe and Brill.
    c.   Holland and Super.
    d.   Tiedman and O'Hara.

The trait-factor model is sometimes classified as a "structural" theory since it emphasizes individual differences or what your exam might call structural differences. Note: Some exams may ask you if the trait-factor model is grounded in "differential psychology" which is the study of individual differences. The answer . . . a resounding "yes" of course. The assumption in this approach is that man is rational. Hence, when the proper information (e.g., from tests, etc.) is available, the individual can make a proper or wise choice of career. C.F. Patterson, from the University of Minnesota, was the other major proponent of this approach and thus, his name could easily be added to choice "a." The theory has been accused of being oversimplified as it subordinated personal choice making and advanced the idea of "a single job for life." In other words, the theory assumes that an individual's traits can be measured so accurately that the choice of an occupation is a one-time process. Moreover, experts began to question the notion that a single "right occupation" existed for each personality profile. Choice "b" mentions Roe and Brill who espoused personality theories of career choice. In choice "c," Holland suggested that a person's personality needs to be congruent with the work environment, while Super emphasized career development rather than career choice. As for choice "d," Tiedeman and O'Hara support a decision-making theory. **(a)**

513. The trait-factor or actuarial approach asserts that

    a.   job selection is a long-term development process.
    b.   relies heavily on testing.
    c.   a counselor can match the correct person with the appropriate job.
    d.   b and c.

Though today's career counselors generally do not practice from a pure trait-factor base, experts insist, nevertheless, that remnants of the trait-factor approach are still evident in some of the modern theories such as those suggested by Crites and Super. **(d)**

514. In 1909 Frank Parsons wrote a landmark book entitled *Choosing A Vocation.* Parsons has been called

a. the Father of Life-style.
b. the Father of Modern Counseling.
c. the Father of Vocational Guidance.
d. the fourth force in counseling.

What's that; you felt you could have answered this one in your sleep? Well don't scold me for being redundant. Instead, why not thank your lucky stars that the repetition could save you a point on the test? The phrase "the fourth force in counseling" referenced in choice "d" has been suggested to describe "multiculturalism." **(c)**

515. Which statement is not true of the trait-factor approach to career counseling?

a. The approach attempts to match the person's traits with the requirements of a job.
b. The approach usually relies on psychometric information.
c. The approach is developmental.
d. The approach is associated with the work of Parsons and Williamson.

Developmental approaches delineate stages or specify vocational choice in terms of a process which can change throughout the life span. Thus, vocational development parallels psychosocial, cognitive, and personality development. Eli Ginzberg, an economist, Sol Ginsburg, a psychiatrist, Sidney Axelrad, a sociologist, and John Herma, a psychologist, are often cited as pioneers in this area, questioning the premise that career choice was a single event. The theories proposed by Super and Tiedeman and O'Hara are also derived from developmental psychology. **(c)**

516. Edmund Griffith Williamson's work (or the so-called Minnesota Viewpoint) purports to be scientific and didactic utilizing test data from instruments like the

a. Rorschach and the TAT.
b. Binet and the Wechsler.
c. BDI and the MMPI.
d. *Minnesota Occupational Rating Scales.*

Suggested memory devices: Minnesota means matching or Minnesota and matching both begin with an "M." Williamson was associated with the University of Minnesota for over 40 years. Remember that you are looking for the best answer. All of the tests listed might be used by a modern-day counselor of the trait-factor persuasion; nevertheless, choice "d" mentions a test specifically aimed at enhancing the actuarial approach to career choice. The Rorschach, TAT, BDI, and MMPI would probably be the favorites of counselors who favor a personality theory of career choice. **(d)**

517. The trait-factor approach fails to take _____ into account.

    a. individual change throughout the life span
    b. relevant psychometric data
    c. personality
    d. job requirements

Choice "b," psychometric data, refers to the use of test results in counseling, a practice which is stressed by trait-factor practitioners. The correct answer (choice "a") has been a major criticism of this model and perhaps accounts for some of the popularity of developmental theories. **(a)**

518. Anne Roe suggested a personality approach to career choice

    a. based on cognitive-behavioral therapy.
    b. based on a model of strict operant conditioning.
    c. based on the premise that a job satisfies an unconscious need.
    d. based on the work of Pavlov.

The American clinical psychologist Anne Roe was one of the first individuals to suggest a theory of career choice based heavily on personality theory. Some exams refer to Roe's work as the "person-environment" theory. The theory is primarily psychoanalytic, though it also draws on Maslow's hierarchy of needs. Roe's major propositions are that needs which are satisfied do not become unconscious motivators; that higher order needs will disappear even if they are rarely satisfied, but low order needs (such as safety) will be the major concern; and that needs which are satisfied after a long delay will become unconscious motivators. Roe emphasized that early child rearing practices influence later career choices since a job is a major source of gratification for an unconscious need. P.S. If you answered "d," salivate and crack open your old career counseling text! You're rusty! **(c)**

519. Roe was the first career specialist to utilize a two-dimensional system of occupational classification utilizing

    a.   unconscious and preconscious.
    b.   fields and levels.
    c.   yin and yang.
    d.   transactional analysis nomenclature.

The eight occupational "fields" include: service, business contact, organizations, technology, outdoor, science, general culture, and arts/entertainment. The six "levels" of occupational skill include: professional and managerial 1, professional and managerial 2, semiprofessional/small business, skilled, semiskilled, and unskilled. **(b)**

520. All of the following are examples of Anne Roe's "fields" except

    a.   service.
    b.   science.
    c.   arts and entertainment.
    d.   unskilled.

See the previous answer. "Unskilled" refers to a "level" of occupational skill and/or responsibility rather than an "occupational field."   **(d)**

521. All of the following are examples of Anne Roe's "levels" except

    a.   outdoor.
    b.   semiskilled.
    c.   semiprofessional/small business.
    d.   professional and managerial.

Review the last two questions and answers unless you chose choice "a." All of the other alternatives describe "levels."   **(a)**

522. Roe spoke of three basic parenting styles: overprotective, avoidant, or acceptant. The result is that the child

    a.   experiences neurosis or psychosis.
    b.   will eventually have a lot of jobs or a lack of employment.
    c.   will develop a personality which gravitates (i.e., moves) toward people or away from people.
    d.   will suffer from depression in the work setting or will be highly motivated to succeed.

Some texts and exams will refer to the avoidant child rearing style as "rejecting" and the acceptant style as "democratic." If the person moves "toward" people, he or she would chose the "fields" of service, business, organization, or general cultural while an individual who moves away from people would gravitate toward outdoor, science, or perhaps technology. Research tends to support the contention that an individual raised in a warm, accepting family where person-to-person interaction was rewarded would tend to seek out careers emphasizing contact with others. A cold "avoiding" family of origin would thus be more likely to produce an individual who would shun person-oriented careers.   **(c)**

523. Roe's theory relies on Abraham Maslow's hierarchy of needs in the sense that in terms of career choice

    a.   lower order needs take precedence over higher order needs.

    b.   self-actualization needs take precedence over lower order needs.

    c.   all needs are given equal consideration.

    d.   the need for self-actualization would overpower a physical need.

The job meets the "most urgent need." **(a)**

524. Some support for Roe's theory comes from

    a.   the BDI.

    b.   the WAIS-R.

    c.   the Rorschach and the TAT.

    d.   the Gestalt Therapy movement.

Suggested memory device: Roe begins with an "r" and so does Rorschach. The TAT is similar in that it is a projective test. **(c)**

525. In terms of genetics Roe's theory would assert that

    a.   genetics play a very minor role in career choice.

    b.   genetics help to determine intelligence and education, and hence this influences one's career choice.

    c.   genetics are important while upbringing is not.

    d.   genetics are important while the unconscious is not.

Time for a Roe Review: career choice is influenced by genetics, parent-child interaction, unconscious motivators, current needs, interests (people/things), education, and intelligence. **(b)**

526. According to Anne Roe who categorized occupations by fields and levels

   a.   the decision to pursue a career is purely a conscious decision.
   b.   using the Strong is the best method of explaining career choice.
   c.   early childhood experiences are irrelevant in terms of career choice.
   d.   the choice of a career helps to satisfy an individual's needs.

Roe determined that choice "a" was incorrect and early childhood experiences are indeed important.   **(d)**

527. A 37-year-old Caucasian male states during a counseling session that he is working as a clerk at Main Street Plumbing. This verbalization depicts the client's

   a.   career.
   b.   life-style.
   c.   job.
   d.   occupation.

Technically, a job refers to a given position while an occupation is broader and refers to groups of positions. Career is the broadest category as it depicts a group of positions within an occupation. Possible memory device to recall the order from most specific to most general: Joc (which sounds like the word Jock).   **(c)**

528. Roe recognized the role of the unconscious mind in terms of career choice. Another theorist who emphasized the unconscious processes in this area of study was

   a.   Krumboltz.
   b.   Parsons.
   c.   Super.
   d.   Bordin.

Choice "a" is decidedly incorrect as Krumboltz worked with a behavioristic model. Bordin, though, felt that career choices could be used to solve unconscious conflicts. Psychoanalytic approaches—used in regard to career choice or other issues—have never been extremely popular with helpers trained in counseling departments since short-term, time efficient modalities are stressed. **(d)**

529. Edwin Bordin felt that difficulties related to job choice

    a.   are indicative of neurotic symptoms.
    b.   are indicative of inappropriate reinforcers in the environment.
    c.   are related to a lack of present moment awareness.
    d.   are the result of irrational cognitions.

This is the kind of exam question you literally could answer correctly via the process of elimination. In the previous question, it was noted that Bordin analyzed career choices using the unconscious mind. Needless to say, this is a psychoanalytic assumption. Hence, choice "b" can be eliminated since "reinforcers" are seen as modifiers in the behaviorist school. Choice "c" also can be eliminated inasmuch as analysis is not a present moment approach. Lastly, "irrational cognitions" are stressed in Rational-Emotive Therapy and some related cognitive schools of intervention. **(a)**

530. Another career theorist who drew upon psychoanalytic doctrines was A.A. Brill. Brill emphasized _____, an ego-defense mechanism.

    a.   subliminal
    b.   sublimation
    c.   repression
    d.   rationalization

Choice "a" is not a defense mechanism. Sublimation occurs when an individual expresses an unacceptable need in a socially acceptable manner. A person, for example, who likes to cut things up might pursue a career as a butcher or perhaps a surgeon. REVIEW THE HELPING RELATIONSHIP SECTION IF YOU DO NOT KNOW THE DEFINITIONS OF THE FOUR ALTERNATIVES. **(b)**

531. A client who becomes a professional football player because he unconsciously likes to hurt people would be utilizing _____ according to Brill's theory of career choice.

    a.   subliminal
    b.   sublimation
    c.   suppression
    d.   introjection

See the explanation to the previous question. **(b)**

532. Today, the most popular approach to career choice reflects

    a.   the work of Anne Roe.
    b.   the work of Donald Super.
    c.   the work of John Holland.
    d.   the work of Jane Loevinger.

Choice "d" is the most outlandish—at least, if you marked any other choice you chose a career theorist. Loevinger is noted for her seven stage transition continuum theory of ego development. John Holland's theory can be best described by his four assumptions. First, in our culture, there are six basic personality types: realistic, investigative, artistic, social, enterprising, or conventional. Second, most work environments correspond to six personality types. Third, people search out an agreeable environment which lets them express their personality type. Fourth, the individual's behavior is determined by an interaction of the personality and the environment. Possible memory device for the six types of personality/environments: "as rice." **(c)**

533. Holland categorized _____ personality orientations which correspond to analogous work environments.

    a.   2
    b.   5
    c.   3
    d.   6

In this theory the counselor attempts to find a job for the client in which the personality/environment interaction is congruent. Holland felt that people try to avoid environments which are disagreeable. A host of studies lends support to his theory of personality types. **(d)**

534. Most experts in the field of career counseling would classify Roe, Brill, and Holland as _____ theorists.

    a.   behavior modification
    b.   ego psychologists
    c.   experiential
    d.   personality

Remember: your exam could use the term "structural theory" in place of the term "personality theory." Don't let it throw you! **(d)**

535. Counselors who support John Holland's approach believe that

    a.   an appropriate job allows one to express his or her personality.
    b.   stereotypes cannot be considered relevant.
    c.   four major personality categories exist.
    d.   sublimation is the major factor in job selection.

Choice "b" is incorrect; Holland did indeed believe in stereotypes, and some critics have thus said his theory is too simplistic and somewhat sexist. Choice "c" would need to read "six major personality categories" to be accurate. **(a)**

536. Holland mentioned six modal orientations: artistic, conventional, enterprising, investigative, realistic, and social. A middle school counselor is most likely

    a.   artistic.
    b.   social.
    c.   enterprising.
    d.   realistic.

Teachers, counselors, speech therapists, and social workers would fit into the social category. Holland said that the person in the "social" category prefers to solve problems using interpersonal skills and feelings. **(b)**

537. Holland's theory would predict that the vice president of the United States would be

    a.   artistic.
    b.   social.
    c.   enterprising.
    d.   realistic.

The "enterprising" person likes to sell to others or perform leadership tasks. He or she tends to value power and status. Other enterprising occupations would include real estate agents, business owners, television producers, and hotel managers. **(c)**

538. A client who wishes to work on an assembly line would fit into Holland's _____ typology.

    a.   artistic
    b.   conventional
    c.   social
    d.   realistic

The "realistic" or "motoric" person likes machines. This individual might become a truck driver, an auto mechanic, or might fancy plumbing. **(d)**

539. Holland's psychological needs theory would say that a research chemist is primarily the _____ type.

    a.   investigative
    b.   social
    c.   enterprising
    c.   artistic

The "investigative" personality type likes to think his or her way through a problem. Occupations congruent with this type include scientists, design engineers, geologists, mathematicians, and philosophers. **(a)**

540. Holland's artistic type seems to value feelings over pure intellect or cognitive ability. Which of the following clients would NOT be best described via the artistic typology?

    a.   A 72-year-old part-time male ballet instructor
    b.   A 29-year-old female fiction writer
    c.   A 33-year-old female drill press operator
    d.   A 41-year-old singer for a heavy metal rock band

Hint: The typist on the NCE or other major exam will probably not be kind enough to type the word "NOT" in uppercase letters, so read the questions carefully. The "artistic" type shuns conformity as well as structure. The emphasis is on self-expression. The drill press operator would be a "realistic" type who likes physical labor and enjoys working with tools. **(c)**

541. Holland did indeed believe in career stereotypes. In other words the person psychologically defines himself or herself via a given job. Thus, a bookkeeper or a clerical worker would primarily fit into the _____ category.

    a.   artistic
    b.   conventional
    c.   realistic
    d.   social

The "conventional" type values conformity, structure, rules, and feels comfortable in a subordinate role. Statisticians, bank clerks, and controllers fit this stereotype. By the way, "conventional" and "conformity" both begin with a "c." Nice memory device, huh? **(b)**

542. In regard to an individual's behavioral style or so-called modal orientation, Holland believed that

    a.   every person has a pure or discrete orientation that fits perfectly into one of the six categories.

    b.   occupational measures like the Strong Vocational are for the most part useless.

    c.   most people are not pure personality types and thus can best be described by a distribution of types such as Realistic, Social, Investigative (RSI).

    d.   a and b.

If you marked "b" try again; the Strong is based on Holland's model. Although each individual has a primary direction or type, the person can be described best using a "profile" over three areas. Graphically, the six types generally are placed on a hexagon such that adjacent or consistent types are next to each other on the geometric figure. Thus RIA would be "consistent" while RAE would be "inconsistent." (See "Graphical Representations" section of this book.) **(c)**

543. Holland believed that

    a.   a given occupation will tend to attract persons with similar personalities.

    b.   a given occupation will tend to attract persons with a very wide range of personality attributes.

    c.   one's personality is, for the most part, unrelated to one's occupational choice.

    d.   b and c.

Like Roe, Holland felt that early childhood development influences adult personality characteristics. **(a)**

544. Holland relied on a personality theory of career choice. Hoppock's theory, based on the work of _____ is also considered a personality approach.

    a.   Donald Super
    b.   Robert Rosenthal
    c.   David Wechsler
    d.   Henry Murray

Henry Murray created the "needs-press" theory and the TAT (along with Christina Morgan) projective test. The occupation is used to meet a person's current need. Rosenthal (choice "b," no relation to me) is famous for his research regarding the "experimenter effect" while David Wechsler (choice "c") is well-known for creating the Wechsler intelligence scales. **(d)**

545. Developmental career theorists view career choice as an ongoing or so-called "longitudinal" process rather than a single decision made at one point in time. The pioneer theorists in this area were

    a.   Super and Roe.
    b.   Hoppock and Holland.
    c.   Ginzberg, Ginsburg, Axelrad, and Herma.
    d.   Brill and Bordin.

In the early 1950s Ginzberg and his associates began to emphasize developmental factors related to occupational choice. Based on a small research sample they concluded that occupational choice takes place over a six to ten year period; the choice is irreversible; and always has the quality of compromise. The theory postulated three stages: fantasy—until age 11, based strongly on impulses; tentative—ages 11 to 17, where interests and abilities are examined; and the realistic period—age 17, where a choice is made by weighing abilities and needs and making a compromise. Exploration was said to lead to crystallization. By 1972, Ginzberg modified his position by stating that the process of choice is open-ended and lifelong. This, of course, refuted the notion of irreversibility. He also replaced "compromise" with the concept of "optimization," meaning that individuals try to make the best of what they have to offer and what is available in the job market. **(c)**

546. Ginzberg and his colleagues now believe in a development model of career choice which asserts that

    a. the process of choosing a career does not end at age 20 or adulthood.
    b. career choice decisions are really made throughout the life span.
    c. career choice is reversible.
    d   all of the above.

See the question and answer to 545. **(d)**

547. Initially, Ginzberg and his associates viewed career choice as irreversible and the result of compromises between wishes and realistic possibilities. This theory identified three stages of career development

    a. informal, formal, and concrete.
    b. fantasy (birth to age 11), tentative (ages 11 to 17), and realistic (age 17 to early 20s).
    c. sensorimotor, formal and concrete.
    d. oral, anal, and phallic.

See the question and answer to 545. **(b)**

548. The most popular developmental career theorist is Donald Super. Super emphasizes

a. id impulses.
b. the critical parent.
c. the self-concept.
d. ego strength.

Super and self-concept both begin with an "s." How convenient! The assumption here is that the individual chooses a career which allows the self-concept to be expressed. **(c)**

549. Super's theory emphasizes _____ life stages.

a. five
b. four
c. three
d. nine

The stages are first, Growth (birth to 14); second, Exploration (15-24); third, Establishment (24-44); fourth, Maintenance (44-64); and fifth, Decline (65+). Suggested memory device: GEE MD. (Note, as far as the two "e's" are concerned, common sense would dictate that exploration would come before establishment.) **(a)**

550. Super's theory includes

a. the life-career rainbow.
b. the life-career stars.
c. the life-career moon.
d. the life-career psychosis.

The person can play a number of potential roles as he or she advances through the five stages mentioned in the previous question; they are parent, homemaker, worker, citizen, leisurite, student, or child. Super called the graphic display of the roles unfolding over the life span, the "career rainbow." The roles are played out in the "theaters" of the home, community, school, and work. **(a)**

551. Research into the phenomenon of career maturity reflects the work of

    a. Crites.
    b. Roe.
    c. Holland.
    d. Schlossberg.

Career maturity might be referred to as "vocational maturity" on your exam. Choice "d" mentions the work of Schlossberg who has focused heavily on adult career development. She suggested five noteworthy factors: behavior in the adult years is primarily determined by social rather than biological factors; behavior can either be a function of one's life stage or his or her age at other times; sex differences are actually more powerful than age or stage differences; adults continually experience transitions which require adaptation and self-assessment; identity, intimacy, and generativity are recurring themes in adulthood.   **(a)**

552. The decision-making theory, which refers to periods of anticipation and implementation/adjustment, was proposed by

    a. Crites.
    b. Holland.
    c. David Tiedman and Robert O'Hara.
    d. Super.

Tiedman and O'Hara suggested that the decision process is best explained by breaking it down into a two part process. In the anticipation stage the individual imagines himself or herself in a given career. In the implementation phase (also sometimes called accommodation or induction) the person engages in reality testing regarding his or her expectations concerning the occupation. ALL DECISION-MAKING THEORIES CONTEND THAT THE INDIVIDUAL HAS THE POWER TO CHOOSE FROM THE VARIOUS CAREER OPTIONS.   **(c)**

553. John Krumboltz postulated a social learning approach to career choice. This model is based mainly on the work of

    a.   Joseph Wolpe.
    b.   Albert Bandura.
    c.   Donald Super.
    d.   Karen Horney.

THE PURPOSE OF THIS QUESTION IS STRAIGHT-FORWARD: YOU MUST KNOW SOMETHING ABOUT THE CONCEPT OF SOCIAL LEARNING THEORY IN ORDER TO DO WELL ON YOUR EXAM! Anita Mitchell, G. Brian Jones, and John Krumboltz utilized the work of Albert Bandura to explain career choice. Bandura emphasized the role of modelling in the acquisition of new behaviors. The theory states that people learn not only from the consequences of their own behavior but also from observing the consequences of others. Learning which takes place by watching others is sometimes called "vicarious learning." Krumboltz felt that interests are the result of "learning," such that changes in interests can be "learned." Thus, actual exposure to a wide range of work settings (i.e., site visits) is highly desirable. Occupational indecisiveness is seen as an indication of an information deficit rather than a lack of career maturity. **(b)**

554. The model Krumboltz suggested is

    a.   a psychoanalytic model of career development.
    b.   a neo-analytic model of career development.
    c.   a Rogerian model of career development.
    d.   a behavioristic model of career development.

Some textbooks and exams may categorize Krumboltz's theory as a decision-making theory. Krumboltz believed that decision making—in terms of career options as well as noncareer options—is a skill which can be learned. Krumboltz acknowledged the role of genetics and the environment but focused on what can be changed via learning. **(d)**

555. A counselor who favors a behavioristic mode of career counseling would most likely

    a.   analyze dreams related to jobs and/or occupations.
    b.   give the client a standardized career test.
    c.   suggest a site visit to a work setting.
    d.   a and b.

Choice "a," come on . . . you didn't really choose it . . . did you? It sounds like something out of a primer on Freudian analysis. Ideally, all individuals should be exposed to as many learning experiences as possible. Another behavioristic strategy known as the "job club" has been suggested by Azrin. The job club operates like a behaviorist group in which members share job leads and discuss and/or role-play specific behaviors (e.g., interviewing skills) necessary for job acquisition. **(c)**

556. The newest model to explain career development is the decision approach. The Gelatt Decision Model refers to information as "the fuel of the decision." The Gelatt Model asserts that information can be organized into three systems

    a.   predictive, value, and decision.
    b.   internal, external, and in between.
    c.   predictive, external, and internal.
    d.   internal, external, and predictive.

Decision-making theory asserts that although occupational choice is an ongoing process, there are times when a key decision must be made. In the Gelatt Model the predictive system is concerned with the probable alternatives, actions, and possibilities. The person's value system is concerned with one's relative preferences regarding the outcomes, while the decision system provides rules and criteria for evaluating the outcome. **(a)**

557. In the Gelatt Model the predictive system deals with

    a.   personal likes, dislikes, and preferences.
    b.   personal rules.
    c.   alternatives and the probability of outcomes.
    d.   the Self Directed Search.

Choice "a" would be the value system while choice "b" refers to the decision system. Prediction focuses on the probability of an outcome. Choice "d," abbreviated SDS, is a self-administered, self-scored interest inventory based on John Holland's theoretical notions. **(c)**

558. Bergland suggested that decision making actually consists of six steps. The first step is _____, while the final step consists of _____.

    a.   generating alternatives; gathering information
    b.   defining the problem; implementation and plan evaluation
    c.   defining the problem; processing information
    d.   making plans and setting goals; processing information

The six steps are: first, the problem is defined; second, alternatives are generated; third, information is gathered; fourth, information is processed; fifth, plans are made and goals selected; and sixth, plans are implemented and evaluated. **(b)**

559. The leading method adults use to find career information in the U.S. is

    a.   to see a state employment counselor.
    b.   to visit a private practice career counselor.
    c.   to undergo counseling with a counselor with NCCC credentials.
    d.   securing information via the newspaper.

According to a report for the National Institute Of Education, newspaper ads ranked first, the U.S. Employment Service was second, while post secondary institutions snared the number three spot. Private employment agencies ranked fifth, while high school counselors and teachers ranked ninth. **(d)**

560. When career counselors speak of the OOH they are referring to

    a. the *Occupational Options Handbook.*
    b. the *Occupational Outlook Handbook.*
    c. the *Dictionary of Occupational Titles.*
    d. the *Optional Occupations Handbook.*

The OOH is published by the U.S. Department of Labor and is used by about nine out of ten high schools since it is so easy to comprehend. The OOH highlights the salient factors of the job, necessary training, earnings, and even advancement opportunities. **(b)**

561. The DOT or *Dictionary of Occupational Titles* lists more than

    a. 10,000 job titles.
    b. 5,000 job titles.
    c. 20,000 job titles.
    d. 50,000 job titles.

This is the largest, most comprehensive source and is used more than any other printed resource in the field. As with the OOH, you can thank the U.S. Department of Labor, who has been publishing the DOT since 1939. **(c)**

562. In the *Dictionary of Occupational Titles* each job is given a _____ digit code.

a. 9
b. 8
c. 6
d. 5

The first three digits designate the occupational category and divisions, whereas the middle three describe tasks in relation to data, people, and things respectively. The final digits help alphabetize the titles. **(a)**

563. The DOT was first published by the Department of Labor in 1939. The first three digits in the current DOT code refer to

a. an occupational group.
b. career options.
c. OOH data.
d. the transfer of skills.

The first digit in the DOT designates one of nine occupational categories: 0/1 Professional, Technical, and Managerial Occupations; 2 Clerical and Sales Occupations; 3 Service Occupations; 4 Agricultural, Fishery, Forestry, and Related Occupations; 5 Processing Occupations; 6 Machine Trade Occupations; 7 Bench Work Occupations; 8 Structural Work Occupations; and 9 Miscellaneous. Thus, in the code for counselor (045.107-010) the first digit (0) is from the Professional, Technical, and Managerial Occupations category. The second digit, for example 04, refers to occupations in life sciences; while the third digit defines the occupational group. In this case, 045 is "Occupations in psychology." The final three digits alphabetize titles designated by the first six digit code groups. Choices "b" and "d" would require information from the middle three digits of the code. **(a)**

564. Which statement regarding the DOT is false?

    a.   The DOT lists over 20,000 job titles.

    b.   The last three digits of the code connote transferable skills.

    c.   The last three digits alphabetize the order of titles.

    d.   The DOT is more comprehensive and more widely used than other career guide books, though the OOH is more readable.

Since the middle three digits connote the transfer of skills choice "b" is false.   **(b)**

565. A counselor who is interested in trends in the job market should consult the

    a.   DOT.

    b.   SOC which relies on DOT codes.

    c.   SIC.

    d.   OOH which relies on DOT codes.

First let's look at choices "b" and "c" which are incorrect in terms of this answer yet excellent resources for the adept career counselor. The SOC (choice "b") is the *Standard Occupational Classification Manual* which codes job clusters via similar worker function. Thus, it is very useful for a counselor who wants to find additional occupations that a worker might already be trained for or could consider with additional training. The SIC (choice "c"), the *Standard Industrial Classification Manual*, classifies businesses in regard to the type of activity they are engaged in (i.e., the type of service or product). "Hopefully, working in industry won't make you sic," is a rather pessimistic, yet useful memory device here! Industry growth is often computed on SIC codes. The OOH as its name implies focuses on "outlook" and useful trends or predictions (hence the word "Outlook" in the title) in the labor market. The OOH is revised every two years.   **(d)**

566. A counselor wants to suggest an easy-to-read source for a client in search of career information. The counselor should recommend the

    a.   DOT.
    b.   SOC.
    c.   SIC.
    d.   OOH.

Most counselors consider the OOH the easiest guide to read and understand. It has been said that statistically speaking high schools are more apt to rely on the OOH than the DOT, face-to-face career counseling, or career days. **(d)**

567. A counselor with a master's degree who is working for minimum wage at a fast-food restaurant due to a lack of jobs in the field is a victim of

    a.   unemployment.
    b.   underemployment.
    c.   the phi phenomenon.
    d.   the risky shift phenomenon.

Underemployment occurs when a worker is engaged in a position which is below his or her skill level. This phenomenon can occur when an abundance of educated people flood a labor market that does not have enough jobs which require a high level of training. Hence, as more people go to college the rate of underemployment is expected to increase. **(b)**

568. The OOH has an index of DOT codes and describes 225 occupations. It also provides addresses for employment offices. One trend suggested in the OOH is that

    a.   less women will be employed.
    b.   less minorities will be employed.
    c.   more women and minorities will be employed.
    d.   many new jobs will spring up in the New York, New Jersey area.

The current 1990-1991 edition of the OOH, which contains an overview of the employment situation through the year 2000, suggests that more jobs will be available in the western states as individuals move away from the Northeast . . . and needless to say an increase in number of women (nearly 50% of all workers by the year 2000) and minorities filling these positions. **A WORD TO THE WISE:** ALTHOUGH THIS IS THE TYPE OF QUESTION YOU COULD ENCOUNTER, DON'T COUNT ON THIS ANSWER SINCE LABOR PATTERNS ARE HARDLY STATIC. CONSULT THE CURRENT EDITION OF THE OOH BEFORE SITTING FOR YOUR EXAM. **(c)**

569. The *Guide for Occupational Exploration* (GOE) was published by the U.S. Department of Labor. The guide lists groups of jobs listed in

    a.   12 interest areas.
    b.   6 interest areas.
    c.   3 interest areas.
    d.   175 interest areas.

Interest areas include artistic, scientific, plants and animals, protective, mechanical, industrial, business detail, selling, accommodating (i.e., services), humanitarian, leading-influencing, and physical-performing. The GOE helps job seekers "explore" jobs that are slanted toward a given "interest area." **(a)**

570. Self-efficacy theory is based on the work of

    a.   the OOH and the DOT.
    b.   Holland.
    c.   the SIC and the SOC.
    d.   Albert Bandura.

Bandura proposed that one's belief or expectation of being successful in an occupation causes the individual to gravitate toward that particular occupation. Bandura felt that "chance factors," such as accidentally being exposed to certain situations, influence career development. **(d)**

571. SIGI, Choices, and Discover are

    a.   Computer Assisted Career Guidance Systems (CACG).

    b.   paper and pencil career tests.

    c.   career theories proposed in the 1940s.

    d.   computer systems which are slower to use than traditional texts such as the DOT or the OOH.

Choice "d" is obviously incorrect since computer programs often speed up information retrieval.   **(a)**

572. A client who likes her flower arranging job begins doing flower arranging in her spare time on weekends and after work. This phenomenon is best described as

    a.   the contrast effect.

    b.   sublimation.

    c.   the compensatory effect.

    d.   spillover.

Let me introduce you to three key terms in the field of career counseling: the contrast effect (choice "a"), the compensatory effect (choice "c"), and spillover (choice "d"). In psychology, contrast refers to a heightened sense of awareness regarding the difference between the successive juxtaposition of two stimuli. The word "juxtaposition" simply means to put side by side. Hence, in career placement settings the term has been used to suggest that an interviewer's impression of an interviewee is often affected by previous interviewees. Thus, a typical applicant would look more impressive if she is interviewed after a string of applicants who are ill qualified for the job. Unfortunately, the converse is also true. An average applicant whose interview comes after several highly qualified (or overqualified) applicants will not be judged as favorably by the person who is doing the interviewing. The "compensatory effect" suggests that a worker compensates or makes up for things he or she can't do on the job. Thus, a librarian who must be quiet from 8 to 5 may go out after work and get wild, crazy, and most importantly LOUD. In essence, the compensatory effect occurs when you engage in on the job. "Spillover" on the other hand is like a glass of water spilling over on to the table. Here, the individual's work spills over, if you will, into his or her time off the job. When spillover takes place the person engages in activities similar to work during periods of leisure. The aforementioned florist or an engineer who is building a satellite in his or her basement would be a victim of spillover. **(d)**

573. A male client who hates his job is trying desperately to be the perfect father, husband, and family man. This phenomenon is best described as

    a.   the recency effect.
    b.   the leniency/strictness bias.
    c.   the compensatory effect.
    d.   spillover.

In some instances, textbooks and exams will refer to the compensatory effect in a psychodynamic fashion, which infers that an individual might tend to compensate for a poor job satisfaction by excelling in his or her activities outside of work. My advice: although the definition given in the previous question is the most common, you should read questions of this ilk very carefully to ascertain the context in which the term "compensatory effect" is being used. Choices "a" and "b" are terms utilized to describe subjective biases of individuals who rate employee performance. The "recency effect" occurs when a rater's judgement of an employee reflects primarily his or her most recent performance. This is, of course, undesirable inasmuch as the employee's performance over the entire rating period should be duly noted. The term was borrowed from memory experiments in psychology demonstrating that numbers toward the end of a list are more likely to be recalled than those in the middle. The "leniency/strictness bias" occurs when a rater tends to give employees very high/lenient or very low/strict ratings while avoiding the middle or so-called average range. Raters who do the opposite (i.e., rate almost everybody in the average range) are said to display a "central tendency bias." **(c)**

574. The National Vocational Guidance Association was founded in 1913. It was fused with other organizations in 1952 to become

    a.   the American Psychological Association.
    b.   AACD.
    c.   APGA.
    d.   NASW.

Did you choose alternative "b"? If so, give yourself a pat on the back for an A- answer. You see, AACD was actually the American Personnel and Guidance Association (APGA) until 1983, making choice "c" an even better response . . . say an A+. In 1983 APGA changed its name to AACD (American Association for Counseling and Development) which was changed in 1992 to ACA (American Counseling Association). **(c)**

575. Life-style includes

    a.   work.
    b.   leisure.
    c.   style of living.
    d.   all of the above.

Life-style is a broad term which describes the overall balance of work, leisure, family, and social activities. Some exams will use the term "avocational" in place of the term "leisure." **(d)**

576. The *Strong-Campbell Interest Inventory* (SCII) is based on John Holland's theory. The test assumes that a person who is interested in a given subject will experience

a. satisfaction in a job with workers who have different interests.
b. satisfaction in a job in which those working in the occupation have similar interests.
c. generalized anxiety if he or she is placed in a job where people have similar interests.
d. the best results if he or she finishes the inventory in one hour or less.

The interest inventory first appeared on the scene in 1927 when E.K. Strong, Jr. developed the *Strong Vocational Interest Blank* (SVIB) for men. The test indicated how an examinee's likes and dislikes were similar to the likes and dislikes of workers in various occupations. Later, in 1933, women's occupations were examined in the same manner using the SVIB for women. Strong died in 1963, and in 1974 the inventory was expanded by David P. Campbell. The inventory has been the subject of over 1700 papers and studies. Recent efforts have focused on eliminating sex bias from the instrument. The test, which consists of 325 items, is based on John Holland's typology (discussed earlier), and is untimed (in other words choice "d" is incorrect). The examinee responds to questions using a forced choice format of "like," "indifferent," or "unlike" to each item. (Each occupational scale for the inventory was created by examining 200 to 300 happily employed men and women in an occupation.) It takes most adults about 30 minutes to finish the inventory. The inventory is suited to high school, college and adult populations and must be computer scored. KEEP IN MIND THAT THE SCII MEASURES INTERESTS, NOT ABILITIES. **(b)**

577. The *Self-Directed Search* (SDS) is

a. based on the work of Holland.
b. self-administered.
c. self-scored and self-interpreted.
d. all of the above.

John Holland introduced the SDS in 1970 to help those who did not have access (or could not afford) professional career counseling. The test takes about 40 minutes and is suitable for ages 15 and older. Holland warned that the test is NOT SUITABLE FOR GROSSLY DISTURBED, UNEDUCATED, OR ILLITERATE PERSONS, ALTHOUGH AN EASY FORM (KNOWN AS FORM "E") IS AVAILABLE FOR THOSE WITH LIMITED READING SKILLS OR THOSE WHO LACK A HIGH SCHOOL EDUCATION. FORM "E" IS SHORTER THAN THE REGULAR SDS AND USES NO WORDS BEYOND THE FOURTH GRADE LEVEL. THE SDS IS SPECIFICALLY NOT RECOMMENDED FOR THOSE WHO HAVE A GREAT DEAL OF DIFFICULTY MAKING DECISIONS. **(d)**

578. At a case staffing one career counselor says to another, "The client's disability suggests she can only physically handle sedentary work." This technically implies

    a.   the client will not need to lift over 10 pounds.
    b.   the client will not need to lift over 100 pounds.
    c.   the client will be standing a lot.
    d.   the client could walk or stand up to six hours daily.

    Sedentary: maximum lifting is 10 pounds. **Light work:** maximum lifting is up to 20 pounds. **Medium work:** maximum lifting is 50 pounds. **Heavy work:** maximum lifting is up to 100 pounds. **Very heavy work:** maximum lifts exceed 100 pounds. The stipulation in choice "d" applies to the "light work" category. **(a)**

579. The notion of the hidden job market would suggest that

    a.   most jobs will appear on college bulletin boards.
    b.   most jobs will appear in supermarket tabloids.
    c.   most jobs will appear in daily newspaper classified ads.
    d.   most jobs are not advertised.

    Perhaps you're shocked but experts say it is true! A high percentage of jobs are NOT ADVERTISED! **(d)**

580. An SDS score will reveal

    a.   career aptitude.
    b.   the personality via projective measures.
    c.   the individual's three highest scores based on Holland's personality types.
    d.   spillover personality tendencies.

The SDS provides the user with a three-letter code that indicates the three personality types the examinee most resembles. An Occupational Finder booklet then describes over 1,300 occupations in order to ascertain which occupations best match the personality type. As of late, the SDS sports a computer version (Form "R") as well as a version for those who speak Spanish. **(c)**

581. As you walk into a professional seminar on career counseling you note that the instructor is drawing a hexagon on the blackboard. The instructor is most likely discussing

    a.   David Tiedman.
    b.   John Holland.
    c.   Anne Roe.
    d.   John Crites.

Was this just an easy question, or could it be that now you really know this material? Come on, how about giving yourself credit for all your knowledge! (See "Graphical Representations" section of this book for a pictorial display of the hexagon.) **(b)**

582. The *Strong* is considered an interest inventory. So is

    a.   the *Kuder*, created by G.F. Kuder.
    b.   the *Wechsler*.
    c.   the *Peabody Picture Vocabulary Test.*
    d.   the *MMPI-2*.

The original version of the *Kuder* appeared during the 1930s. Today the *Kuder Occupational Interest Survey* (KOIS) has been called a "triad inventory" as the respondent chooses which of three activities he or she prefers. A form "DD" of the *Kuder* allows the examinee to be compared to college major groups. The PPVT noted in choice "c" is an example of an IQ test which would be suitable for a child with linguistic impairments or who is deaf. **(a)**

583. The United States Employment Service created the

       a.   ASVAB.
       b.   DAT.
       c.   GATB.
       d.   SCII.

Choice "a" is short for the *Armed Services Vocational Aptitude Battery*, often administered at recruiting stations or to high school seniors interested in the military. The reliability and validity of this measure have recently come under fire despite the fact that over one million ASVAB's are given yearly. Choice "b" is the *Differential Aptitude Test* first published in 1947 and revised three times since. This measure helps students decide whether a student should attend college, and if so, where he or she might excel the most. It is suitable for students in grades 8 through 12 and takes about three hours to complete. The GATB or *General Aptitude Test Battery* is the test utilized by state employment security offices, Veterans Administration hospitals, and related government agencies. The battery measures 12 job-related aptitudes including intelligence/general learning ability, verbal aptitude, numerical aptitude, spatial aptitude, clerical perception, form perception, motor coordination, manual dexterity, and finger dexterity. **(c)**

584. Occupational aptitude tests such as the DAT, the ASVAB, and the GATB grew out of the

a. cognitive therapy movement.
b. humanistic psychology movement.
c. individual psychology movement.
d. trait-factor movement related to career counseling.

The primary purpose of any aptitude test is to predict future performance, though career placement should never rest solely on a single source of data such as the aforementioned tests. **(d)**

585. A client says she has always stayed home and raised her children. Now the children are grown and she is seeking employment. She is best described

    a.   as a displaced homemaker.
    b.   as a victim of underemployment.
    c.   by a DSM diagnosis.
    d.   as a victim of the hidden job market.

This is the definition of a displaced homemaker who also could be divorced or widowed. **(a)**

586. According to the concept of wage discrimination

    a.   women make more than men for doing the same job.
    b.   women make less than men for doing the same job.
    c.   men and women make identical salaries thanks to legislation.
    d.   women who are seen as attractive still make 6% more than men for doing the same job.

Although in a fair world choice "c" would be true, choice "b" still depicts reality. **(b)**

587. According to the concept of occupational sex segregation

    a.   most women hold high paying executive jobs.

    b.   most women hold low paying jobs with low status.

    c.   most women hold jobs which require a college degree.

    d.   men still make considerably less than women.

The concept of "occupational sex segregation" suggests that female occupations generally pay less and lack the status of male occupations. **(b)**

588. A counselor advises a female to steer clear of police work as he feels this is a male occupation. This suggests

    a.   positive transference

    b.   negative transference

    c.   counselor bias based on gender bias

    d.   sex wage discrimination

But wait . . . don't jump to conclusions here. It's not just male counselors who are the culprit here! Not by a long shot. Research indicates that female counselors urge females to seek out traditionally feminine occupations, and worse yet some tests in the area of career counseling are guilty of gender bias! **(c)**

589. Most research would suggest that a woman who has the same intelligence, skills, and potential as a man will often

    a.   make the same job choice as a man.

    b.   choose a supervisory position more often than a man.

    c.   have lower career aspirations than a man.

    d.   choose a career well above her ability level.

Fitzgerald and Crites discovered that even when girls manifest higher career maturity than boys, their aspirations are lower. **(c)**

590. A displaced homemaker might have grown children or

    a.   be widowed.
    b.   be divorced.
    c.   a and b.
    d.   have extensive supervisory experience.

See question 585. The high divorce rate and the declining birthrate have increased the number of women seeking employment in recent years. **(c)**

591. Mid-life career change

    a.   is not that unusual.
    b.   is often discussed, but in reality is very rare.
    c.   would be extremely rare after the death of a spouse.
    d.   would be extremely rare after all the children leave home.

This generally takes place between ages 35 and 45 and additional training is often needed. Precipitating factors for the change include divorce, empty nest syndrome, and perhaps most important, job dissatisfaction. Choices "c" and "d" are typical motivators and thus constitute incorrect answer choices. **(a)**

592. The term reentry woman would best describe a

    a.   a 32-year-old female police officer promoted to sergeant.
    b.   a 22-year-old female teacher who becomes a school counselor.
    c.   a 59-year-old female administrative assistant who switched positions for 2 years and will return to her job.
    d.   a 29-year-old female who was babysitting in her home but is currently working at a fast-food restaurant.

The term "reentry women" refers to women who go from working within the home to outside the home. Counselors need to be aware of the fact that reentry women typically experience an extremely high degree of career indecision. MY PREDICTION: IN THE COMING YEARS EXPECT TO SEE MORE AND MORE QUESTIONS ON THE CAREER AREA OF COMPREHENSIVE AND LICENSING EXAMS RELATED TO WOMEN, OLDER ADULTS, MINORITY GROUPS, AND DISABLED PERSONS. **(d)**

593. A counselor doing multicultural career counseling should be aware

    a.   of his or her own ethnocentric biases.

    b.   that Asian Americans rarely choose scientific careers.

    c.   that Black males will often choose enterprising jobs in terms of Holland's typology.

    d.   that career inventories have eliminated cultural biases.

Actually, Asian Americans (see choice "b") are the only minority that has a large number of individuals in the scientific community. Black males are highly represented in realistic rather than enterprising occupations (see choice "c"). Thus the counselor has to be aware of his or her own stereotypical attitudes (e.g., Black women make good housekeepers or Hispanic women are best off working in secretarial jobs). **(a)**

594. In terms of the labor market

    a.   music is very effective in terms of increasing the worker's output.

    b.   the number of employees employers want to hire goes down as salary goes up.

    c.   the number of employees willing to work for you goes up as the salary increases.

    d.   b and c.

Choice "a" is false. Music is generally ineffective in terms of significantly boosting a worker's level of production. The lack of effectiveness is thought to be the result of "habituation." Habituation—which will be referred to as "adaptation" on some exams—indicates a decrease in response to a constant stimulus or a stimulus that is repeated too frequently. Thus, as the music becomes a familiar stimulus, the employees will not really notice it, and its positive effects are minimal. Career counselors often refer to the phenomenon described in choices "b" and "c" as the "supply and demand curve," a concept borrowed from economics. **(d)**

595. SIGI Plus is

  a.   a Black male teacher who makes less than an Asian teacher.
  b.   a single female who holds down two part-time jobs.
  c.   a computer career program known as the System of Interactive Guidance and Information.
  d.   a computerized projective test for career counseling.

SIGI, or the system of Interactive Guidance and Information, created by the Educational Testing Service, is intended for college students. DISCOVER (named after its inventor, the DISCOVER Foundation in Maryland) and CHOICES are two other well-known computerized career development programs. **(c)**

596. A career counselor who is helping a client design a resume

  a.   should downplay the value of the cover letter.
  b.   should emphasize that a lengthy resume is invariably more effective.
  c.   should emphasize the importance of listing height and weight data.
  d.   should emphasize the importance of a cover letter.

Choices "a," "b," and "c" all would be considered counterproductive. The resume should always be accompanied by a cover letter. Many personnel workers will not read a resume which is received without a cover letter. The letter should be brief (i.e., generally about three short paragraphs) and ideally the paper and type should match the resume and be of excellent quality. **(d)**

597. Most experts would agree that a resume

    a.   is like an art project and must look good.

    b.   is not an art project and looks have little if anything to do with effectiveness.

    c.   need not utilize bold headings as personnel officers often spend an extensive amount of time reading them.

    d.   contrary to popular opinion, can sport typos and spelling errors yet still have a powerful impact on future employers.

Just in case good old common sense failed you here your advice to clients preparing a resume should be make it look good, use bold headings or fonts which catch the eye whenever possible, and avoid typos and spelling errors because they can greatly reduce the impact of a resume even if everything else is up to snuff. And if you chose alternative "d," let's at least keep it a secret from your former English teachers! **(a)**

598. The concept of job clubs as promoted by Azrin et al.

    a.   is very behavioristic.

    b.   is indicative of a client-centered approach.

    c.   is psychodynamic.

    d.   is appropriate, but not with disabled populations.

Choice "b" is roughly the opposite of the so-called "selective placement" philosophy. In the client-centered approach to career counseling the counselor lets the client find his or her own leads and job contacts. A counselor who believes in the "selective placement" philosophy may give the client job leads and may take an active stance in terms of working with the client. The selective approach is preferable with clients who lack the concrete skills necessary to land a job. The job finding club is an example of a behavioristic group strategy in that the clients share job leads and work on actual skills (e.g., interviewing) which are necessary in order to secure work. Job clubs are highly recommended for the disabled. **(a)**

599. Schlossberg's theory refers to adult changes as

    a.   concrete operations.
    b.   formal operations.
    c.   SIGI.
    d.   transitions.

Choice "c" is a computer system designed by Katz which helps college students clarify values to enhance the process of career choice. **(d)**

600. All of the following are difficulties with career testing except

    a.   stereotyping.
    b.   the tests all take at least 3 hours to administer.
    c.   the counselor may rely too heavily on test results.
    d.   many tests are biased in favor of White middle-class clients.

With the exception of the DAT which is quite lengthy and may take 3 hours to complete, most of the other tests utilized take an hour or less. **(b)**

CHAPTER 9

APPRAISAL

601. Appraisal can be defined as

    a.   the process of assessing or estimating attributes.
    b.   testing which is always performed in a group setting.
    c.   testing which is always performed on a single individual.
    d.   a pencil and paper measurement of assessing attributes.

Appraisal is a broad term which includes more than merely "testing clients." Appraisal could include a survey, observations, or even clinical interviews. Choices "b," "c," and "d" are thus too limited. A test is simply an instrument which measures a given sample of behavior. **(a)**

602. A test can be defined as a systematic method of measuring a sample of behavior. Test format refers to the manner in which test items are presented. The format of an essay test is considered a(n) _____ format.

    a.   subjective
    b.   objective
    c.   very precise
    d.   concise

A "subjective" paradigm relies mainly on the scorer's opinion. If the rater knows the test taker's attributes, the rater's "personal bias" can significantly impact upon the rating. For example, an attractive examinee or an individual of the same race might be given a higher rating. (This is the so-called "halo effect.") In job settings, peers generally rate their colleagues higher than do their supervisors. In an "objective" test (choice "b") the rater's judgment plays little or no part in the scoring process.   **(a)**

603. The NCE (National Counselor Exam) is a(n) _____ test as the scoring procedure is specific.

        a.   subjective
        b.   objective
        c.   projective
        d.   subtest

Since the NCE uses an a,b,c,d alternative format the rater's "subjective" feelings and thoughts would not be an issue.   **(b)**

604. A short answer test is a(n) _____ test.

        a.   objective
        b.   culture free
        c.   forced choice
        d.   free choice.

Some exams will call this a "free response" format. In any case, the salient point is that the person taking the test can respond in any manner he or she chooses. Although free choice response patterns can yield more information, they often take more time to score and increase subjectivity (i.e., there is more than one correct answer).   **(d)**

605. The NCE is a(n) _____ test.

    a.   free choice
    b.   forced choice
    c.   projective
    d.   intelligence test

"Forced choice" items are sometimes known as "recognition items." This book is composed of forced choice/recognition items. On some tests this format is used to control for the "social desirability phenomenon" which asserts that the person puts the answer he or she feels is socially acceptable (i.e., the test provides alternatives that are all equal in terms of social desirability). The MMPI or *Minnesota Multiphasic Personality Inventory*, for example, uses forced choices to create a "lie scale" composed of human frailties we all possess. This scale, therefore, ferrets out those individuals who tried to make themselves look good (i.e., the way they believe they "should" be). **(b)**

606. The _____ index indicates the percentage of individuals who answered each item correctly.

    a.   difficulty
    b.   critical
    c.   intelligence
    d.   personal

The higher the number of people who answer a question correctly, the easier the item is—and vice versa. A .5 difficulty index would suggest that 50% of those tested answered the question correctly, while 50% did not. Most theorists agree that a "good measure" provides a wide range of items that even a poor performer will answer correctly. **(a)**

607. Short answer tests and projective measures utilize free response items. The NCE uses forced choice or so-called _____ items.

- a. vague
- b. subjective
- c. recognition
- d. numerical

See the answer to 606. Recognition items give the examinee two or more alternatives. **(c)**

608. A true/false test has _____ recognition items.

- a. similar
- b. free choice
- c. dichotomous
- d. no

"Dichotomy" simply means that you are presented with two opposing choices. This explains why choice "a" is definitely incorrect. When a test gives the person taking the exam three or more forced choices (e.g., the NCE, the EPPP, or this book) then psychometricians call it a "multipoint item." Choice "b" describes a situation in which the examinee can respond in any way he or she chooses. **(c)**

609. A test format could be normative or ipsative. In the normative format

- a. each item depends on the item before it.
- b. each item depends on the item after it.
- c. the client must possess an IQ within the normal range.
- d. each item is independent of all other items.

Ipsative measures compare traits within the same individual. The *Kuder Vocational* measure is one such example. The ipsative test allows the person being tested to compare items. **(d)**

610. A client who takes a normative test

    a. cannot legitimately be compared to others who have taken the test.

    b. can legitimately be compared to others who have taken the test.

    c. could not have taken an IQ test.

    d. could not have taken a personality test.

First, forget about choice "a" . . . it's ipsative. Technically, a normative interpretation is one in which the individual's score is evaluated by comparing it to others who took the same test. A percentile rank is an excellent example. Say your client scores an 82 on a nationally normed test and this score corresponds to the percentile rank of 60. This tells you that 60% of the individuals who took the test scored 82 or less. If it's still a bit fuzzy don't sweat it! There's more where this one came from in the next section! **(b)**

611. In an ipsative measure the person taking the test must compare items to one another. The result is that

    a. an ipsative measure cannot be utilized for career guidance.

    b. you cannot legitimately compare two or more people who have taken an ipsative test.

    c. an ipsative measure is never valid.

    d. an ipsative measure is never reliable.

Since the ipsative measure does NOT REVEAL ABSOLUTE STRENGTHS, comparing one person's score to another is relatively meaningless. The person is measured in response to his or her own standard of behavior. The ipsative points out highs and lows between a single individual. Hence, when a colleague tells you that Mr. Johnson's anxiety is improving, she has given you an "ipsative" description. This description, however, would not lend itself to comparing Mr. Johnson's anxiety to Mrs. McBee's. **(b)**

612. Tests are often classified as speed tests versus power tests. A timed typing test used to hire secretaries would be

    a.   a power test.
    b.   neither a speed test nor a power test.
    c.   a speed test.
    d.   a fine example of an ipsative measure.

In terms of difficulty, a speed test is really intended to be very easy. The difficulty is induced by time limitations, not the difficulty of the tasks or the questions themselves. (Try giving your secretary a timed typing test and give him or her three hours to complete it and you'll see what I mean.) A GOOD TIMED/SPEED TEST IS PURPOSELY SET UP SO THAT NOBODY FINISHES IT. A "power test" (see choice "a") is designed to evaluate the level of mastery without a time limit. **(c)**

613. A counseling test consists of 300 forced response items. The person taking the test can take as long as he or she wants to answer the questions.

    a.   This is most likely a projective measure.
    b.   This is most likely a speed test.
    c.   This is most likely a power test.
    d.   This is most likely an invalid measure.

Like the speed test, it will ideally be designed so that nobody receives a perfect score. Choice "a," projective measure, stands incorrect since the projective tests rely on a "free response" format. **(c)**

614. An achievement test measures maximum performance while a personality test or interest inventory measures

    a.   typical performance.
    b.   minimum performance.
    c.   unconscious traits.
    d.   self-esteem by always relying on a Q-Sort design.

Choice "d," the Q-Sort, involves a procedure in which an individual is given cards with statements and asked to place them in piles of "most like me" to "least like me." Then the subject compiles them to create the "ideal self." The ideal self can then be compared to his or her current self-perception in order to assess self-esteem. **(a)**

615. In a spiral test

    a.   the items get progressively easier.
    b.   the difficulty of the items remains constant.
    c.   the client must answer each question in a specified period of time.
    d.   the items get progressively more difficult.

Just remember that a spiral staircase seems to get more difficult to climb as you walk up higher. **(d)**

616. In a cyclical test

    a.   the items get progressively easier.
    b.   the difficulty of the items remains constant.
    c.   you have several sections which are spiral in nature.
    d.   the client must answer each question in a specified period of time.

In each section the questions would go from easy ones to those which are more difficult. **(c)**

617. A test battery is considered

    a.   a horizontal test.
    b.   a vertical test.
    c.   a valid test.
    d.   a reliable test.

Say, this can get confusing. Remember that in the section on group processes I talked about vertical and horizontal interventions. In testing, a vertical test would have versions for various age brackets or levels of education (e.g., a math achievement test for pre-schoolers and a version for middle-school children). A horizontal test measures various factors (e.g., math and science) during the same testing procedure. **(a)**

618. In a counseling research study two groups of subjects took a test with the same name. However, when they talked with each other they discovered that the questions were different. The researcher assured both groups that they were given the same test. How is this possible?

    a.   The researcher is not telling the truth. The groups could not possibly have taken the same test.
    b.   The test was horizontal.
    c.   The test was not a power test.
    d.   The researcher gave parallel forms of the same test.

When a test has two versions or forms that are interchangeable they are termed "parallel forms" or "equivalent forms" of the same test. From a statistical standpoint each form must have the same mean, standard error, and other statistical components. **(d)**

619. The most critical factors in test selection are

    b.   horizontal versus vertical.
    c.   validity and reliability.
    d.   spiral versus cyclical format.

Validity refers to whether the test measures what it says it measures while reliability tells how consistent a test measures an attribute. **(c)**

620. Which is more important, validity or reliability?

    a. Reliability
    b. They are equally important.
    c. Validity
    d. It depends on the test in question.

EXPERTS NEARLY ALWAYS CONSIDER VALIDITY THE NUMBER ONE FACTOR IN THE CONSTRUCTION OF A TEST. A TEST MUST MEASURE WHAT IT PURPORTS TO MEASURE. Reliability, choice "a," is the second most important concern. A bathroom scale, for example, must measure body weight if it is a valid instrument. In order to be reliable, it will need to give repeated readings which are nearly identical for the same person if the person keeps stepping on and off the scale.   **(c)**

621. In the field of testing, validity refers to

    a. whether the test really measures what it purports to measure.
    b. whether the same test gives consistent measurement.
    c. the degree of cultural bias in a test.
    d. the fact that numerous tests measure the same traits.

TO BE VALID THE TEST MUST MEASURE WHAT YOU WANT IT TO MEASURE! Incidentally, a test which is valid for one population is not necessarily valid for another group. THERE ARE FOUR BASIC TYPES OF VALIDITY YOU SHOULD FAMILIARIZE YOURSELF WITH FOR YOUR EXAM. First, content validity or what is sometimes called rational or logical validity. Does the test examine or sample the behavior under scrutiny? An IQ test, for example, that did not sample the entire range of intelligence (say the test just sampled memory and not vocabulary, math, etc.) would have poor content validity. In this case an idiot savant might truly score higher than a well-rounded individual with genius level mentality. Second, construct validity which refers to a test's ability to measure a theoretical construct like intelligence, self-esteem, artistic talent, mechanical ability, or managerial potential. Third, concurrent validity which deals with how well the test compares to other instruments that are intended for the same purpose. Fourth, predictive validity, also known as empirical validity, which reflects the test's ability to predict future behavior according to established criteria. On some exams, concurrent validity and predictive validity are often lumped under the umbrella of "criterion validity," since concurrent validity and predictive validity are actually different types of criterion-related validity. **(a)**

622. A counselor peruses a testing catalog in search of a test which will repeatedly give consistent results. The counselor

    a.   is interested in reliability.
    b.   is interested in validity.
    c.   is looking for information which is not available.
    d.   is magnifying an unimportant issue.

BEWARE: A TEST CAN INDEED BE RELIABLE YET NOT VALID. A highly reliable test could conceivably prove invalid. A bathroom scale that invariably reads 109 lb. when you weigh 143 lb. would hardly be providing you with a valid assessment of your true weight. The score, nevertheless, is consistent (reliable). Thus, a test can have a high reliability coeffecient but still have a low validity coefficient. Reliability places a ceiling on validity, but validity does not set the limits on reliability. **(a)**

623. Which measure would yield the highest level of reliability?

    a.   A TAT
    b.   The WAIS-R
    c.   The MMPI-2
    d.   A bathroom scale

In the real world physical measurements are more reliable than psychological ones. **(d)**

624. Construct validity refers to the extent that a test measures an abstract trait or psychological notion. An example would be

    a.   height.
    b.   weight.
    c.   ego strength.
    d.   the ability to name all men who have served as U.S. presidents.

Any trait you cannot "directly" measure or observe can be considered a construct. **(c)**

625. Face validity refers to the extent that a test

    a.   looks or appears to measure the intended attribute.
    b.   measures a theoretical construct.
    c.   appears to be constructed in an artistic fashion.
    d.   can be compared to job performance.

Okay, so I lied . . . well, kind of lied on the answer to question 621 when I told you there were four basic types of validity. You see, most experts technically no longer list "face validity" as a fifth type of validity. Face validity—like a person's face—merely tells you whether the test looks like it measures the intended trait. Does your therapist look like a therapist? Does the Wechsler appear to be an IQ test? The obvious answer is "In most cases who cares; it's not that important"! And if a therapist looks like a good therapist, does that necessarily mean he is an adept therapist? Of course not. And the same is true of testing. Face validity is not required test information according to the 1974 committee that drafted Standards for Educational and Psychological Tests. **(a)**

626. A job test which predicted future performance on a job very well would

a.   have high criterion/predictive validity.
b.   have excellent face validity.
c.   have excellent construct validity.
d.   not have incremental validity or synthetic validity.

Here you are concerned that the test will measure an independent or external, outside "criterion," in this case the "future prediction" of the job performance. **(Note:** Choice "a" would be incorrect on a question such as this if the question specified current job performance. If this were the case then technically only the term "criterion" would apply.) Choice "d" introduces you to the terms "incremental validity" and "synthetic validity." Although incremental validity and synthetic validity are not considered two of the four or five major types of validity, don't be too surprised if they pop up on an exam question. The term incremental validity has been used to describe a number of testing phenomena. First and foremost, incremental validity has been used to describe the process by which a test is refined and becomes more valid as contradictory items are dropped. Incremental validity also refers to a test's ability to improve predictions when compared to existing measures that purport to facilitate selection in business or educational settings. When a test has incremental validity, it provides you with additional valid information that was not attainable via other procedures. Synthetic validity is derived from the word "synthesized." Synthetic validity was popularized by industrial psychologists who felt the procedure had merit, especially when utilized for smaller firms who did not hire a large number of workers. In synthetic validity, the helper or researcher looks for tests that have been shown to predict each job element or component (e.g., typing, filing, etc.). Tests that predict each component (criterion) can then be combined to improve the selection process.   **(a)**

627. A new IQ test which yielded results nearly identical to other standardized measures would be said to have

a. good concurrent validity.
b. good face validity.
c. superb internal consistency.
d. all of the above.

Criterion validity could be "concurrent" or "predictive." Concurrent validity answers the question of how well your test stacks up against a well-established test that measures the same behavior, construct, or trait. Evidence for reliability and validity is expressed via correlation coefficients. Suffice to say that the closer they are to 1.00 the better. You also should be familiar with the terms "convergent" and "discriminant" validity. These terms relate to both criterion validity and construct validity. The relationship or correlation of a test to an independent measure or trait is known as convergent validity. Convergent validity is actually a method used to assess a test's construct/criterion validity by correlating test scores with an outside source. Say, for example, that a measure purports to measure phobic responses. A client, who has a snake phobia, is then exposed to a snake and experiences extreme panic. If the client scores higher on the test than he would in a relaxed state, then this would display convergent validity. The test also should show discriminant validity. This means the test will NOT REFLECT unrelated variables. Hence, if phobias are unrelated to IQ, then when one correlates clients' IQ scores to their scores on the test for phobias, this should produce a near zero correlation. Similarly, a counselor who is genuinely qualified to sit for a state licensing exam should score higher on the exam than a student who flunked an introductory counseling course, if discriminant validity is evident. When a researcher is engaged in test validation, both convergent and discriminant validity should be thoroughly examined.   **(a)**

628. When a counselor tells a client that the *Graduate Record Examination* (GRE) will predict her ability to handle graduate work, the counselor is referring to

a. good concurrent validity.
b. construct validity.
c. face validity.
d. predictive validity.

The GRE, the SAT *(Scholastic Aptitude Test)*, the ACT *(American College Test)*, and public opinion polls are effective only if they have high predictive validity which is the power to accurately describe future behavior or events. Again the subtypes of criterion validity are concurrent and predictive. **(d)**

629. A reliable test is _____ valid.

    a. always
    b. 90%
    c. not always
    d. 80%

Reliability, nonetheless, determines the upper level of validity. **(c)**

630. A valid test is _____ reliable.

    a. not always
    b. always
    c. never
    d. 80%

Choice "b" is true because a test that measures a given trait well does so repeatedly. Remember that a reliable test, however, is not necessarily always valid. After all, a depression scale that was invalid and really measuring anxiety could produce consistent reliable anxiety data. **(b)**

631. One method of testing reliability is to give the same test to the same group of people two times and then correlate the scores. This is called

a.   test-retest reliability.
b.   equivalent forms reliability.
c.   alternate forms reliability.
d.   the split-half method.

All right, I've got to hand it to you . . . you're very perceptive. You've figured out that I'm banking on the fact that your exam will spring a few reliability and/ or validity questions on you. The well-known test-retest method discussed here tests for "stability," which is the ability of a test score to remain stable or fluctuate over time when the client takes the test again. When using the test-retest paradigm the client generally takes the same test after waiting at least seven days. The test-retest procedure is only valid for traits such as IQ which remain stable over time and are not altered by mood, memory, or practice effects.   **(a)**

632. One method of testing reliability is to give the same population alternate forms of the identical test. This is known as

a.   test-retest reliability.
b.   equivalent or alternate forms reliability.
c.   the split-half method.
d.   internal consistency.

Here a single group of examinees takes parallel forms of a test and a reliability correlation coefficient is figured on the two sets of scores. Counterbalancing is necessary when testing reliability in this fashion. That is to say, half of the individuals get parallel form A first and half get form B initially. This controls for variables such as fatigue, practice, and motivation.   **(b)**

633. A counselor doing research decided to split a standardized test in half by using the even items as one test and the odd items as a second test and then correlate them. The counselor

a. used an invalid procedure to test reliability.
b. was testing reliability via the split-half method.
c. was testing reliability via the equivalent forms method.
d. was testing reliability via the inter-rater method.

In this situation the individual takes the entire test as a whole and then the test is divided into halves. The correlation between the half scores yields a reliability coefficient. When a researcher does not use even versus odd questions to split the test, he or she may do so using random numbers (merely dividing a test according to first half versus second half could confound the data due to practice and fatigue effects). **(b)**

634. Which method of reliability testing would be useful with an essay test but not with a test of algebra problems?

   a. test-retest
   b. alternate forms
   c. split-half
   d. inter-rater/inter-observer

Using choice "d," several raters assess the same performance. This method has been called "scorer reliability" and is utilized with subjective tests such as projectives to ascertain whether the scoring criteria are such that two persons who grade or assess the responses will produce roughly the same score. **(d)**

635. A reliability coefficient of 1.00 indicates

   a. a lot of variance in the test.
   b. a score with a high level of error.
   c. a perfect score which has no error.
   d. a typical correlation on most psychological and counseling tests.

As stated earlier, this generally occurs only in physical measurement. **(c)**

636. An excellent psychological or counseling test would have a reliability coefficient of

    a.   .50.
    b.   .90.
    c.   1.00.
    d.   -.90.

90% of the score measured the attribute in question, while 10% of the score is indicative of error. **(b)**

637. A researcher working with a personality test discovers that the test has a reliability coefficient of .70 which is somewhat typical. This indicates that

    a.   70% of the score is accurate while 30% is inaccurate.
    b.   30% of the people who are tested will receive accurate scores.
    c.   70% of the people who are tested will receive accurate scores.
    d.   30% of the score is accurate while 70% is inaccurate.

70% of the obtained score on the test represented the true score on the personality attribute, while 30% of the obtained score could be accounted for by error. 70% is true variance while 30% constitutes error variance. **(a)**

638. A career counselor is using a test for job selection purposes. An acceptable reliability coefficient would be ____ or higher.

    a.   .20
    b.   .55
    c.   .80
    d.   .70

This is a tricky question. Although .70 is generally acceptable for most psychological attributes admissions for jobs, schools, etc., it should be a least .80 and some experts will not settle for less than .90. **(c)**

639. The same test is given to the same group of people using the test-retest reliability method. The correlation between the first and second administration is .70. The true variance is

    a.   70%.
    b.   100%.
    c.   .50%.
    d.   .49%.

Here's the key to simplifying a question such as this. To demonstrate the variance of one factor accounted for by another you merely square the correlation (i.e., reliability coefficient). So, .70 x .70 = .49. **(d)**

640. IQ means

    a.   a query of intelligence.
    b.   indication of intelligence.
    c.   intelligence quotient.
    d.   intelligence questions for test construction.

A quotient is the result when you perform division. The early ratio formula for the Binet IQ score was MA/CA (i.e., mental age divided by your chronological age) x 100. The score indicated how you compared to those in your age group. Memory device: An MA is a high degree so put it on top of the equation as the numerator. **(c)**

641. _____ did research and concluded that intelligence was normally distributed like height or weight and that it was primarily genetic.

a.   Spearman
b.   Guilford
c.   Williamson
d.   Francis Galton

Galton felt intelligence was a single or so-called "unitary" factor.   **(d)**

642. Francis Galton felt intelligence was

a.   a unitary faculty.
b.   best explained via a two factor theory.
c.   best explained via the person's environment.
d.   fluid and crystallized in nature.

Sir Francis Galton of England has been recognized as one of the major pioneers in the study of individual differences. A half cousin himself to Charles *Origin of Species* Darwin, he believed that exceptional mental abilities were genetic and ran in families, and said just that in his 1869 work *Hereditary Genius*. Choice "b" illuminates the position of Charles Spearman who in 1904 postulated two factors—a general ability G and a specific ability S which were thought to be applicable to any mental task. (Wasn't psychological theory simple in those days?) As for choice "d," it pops up on exams from time to time. Fluid intelligence is flexible (terrific they both begin with an F), culture-free, and adjusts to the situation, while crystallized is rigid and does not change or adapt.   **(a)**

643. J.P. Guilford isolated 120 factors which added up to intelligence. He also is remembered for his

a.   thoughts on convergent and divergent thinking.
b.   work on cognitive therapy.
c.   work on behavior therapy.
d.   work to create the first standardized IQ test.

Using factor analysis Guilford determined that there were 120 elements/abilities which added up to intelligence. Two of the dimensions—convergent and divergent thinking—are still popular terms today. Convergent thinking occurs when divergent thoughts and ideas are combined into a singular concept. Divergent thinking is the ability to generate a novel idea. Choice "d" would reflect primarily the work of Alfred Binet and Theodore Simon. **(a)**

644. A counselor is told by his supervisor to measure the internal consistency reliability (i.e., homogeneity) of a test but not to divide the test in halves. The counselor would need to utilize

    a.   the split-half method.
    b.   the test-retest method.
    c.   the Kuder-Richardson coefficients of equivalence.
    d.   cross validation.

Internal consistency or homogeneity of items also is known as "inter-item consistency." In plain everyday verbiage, the supervisor wants the counselor to find out if each item on the test is measuring the same thing as every other item. Is performance on one item truly related to performance on another? This can be done by using the Kuder-Richardson estimates which are often denoted on exams as the KR-20 or KR-21 formulas. Another statistic, Lee J. Cronbach's alpha coefficient, also has been used in this respect. Choice "a" is incorrect. Yes, the split-half method does investigate internal consistency reliability, but it relies on (as its name implies) splitting the test in halves (e.g., even versus odd scores). Cronbach's alpha and the KR-20 or KR-21 are alternatives to the split-half method. Choice "d," "cross validation," is another popular term used in this area of study. Cross validation takes place when a researcher further examines the criterion validity (and in rarer instances, the construct validity) of a test by administering the test to a new sample. This procedure is necessary to ensure that the original validity coefficient is applicable to others who will take the exam. This method helps guard against error factors, which are likely to be present if the original sample size is small. IN MOST CASES A CROSS VALIDATION COEFFICIENT IS INDEED SMALLER THAN THE INITIAL VALIDITY COEFFICIENT. THIS PHENOMENON IS CALLED "SHRINKAGE." **(c)**

645. The first intelligence test was created by

    a.   David Wechsler.
    b.   J.P. Guilford.
    c.   Francis Galton.
    d.   Alfred Binet and Theodore Simon.

The year was 1904 and the French Government appointed a commission to ferret out feeble-minded Parisian children from those who were normal. Alfred Binet led the committee and the rest is history. By 1905, Binet, along with his coworker Simon, created a 30-question test with school related items of increased difficulty. Binet used his own daughters as test subjects in order to investigate mental processes and also is cited as one of the pioneers in projective testing based on his work with inkblots. After testing nearly 3,000 children in the U.S. in 1916, Lewis M. Terman of Stanford University published an American version of the Binet that was translated into English and adopted to American children. And in case you haven't already guessed, the word "Stanford" was added to the name. **(d)**

646. Today, the Stanford-Binet IQ test is

    a.   a nonstandardized measure.
    b.   a standardized measure.
    c.   a projective measure.
    d.   b and c.

The Stanford-Binet is standardized since the scoring and administration procedures are formal and well delineated. Measures which are not standardized (choice "a") lack procedural guidelines for scoring and/or administration and do not include quantitative information related to "standards" of performance. **(b)**

647. IQ stands for intelligence quotient which is expressed by

    a.   CA/MA x 100.
    b.   CA/MA x 100.
    c.   MA/CA x 50.
    d.   MA/CA x 100.

The test is Binet's, but the famous formula was created by the German, Wilhelm Stern. The formula produced what is known as a "ratio IQ." Today, a "deviation IQ" is utilized which compares the individual to a norm (i.e., the person is compared to others in his or her age group). Thus, the present score indicates "deviation" from the norm. Okay, now just to be sure that you are really picking this up let me say it in a little different way: ALTHOUGH WE STILL USE THE TERM IQ, THE BINET TODAY ACTUALLY RELIES ON A STANDARD AGE SCORE (SAS) WITH A MEAN OF 100 AND A STANDARD DEVIATION OF 16. So then you see, the IQ isn't really an IQ after all . . . right?   **(d)**

648. The Binet stressed age-related tasks. Utilizing this method, a 9-year-old task would be one which

    a.   only a 10-year-old child could answer.
    b.   only an 8-year-old child could answer.
    c.   50% of the 9-year-olds could answer correctly.
    d.   75% of the 9-year-olds could answer correctly.

A 9-year-old task was defined as one in which 1/2 of the 9-year-olds tested could answer successfully.   **(c)**

649. Simon and Binet pioneered the first IQ test around 1905. The test was created to

a. assess high school seniors in America.
b. assess U.S. military recruits.
c. discriminate normal from retarded Parisian children.
d. measure genius in the college population.

The Minister of Public Instruction for the Paris schools wanted a test to identify mentally retarded children so that they could be taught separately. The assumption was made that intelligence was basically the ability to understand school related material. In regard to choice "d" some experts believe that the Wechsler is a better test for those who fall in the average range, while the Stanford-Binet is more accurate for assessing extremes of intellect. **(c)**

650. Today the Stanford-Binet is used from ages 2 to adulthood. The IQ formula has been replaced by the

    a. SAS.
    b. SUDS.
    c. AAS.
    d. ACPA.

Review question 647. SAS stands for "standard age score." **(a)**

651. Most experts would agree that the Wechsler IQ tests gained popularity as the Binet

    a. must be administered in a group.
    b. favored the geriatric population.
    c. didn't seem to be the best test for adults.
    d. was biased toward women.

Choice "a" is incorrect—both the Binet and the Wechsler are individual tests which require specific training beyond that required for a group IQ test. David Wechsler felt the Binet was slanted toward verbal skills and thus he added "performance" skills to ascertain attributes which might have been cultivated in a background which did not stress verbal proficiency. The Wechsler yields a verbal IQ, performance IQ, and a full scale IQ. The WAIS-R is organized into eleven subtests. **(c)**

652. The best IQ test for a 22-year-old single male would be the

    a.   WPPSI.
    b.   WAIS-R.
    c.   WISC-R.
    d.   TAT.

Choice "a," the WPPSI or the *Wechsler Preschool and Primary Scale of Intelligence,* is suitable for children ages 4 to 6 1/2. Choice "b," the *Wechsler Adult Intelligence Scale Revised,* is intended for ages 16 and beyond. Choice "c," the *Wechsler Intelligence Scale for Children Revised,* is appropriate for kids 6 to 17. **(b)**

653. The best intelligence test for a sixth-grade girl would be the

    a.   WPPSI.
    b.   WAIS-R.
    c.   WISC-R.
    d.   Merrill Palmer.

Review the answer to the previous question. The *Merrill-Palmer Scale of Mental Tests* is an intelligence test for infants. **(c)**

654. The best intelligence test for a kindergartner would be the

    a.   WPPSI.
    b.   WAIS-R.
    c.   WISC-R.
    d.   *Myers-Briggs Type Indicator.*

Since the child most likely would be between 4 and 6 1/2 the WPPSI would be the only possible choice. Choice "d," the MBTI, is based on Carl Jung's analytic psychology. The MBTI uses dichotomous types: extraversion versus introversion, sensing versus intuition, thinking versus feeling, and judging versus perceiving. The test results in a four letter type score such as ISFJ (i.e., introversion, sensing, feeling, judging). (**Note:** Intuition, though it begins with an "I" is coded using an "N" since Introversion begins with an "I.") In a November 22, 1990 article entitled *MBTI: Test's Popularity Raises Concerns*, senior staff writer for the "Guidepost" explores the issue of whether the MTBI is being overused as well as misused (e.g., hiring employees based on whether their MBTI profile matches others engaging in the work). Keeping up with current issues in testing is highly recommended when studying for the Appraisal section of comprehensive exams. **(a)**

655. The mean on the Wechsler and the Binet is _____ and the standard deviation is _____.

    a.   100; 100
    b.   100; 15 Wechsler, 16 Stanford-Binet
    c.   100; 20
    d.   100; 1

IQs above 100 are above average and those shy of 100 are below average. **(b)**

656. Group IQ tests like the *Otis Lennon*, the *Lorge-Thorndike*, and the *California Test of Mental Abilities* are popular in school settings. The advantage is that

    a.   group tests are quicker to administer.
    b.   group tests are superior in terms of predicting school performance.
    c.   group tests always have a higher degree of reliability.
    d.   individual IQ tests are not appropriate for school children.

World War I provided the impetus for the group testing movement. Approximately two million men were tested using the *Army Alpha* for literates and the *Army Beta* for illiterates and those from other countries. School districts, government, and industry prefer tests which can be administered to many individuals simultaneously. The catch is that group tests are less accurate and have lower reliability. **(a)**

657. The group IQ test movement began

    a.   in 1905.
    b.   with the work of Binet.
    c.   with the *Army Alpha* and *Beta* in World War I.
    d.   with the AGCT in World War II.

Note the word "group." **(c)**

658. In a culture-fair test

    a.   items are known to the subject regardless of his or her culture.
    b.   the test is not standardized.
    c.   culture-free items cannot be utilized.
    d.   Blacks generally score higher than Whites.

The culture-fair test attempts to expunge items which would be known only to an individual due to his or her background. **(a)**

659. The Black versus White IQ controversy was sparked mainly by a 1969 article written by _____.

    a.   John Ertl
    b.   Raymond Cattell
    c.   Arthur Jensen
    d.   Robert Williams

Here are four names to be familiar with. Choice "a," John Ertl, claimed he invented an electronic machine to analyze neural efficiency and take the place of the paper and pencil IQ test. The device relies on a computer, an EEG, a strobe light, and an electrode helmet. The theory is that the faster one processes the perception the more intelligence he or she has. I might add that thus far, counselors don't seem to be buying the idea! Choice "b," Raymond B. Cattell, is responsible for the fluid (neurological which decreases with age) and crystallized (intelligence from experiential and educational interaction) distinctions. Crystallized intelligence is measured by tests that focus on content. Fluid intelligence is tested by what has been called "content free reasoning" such as a block design or a pictorial analogy problem. Jensen, choice "c" mentioned earlier, sparked tremendous controversy—actually that's putting it mildly—when he suggested in a 1969 *Harvard Educational Review* article ("How Much Can We Boost IQ and Scholastic Performance?") that the closer people are genetically, the more alike their IQ scores. Adopted children, for example, will sport IQs closer to their real parents than adopted ones. Jensen then leveled the charge that Whites score 11 to 15 IQ points higher than Blacks (regardless of social class). His theory stated that due to slavery it was possible that Blacks were bred for strength rather than intelligence. He estimated that heredity contributed 80%, while environment influenced 20% of the IQ. Uri Bronfenbrenner, who could be included here if we had a choice "e," claimed that Jensen relied on twin studies with poor internal validity. Other researchers (e.g., Newman, Freeman and Holzinger, Fehr) felt that genetic influences contributed less than 50% to IQ. In the final choice, Black psychologist Robert Williams created the BITCH *(Black Intelligence Test of Cultural Homogeneity)* to demonstrate that Blacks often excelled when given a test laden with questions familiar to the Black community. Williams charged that tests like the *Binet* and the *Wechsler* were part of "scientific racism." Williams—a victim of the system himself—scored an 82 on an IQ test at age 15 and his counselor suggested bricklaying since he was good with his hands! Williams rejected the advice and went on to put Ph.D. after his name! IQ tests are, however, excellent predictors of school success in most cases since school emphasizes White values. **(c)**

660. The MMPI-2 is

    a.   an IQ test.
    b.   a neurological test.
    c.   a projective personality test.
    d.   a standardized personality test.

The *Minnesota Multiphasic Personality Inventory-2* is known as a "self-report" personality inventory. The client can respond with "true," "false," or "cannot say" to 567 questions (10 more than the traditional MMPI which was the most researched test in history as well as the most useful for assessing emotional disturbance). The "new" MMPI designated via the 2 is intended to help clinicians diagnose and treat patients. The test is said to have retained the best factors of the MMPI, while updating the test and eliminating sexist wording. The MMPI-2 is suitable for those over 18. An eighth-grade reading level is required and testing time varies from 60 to 90 minutes. The test restandardization committee reported that the norming sample for the MMPI-2 is larger and more representative than the old measure. By the time you sit for your exam an adolescent version could be released. Until that time the traditional MMPI should be utilized for adolescents. The MMPI offers computer report packages for specialized settings such as college counseling, chronic pain programs, or outpatient mental health centers. MY ADVICE: THUMB THROUGH A FEW MAJOR TESTING CATALOGS BEFORE TAKING THE EXAM. **(d)**

661. The word psychometric means

    a.   a form of measurement used by a neurologist.
    b.   any form of mental testing.
    c.   a mental trait which cannot be measured.
    d.   the test relies on a summated or linear rating scale.

Psychometrics literally refers to the branch of counseling or psychology which focuses on testing. Choice "d" is used to describe answer scales in which various values are given to different responses. For example, on a Likert Scale a "strongly agree" might be given a 5, yet an "agree response" might be rated a 4. The clients score is the "sum" of all the items.   **(b)**

662. In a projective test the client is shown

    a.   something which is highly reinforcing.
    b.   something which is highly charged from an emotional standpoint.
    c.   a and b.
    d.   neutral stimuli.

The idea here is that the client will "project" his or her personality if given an unstructured task. More specifically, there are several acceptable formats for projective tests. First, ASSOCIATION—such as "What comes to mind when you look at this inkblot?" Second, COMPLETION—"Complete these sentences with real feelings." Third, CONSTRUCTION—such as drawing a person. The theory is that self-report inventories like the MMPI do not reveal hidden unconscious impulses. In order to accomplish this the client is shown vague, ambiguous stimuli such as a picture or an inkblot. Some counselors believe that by using projective measures a client will have more difficulty faking his or her responses and that he or she will be able to expand on answers. It should be noted that examiner bias is common when using projectives, and a therapist using projectives needs more training than one who merely works with self-report tests.   **(d)**

663. The 16 PF reflects the work of

    a.   Raymond B. Cattell.
    b.   Carl Jung.
    c.   James McKeen Cattell.
    d.   Oscar K. Buros.

The *16 Personality Factor Questionnaire* is suitable for persons 16 and above and has been the subject of over 2,000 writings! The test measures key personality factors like assertiveness, emotional maturity, and shrewdness. A couple can even decide that each party will take the 16 PF, and an individual as well as a joint profile will be compiled which can be utilized for marital counseling. Choice "c" is the other Cattell, who coined the term "mental test" and spent time researching mental assessment and its relation to reaction time at the University of Pennsylvania. James Cattell had originally worked with Wundt and later Galton.   **(a)**

664. The *Myers-Briggs Type Indicator* reflects the work of

    a.   Raymond B. Cattell.
    b.   Carl Jung.
    c.   William Glasser.
    d.   Oscar K. Buros.

Review question 654. Buros, mentioned in choice "d" of this question as well as the last, is noted for his *Mental Measurements Yearbook* which was the first major publication to review available tests. After his death, the University of Nebraska set up the Oscar K. Buros Center which continued his valuable contribution to the field.   **(b)**

665. The counselor who favors projective measures would most likely be a

a. Rogerian.
b. strict behaviorist.
c. TA therapist.
d. psychodynamic clinician.

Choices "a," "b," and "c" all reflect positions that do not rely heavily on the unconscious mind (especially the behaviorists who believe that if you can't directly measure the behavior, it is not meaningful). Some theorists (e.g., Allport) would contend that even if it is true that unconscious impulses exist, they are not very important. **(d)**

666. An aptitude test is to _____ as an achievement test is to _____.

a. what has been learned; potential
b. potential; what has been learned
c. profit from learning; potential
d. a measurement of current skills; potential

An aptitude test assesses "potential" and "predicts." An achievement test examines what you know (e.g., the NCE). PREDICTIVE VALIDITY IS PARTICULARLY IMPORTANT WHEN CHOOSING AN APTITUDE TEST. **(b)**

667. Both the *Rorschach* and the TAT are projective tests. The *Rorschach* uses 10 inkblot cards while the *Thematic Apperception Test* uses

a. a dozen inkblot cards.
b. verbal and performance IQ scales.
c. pictures.
d. incomplete sentences.

The *Thematic Apperception Test* or TAT consists of 30 cards plus one blank card. The test, which is intended for ages 4 and beyond, uses up to 20 cards when administered to any given individual (i.e., 19 selected to fit the age and sex of the client, plus one blank card). The pictures on each card are intentionally ambiguous, and the client is asked to make up a story for each of them. Choice "d" would describe a projective test such as the *Rotter Incomplete Sentence Blank* (Rotter ISB) in which the subject completes an incomplete sentence with a real feeling. **(c)**

668. Test bias primarily results from

    a.   a test being normed solely on White middle-class clients.
    b.   the use of projective measures.
    c.   using Whites to score the test.
    d.   using IQ rather than personality tests.

This bias should be communicated to the client when the results are explained. **(a)**

669. A counselor who fears the client has an organic, neurological, or motoric difficulty would most likely use the

    a.   *Bender Gestalt.*
    b.   *Rorschach.*
    c.   *Minnesota Multiphasic Personality Inventory.*
    d.   *Thematic Apperception Test.*

The *Bender Visual Motor Gestalt Test* (named after Loretta Bender) is actually an expressive projective measure, though first and foremost it is known for its ability to discern whether brain damage is evident. Suitable for ages four and beyond the client is instructed to copy nine geometric figures which the client can look at while constructing his or her drawing. **(a)**

670. An interest inventory would be least valid when used with

a. a first-year college student majoring in philosophy.
b. a third-year college student majoring in physics.
c. an 8th-grade male with an IQ of 136.
d. a 46-year-old White male construction worker.

Interest inventories work best with individuals who are of high school age or above inasmuch as interests are not extremely stable prior to that time. Interests become quite stable around age 25. **(c)**

671. One major criticism of interest inventories is that

a. they have far too many questions.
b. they are most appropriate for very young children.
c. they emphasize professional positions and minimize blue-collar jobs.
d. they favor female pursuits.

ALSO TAKE NOTE OF THE FACT THAT CONTRARY TO POPULAR OPINION INTERESTS AND ABILITIES ARE NOT—THAT'S RIGHT NOT—HIGHLY CORRELATED. A client, for example, could have tremendous musical ability yet could thoroughly dislike being a musician. **(c)**

672. Interest inventories are positive in the sense that

a. they are reliable and not threatening to the test taker.
b. they are always graded by the test taker.
c. they require little or no reading skills.
d. they have high validity in nearly all age brackets.

Generally, an interest inventory would be the least threatening variety of test. **(a)**

673. A counselor who had an interest primarily in testing would most likely be a member of

a. ASGW.
b. AMECD.
c. NASW.
d. AHEAD.

This ACA Division is the Association for Measurement and Evaluation in Counseling and Development. Can you name the other choices? **(b)**

674. The NCE is

a. an intelligence test.
b. an aptitude test.
c. a personality test.
d. an achievement test.

The NCE is testing your knowledge and application of material in the counseling profession. **(d)**

675. The _____ are examples of aptitude tests.

a. GATB and the MCAT
b. GZTS and the MMPI
c. CPI and the MMPI
d. Strong and the LSAT

Plenty of alphabet soup here! You can find the correct choice, the *General Aptitude Test Battery*, at your friendly neighborhood State Employment Office who will use it to try to help you secure an appropriate job. Here I've teamed it up with the new *Medical College Admission Test*. Choice "b," the *Guilford-Zimmerman Temperament Survey*, is a personality measure for persons who do not have severe psychiatric disabilities. Lastly, the final alternative introduces you to the new *Law School Admission Test* which of course qualifies as a bona fide aptitude test. So why is choice "d" incorrect? Well, if any portion of a response is incorrect, then the entire choice is erroneous. If you marked choice "d" you can blame it on the Strong! EXAM HINT: SCHOOL SELECTION TESTS ASSESS APTITUDE. **(a)**

676. One problem with interest inventories is that the person often tries to answer the questions in a socially acceptable manner. Psychometricians call this response style phenomenon

     a.   standard error.
     b.   social desirability (the right way to feel in society).
     c.   cultural bias.
     d.   acquiescence.

The converse of choice "b" occurs when an individual purposely, or when in doubt, gives unusual responses. This phenomenon is known as "deviation." Choice "d" manifests itself when a client always agrees with something. **(b)**

677. An aptitude test predicts future behavior while an achievement test measures what you have mastered or learned. In the case of a test like _____ the distinction is unclear.

     a.   Binet
     b.   Wechsler
     c.   GRE
     d.   Bender

Sure, the test attempts to predict graduate school performance, but it also tests your level of knowledge. Some exams will refer to tests like the GRE, MAT, MCAT, SAT, etc. as "aptitude-achievement tests." Now here's where a counselor's life gets really complicated. Say your exam presents you with one of the aforementioned tests and gives you "aptitude" as one choice, and "achievement" as another, but does not give you "aptitude-achievement" as an alternative (yipes!). Well, I certainly won't condone the practice, but based on my investigation of the textbook taxonomy of tests I'd opt for the "aptitude" option and latch on to the first good four-leaf clover I could get my hands on. **(c)**

678. Your supervisor wants you to find a new personality test for your counseling agency. You should read

    a.   professional journals.
    b.   the *Buros Mental Measurements Yearbook*.
    c.   classic textbooks in the field as well as test materials produced by the testing company.
    d.   all of the above.

Moreover, it has been discovered that if the counselor involves the client in the process of test selection it will improve his or her cooperation in the counseling process. **(d)**

679. The standard error of measurement tells you

    a.   how accurate or inaccurate a test score is.
    b.   what population responds best to the test.
    c.   the accuracy for personality but not IQ tests.
    d.   the number of people used in norming the test.

If a client decided to take the same test over and over and over again you could plot a distribution of scores. This would be the standard error of measurement for the instrument in question. Suffice it to say, the lower the better. A low standard error means high reliability. Say, that's a pretty important concept; I better explain it again with a slightly different twist in the "Research And Evaluation" section of this book. **(a)**

680. A new IQ test has a standard error of measurement of 3. Tom scores 106 on the test. If he takes the test a lot, we can predict that about 68% of the time

    a.   Tom will score between 100 and 103.
    b.   Tom will score between 100 and 106.
    c.   Tom will score between 103 and 109.
    d.   Tom will score higher than Betty who scored 139.

Calculated simply by taking: 106 - 3 = 103 and 106 + 3 = 109. Hint: Your exam could refer to this as the 68% confidence interval (i.e., 103 to 109). Classical test theory suggests the formula, X = T + E, where X is the obtained score, T is the true score, and E is the error. Hence, psychometricians know that if a client takes the same test over and over, random error (i.e., E in the formula) will cause the score to fluctuate. **(c)**

681. A counselor created an achievement test with a reliability coefficient of .82. The test is shortened since many clients felt it was too long. The counselor shortened the test but logically assumed that the reliability coefficient would now

    a.   be approximately .88.
    b.   remain at .82.
    c.   be at least 10 points higher or lower.
    d.   be lower than .82.

INCREASING A TEST'S LENGTH RAISES RELIABILITY. SHORTEN IT AND THE ANTITHESIS OCCURS. NOTE: The Spearman Brown formula is used to estimate the impact that lengthening or shortening a test will have on a test's reliability coefficient. **(d)**

682. A counselor can utilize psychological tests to help secure a _____ diagnosis if third party payments are necessary.

    a.   AACD
    b.   DSM or ICD
    c.   percentile
    d.   standard error

Diagnosis is a medical term which asserts that you classify a disease based on symptomatology. **(b)**

683. A colleague of yours invents a new projective test. Seventeen counselors rated the same client using the measure and came up with nearly identical assessments. This would indicate

    a.   high validity.
    b.   high reliability.
    c.   excellent norming studies.
    d.   culture fairness.

This is known as "inter-rater" reliability.   **(b)**

684. Counselors often shy away from self-reports since

    a.   clients often give inaccurate answers.
    b.   ACA ethics do not allow them.
    c.   clients need a very high IQ to understand them.
    d.   they are generally very lengthy.

Say a client is monitoring her behavior and does not wish to disappoint her therapist. The report could be biased. This is a "reactive effect" of the self-monitoring.   **(a)**

685. In most instances, who would be the best qualified to give the *Rorschach Inkblot Test?*

    a.   A counselor with NCC, NCCC after his or her name.
    b.   A clinical psychologist.
    c.   A D.O. psychiatrist.
    d.   A social worker with ACSW after his or her name.

Generally, a clinical psychologist would have the most training in this area while the social worker would have the least education regarding tests and measurements.   **(b)**

686. Your client, who is in an out-patient hospital program, is keeping a journal of irrational thoughts. This would be

a. an unethical practice based on NBCC ethical guidelines.
b. considered a standardized test.
c. an informal assessment technique.
d. an aptitude measure.

Self-reports, case notes, checklists, sociograms of groups, interviews, and professional staffings would also fall into this category. **(c)**

687. You are uncertain whether a test is intended for the population served by your not-for-profit agency. The best method of researching this dilemma would be to

a. contact a local APA clinical psychology graduate program.
b. make a long distance call to the person who created the test.
c. read the test manual included with the test.
d. give the test to six or more clients at random.

The manual should specify the target population for the test in question. **(c)**

688. Clients should know that

a. validity is more important than reliability.
b. projective tests favor psychodynamic theory.
c. face validity is not that important.
d. a test is merely a single source of data and not infallible.

Although the first three choices are important to the counselor, the final statement should be explained to the client. An extremely high score say on a mechanical aptitude test does not automatically imply that the client will prosper as a mechanic. **(d)**

689. One major testing trend is

    a.   computer-assisted testing and computer interpretations.
    b.   more paper and pencil measures.
    c.   to give school children at least three IQ tests per year.
    d.   to train pastoral counselors to do projective testing.

But don't take my word for it. Pick up any modern testing catalog and you might erroneously think you've picked up a computer software directory! **(a)**

690. One future trend which seems contradictory is that some experts are pushing for

    a.   a greater reliance on tests while others want to rely on them less.
    b.   social workers to do most of the testing.
    c.   psychiatrists to do most of the testing.
    d.   counselors to ban all computer-assisted tests.

It seems we counselors just can't agree on anything. Many counselors would like to see a greater emphasis in the future on tests which assess creative and motivational factors. **(a)**

691. Most counselors would agree that

    a.   more preschool IQ testing is necessary.
    b.   teachers need to give more personality tests.
    c.   more public education is needed in the area of testing.
    d.   the testing mystique has been beneficial to the general public.

Again, the public needs to know the limitations of testing (i.e., that they are fallible). If you've been doing counseling for any length of time then you've surely come in contact with clients who have been harmed by hearing a score (e.g., their IQ) and then reacting to it such that it becomes a negative self-fulfilling prophecy. **(c)**

692. _____ would be an informal method of appraisal.

    a.   IQ testing
    b.   Standardized personality testing
    c.   GRE scores
    d.   A checklist

Unlike choices "a," "b," and "c," the informal method does not use standard administration or scoring procedures. I might tell a client to do her checklist or diary one way and you would go about it in a totally different manner. **(d)**

693. The WAIS-R is given to 100,000 individuals in the U.S. who are picked at random. A counselor would expect that

    a.   approximately 68% would score between 85 and 115.
    b.   approximately 68% would score between 70 and 130.
    c.   the mean IQ would be 112.
    d.   50% of those tested would score 112 or above.

I know . . . I see it too . . . a question with numbers . . . lots of numbers, but don't panic. Let's walk through this one together. First, the Wechsler IQ test has been administered to a very large group of people so chances are the distribution of scores will be normal. This tells you that the mean score will be 100 (i.e., the average IQ) and the standard deviation will be 15 (if the question asked about the Binet you'd use 16 as the standard deviation). In a normal distribution approximately 68% of the population will fall between plus/minus 1 standard deviation of the mean. With a standard deviation of 15 you simply subtract 15 from 100 to get the low score (i.e., 85) and add 15 to 100 to get 115. Choice "b" would be correct if the 68% was changed to 96%, since about 96% of the people in a normal distribution fall between plus/minus 2 standard deviations of the mean. (You simply subtract 30 from 100 to get 70 and add 30 to 100 to yield the upper IQ score of 130.) Keep in mind that choice "c" should read 100 while choice "d" ought to indicate that 50% would score above 100.　　　**(a)**

694. A word association test would be an example of

    a.　a neuro-psychological test.
    b.　a motoric test.
    c.　an achievement test.
    d.　a projective test.

Although it is rare, some texts and exams take issue with the archaic word "projective" and refer to such tests as "self-expressive."　　　**(d)**

695. Infant IQ tests are

    a.　more reliable than those given later in life.
    b.　more unreliable than those given later in life.
    c.　not related to learning experiences.
    d.　never used.

These "toddler tests" are sometimes capable of picking up gross abnormalities such as serious mental retardation.　　　**(b)**

696. A good practice for counselors is to

    a.　always test the client yourself rather than referring the client for testing.
    b.　never generalize on the basis of a single test score.
    c.　stay away from culture-free tests.
    d.　stay away from scoring the test yourself.

Also, although choice "c" represents an ideal measure, most experts believe that as of this date no such animal exists. **(b)**

697. You want to admit only 25% of all counselors to an advanced training program in psychodynamic group therapy. The item difficulty on the entrance exam for applicants would be best set at

    a.   0.0.
    b.   .5 regardless of the admission requirement.
    c.   1.0.
    d.   .25.

In most tests the level is set at .5 (i.e., 50% of the examinees will answer correctly while 50% will not). However, in this case the .25 level would allow you to ferret out the lower 75% you do not wish to admit. Item difficulty ranges from 0.0 (choice "a") to 1.0 (choice "c"). **(d)**

698. According to Public Law 93-380, also known as the Buckley Amendment, a 19-year-old college student attending college

    a.   could view her record which included test data.
    b.   could view her daughter's infant IQ test given at preschool.
    c.   could demand a correction she discovered while reading a file.
    d.   all of the above.

Persons over 18 can inspect their own records and those of their children. The Family Education Rights and Privacy Act also stipulates that information cannot be released without adult consent. **(d)**

699. Lewis Terman

    a.   constructed the Wechsler tests.
    b   constructed the initial Binet prior to 1910.
    c.   constructed the Rorschach.
    d.   Americanized the Binet.

Since Terman was associated with Stanford University the test became the Stanford-Binet. **(d)**

700. In constructing a test you notice that all 75 people correctly answered item number 12. This gives you an item difficulty of

    a.   1.2.
    b.   .75.
    c.   1.0.
    d.   0.0.

The item difficulty index is calculated by taking the number of persons tested who answered the item correctly/ total number of persons tested. Hence, in this case 75/75 = 1.0. This maximum score for item 12 tells you it is probably much too easy for your examinees. **(c)**

CHAPTER **10**

RESEARCH
AND
EVALUATION

701. The most common type of research is

    a.   conducted using factor analysis.
    b.   conducted using the chi-square.
    c.   the experiment, used to discover cause-and-effect relationships.
    d.   the quasi-experiment.

A MINI PEP TALK FROM ME TO YOU. JUST THINK OF STATISTICS AND RESEARCH AS ANOTHER AREA ON THE TEST—NO EASIER AND NO HARDER. MOST OF THE STUDENTS I'VE SPOKEN TO WHO STUDIED FOR MAJOR EXAMS WERE SURPRISED TO FIND THAT THIS SECTION OF THE TEST WAS NOT THAT DIFFICULT!!! I SHALL TRY TO KEEP MY EXPLANATIONS SIMPLE AND WILL VARY THE PRESENTATION OF THE MATERIAL SO THAT IF YOU DON'T UNDERSTAND IT IN ONE WAY, YOU'LL COMPREHEND IT WHEN IT IS EXPLAINED IN A DIFFERENT MANNER. AND LASTLY, I PROMISE REPETITION, REPETITION, AND MORE REPETITION!!! Experimental research is the process of gathering data in order to make evaluative comparisons regarding different situations. An experiment must have the conditions of treatment controlled via the experimenter and random assignments (also called randomization) used in the groups. An experiment attempts to eliminate all extraneous variables. In the quasi-experiment (choice "d") the researcher uses preexisting groups, and hence the IV (independent variable) cannot be altered (e.g., gender or ethnicity). In a quasi-experiment you cannot state with any degree of statistical confidence that the IV caused the DV (dependent variable). One popular type of quasi-experiment is known as the "ex post facto study." Ex post facto literally means "after the fact," connoting a correlational study or research in which intact, preexisting groups are utilized. In the case of the ex post facto study the IV was administered before the research began. When conducting or perusing a research study a counselor is very concerned with "internal and external validity." Threats to internal validity include maturation of subjects, mortality (i.e., subjects withdrawing), instruments used to measure the behavior or trait, and statistical regression (i.e., the notion that extremely high or low scores would move toward the mean if the measure is utilized again). Internal validity refers to whether the DVs were truly influenced by the experimental IVs or whether other IVs had an impact. External validity, on the other hand, refers to whether the experimental research results can be generalized to larger populations. Thus, if the results of the study only apply to the population in the study itself then the external validity is said to be low. P.S. If it's been a while and you've forgotten terms like IV and DV just hold your pants on; we'll get to you in a minute. As for the other incorrect choices a "factor analysis" (choice "a") refers to statistical procedures which attempt to summarize a lot of variables using the important or underlying "factors." Hence, a test which measures a counselor's ability may try to describe the three most important variables (factors) which make an effective helper, although literally hundreds of factors may exist. Using factor analysis procedures, a short test that measures the three major factors may be able to predict who will be the an effective counselor as accurately as 10 other tests that examine hundreds of variables or so-called factors. Choice "b" mentions the "chi-square." The chi-square is a non-parametric statistical measure that tests whether a distribution differs significantly from an expected theoretical distribution. **(c)**

702. Experiments emphasize parsimony which means

    a.   interpreting the results in the simplest way.
    b.   interpreting the results in the most complex manner.
    c.   interpreting the results using a correlation coefficient.
    d.   interpreting the results using a clinical interview.

Parsimonious literally means a tendency to be miserly and not overspend. A parsimonious individual is said to be overly economical and stingy. In research, we strive for parsimony in the sense that the easiest and less complex explanation is said to be the best, an economical description if you will. Simply put, the simplest explanation of the findings is always preferred. The factor analysis mentioned in the previous answer is parsimonious in the sense that 10 tests which measure the dimensions of an effective counselor can be explained via a short measure which describes three underlying variables. Factor analysis then, is concerned with data reduction. **(a)**

703. Occam's Razor suggests that experimenters

    a.   interpret the results in the simplest manner.
    b.   interpret the results in the most complex manner.
    c.   interpret the results using a correlation coefficient.
    d.   interpret the results using a clinical interview.

A word to the wise: exams often refer to parsimony as Occam's Razor, the principle of economy, or Lloyd Morgan's 1894 Canon (canon in this sense means "law"). Conway Lloyd Morgan was an English Psychologist/Physiologist, while William of Occam was a 14th-century philosopher and theologian. The early behaviorists (e.g., Watson) adhered closely to this principle. **(a)**

704. A counselor educator is running an experiment to test a new form of counseling. Unbeknownst to the experimenter one of the clients in the study is secretly seeing a gestalt therapist. This experiment

    a.   is parsimonious.
    b.   is an example of Occam's Razor.
    c.   is confounded/flawed.
    d.   is valid and will most likely help the field of counseling.

The experiment is said to be invalid (so much for choice "d") due to an extraneous independent variable (e.g., the gestalt therapy). Variables which are undesirable confound or "flaw" the experiment. The only experimental variable should be the independent variable—in this case the new form of counseling. The IV must have the effect on the dependent variable (here the DV would be some measure of the client's mental health). In this experiment any changes could not be attributed with any degree of certainty to the new form of counseling since dependent variable changes could be due to the gestalt intervention (an extraneous confounding variable). All correlational research is said to be confounded. **(c)**

705. Nondirective is to person-centered as

    a.   psychological testing is to counseling.
    b.   confounding is to experimenting.
    c.   appraisal is to research.
    d.   parsimony is to Occam's Razor.

A simple analogy question. Nondirective and person-centered therapy are synonymous; both refer to names given to Rogerian counseling. Parsimony is roughly synonymous with Occam's Razor. **(d)**

706. An experiment is said to be confounded when

    a.   undesirable variables are not kept out of the experiment.
    b.   undesirable variables are kept out of the experiment.
    c.   two researchers are utilized.
    d.   the sample is random.

I hope you didn't mark choices "b" and "d" since they are necessary for a proper experiment. Confounding is said to occur when a undesirable variable which is not controlled by the researcher is introduced in the experiment. If you missed this one, fess up and review question 704.   **(a)**

707. In experimental terminology IV stands for _____ and DV stands for _____.

    a.   independent variable; dependent variable
    b.   dependent variable; independent variable
    c.   individual variable; dependent variable
    d.   independent variable; designer variable

Variables in an experiment are categorized as IVs (independent variables) or DVs (dependent variables). A variable is merely a behavior or a circumstance that can exist in at least two levels or conditions. In plain simple everyday English, a variable is a factor that "varies" or is capable of change. In an experiment the IV is the variable that the researcher manipulates, controls, alters, or wishes to experiment with. A neat little memory device is that IV begins with an "I," so imagine yourself as the researcher and remember "I manipulate the IV" or "I experiment with the IV." The DV expresses the outcome or the data. Here the memory device is a cinch: DV begins with a "D" and so does the word "data." The DV expresses the data regarding factors you wish to measure. IVs and DVs— the variables of the experimental trade—can be discrete (e.g., a brand of counseling or occupation) or continuous (e.g., height or weight).   **(a)**

708. A professor of counselor education hypothesized that biofeedback training could reduce anxiety and improve the average score on written board exams. If this professor decides to conduct a formal experiment the IV will be the _____, and the DV will be the _____.

    a.   professor; anxiety level
    b.   anxiety level; board exam score
    c.   biofeedback; board exam score
    d.   board exam score; biofeedback

Ah, here we have it: the old standby in the field of comprehensive exams. The examinee is given an experiment to ferret out the IV and DV. Now I've got this uncanny feeling that you won't be caught by surprise when you see it! Okay, time to plug in your memory devices. "I manipulate . . . or I experiment with . . . well the biofeedback training, of course." The "I" statement here gives you your "IV." For your "DV" (remember DV begins with a "D" like "data") your data is provided by the board exam score. True, the researcher here hypothesized that the training lowers anxiety, but you won't have any direct data regarding this trait. Hence it will not be your DV in this experiment. **(c)**

709. Experimenters should always abide by a code of ethics. The variable you manipulate/control in an experiment is the

    a.   DV.
    b.   dependent variable.
    c.   the variable you will measure to determine the outcome.
    d.   IV or independent variable.

Again, repeat after me: "I am the researcher so I manipulate or experiment with the IV." Choices "a," "b," and "c" all mention the DV which deals with outcome "data." Now in any experiment the counselor researcher is guided by ethics. Ethics suggest first, that subjects are informed of any risks; second, that negative after effects are removed; third, that you will allow subjects to withdraw at any time; fourth, that confidentiality of subjects will be protected; fifth, that research report results will be presented in an accurate format that is not misleading; and sixth, that you will use only techniques that you are trained in. Research is considered a necessary factor for professionalism in counseling. **(d)**

710. In order for the professor of counselor education (see question 708) to conduct an experiment regarding his hypothesis he will need a(n) _____ and a(n) _____.

    a.   biofeedback group; systematic desensitization group
    b.   control group; systematic desensitization group
    c.   control group; experimental group
    d.   at least 60 subjects

The control group and the experimental group both have the same characteristics except that members of the control group will not have the experimental treatment applied to them. In this case, for example, the control group will not receive the biofeedback training. THE CONTROL GROUP DOES NOT RECEIVE THE IV. THE EXPERIMENTAL GROUP RECEIVES THE IV. The basic presupposition is that the averages (or means) of the groups do not differ significantly at the beginning of the experiment. **(c)**

711. In order for the professor of counselor education to conduct the experiment suggested in question 708 the experimental group would need to receive

    a.   the manipulated IV.
    b.   the biofeedback training.
    c.   a and b.
    d.   the organismic IV.

The experimental group receives the IV which in this case is the biofeedback training. An organismic variable is one the researcher cannot control yet exists such as height, weight, or gender. To determine whether an organismic IV exists you simply ask yourself if there is an experimental variable being examined which you cannot manipulate. In most cases, when you are confronted with IV/DV identification questions, the IV will be of the "manipulated variety." **(c)**

712. Hypothesis testing is most closely related to the work of

    a.   Hoppock.
    b.   Freud.
    c.   Lloyd Morgan.
    d.   R.A. Fisher.

Hypothesis testing was pioneered by R.A. Fisher. An hypothesis is a hunch or an educated guess which can be tested utilizing the experimental model. An hypothesis might be that biofeedback raises board exam scores; or that reality therapy reduces dysfunctional classroom behavior in high school students; or perhaps that cognitive therapy relieves depression in males in the midst of a divorce. AN HYPOTHESIS IS A STATEMENT WHICH CAN BE TESTED REGARDING THE RELATIONSHIP OF THE IV AND THE DV. **(d)**

713. The null hypothesis suggests that there will not be a significant difference between the experimental group who received the IV and the control group who did not. Thus, if the experiment in question 708 was conducted, the null hypothesis would suggest that

    a.   all students receiving biofeedback training would score equally well on the board exam.
    b.   systematic desensitization might work better than biofeedback.
    c.   biofeedback will not improve the board exam scores.
    d.   SUDS will increase significantly.

The null hypothesis asserts that the samples will not change (i.e., they will still be the same) even after the experimental variable is applied. Let me say that in a little different way: according to the null hypothesis the control group and the experimental group will not differ at the end of the experiment. The null hypothesis is simply that THE IV DOES NOT EFFECT THE DV. Null means "nil" or "nothing." Null is a statement of "no difference." **(c)**

714. The hunch is known as the experimental or alternative hypothesis. The experimental hypothesis suggests that a difference will be evident between the control group and the experimental group (i.e., the group receiving the IV). Thus, if the experiment in question 708 were conducted, the experimental hypothesis would suggest that

    a.   the biofeedback would raise board scores.
    b.   the control group will score better on the board exam.
    c.   there will be no difference between the experimental and the control groups.
    d.   the experiment has been confounded.

An alternative hypothesis—which may be called the "affirmative hypothesis" on your exam—asserts that the IV has indeed caused a change. **(a)**

715. From a purely statistical standpoint, in order to compare a control group (which does not receive the IV or experimental manipulation) to the experimental group the researcher will need

    a.   a correlation coefficient.
    b.   only descriptive statistics.
    c.   percentile rank.
    d.   a test of significance.

Let's go through each possible alternative here. Choice "a" or correlational research does not make use of the paradigm in which an IV is experimentally introduced. Descriptive statistics (choice "b"), as the name implies, merely describes data (e.g., the mean, the median, or the mode). In order to compare two groups "inferential statistics," which infer something about the population as a whole based on sampling statistics, are necessary. Choice "c," percentile rank, is a descriptive statistic that tells the counselor what percentage of the cases fell below a certain level. Hence, if Joe's score puts him at the 50th percentile, than 50 percent of the people had raw scores lower than his particular score. DO NOT CONFUSE PERCENTILES WITH PERCENTAGE SCORES. A PERCENTAGE SCORE IS JUST ANOTHER WAY OF STATING A RAW SCORE. A PERCENTAGE SCORE OF 50 COULD BE A VERY HIGH, A VERY LOW, OR AN AVERAGE SCORE ON THE TEST. IT MERELY SAYS THAT THE EXAMINEE GOT HALF OF THE ANSWERS CORRECT. Graphically speaking, a distribution of percentile scores will always appear rectangular and flat. The correct answer is that the researcher in this experiment will need a test of significance. Such statistical tests are used to determine whether a difference in the groups' scores are "significant" or just due to chance factors. In this case a t-test would be used to determine if a significant difference between two means exists. This has been called the "two-groups" or "two-randomized-groups" research design. In this study, the two groups were independent of each other in the sense that the change (or lack of it) in one group did not influence the other group. Thus, this is known as an "independent group comparison design." If the researcher had measured the same group of subjects without the IV and with the IV, then the study would be a "repeated-measures comparison design." Exam hint: When a research study uses different subjects for each condition, some exams refer to the study as a "between-subjects design." If the same subjects are employed (e.g., such as in repeated measures), your exam could refer to it as a "within-subjects design." Stated in a different manner: In a between-subjects design, each subject receives only one value of the IV. In a within-subjects design, two or more values or levels of the IV are administered to each subject. **(d)**

716. When you see the letter "p" in relation to a test of significance it means

    a.   portion.
    b.   population parameter.
    c.   probability.
    d.   person-centered counseling experimentation.

Don't be surprised if the word "parameter" makes its way into your exam. A parameter is technically a value obtained from a population while a statistic is a value drawn from a sample. A parameter summarizes a characteristic of a population (e.g., the average male's height is 5'11"). The correct answer is choice "c" which refers to the probability or the level of significance. Traditionally, the probability in social science research (often indicated by a P) has been set at .05 or lower. The .05 level indicates that differences would occur via chance only 5 times in 100. The significance level must be set before the experiment begins! **(c)**

717. In the social sciences the accepted probability level is usually

    a.   .05 or less.
    b.   1.0 or higher.
    c.   .0001 or less.
    d.   5.0.

.05 and .01 are the two most popular levels of significance. **(a)**

718. P=.05 really means that

    a.   five subjects were not included in the study.
    b.   there is only a 5% chance that the difference between the control group and the experimental groups is due to chance factors.
    c.   the level of significance is .01.
    d.   no level of significance has been set.

Important note: Many experts in the field feel it is misleading when many exams still refer to this as the "95% confidence interval," meaning that the results would be due to chance only five times out of 100. When P=.05, differences in the experimental group and the control group are evident at the end of the experiment, and the odds are only one in 20 that this can be explained by chance. So once more for good measure (no pun intended!), your exam could refer to the "level of significance" as the level of confidence or simply the confidence level. The meaning is intended to be the same. **(b)**

719. P = .05 really means that

    a.   differences truly exist; the experimenter will obtain the same results 95 out of 100 times.
    b.   differences truly exist; the experimenter will obtain the same results 99 out of 100 times.
    c.   there is a 95% error factor.
    d.   there is a 10% error factor.

Review the previous three questions and answers if you missed this question. **(a)**

720. The study that would best rule out chance factors would have a significance level of P =

    a.   .05.
    b.   .01.
    c.   .001.
    d.   .08.

The smaller the value for P the more stringent the level of significance. Here, the .001 level is the most stringent level listed, indicating that there is only one chance in 1,000 that the results are due to chance, versus one in 20 for .05, and one in 100 for .01. In plain simple everyday English it is easier to get significant results using .08, .05, or .01, than it is using .001.   **(c)**

721. Type I and Type II errors are called _____ and _____ respectively.

    a.   beta; alpha
    b.   .01; .05
    c.   a and b
    d.   alpha; beta

If it sounds a little like Greek that's because it is. Alpha and beta are the first and second letters of the Greek alphabet. A Type I (alpha error) occurs when a researcher rejects the null hypothesis when it is true; and a Type II error (beta error) occurs when you accept null when it is false. The memory device RA (as in "residence advisor") works well here so you can remember the principle as well as the sequence. Let "R" signify "reject when true" and "A"—which comes after "R"—signify "accept when false." If that memory device leaves you feeling apprehensive, here's another one using the "RA" abbreviation. Let "RA" be your first error (i.e., alpha, Type I) and remember this error occurs when you "R" (reject) null when you should "A" for accept it. Or better still, use both "RA" devices. THE PROBABILITY OF COMMITTING A TYPE I ERROR EQUALS THE LEVEL OF SIGNIFICANCE MENTIONED EARLIER. THEREFORE, THE LEVEL OF SIGNIFICANCE IS OFTEN REFERRED TO AS THE "ALPHA LEVEL." BETA MINUS ONE IS CALLED "THE POWER OF A STATISTICAL TEST." IN THIS RESPECT, POWER CONNOTES A STATISTICAL TEST'S ABILITY TO REJECT CORRECTLY A FALSE NULL HYPOTHESIS. PARAMETRIC TESTS HAVE MORE POWER THAN NONPARAMETRIC STATISTICAL TESTS. PARAMETRIC TESTS ARE USED ONLY WITH INTERVAL AND RATIO DATA.   **(d)**

722. A Type I error occurs when

    a.   you have a beta error.
    b.   you accept null when it is false.
    c.   you reject null when it is true.
    d.   you fail to use a test of significance.

Okay, here it is. Time to plug in your handy dandy memory formula . . . "RA" or "reject when applicable/true." Since all statistical tests rely on probability there is always the chance that the results were merely chance occurrences. Researchers call these chance factors "errors." **(c)**

723. A Type II error

    a.   is also called a beta error.
    b.   means you reject null when it is applicable.
    c.   means you accept null when it is false.
    d.   a and c.

Although lowering the significance level (e.g., .01 to .001) lowers Type I errors, it "raises" the risk of committing a Type II or so-called beta error. Simply think of the Type I, Type II relationship as a seesaw in the sense that when one goes up the other goes down. Hence, in determining an alpha level, the researcher needs to decide which error results in the most serious consequences. The safest bet is to set alpha at a very stringent level and then use a large sample size. If this can be accomplished, it is possible to make the correct decision (i.e., accept or reject null) the majority of the time. **(d)**

724. Assume the experiment in question 708 is conducted. The results indicate that the biofeedback helped raise written board exam scores but in reality this is not the case. The researcher has made a

a. Type I error.
b. Type II error.
c. beta error.
d. b and c.

QUESTIONS LIKE THIS CAN BE VERY DIFFICULT. BE SURE TO UTILIZE SCRATCH PAPER TO WRITE DOWN YOUR THOUGHTS IF YOUR EXAM ALLOWS YOU TO DO SO! First, write down (or mentally picture) the null hypothesis regarding the experiment in question. In this case null would mean that biofeedback did not raise board exam scores. This question tells you that the experimental results revealed that biofeedback did raise board scores, so you will reject the null hypothesis. The question then goes on to say that in reality the biofeedback did not really cause the results. Therefore, you have rejected null when it is true/applicable. This is the definition of a Type I or alpha error. Since the experimenter sets the alpha level, he or she is always cognizant of the probability of making a Type I error. **(a)**

725. A counselor educator decides to increase the sample size in her experiment. This will

a. confound the experiment in nearly every case.
b. raise the probability of Type I and Type II errors.
c. have virtually no impact on Type I and Type II errors.
d. reduce Type I and Type II errors.

Raising the size of a sample helps to lower the risk of chance/error factors. Simply put: differences revealed via large samples are more likely to be genuine than differences revealed using a small sample size. **(d)**

726. If a researcher changes the significance level from .05 to .001, then

a. alpha and beta errors will increase.
b. alpha errors increase but beta errors decrease.
c. alpha errors decrease; however, beta errors increase.
d. This will have no impact on Type I and Type II errors.

Review question 723. **(c)**

727. A counselor believes that clients who receive assertiveness training will ask more questions in counseling classes. An experimental group receives assertiveness training while a control group does not. In order to test for significant differences between the groups the counselor should utilize

a. the student's t-test.
b. a correlation coefficient.
c. a survey.
d. an analysis of variance or ANOVA.

When comparing two sample groups the t-test, which is a simplistic form of the analysis of variance, is utilized. The t-test is used to ascertain whether two sample means are significantly different. The researcher sets the level of significance and then runs the experiment. The t-test is computed and this yields a t value. The researcher then goes to a t-table found in the index of most statistic's texts. If the t value obtained statistically is lower than the ·t value (sometimes called "critical t") in the table, then you accept the null hypothesis. YOUR COMPUTATION MUST EXCEED THE NUMBER CITED IN THE TABLE IN ORDER TO REJECT NULL. If there are more than two groups, then the analysis of variance (choice "d") is utilized. The results of an ANOVA yield an F-statistic. The researcher then consults an F-table for a critical value of F. If F obtained (i.e., computed) exceeds the critical F-value in the table, then the null hypothesis is rejected. The other major statistical tests likely to show up on your exam include the following six: the analysis of covariance or ANCOVA, which tests two or more groups while controlling for extraneous variables that are often called "co-variates"; the Kruskal-Wallis, which is used instead of the one-way ANOVA when the data are nonparametric; the Wilcoxon signed rank test, used in place of the t-test when the data are nonparametric and you wish to test whether two correlated means differ significantly (use the "co" to remind you of "correlated"); the Mann-Whitney U-Test, to determine whether two uncorrelated means differ significantly when data are nonparametric (the "u" can remind you of "uncorrelated"); the Spearman correlation or Kendall's tau, which is used in place of the Pearson r when parametric assumptions cannot be utilized; and the Chi-Square nonparametric test, which examines whether obtained frequencies differ significantly from expected frequencies. NOTE THAT STATISTICIANS HAVE CREATED NONPARAMETRIC TESTS THAT PARALLEL THE POPULAR PARAMETRIC MEASURES.   **(a)**

728. The researcher in question 727 now attempts a more complex experiment. One group receives no assertiveness training, a second group receives four assertiveness training sessions, and a third receives six sessions. The statistic of choice would

    a.   be the mean.
    b.   be the t-test.
    c.   be the two-way ANOVA.
    d.   be the ANOVA.

This is a tough question. A one-way analysis of variance is used for testing one independent variable, while a two-way analysis of variance is used to test two independent variables. When a study has more than one DV the term "multivariate analysis of variance" or MANOVA for short is utilized. THE ANSWER IS CHOICE "D" SINCE THE SIMPLE ANOVA OR ONE-WAY ANALYSIS OF VARIANCE IS USED WHEN THERE IS MORE THAN ONE LEVEL OF A SINGLE IV, WHICH IN THIS CASE IS THE ASSERTIVENESS TRAINING.   **(d)**

729. If the researcher in the previous question utilized two IVs then the statistic of choice would be

    a.   the median.
    b.   the t-test.
    c.   the two-way ANOVA or MANOVA.
    d.   the ANOVA.

Two IVs requires a two-way ANOVA, three IVs, a three-way ANOVA, etc. **(c)**

730. To complete a t-test you would consult a tabled value of t. In order to see if significant differences exist in an ANOVA you would

    a.   consult the mode.
    b.   consult a table for t values.
    c.   consult a table for F values.
    d.   compute the chi-square.

More elaborate tests (e.g., Tukey's, Duncan's multiple range, and Scheffe's test) can determine whether a significant difference exists between specific groups. Group comparison tests such as these are called "post hoc" or "a posteriori" tests for ANOVA calculations. **(c)**

731. Which level of significance would best rule out chance factors?

    a.   .05
    b.   .01
    c.   .2
    d.   .001

Some researchers refer to the level of significance as where "one draws the line" or the "cutoff point" between findings that should or should not be ascribed to chance factors. The significance level must be set low. If, for example, a researcher foolishly set the level at .50, then the odds would be 50-50 that the results were due to pure chance. I guarantee you a reputable journal would never touch an article with statistics like that! If you marked anything other than choice "d," you also should review question 720. **(d)**

732. When there is no direct manipulation of the IV, then the experiment uses correlation. A researcher might ask, for example, how IQ correlates with the incidence of panic disorder. Again, nothing is manipulated; just measured. In cases such as this a correlation coefficient will reveal

    a.   the relationship between IQ and panic disorder.
    b.   the probability that a significant difference exists.
    c.   an F test.
    d.   percentile rank.

A statistic that indicates the degree or magnitude of relationship between two variables is known as a "correlation coefficient" and is often abbreviated using a lower case r. A coefficient of correlation makes a statement regarding the association of two variables and how a change in one is related to the change in another. Correlations range from 0.00, no relationship, to 1.0 or -1.0 which signify perfect relationships. **IMPORTANT: A POSITIVE CORRELATION IS NOT A STRONGER RELATIONSHIP THAN A NEGATIVE ONE OF THE SAME NUMERICAL VALUE. A CORRELATION OF -.70 IS STILL INDICATIVE OF A STRONGER RELATIONSHIP THAN A POSITIVE CORRELATION OF .60. THE MINUS SIGN MERELY DESCRIBES THE FACT THAT AS ONE VARIABLE GOES UP THE OTHER GOES DOWN.** **(a)**

733. If data indicate that students who study a lot get very high scores on state counselor licensing exams, then the correlation between study time and LPC exam scores would be

a. positive.
b. negative.
c. 0.00.
d. impossible to ascertain.

A POSITIVE CORRELATION IS EVIDENT WHEN BOTH VARIABLES CHANGE IN THE SAME DIRECTION. A NEGATIVE CORRELATION IS EVIDENT WHEN THE VARIABLES ARE INVERSELY ASSOCIATED; ONE GOES UP AND THE OTHER GOES DOWN. In this case the relationship is positive since as study time increases, LPC exam scores also increase. A negative correlation (choice "b") would be expected when correlating an association like the number of dental caries and time spent brushing one's teeth; as brushing time goes up dental cavities probably go down. Choice "c" or a zero correlation indicates an absence of a relationship between the variables in question. **NOTE:** YOUR EXAM COULD THROW THE TERM BISERIAL CORRELATION AT YOU. THIS MERELY INDICATES THAT ONE VARIABLE IS CONTINUOUS (I.E., MEASURED USING AN INTERVAL SCALE) WHILE THE OTHER IS DICHOTOMOUS. AN EXAMPLE WOULD BE EVIDENT IF YOU DECIDED TO CORRELATE STATE LICENSING EXAM SCORES TO NCC STATUS (HERE THE DICHOTOMY IS LICENSED/UNLICENSED). IF BOTH VARIABLES ARE DICHOTOMOUS (I.E., TWO VALUED) THEN A PHI-COEFFICIENT CORRELATION IS NECESSARY. IMAGINE A RESEARCHER WHO WANTS TO CORRELATE NCC STATUS WITH CCMHC STATUS OR PERHAPS GENDER WITH CERTIFICATION STATUS (HAS CERTIFICATION/DOES NOT HAVE CERTIFICATION).   **(a)**

734. Which of the following would most likely yield a perfect correlation of 1.00?

a. IQ and salary
b. ICD diagnosis and salary
c. length in inches and length in centimeters
d. height and weight

In the real world correlations may be strong (e.g., choice "d"), yet they are rarely 1.00. Correlation is concerned with what statisticians call "covariation." When two variables vary together statisticians say the variables "covary positively," and when one increases while the other decreases they are said to "covary negatively." **(c)**

735. A good guess would be that if you would correlate the length of CACREP graduates' baby toes with their NCE scores the result would

    a.   be close to 0.00.
    b.   be close to a perfect 1.00.
    c.   be close to a perfect negative correlation of -1.00.
    d.   be about +.70.

There is an absence of association here because as one variable changes the other variable varies randomly. The variation of one variable is most likely totally unrelated to the variation of the other. **(a)**

736. Dr. X discovered that the correlation between therapists who hold NCC status and therapists who practice systematic desensitization is .90. A student who perused Dr. X's research told his fellow students that Dr. X had discovered that attaining NCC status causes therapists to become behaviorally oriented. The student is incorrect because

    a.   systematic desensitization is clearly not a behavioral strategy.
    b.   this can only be determined via a histogram.
    c.   the study suffers from longitudinal and maturational effects.
    d.   correlation does not imply causal.

CORRELATION DOES NOT MEAN CAUSAL! CORRELATIONAL RESEARCH IS QUASI-EXPERIMENTAL, AND HENCE, IT DOES NOT YIELD CAUSE-EFFECT DATA.

A major research study, for example, might discover a very high correlation between the number of college students in a given geographical area and number of writing utensils owned. Yet it would certainly be misleading to conclude owning a lot of writing utensils causes one to become a college student. Exam hint: When correlational data describe the nature of two variables, the term "bivariate" is utilized. If more than two variables are under scrutiny, then the term "multivariate" is used to describe the correlational paradigm. **(d)**

737. Behaviorists often utilize N = 1, which is called intensive experimental design. The first step in this approach would be to

    a.   consult a random number table.
    b.   decide on a nonparametric statistical test.
    c.   take a baseline measure.
    d.   compute the range.

"N," or the number of persons being studied, is one. This is a "case study" of one approach. This method is popular with behaviorists who seek overt (measurable) behavioral changes. The client's dysfunctional behavior is measured (this is called a baseline measure), the treatment is implemented, and then the behavior is measured once again (i.e., another baseline is computed). Exams sometimes delineate this paradigm using upper case A's and B's and C's such that A's signify baselines, B's intervention implementation, and C a second or alternative form of intervention. Single case investigations are often called "idiographic studies" or "single-subject designs." The original case study methodology was popularized by Freud, though needless to say, unlike the behaviorists Freud did not rely on numerical baseline measures. Case studies are often misleading because the results are not necessarily generalizable. **(c)**

738. In a new study the clients do not know whether they are receiving an experimental treatment for depression or whether they are simply part of the control group. This is, nevertheless, known to the researcher. Thus, this is a

    a. double blind study.
    b. single blind study.
    c. baseline for an intensive N=1 design.
    d. confounded.

In the single blind study the subject would not know whether he or she is a member of the control group or the experimental group. This strategy helps eliminate "demand characteristics" which are clues or features of a study which suggest a desired outcome. In other words a subject can manipulate and confound an experiment by purposely trying to confirm or disprove the experimental hypothesis. Let us say that in the above-referenced experiment a subject is fond of the researcher. And let us further assume that a score on a standardized depression inventory will be used as the DV. Our subject might purposely answer the questions as if he is less depressed than he really is. A subject who disliked the researcher could present himself as even more depressed. Just in case you erroneously chose choice "c" please notice that the question used the word "clients" which is plural. N=1 designs rely on a single individual for investigation purposes. Choice "d" could be eliminated on the basis that a single blind study would be used to abate confounding factors.   **(b)**

739. A large study at a major university gave an experimental group of clients a new type of therapy that was intended to ameliorate test anxiety. The control group did not receive the new therapy. Neither the clients nor the researchers knew which students received the new treatment. This was a

a. double blind study.
b. single blind study.
c. typical AB design.
d. case of correlational research.

A double blind study goes one step beyond the single blind version by making certain that the experimenter is also unaware of the subjects' status. In fact, in the double blind situation the persons assigned to rate or judge the subjects are often unaware of the hypothesis. This procedure helps eliminate confounding caused by "experimenter effects." EXPERIMENTER EFFECTS CAN FLAW AN EXPERIMENT AS THE EXPERIMENTER MIGHT UNCONSCIOUSLY COMMUNICATE HIS OR HER INTENT OR EXPECTATIONS TO THE SUBJECTS. Choice "c," though incorrect, is a must know concept. An AB or ABA design is the simplest type of single-subject research. The AB and ABA rely on "continuous-measurement." A baseline is secured (A); intervention is implemented (B); and the outcome is examined via a new baseline (A) in the case of the ABA design. In order to improve the research process, an ABAB design can be utilized to better rule out extraneous variables. If the pattern for the second AB administration mimics that of the first AB, then the chances increase that B (the intervention or so-called treatment) caused the changes rather than an extraneous variable. Some exams will refer to ABA or ABAB paradigms as "withdrawal designs." The rationale is that the behavior will move in the direction of the initial baseline each time the treatment is withdrawn if the treatment IV is responsible for the change. The ethical counselor must forego using a withdrawal or reversal design (as they are sometimes called) if the removal of the treatment variable could prove harmful to the subject or those who come in contact with the individual. Here, a simple AB must suffice. Remember that when a researcher employs more than one target behavior, the term "multiple-baseline design" probably will be used on your exam. **(a)**

740. Experimental is to cause and effect as correlational is to

a.   blind study.
b.   double blind study.
c.   N=1 design.
d.   degree of relationship.

A correlation coefficient is a descriptive statistic which indicates the degree of "linear relationship" between two variables. Statisticians use the phrase "linear relationship" to indicate that when a perfect relationship exists (i.e., a correlation of 1.0 or -1.0) and it is graphed, a straight line is formed. (See the "Graphical Representations" section of this book.) The Pearson Product-Moment correlation r is used for interval or ratio data while the Spearman rho correlation is used for ordinal data. Correlational research is not experimental and hence does not imply causality. So what do you do if your exam sneaks in a question regarding the type of data which must be used with the Pearson r versus the Spearman rho? I'd opt for a memory device. Pearson r, the most common correlation coefficient, uses I and R (interval and ratio data) as in "information and referral." Spearman rho ends in "o" as in ordinal. YES YOU CAN DO WELL ON THIS SECTION OF THE EXAM!   **(d)**

741. In a normal curve the mean, the median, and the mode all fall precisely in the middle of the curve. From a graphical standpoint the so-called normal or Gaussian curve (named after the astronomer/mathematician K.F. Gauss) looks like

    a.   a symmetrical bell.
    b.   the top half of a bowling ball.
    c.   the top half of a hot dog.
    d.   a mountain which is leaning toward the left.

The normal curve is a theoretical notion often referred to as a "bell-shaped curve." The bell is symmetrical. Most physical and psychological traits are normally distributed. In other words, if enough data are collected in regard to a given trait, and a frequency polygon is constructed, it will resemble the bell shaped curve. Curves that are not symmetrical (i.e., those which are asymmetrical) are called "skewed distributions." (See Graphical Representations" section of this book.) **(a)**

742. The most common measures of central tendency are the mean, the median, and the mode. The mode is

    a. the most frequently occurring score and the least important measure of central tendency.
    b. always 10% less than the mean.
    c. the arithmetic average.
    d. the middle score in the distribution of scores.

The mode is the highest or maximum point of concentration. The French phrase a la mode means "in style" or "in vogue." The mode is the score that is most "in style" or occurs the most. Just remember that pie a la mode has a "high concentration of calories." The modal score is the highest point on the curve. Hence, a test might tell you that a population of schizophrenics consists of 400 Whites, 60 Asian Americans, and 100 Blacks and ask you to pick out the so-called "modal category," rather than the modal score. In this case the highest value is held by the White population. Statisticians refer to choice "c" as the "mean" and choice "d" as the "median." **(a)**

743. A bimodal distribution has two modes (i.e., most frequently occurring scores). Graphically, this looks roughly like

    a. a symmetrical bell-shaped curve.
    b. a camel's back with two humps.
    c. the top half of a bowling ball.
    d. a mountain which is leaning toward the left.

Come on, admit it now . . . the camel's back makes a nice little memory device doesn't it? If you decided to give the NCE to first-year counseling students and counselor educators teaching in CACREP programs the distribution of scores would probably be bimodal. So would a distribution of men and women's weights. Chances are that in both of the aforementioned situations two peaks would be evident. When a curve exhibits more than two peaks it is known as a "multimodal" distribution. This can be contrasted to the curve with just a single peak (e.g., the normal curve) which is said to be "unimodal." (See Graphical Representations" section of this book.)   **(b)**

744. In a basic curve or so-called frequency polygon the point of maximum concentration is the

   a.   mean.
   b.   median.
   c.   mode.
   d.   range.

Say your exam provides you with a list of test scores such as this: 1, 10, 19, 1, 10, 19, 19, 19, 6, 54. You are then asked to delineate the mode. Your answer will simply be determined by finding the score that appears the most, which in this example would be 19 since four individuals scored 19. The mean, choice "a," would be computed by adding the numbers provided (i.e., the scores) and then dividing by the number of scores which in this case is 10. Here the sum of the scores equals 158 divided by 10 which yields a mean value of 15.8. The median, choice "b," is defined as the score which is the exact middle of the distribution. (Just remember that the median is in the middle of the highway.) Choice "d," the range, which is a measure of variability, is the distance between the largest and the smallest scores (i.e., 54 and 1). To compute the range you would take 54 minus 1 and get a range of 53. THE LARGER THE RANGE THE GREATER THE DISPERSION OR SPREAD OF SCORES FROM THE MEAN. Since the computation of the range is based solely on the computation of two scores, the variance and the standard deviation (the square root of the variance) are more stable statistics.   **(c)**

745. The most useful measure of central tendency is the

    a.   mean often abbreviated by an X with a bar over it.
    b.   median often abbreviated by Md. or Mdn.
    c.   mode often abbreviated by Mo.
    d.   point of maximum concentration.

In everyday life when we use the word average we are referring to the "mean." Perhaps this is because in most instances it is the most useful of the three measures of central tendency. Nevertheless, if a distribution is plagued with extreme scores then the "median" is the statistic of choice. The median is best for skewed distributions. If a counselor decides to figure the average income of incoming undergraduate freshmen in a crisis intervention class, and one of the students is a millionaire, then the median will be a more valuable statistic than the mean since the mean would be raised significantly by the millionaire's income. And of course, you were able to discern that choice "d" is a definition of choice "c," mode, which researchers consider the least important measure of central tendency. **(a)**

746. In a career counseling session an electrical engineer mentions three jobs he has held. The first paid $10 per hour, the second paid $30 per hour, and the third paid a higher rate of $50 per hour. The counselor responds that the client is averaging $30 per hour. The counselor is using

    a.   a Pearson product-moment correlation coefficient.
    b.   the median.
    c.   the harmonic mean.
    d.   the mean.

The mean is the sum of scores divided by the number of scores. $10 + $30 + $50 = $90. $90 divided by 3 jobs = $30. Choice "c," the harmonic mean, refers to a central tendency statistic that is the reciprocal of the arithmetic mean of the reciprocals of the set of values. Say, for example, that your exam asks you to calculate the harmonic mean for 3 scores of: 2, 2, and 4. First you would convert them to reciprocals: ½, ½, and ¼. The arithmetic mean then is ½ + ½ + ¼ = 1¼ or 1.25/ 3 = .4166. The reciprocal of this gives you a harmonic mean of 1/.4166. The statistic has limited usage; however, it is occasionally called for if measurements were not made on an appropriate scale (e.g., data revealed the number of behaviors per hour, when the number of minutes per behavior would be more useful). The harmonic cannot be utilized with negative numbers or if the data include a score of zero. **(d)**

747. From a mathematical standpoint, the mean is merely the sum of the scores divided by the number of scores. The mean is misleading when

    a.   the distribution is skewed.
    b.   the distribution has no extreme scores.
    c.   there are extreme scores.
    d.   a and c.

See question 745 for an explanation. **(d)**

748. When a distribution of scores is not distributed normally statisticians call it

    a.   Gauss's curve.
    b.   a symmetrical bell-shaped curve.
    c.   a skewed distribution.
    d.   an invalid distribution.

Your exam might show you a graphic representation of a distribution and ask you whether the distribution is skewed. IN A SKEWED DISTRIBUTION THE LEFT AND RIGHT SIDE OF THE CURVE ARE NOT MIRROR IMAGES. IN A SKEWED DISTRIBUTION THE MEAN, THE MEDIAN, AND THE MODE FALL AT DIFFERENT POINTS. IN A NORMAL CURVE THEY WILL FALL AT THE SAME POINT. (See Graphical Representations" section of this book.) **(c)**

749. The median is

    a.   the middle score when the data are arranged from highest to lowest.
    b.   the arithmetic average.
    c.   the most frequent value obtained.
    d.   never more useful than the mean.

Use your memory device: the median is the exact "middle of the highway" . . . it is the "middle score." In studies measuring variables with extreme scores (e.g., family size or income), the median would be the best statistic. Your exam could specify a distribution of scores and ask you to name the median score. Say, for example, your exam provides these scores: 1, 90, 12, 90, 6, 8, 7. First rank the scores from the lowest to the highest: 1, 6, 7, 8, 12, 90, 90. In this case, the median score is 8 since there are three scores above 8 (12, 90, 90) and three scores below it (1, 6, 7). Now let's assume that the test construction committee isn't so kind. In fact, maybe they are feeling a little sadistic that day. This time they add another score so there are eight scores rather than seven in the distribution. Now the distribution has an even rather than an odd number of scores. Assume the score of 10 was added. Thus when you rank order the distribution, it now looks like this: 1, 6, 7, 8, 10, 12, 90, 90. Do I hear some head-scratching here. . .maybe even a tinge of panic? What's that you say? You can't find a value that has an equal number of scores above and below it. Well you're correct—it doesn't exist. The trick here is to know that the median is a score or a "potential score" that divides the distribution in half. Therefore, when a distribution has an even number of scores, you take the arithmetic mean of the two middle scores and use this as the median. In this case: 8 + 10 = 18 and 18/2 = 9. The median of 9 lies midway between the middle scores of 8 and 10. In some cases, your computation could yield legitimately a fraction (e.g., 9 ½). **(a)**

750. In a new experiment, a counselor educator wants to ferret out the effects of more than one IV. She will use a _____ design.

    a.   Pearson product-moment r
    b.   Spearman rank order rho
    c.   factorial
    d.   Solomon four-group design

In a factorial experiment, several experimental variables are investigated and interactions can be noted. Factorial designs, therefore, include two or more IVs. Choices "a" and "b" are not considered pure experimental. Now even though choice "d" is incorrect, it is indeed a must know term. In the Solomon four-group design, the researcher uses two control groups. Only one experimental group and one control group are pretested. The other control group and experimental group are merely post-tested. The genius of the design is that it lets the researcher know if results are influenced by pretesting. The two control groups as well as the two experimental groups can then be compared. **(c)**

751. Regardless of the shape, the _____ will always be the high point when a distribution is displayed graphically.

    a.   df
    b.   mean
    c.   median
    d.   mode

The mode will be highest because it is the point where the most frequently occurring score falls. **(d)**

752. If a group of first semester graduate students in counseling took the NCE exam, a distribution of scores would be

a. a bell-shaped curve.
b. positively skewed.
c. negatively skewed.
d. more information obviously is needed.

Try to imagine this in your mind or roughly graph it on scratch paper. First semester students (assuming they were allowed to take the NCE which they are not) would probably have little information on the more advanced points of counseling; and thus, we would expect them to score very poorly. Hence, most of the scores would fall on the left or the low side of the distribution. Graphically then, the "tail" of the distribution would point to the right or the positive side. MEMORY DEVICE: THE TAIL INDICATES WHETHER THE DISTRIBUTION IS POSITIVELY OR NEGATIVELY SKEWED. (See the "Graphical Representations" section of this book.) **(b)**

753. Nine of the world's finest counselor educators are given an elementary exam on counseling theory. The distribution of scores would most likely be

a. a bell-shaped curve.
b. positively skewed.
c. negatively skewed.
d. more information would be necessary.

We would expect these folks to score really high; and thus, the right side of the curve would be packed with high values. This gives you a long tail that points to the left, which indicates a negative skew. The tail points you in the direction of the correct answer! (See "Graphical Representations" section of this book.) **(c)**

754. Billy received an 82 on his college math final. This is Billy's raw score on the test. A raw score simply refers to the number of items correctly answered. A raw score is expressed in the units by which it was originally obtained. The raw score is not altered mathematically. Billy's raw score indicates that

a.   he is roughly a B student.
b.   he answered 82% correctly.
c.   his percentile rank is 82.
d.   more information is obviously necessary.

Don't get burnt on a question like this; the fact that Billy scored an 82 tells you next to nothing. Raw data is like a raw piece of meat; it is uncooked and nothing has been done to it. How many questions are on the test? Well, you don't know, do you? So, you couldn't choose choice "b" since you don't have enough information to figure out the percentage. The question doesn't specify this critical fact. You see, if Billy scored an 82 on a test with 82 questions, then he had a perfect score. If, however, the exam had several thousand items, his score may not have been all that high. I say "may not have been all that high," since a raw score of 82 might have been the highest score of anybody tested. You would need a "transformed score" (such as choice "c") to make this determination. **(d)**

755. A distribution with class intervals can be graphically displayed via a bar graph also called a

a.   histogram.
b.   sociogram.
c.   genogram.
d.   genus.

Most bar graphs are drawn in a vertical fashion. When the bars are drawn horizontally it is sometimes called a "horizontal bar chart." A "double-barred histogram" can be used to compare two distributions of scores such as pre and post test scores. (See "Graphical Representations" section of this book.) **(a)**

756. When a horizontal line is drawn under a frequency distribution it is known as

a. mesokurtic.
b. the y axis.
c. the ordinate.
d. the x axis.

Choice "a" is from the Latin root "meso" or middle, and kurtic refers to the peakedness of a curve. The normal Gaussian curve is said to be mesokurtic since the peak is in the middle. When graphically representing data, the "x axis" (also called the abscissa) is used to plot the independent variable. The x axis is the horizontal axis. The "y axis" (also called the ordinate) is the vertical axis which is used as a scale for the dependent variable.   **(d)**

757. The x axis is used to plot the IV scores. The x axis is also known as

a. the y axis.
b. the abscissa.
c. the DV.
d. the vertical axis.

Again, it is the horizontal axis which plots the IV—the factor manipulated via the experimenter.   **(b)**

758. The y axis is used to plot the frequency of the DVs. The y axis is also known as the

a. ordinate.
b. abscissa.
c. the IV.
d. the horizontal axis.

The ordinate plots the DV or experimental data. A simple memory device might be that the y axis is vertical like the letter "y."   **(a)**

759. If a distribution is bimodal, then there is a good chance that

a.   the curve will be normal.
b.   the curve will be shaped like a symmetrical bell.
c.   the researcher is working with two distinct populations.
d.   the research is useless in the field of counseling.

Imagine, if you will, that you are plotting the average weights of adult men and women. In all probability, two distinct points of concentration would be evident on the curve. (See "Graphical Representations" section of this book.)   **(c)**

760. If an experiment can be replicated by others with almost identical findings, then the experiment

     a.   is confounded.
     b.   is said to be a naturalistic observation.
     c.   is the result of ethological observation.
     d.   is said to be reliable.

You will recall that the term reliability in the social sciences is also used in regard to testing to indicate consistency in measurement. Choice "b" occurs when clients are observed in a "natural" setting or situation. Choice "c" relates to the observation of animals.   **(d)**

761. The range is a measure of variance and usually is calculated by determining the difference between the highest and the lowest score. Thus, on a test where the top score was a 93 and the lowest score was a 33 out of 100, the range would be

     a.   61.
     b.   77.
     c.   59.
     d.   more information is necessary.

The range is the simplest way to measure the spread of scores. Technically, statistics that measure the spread of scores are known as "measures of variability." The range is usually calculated by subtracting the lowest score from the highest score (e.g., 93-33 = 60). But wait . . . 60 is not a choice! Well, I purposely gave you this example to point out that some tests and statistics books define the range as the highest score minus the lowest score plus 1. If the test specifies the "inclusive range" then use the formula with plus 1. If not, I'd go with the "exclusive range" formula which does not include it. My guess is that most counseling tests would give you either 60 or 61 as a choice (probably 60) but not both. **(a)**

762. A sociogram is to a counseling group as a scattergram is to

    a.   the normal curve.
    b.   the range.
    c.   a correlation coefficient.
    d.   the John Henry Effect.

A scattergram—also known as a scatterplot—is a pictorial diagram or graph of two variables being correlated. (See "Graphical Representations" section of this book.) And yes, my dear reader, choice "d" is for real. There really is a John Henry Effect. The John Henry Effect (also called compensatory rivalry of a comparison group) is a threat to the internal validity of an experiment that occurs when subjects strive to prove that an experimental treatment that could threaten their livelihood really isn't all that effective. (An old railroad song asserts that John Henry died with a steam drill in his hand to prove he could outwork the machine.) Say, for example, that counselor educators were asked to use computers as part of the teaching experience but were worried that the computers might ultimately take their jobs! The counselor educators in the comparison control group might purposely spend more time preparing their materials and give students more support than they normally would. One way for the researcher to handle this problem is to make observations before the experiment begins. Another control group phenomenon that threatens internal validity in research is the "Resentful Demoralization of the Comparison Group" (as called "compensatory equalization"). Here, the comparison group lowers their performance or behaves in an inept manner because they have been denied the experimental treatment. When this occurs, the experimental group looks better than they should. If the comparison group deteriorates throughout the experiment while the experimental group does not, then demoralization could be noted. This could be measured via a pretest and a post-test.   **(c)**

763. A counselor educator is teaching two separate classes in individual inventory. In the morning class the counselor educator has 53 students and in the afternoon class she has 177. A statistician would expect that the range of scores on a test would be

    a.   greater in the afternoon class than the morning class.
    b.   smaller in the afternoon class.
    c.   impossible to speculate about without more data.
    d.   nearly the same in either class.

The range generally increases with sample size.   **(a)**

764. The variance is a measure of dispersion of scores around some measure of central tendency. The variance is the standard deviation squared. A popular IQ test has a standard deviation (SD) of 15. A counselor would expect that if the mean IQ score is 100, then

    a.   the average score on the test would be 122.
    b.   95% of the people who take the test will score between 85 and 115.
    c.   99% of the people who take the test will score between 85 and 115.
    d.   68% of the people who take the test will score between 85 and 115.

Statistically speaking 68.26% of the scores fall within plus or minus 1 SD of the mean, 95.44% of the scores fall within plus or minus 2 SD of the mean, and 99.74%

of the scores fall within plus or minus 3 SD of the mean. **(d)**

765. Using the data in question 764 one could say that a person with an IQ score of 122 would fall within

    a.   plus or minus 1 SD of the mean.
    b.   the average IQ range.
    c.   an IQ score which is more that 2 SD above the mean.
    d.   plus or minus 2 SD of the mean.

Two SD would be IQ's from 70 to 130 since 2 SD would be 30 IQ points. Please note that if everybody scored the same on the test then the SD would be zero. An SD, for example, of 1.8 has scores closer to the mean (i.e., not as spread out or scattered) then an SD of 2.8. THE GREATER THE SD THE GREATER THE SPREAD. **(d)**

766. The standard deviation is the square root of the variance. A Z-score of +1 would be the same as

    a.   one standard deviation above the mean.
    b.   one standard deviation below the mean.
    c.   the same as a so-called T-score.
    d.   the median score if the population is normal.

Z-scores are the same as standard deviations! A Z-score is the most elementary type of standard score. It is possible your exam will refer to it merely as a standard score. Just say it in slang: "Z-score" (sounds rather like saying "the score") is simply the SD. A Z-score of plus one or 1 SD would include about 34% of the cases in a normal population. For those with a fear of negative integers, the normal distribution also can be described using T-scores sometimes called "transformed scores." The T-score uses a mean of 50 with each SD as 10. Hence, a Z-score of -1.0 would be a T-score of 40. A Z-score of -1.5 would be a T-score of 35 and so on. If double digit figures intimidate you, then you might want to analyze the normal distribution using a "stanine" score which divides the distribution into nine equal parts with 1 the lowest and 9 the highest portion of the curve. **(a)**

767. Z-scores are the same as standard deviations. Thus a Z-score of -2.5 means

    a.   2 1/2 SD below the mean.
    b.   2.5 SD above the mean.
    c.   a CEEB score of 500.
    d.   .05% of the population falls within this area of the curve.

This would be a T-score of 25. Now, let's examine choice "c" which expresses the abbreviation for the "College Entrance Examination Board" scores by the Educational Testing Service (ETS) of Princeton, New Jersey. This standard score is used for tests such as the GRE or the SAT. The scale ranges from 200 to 800 with a mean of 500. CEEB scores use a standard deviation of 100. Scores lower than 200 or above 800 are simply rated as end point scores. A score of 200 corresponds to 3 SD below the mean with 800 landing at a point 3 SD above the mean. Therefore, in this case, choice "c" would need to read "a CEEB score of 250" to be accurate. (That is to say, you would take the CEEB mean of 500 and subtract 2 1/2 SD. Since each SD on the CEEB scale is 100 you would subtract 250 from 500 which gives you a CEEB score of 250.) IT IS CONCEIVABLE THAT YOUR EXAM COULD REFER TO A CEEB SCORE AS AN ETS SCORE. **(a)**

768. A T-score is different than a Z-score. A Z-score is the same as the standard deviation. A T-score, however, has a mean of 50 with every 10 points landing at a standard deviation above or below the mean. Thus a T-score of 60 would equal +1 SD while a T-score of 40 would

a. be -2 SD.
b. be -1 SD.
c. be a Z-score of +2.
d. be a Z-score of +1.

Note that the T-score isn't as mathematically threatening since it is never expressed as a negative number. Choice "a" would be a T-score of 30, choice "c" a T-score of 70, and choice "d" a T-score of 60. **(b)**

769. An IQ score on an IQ test which was three standard deviations above the mean would be

a. about average.
b. slightly below the norm for adults.
c. approximately 110.
d. near the genius level.

Think of it this way. Over 99% of the population will score between plus or minus 3 SD of the mean. Therefore, less than 1% of the population would score at a level 3 SD above the mean. Now that would be a very high IQ score; 145 on the WAIS-R to be exact. **(d)**

770. A platykurtic distribution would look approximately like

a. the upper half of a bowling ball.
b. the normal distribution.
c. the upper half of a hot dog, lying on its side over the abscissa.
d. a camel's back.

If you see the word "kurtosis" on your exam, it refers to the peakedness of a frequency distribution. A "platykurtic" distribution is flatter and more spread out than the normal curve. This is easy to remember if you consider that "plat" sounds rather like "flat." When a curve is very tall, thin, and peaked it is considered "leptokurtic." Suggested memory device: A leptokurtic distribution leaps tall buildings in a single bound. Well, Superman fans, how about it; does that do it justice? **(c)**

771. Test scores on an exam that fell below three standard deviations of the mean or above three standard deviations of the mean could be described as

    a.   extreme.
    b.   very typical or within the average range.
    c.   close to the mean.
    d.   very low scores.

If you graph this situation you will note that these scores would be unusually high (which negates choices "b," "c," and "d") or very low. **(a)**

772. In World War II the Air Force used stanine scores as a measurement. Stanine scores divide the distribution into nine equal intervals with stanine 1 as the lowest ninth and 9 as the highest ninth. In this system 5 is the mean. Thus a Binet IQ score of 101 would fall in stanine

    a.   1.
    b.   9.
    c.   5.
    d.   7.

Stanine is the contraction of the words standard and nine. The mean or average score on the Binet is 100. **(c)**

773. There are four basic measurement scales: the nominal, the ordinal, the interval, and the ratio. The nominal scale is strictly a qualitative scale. It is the simplest type of scale. It is used to distinguish logically separated groups. Which of the following illustrates the function of the nominal scale?

    a.   A horse categorized as a second place winner in a show.
    b.   An ICD diagnostic category.
    c.   An IQ score of 111.
    d.   The weight of an Olympic barbell set.

The order of complexity of S.S. Steven's four types of measurement scales can be memorized by noting the French word "noir" meaning black. Parametric tests rely strictly on interval and ratio data, while nonparametric tests are designed only for nominal or ordinal information. The nominal scale is the most elementary as it does not provide "quantitative" (measurable) information. The nominal scale merely classifies, names, labels, or identifies by group. Other examples would be a street address, telephone number, political party affiliation, gender, brand of therapy, or number on a player's uniform. Adding, subtracting, multiplying, or dividing the aforementioned nominal categories would prove meaningless.   **(b)**

774. The ordinal scale rank-orders variables, though the relative distance between the elements is not always equal. An example of this would be

      a.   a horse categorized as a second place winner in a race.
      b.   an IQ score of 111.
      c.   the weight of an Olympic barbell set.
      d.   a temperature of 78 degrees Fahrenheit.

This is the second level of measurement. Nominal data does not rank-order the data like ordinal data. The rank does not indicate absolute differences. Thus, you could not say that the first, second, and third place horses were equidistant apart. The ordinal scale provides relative placement or standing but does not delineate absolute differences. Again, adding, subtracting, multiplying, or dividing is a no-no with this scale. Ordinal sounds like "order" so you should have no problem committing this scale to memory.   **(a)**

775. The interval scale has numbers scaled at equal distances but has no absolute zero point. Most tests used in school fall into this category. You can add and subtract using interval scales but cannot multiply or divide. An example of this would be

a. that an IQ of 70 is 70 points below an IQ of 140 yet a counselor could not assert that a client with an IQ of 140 is twice as intelligent as a client with an IQ of 70.
b. that a 20 lb. weight is twice as heavy as a 40 lb. weight.
c. that a first place runner is three times as fast as the third place finisher.
d. that a baseball player with number 9 on his uniform can get 9 times more hits than player number 1.

Since the intervals are the same, the amount of difference can be stipulated (e.g., 3 IQ points). Using this scale, distances between each number are equal yet it is unclear how far each number is from zero. Division is not permissible inasmuch as division assumes an absolute zero. (If you had an absolute zero then you could in fact assert that a person with an IQ of 140 would be twice as smart as someone with an IQ of 70. But of course, zero on an IQ test does not equal zero knowledge; hence, IQ tests provide ordinal measurement.)   **(a)**

776. A ratio scale is an interval scale with a true zero point. Ratio measurements are possible using this scale. Addition, subtraction, multiplication and division all can be utilized on a ratio scale. In terms of counseling research

a. the ratio scale is the most practical.
b. all true studies utilize the ratio scale.
c. a and b
d. most psychological attributes cannot be measured on a ratio scale.

If you remember your memory device "noir" you'll recall that the final letter "r" stands for the ratio scale, which is the highest level of measurement. Time, height, weight, temperature on the Kelvin scale, volume, and distance meet the requirements of this scale. Please note the word "most" in the correct choice (i.e., choice "d").

Occasionally, a trait such as GSR (galvanic skin response) biofeedback could be classified as a ratio scale measurement. Since most measurements used in counseling studies do not qualify as ratio scales, choices "a" and "b" are misleading. **(d)**

777. Researchers often utilize naturalistic observation when doing ethological investigations or studying children's behavior. In this approach

    a.   the researcher manipulates the IV.
    b.   the researcher manipulates the IV and the DV.
    c.   the researcher does not manipulate or control variables.
    d.   the researcher will rely on the ANOVA.

WHEN UTILIZING NATURALISTIC OBSERVATION THE RESEARCHER DOES NOT INTERVENE. PREFERABLY, THE SETTING IS "NATURAL" RATHER THAN AN ARTIFICIAL LABORATORY ENVIRONMENT. HISTORICALLY SPEAKING, THIS IS THE OLDEST METHOD OF RESEARCH. **(c)**

778. The simplest form of descriptive research is the _____, which requires a questionnaire return rate of _____ to be accurate.

    a.   survey; 5%
    b.   survey; 10%-25%
    c.   survey; 50-75%
    d.   survey; 95%

Unfortunately, it has been estimated that in most surveys the return rate hovers around the 40% mark. In a survey, the researcher attempts to gather large amounts of data, often utilizing a questionnaire or an interview, in order to generate generalizations regarding the behavior of the population as a whole. Ideally, the sample size will be at least 100. (Compare this to an experimental study which can generally get by with a sample size of 15 per group.) A public opinion poll such as the Gallup is an example of a survey. **(c)**

779. A researcher gives a depressed patient a sugar pill and the individual's depression begins to lift. This is known as

    a. the Hawthorne Effect.
    b. the Halo Effect.
    c. the placebo effect.
    d. the learned helplessness syndrome.

A student once told me that while he was preparing for final exams his roommate suggested that he "pop a couple uppers" for energy. The student did indeed pop the pills, studied like a whirlwind and aced all his finals. He was sold on the pills until his roommate discovered that the two amphetamine capsules were still sitting on the table—the student had swallowed two ordinary breath mints lying next to the drugs!!! The student thought the pills would work and so they did. Researchers often give clients involved in studies an inert substance (i.e., a placebo) so it can be compared with the real drug or treatment procedure. **(c)**

780. A researcher notes that a group of clients who are not receiving counseling, but are observed in a research study, are improving. Her hypothesis is that the attention she has given them has been curative. The best explanation of their improvement would be

    a. the Hawthorne Effect.
    b. the Halo Effect.
    c. the Rosenthal Effect.
    d. a Type II error in the research.

Ah yes, this relates to the famous 1939 study by Roethlisberger and Dickson at the Hawthorne Works of the Western Electric Company which indicated that work production tended to increase with better lighting or worse lighting conditions. The verdict: simply that if subjects know they are part of an experiment—or if they are given more attention because of the experiment—their performance sometimes improves. When observations are made and the subjects' behavior is influenced by the very presence of the researcher, it is often called a "reactive effect" of observation/experimentation. The subject is said to be REACTING TO THE PRESENCE OF THE INVESTIGATOR. A comprehensive test without at least one question on the Hawthorne Effect . . . no way! **(a)**

781. An elementary school counselor tells the third grade teacher that a test revealed that certain children will excel during the school year. In reality, no such test was administered. Moreover, the children were unaware of the experiment. By the end of the year, all of the children who were supposed to excel did excel! This would best be explained via

        a.   the Hawthorne Effect.
        b.   the Halo Effect.
        c.   the Rosenthal Effect.
        d.   a type II error in the research.

Well, forget the Hawthorne Effect this time around since the kids don't even know an experiment is in progress. Here the "Rosenthal Effect," or experimenter effect (mentioned previously), is probably having the impact. The Rosenthal Effect asserts that the experimenter's beliefs about the individual may cause the individual to be treated in a special way so that the individual begins to fulfill the experimenter's expectations. Hint: When you see the Hawthorne Effect question on your exam you can bet that the Rosenthal Effect question is within shouting distance. **(c)**

782. A panel of investigators discovered that a researcher who completed a major study had unconsciously rated attractive females as better counselors. This is an example of

a.   the Hawthorne Effect.
b.   the Halo Effect.
c.   the Rosenthal Effect.
d.   trend analysis

The Halo Effect occurs when a trait which is not being evaluated influences a researcher's rating on another trait. Choice "d," trend analysis, refers to a statistical procedure performed at different times to see if a trend is evident. Some exams use the term to describe an application of the ANOVA to see if performance on one variable mimics the same trend on a second variable. Say you have arranged three groups of subjects in regard to their ability to respond to reality therapy (i.e., poor clients, average clients, and good clients). Your hypothesis is that clients at each level also will respond better to RET than will those on the level below them. (For example, good reality therapy clients will be better RET clients than average or poor reality therapy clients.) Here the ANOVA allows you to statistically test this hypothesis.   **(b)**

783. All of the following describe the analysis of covariance technique **except**

a.   it is a correlation coefficient.
b.   it controls for sample differences which exist.
c.   it helps to remove confounding, extraneous variables.
d.   it statistically eliminates differences in average values influenced by covariates.

Just what is the analysis of covariance or the ANCOVA/ ANACOVA as they say in the statistical circles? First and foremost, the ANCOVA is similar to the ANOVA yet more powerful, as it can help to eliminate differences between groups which otherwise could not be solely attributed to the experimental IVs. In other words, although ideally each random sample will be equal to every other random sample this is not always the case. A so-called CO-VARIATE, which correlates with the DV, could be present. Let's take this very simple example. Imagine that you are using an ANOVA to test the null hypothesis regarding three groups of college students. First, a random sample of college students is selected. Next, the sample is randomly divided into three groups. Group A receives biofeedback, Group B receives meditation, and Group C receives instruction in self-hypnosis. All are intended to reduce test anxiety. At the end of the semester a test which measures test anxiety will be administered to all three groups. The ANOVA would then be applied to test the null hypothesis. Null, of course, would be rejected if a significant difference between the three groups' means was evident on the test anxiety measure. Here comes the problem, however; your random groups, as pointed out earlier, may not really be all that identical. You might suspect, for example, that athletic training is a covariate and thus impacts upon the measure of test anxiety; your DV. The ANCOVA allows you to correct for the differences in the groups (possibly due to prior athletic training). By making the groups more alike upfront, it will enhance the possibility that the IVs (biofeedback, meditation, and self-hypnosis instruction) rather than a covariate or DV (athletic training) caused the differences in the groups. In summary, the ANCOVA tests a null hypothesis regarding the means of two or more groups AFTER THE RANDOM SAMPLES ARE ADJUSTED TO ELIMINATE AVERAGE DIFFERENCES. It is often referred to as an "adjusted average" statistical procedure.　　　　**(a)**

784. A percentile score is not the same as the percentage of questions answered correctly. For example, a student who answered 42 questions out of 100 correctly (i.e., 42% correct) might be at the 50th percentile. This technically would indicate that

    a.   the student's NCE score would be 50.
    b.   his or her score was well below average.
    c.   50% of the persons taking the test had scores equal to or below his raw score 42.
    d.   a and c.

Actually, I'm ashamed of myself for being incredibly sneaky . . . so ashamed that if you chose alternative "c," go ahead and count it as correct even though technically choice "d"—that's right, choice "d"!—is the correct answer. You see, my guess is that 99.99% of those reading this text saw the letters NCE for perhaps the 500th time now and said, "Oh yeh, the National Counselor's Exam again, so what else is new?" You then decided to axe choice "a" based on the knowledge that the NCE has more then 100 questions or some such logic. The fact is that there is A STANDARD SCORE CALLED THE "NORMAL CURVE EQUIVALENT SCALE" THAT ALSO IS ABBREVIATED NCE! THE SCALE—WHICH HAS NOTHING TO DO WITH THE NATIONAL COUNSELOR EXAMINATION—WAS THE BRAINCHILD OF THE U.S. DEPARTMENT OF EDUCATION WHO REQUIRES ITS USE IN SOME FORMS OF REPORTING. THE NORMAL CURVE EQUIVALENT SCALE USES A MEAN OF 50 AND A STRANGE STANDARD DEVIATION OF 21.06. IF I WERE YOU I'D FORGET ABOUT THE STANDARD DEVIATION AND JUST RECALL THAT NCE SCORES MATCH PERCENTILE RANKS. IN OTHER WORDS, AN NCE SCORE OF 50 CORRESPONDS TO THE 50TH PERCENTILE RANK (AN NCE SCORE OF 1 TO A PERCENTILE RANK OF 1 AND SO ON) RENDERING CHOICE "A" RIGHT ON TARGET. A percentile score or "percentile rank" merely refers to the number of people who scored equal to or below a given raw score. In this example the raw score of 42 corresponded to the percentile rank of 50. The 50th percentile is the median. Percentile ranks allow you to analyze more effectively raw scores in comparison to others. (See "Graphical Representations" section of this book.) **(d)**

785. The WAIS-R IQ test is given to 100 adults picked randomly. How many of the adults most likely would receive an IQ score between 85 and 115?

    a.   7 people.
    b.   99 people.
    c.   95 people.
    d.   68 people.

This is really an easy question to answer if you remember that in a normal distribution approximately 68% of the population will fall between plus/minus 1 SD of the mean. One SD on most popular IQ tests is 15 or 16, and the mean score is generally 100. Choice "c" is indicative of plus/minus 2 SD, while choice "b" approximates plus/minus 3 SD.   **(d)**

786. A researcher creates a new motoric test in which clients throw a baseball at a target 40 feet away. Each client is given 100 throws, and the mean on the test is 50. (In other words, out of 100 throws the mean number of times the client will hit the target is 50 times.) Sam took the test and hit the target just two times out of the 100 throws allowed. Jeff, on the other hand, hit the target an amazing 92 out of 100 trials. Using the concept of statistical regression toward the mean the research would predict that

    a.   Sam and Jeff's scores will stay about the same if they take the test again.
    b.   Sam and Jeff will both score over 95 next time.
    c.   Sam's score will increase while Jeff's will go down.
    d.   Sam will beat Jeff if they both are tested again.

Statistical regression is a threat to internal validity. Statistical regression predicts that very high and very low scores will move toward the mean if a test is administered again. This concept is based on "the law of filial regression," which is a genetic principle that asserts that generational traits move toward the mean. If a father is seven feet tall, then the chances are that his son will be shorter (though still much taller than the average person), whereas if a father is four foot ten, the chances are his son will have a few inches on his father. The statistical analogy suggests that extremely low scores on an exam or a pretest will improve while the unusually high scores will get lower. Statistical regression results from errors (i.e., lack of reliability) in measurement instruments and must be taken into account when interpreting test data. Now as for alternative "d" I can only say don't bet on it. Most scores don't change that much, and although Sam's score will probably inch up a bit and Jeff's will lose a little ground, Sam will probably still be in the lower quartile and Jeff the upper quartile. YOU MUST KNOW THE STATISTICAL LINGO: THE TERM QUARTILE IS COMMON AND REFERS TO THE POINTS THAT DIVIDE A DISTRIBUTION INTO FOURTHS. THIS INDICATES THAT THE 25TH PERCENTILE IS THE FIRST QUARTILE, THE SECOND QUARTILE IS THE MEDIAN, AND THE THIRD LIES AT THE 75TH PERCENTILE. THE SCORE DISTANCE BETWEEN THE 25TH PERCENTILE AND THE 75TH PERCENTILE IS CALLED THE INTERQUARTILE RANGE. **(c)**

787. Standardized tests always have

   a.   formal procedures for test administration and scoring.
   b.   a mean of 100 and an SD of 15.
   c.   a mean of 100 and a standard error of measurement of 3.
   d.   a reliability coefficient of +.90 or above.

Standardization implies that the testing format, the test materials, and the scoring process are consistent.   **(a)**

788. There are two distinct types of developmental studies. In a cross-sectional study, clients are assessed at one point in time. In a longitudinal study, however,

   a.   the researcher has an accomplice pose as a client.
   b.   the same people are studied over a period of time.
   c.   the researcher relies on a single observation of a variable being investigated.
   d.   all of the above.

Some exams refer to the cross-sectional method as the "synchronic method" and the longitudinal as the "diachronic method." The longitudinal study is beneficial in the sense that age itself can be used as an IV. In a longitudinal study data are collected at different points in time. In the cross-sectional method, data are indicative of measurements or observations at a single point in time, and thus it is preferable in terms of time consumption. The person in choice "a" is known as a "confederate" or a "stooge." Social psychology studies routinely employ "confederates" or "stooges" who are not real subjects. **(b)**

789. A counselor educator, Dr. Y, is doing research on his classes. He hypothesizes that if he reinforces students in his morning class by smiling each time a student asks a relevant question, then more students will ask questions and exam grades will go up. Betty and Linda accidentally overhear Dr. Y discussing the experiment with the department chairman. Betty is a real people pleaser and decides that she will ask lots of questions and try to help Dr. Y confirm his hypothesis. Linda, nevertheless, is angry that she is being experimented on and promises Betty that Dr. Y could smile until the cows came in but she still wouldn't ask a question. Both Linda and Betty exemplify

   a.   internal versus external validity.
   b.   ipsative versus normative interpretation of test scores.
   c.   the use of the nonparametric chi-square test.
   d.   demand characteristics of experiments.

Choice "b" refers to whether you are looking at an individual's own patterns revealed via measurement (e.g., highs and lows) or whether his or her score is compared to others evaluated by the same measure. The former is "ipsative" while the latter is "normative." Choice "c" mentions what is perhaps the most popular nonparametric (i.e., a distribution which is not normal) statistical test, the chi-square. The chi-square—threatening as it sounds— is merely used to determine whether an obtained distribution differs significantly from an expected distribution. A chi-square might answer the question whether being a man or a woman determines whether you will seek therapy for an elevator phobia. You must be able to have mutually exclusive categories to use the chi-square (such as "will seek therapy" or "won't seek therapy"). The answer to this question, nevertheless, is choice "d." A demand characteristic relates to any bit of knowledge—correct or incorrect—that the subject in an experiment is aware of that can influence his or her behavior. DEMAND CHARACTERISTICS CAN CONFOUND AN EXPERIMENT. Deception has been used as a tactic to reduce this dilemma. **(d)**

790. If an ANOVA yields a significant F value, you could rely on _____ to test significant differences between group means.

   a. one- and two-tailed t-tests
   b. percentile rank
   c. Duncan's multiple range, Tukey's, or Scheffe's test
   d. summative or formative evaluation

Choice "a" refers to whether a statistical test places the rejection area at one end of the distribution (one-tailed) or both ends of the distribution curve (two-tailed). A two-tailed test is often called a "nondirectional experimental hypothesis," while a one-tailed test is a "directional experimental hypothesis." In a one-tailed test your hypothesis specifies that one average mean is larger than another. So, a two-tailed hypothesis would be, "The average patient who has completed psychoanalysis will have a statistically *different* IQ than the average patient who has not received analysis." The one-tailed hypothesis would be, "The average patient who has completed psychoanalysis will have a statistically, significantly *higher* IQ than the average patient who has not received analysis." When appropriate, one-tailed tests have the advantage of having more "power" (i.e., the statistical ability to reject correctly a false hypothesis) than the two-tailed design. In choice "d" you should be aware that summative evaluation is used to assess a final product (e.g., How many high school students are not indulging in alcoholic beverages after completing a yearly program focusing on drug awareness education?). Summative research attempts to ascertain how well the goal has been met. Formative process research, on the other hand, is ongoing while the program is underway (e.g., After three weeks of a proposed year long drug awareness education program how many high school students are taking drugs?). The correct answer to this question, of course, is alternative "c." An F test for the ANOVA is analogous to the student's t-test table when performing a t-test. In order to further discriminate between the ANOVA groups the post hoc measures mentioned in choice "c" would be appropriate. **(c)**

791. Switching the order that stimuli are presented to a subject in a study is known as

    a.   the Pygmalion Effect.
    b.   counterbalancing.
    c.   ahistoric therapy.
    d.   multiple treatment interference.

Let choice "a" come as no surprise if it shows up on your exam. The Rosenthal/Experimenter Effect often shows up wearing this name tag. The experimenter falls in love with his or her own hypothesis and the experiment becomes a self-fulfilling prophecy. Choice "b," the correct answer, is used to control for the fact that the order of an experiment could impact upon its outcome. The solution is merely to change the order of the experimental factors. Choice "c," "ahistoric therapy," connotes any psychotherapeutic model that focuses on the here-and-now rather than the past. This of course has nothing to do with answering the question. Choice "d" warns us that if a subject receives more than one treatment, then it is often tough to discern which modality truly caused the improvements. **(b)**

792. A doctoral student who begins working on his bibliography for his thesis would most likely utilize

    a.   SPSS.
    b.   ERIC.
    c.   the DOT.
    d.   a random number table or random number generation computer program.

Here's a must know question for anyone seriously contemplating a dissertation. ERIC, the Educational Resources Information Center, is a resource bank of scholarly literature and resources to help you complete your literature search before you begin writing. SPSS, the Statistical Package for the Social Sciences, is a popular computer software program that can ease the pain of computing your statistics by hand in case you happen to have an aversion to numbers. Actually, most large studies do rely on computers since they are faster and more accurate than scratch paper calculations. There are many other similar programs, yet at this point in time SPSS is still the most popular. And if you marked choice "c" then you must have slept through my chapter on career development! **(b)**

793. In a random sample each individual in the population has an equal chance of being selected. Selection is by chance. In a new study, however, it will be important to include 20% Blacks. What type of sampling procedure will be necessary?

    a.   Standard (i.e., simple) random sampling is adequate.
    b.   Cluster sampling is called for.
    c.   Stratified sampling would be best.
    d.   Horizontal sampling is required.

Remember: Random sampling (choice "a") is like sticking your hand in a fish bowl to pick a winning ticket. In the random sample each subject has the same probability of being selected, and the selection of one subject does not affect the selection of another subject. The simple random sampling procedure eliminates the researcher's tendency to pick a biased sample of subjects. In this case, nevertheless, a simple random sampling procedure will not suffice, since a "stratum" (plural "strata") or a "special characteristic" needs to be represented. In this case it is race. In other studies it might be gender, educational degree, age, or perhaps therapeutic affiliation. The stratification variable in your sample should mimic the population at large. Thus, if 20% of all Rogerian counselors are Black, then your study on Rogerian counselors should have 20% Black counselors in your sample. In a research situation where a specific number of cases are necessary from each stratum, the procedure often is labelled as "quota sampling." Quota sampling is merely a type of stratified sampling procedure. The "cluster sample" (choice "b") is utilized when it is nearly impossible to find a list of the entire population. The cluster sample solves the problem by using an existing sample or cluster of people or selects a portion of the overall sample. A cluster sample will not be as accurate as a random sample yet it is often used due to time and practical considerations. Imagine trying to secure a list of everybody in the U.S. securing treatment for heroine addiction so you can pick a random sample utilizing a random number generator. Instead, you might rely on the population in your home town chemical dependency unit. And yes there really is a procedure called "horizontal sampling," mentioned in choice "d." Horizontal sampling occurs when a researcher selects subjects from a single socioeconomic group. Horizontal sampling can be contrasted with "vertical sampling," which occurs when persons from two or more socioeconomic classes are utilized. SINCE THIS QUESTION DOES NOT SPECIFY SOCIOECONOMIC FACTORS, YOU COULD HAVE ELIMINATED CHOICE "D." **(c)**

794. A researcher wants to determine why some counselors stay at the Acme Counseling Center for years while others quit within a week or so. The researcher thus looks at 17 variables including age, gender, GRE scores, and financial obligations. Statistically speaking a _____ would be utilized.

    a.   measure of variability
    b.   simple linear regression analysis
    c.   multiple regression analysis
    d.   a t-test

A "simple linear regression analysis" based on correlation (choice "b") is implemented when a researcher attempts to predict an individual's DV performance based on a single IV. A researcher might wish to use GRE scores to predict employees' length of stay at the Acme Counseling Center. "Multiple regression analysis" goes a step further and predicts DV performance based on several IV measures (e.g., the 17 variables mentioned here). **(c)**

795. An operational definition

    a.   outlines a procedure.
    b.   is theoretical.
    c.   outlines a construct.
    d.   is synonymous with the word axiom.

It is very important that researchers "operationally define" procedures so that other researchers can attempt to "replicate" an experimental procedure. Replication implies that another researcher can repeat the experiment exactly as it was performed before. In most cases, counselors would not accept a finding as scientific unless an experiment has been replicated. This means that a researcher should never say something like, "we reinforced children for good classroom behavior." Instead, the procedure must be carefully delineated into terms of the exact terms and actions. For example: "We reinforced each child with 3 M&M's within 30 seconds after he or she answered five addition problems on the ABC Test correctly" . . . etc. **(a)**

796. In a parametric test the assumption is that the scores are normally distributed. In nonparametric testing the curve is not a normal distribution. Which of these tests are nonparametric statistical measures?

    a.   Mann-Whitney U-test, often just called the U-test.
    b.   Wilcoxon signed-rank test for matched pairs.
    c.   Soloman and the Kruskal-Wallis H-test.
    d.   All of the above are nonparametric measures.

All of the above referenced tests are categorized as "nonparametric." Many exams refer to nonparametric statistical tests as "distribution-free" tests. Before I explicate their differences I want to familiarize you with the term "matched design." In a matched design the subjects are literally "matched" in regard to any variable that could be "correlated" with the DV, which is really the post experimental performance. If you wanted to test a hypothesis concerning a new treatment for manic-depression but felt that IQ might be correlated with the DV, then you would try to match subjects based on IQ. This procedure is logically termed "matched sampling." Hence, whether the experiment concluded that the IV did or did not have an impact, the researcher could breathe a little easier knowing that the IQ variable did not confound the study. A special kind of "matched subjects design" is the "repeated-measures" or "within-subjects" design in which the same subjects are used, once for the control condition and again for the experimental IV conditions. The theory here is that ultimately a subject is best matched by himself/herself assuming that counterbalancing is implemented. Now the Mann-Whitney U-test (choice "a") is used to determine whether two uncorrelated/unmatched means differ significantly, while the Wilcoxon signed-rank test examines whether two correlated means differ significantly from each other. By employing ranks, it is a good alternative to the correlated t-test. Why not remind yourself that the "U" in Mann-Whitney U is like the "u" in uncorrelated/unmatched to help you distinguish it from the Wilcoxon? (NOTE: UNMATCHED/UNCORRELATED GROUPS COULD BE TERMED INDEPENDENT GROUPS ON YOUR EXAM.) The U-test, like the Wilcoxon, is an alternative to the t-test when parametric precepts cannot be accepted. Now think back for just a moment and you will recall that if you were using a parametric test to examine a null hypothesis for two means, you could rely on the t-test. If, however, you had three or more groups, then the ANOVA and the F test would be required. A similar situation is in order here. If parametric assumptions are in doubt, the Mann-Whitney U-test or the Wilcoxon can be used for two groups; however, when the number of groups reaches three or above, the Kruskal-Wallis one-way ANOVA H-test noted in choice "c" is utilized. The Soloman, you will recall, controls for pretest effects. **HINT:** MOST COMPREHENSIVE COUNSELING EXAMS WILL HAVE SEVERAL QUESTIONS IN WHICH THE EXAMINEE IS GIVEN THE BASIC FACTORS CONCERNING A RESEARCH STUDY AND THEN IS ASKED TO PICK THE APPROPRIATE STATISTICAL TEST.   **(d)**

797. A researcher studies a single session of counseling in which a counselor treats a client's phobia using a paradoxical strategy. He then writes in his research report that paradox is the treatment of choice for phobics. This is an example of

   a.   deductive logic or reasoning.
   b.   inductive logic or reasoning.
   c.   an N=1 design.
   d.   construct validity.

This is inductive since the research goes from the specific to a generalization. Deductive—which sounds a bit like "reductive"—reduces the general to the specific. This question would have been answered using "deductive" if the researcher observed many clients being cured of their phobias via paradox and so he assumed that Mr. Smith's phobia would be cured in the same manner.   **(b)**

798. A client goes to a string of 14 chemical dependency centers that operate on the 12-step model. When his current therapist suggests a new inpatient program the client responds with, "What for, I already know the twelve steps?" This client is using

   a.   deductive logic.
   b.   inductive logic.
   c.   an empathic assertion.
   d.   an I statement.

Review the previous question if you missed this one. Here the client assumes that the general (his experience in 14 treatment facilities) can be reduced (deduction . . . remember your memory device) to the specific (the new treatment program). **(a)**

799. Mike takes a math achievement test. In order to predict his score if he takes the test again the counselor must know

    a.   the range of scores in his class.
    b.   the standard deviation.
    c.   the standard error of measurement.
    d.   the mode for the test.

The standard error is all you need to know. The question does not ask how well he did on the test, nor does it ask you to compare him to others. **(c)**

800. A researcher performs a study that has excellent external or so-called population validity, meaning that the results have generalizability. To collect his data the researcher gave clients a rating scale in which they were to respond with strongly agree, somewhat agree, neutral, somewhat disagree or strongly disagree. This is

    a.   a projective measure.
    b.   unacceptable for use in standardized testing.
    c.   a speed test.
    d.   a Likert scale.

Created by Rensis Likert in the early 1930s, this scale helps improve the overall degree of measurement. Response categories include such choices as strongly agree, agree, disagree or strongly disagree. (Hmmm . . . that's easy enough to remember . . . How much do you like/Likert something?) **(d)**

CHAPTER 11

PROFESSIONAL ORIENTATION

SPECIAL NOTE: Ethical questions and answers in this chapter are geared toward ACA/NBCC ethical standards. Professional counselors studying for exams other than counselor licensure or certification should consult ethical guidelines in their areas of expertise (e.g., psychologists should use APA's "Ethical Principles of Psychologists"; social workers the "Code of Ethics," written by NASW; etc.). Readers must note that ethical standards are updated routinely.

801. Which group has been most instrumental in opposing counselor licensure?

   a.   Social workers.
   b.   Psychiatrists.
   c.   Psychologists.
   d.   AAMFT members.

We have seen the opponents to counselor licensure, and they call themselves psychologists. Some hypothesize that psychologists wanted a monopoly on nonmedical mental health services, especially the right to collect third-party payments. Others point out that at one time psychologists were debased and called "junior psychiatrists," and now the psychologists are doing to the counselors what psychiatrists did to them. In any case, the tide appears to be changing as "mental health coalitions" are popping up in which psychiatrists, psychologists, counselors, social workers, and related specialists (e.g., choice "d" The American Association for Marriage and Family Therapy) meet to discuss mutual professional concerns. **(c)**

802. In the late 1970s, AACD (now ACA) began to focus very heavily on professional credentialing. This lead to the formation of

    a.   CCMHC.
    b.   NBCC.
    c.   CACREP.
    d.   APGA.

In 1982 AACD, or the American Association for Counseling and Development (now the American Counseling Association), formed the National Board for Certified Counselors or NBCC for short. If you meet the educational/ skill requirements and pass an exam (come on now you remember . . . probably the exam you are studying for this very minute!) you can use the title NCC which stands for National Certified Counselor. The designation lasts for five years at which time the counselor must have 100 approved hours of continued professional development (e.g., workshops) or sit for the test again. (For some strange reason I'm guessing you'll choose the first option.) Other alphabet soup acronyms include choice "a," which stands for Certified Clinical Mental Health Counselor; choice "c," the Council for the Accreditation of Counseling and Related Educational Programs, which is an AACD (ACA) affiliate formed in 1981; and choice "d," the major counseling organization, the American Personnel and Guidance Association, which later became AACD and is now ACA. **(b)**

803. By passing the NCE, a counselor can attain _____,
given via NBCC.

    a.   NCC, a generic certification for counselors
    b.   NCC, a mental health certification for counselors
    c.   NCC, national certification for school counselors
    d.   CCMHC, clinical mental health counselor certification

Again, here is one of those must know concepts, especially since many readers are striving to put NCC after their names. NCC constitutes a "generic" certification. The word generic literally means "general" or "referring to all types of counselors." Look at choice "c" and ask yourself: What is incongruent about this item? The answer is simply that the acronym for National Certified School Counselor is NCSC. NBCC offers two other specialty certifications; the National Certified Career Counselor (NCCC) and the National Certified Gerontological Counselor (NCGC). Choice "d" is also an example of a specialty certification. Another example would be a Certified Rehabilitation Counselor (CRC). And oh yes, one more very, very important point: just because you are certified does not mean you can call yourself a licensed counselor. National certifications can (as the name suggests) be used on a national basis unlike licenses which tend to be state specific. **(a)**

804. ACA, which was once APGA and then AACD, has approximately _____ members.

    a.   10,000
    b.   9,000
    c.   110,000
    d.   57,000

Perhaps you've heard the old adage which suggests that an educated man or woman knows where to go for answers. This question provides an excellent case in point. Prior to sitting for any major exam, a good idea is to read the major publications in the field. The August, 1992 issue of the ACA "Guidepost" listed the total AACD membership as of 6/30/92 as 56,463. If you just said to yourself, "Fine, I'll just remember that ACA membership is about 57,000," then I would hasten to inform you that you've missed the point! This number could go up or down by the time you take the test. The moral of the story is that perusing the major publications could be worth a few much needed points come test time. **(d)**

805. Ethics describe

    a.   laws.
    b.   universal principles which apply to all helpers.
    c.   standards of conduct.
    d.   all of the above.

Let's examine precisely why choices "a," "b," and "d" are incorrect. In regard to choice "a," I doubt seriously whether you'll find a law on the books that explicitly states that you can't date a counselee, yet I can almost guarantee you your licensing board will see it as a so-called "dual relationship," which could be an ethics violation. Ethics define standards of behavior set forth by organizations and certification bodies. Ethics are not state or federal mandated laws. Unlike many laws, ethical guidelines generally do not spell out penalties for violations. Hence, the aforementioned counselor who is dating a client might lose his or her license but will not be serving time in a city jail or a federal penitentiary. Choice "b" is misleading since ethics are not universal. That is to say, the ethics set forth by one organization may not be identical to those spelled out by another organization. **(c)**

806. Most ethical dilemmas are related to

    a.   confidentiality.
    b.   testing.
    c.   diagnosis.
    d.   research.

Confidentiality implies that the counselor will not reveal anything about a client unless he or she is given specific authorization to do so. Some of the literature in the field refers to confidential material as "entrusted secrets." What goes on in the counseling relationship remains private rather than public. Helpers must, nevertheless, be aware that there are exceptions to this principle. The exceptions illuminate the fact that confidentiality is relative to the situation. **(a)**

807. The landmark 1969 case, *Tarasoff versus the Board of Regents of the University of California* illuminated

   a.   difficulties involved in client/counselor sexual behavior.
   b.   ethical issues in relation to research.
   c.   the duty to warn.
   d.   the impact of an impaired professional.

For the most part, I wouldn't go around memorizing court cases for exams; however, the *Tarasoff* case is now so well known in the behavioral sciences that it is the exception to the rule. In 1969 a student named Prosenjit Poddar at Berkeley was receiving counseling on an outpatient basis. During the course of the treatment he revealed that he was going to kill a woman (Tatiana Tarasoff) when she returned from Brazil. The therapist consulted with other professionals and called the campus police. The therapist wanted Poddar hospitalized. Campus police spoke with Poddar but did not hospitalize him. A letter also was sent to the chief of campus police regarding this dangerous situation. Despite all the actions taken, Poddar did indeed kill Tarasoff, and Ms. Tarasoff's parents filed suit against the Board of Regents as well as the university employees. The charge was failure to warn an intended victim. Although a lower court dismissed the suit, the parents appealed the decision, and the California Supreme Court ruled in favor of the parents in 1976. This case is often cited as an example of a professional helper's "duty to warn." Choice "d," impaired professional, connotes a helper who has personal issues (e.g., substance abuse or brain damage) that would hinder the quality of services rendered. **(c)**

808. State laws govern the process of counselor licensure. These laws

    a.   often go against professional ethics.
    b.   are identical to professional ethics.
    c.   are in fact dictated by professional ethics.
    d.   are neutral or supportive of professional ethics.

State laws support ethics via minimum standards for helpers such as licensing for counselors, social workers, and psychologists. They are neutral in the sense that they do not dictate specific behaviors but rather allow the profession to do so via ethical guidelines. Laws may override a code of ethics if the code does not protect citizens adequately. **(d)**

809. State laws do not govern

    a.   accreditation.
    b.   counselor licensure.
    c.   psychologist licensure.
    d.   involuntary commitment to state psychiatric facilities.

State laws regulate "licensing" of professionals such as choice "b" counselors, and choice "c" psychologists, and commitment procedures (choice "d"). Accreditation, however, is not the law. In fact, you need to be aware of the fact that "most" counselor preparation programs are not accredited. Accreditation is a process whereby an agency or school (not an individual) meets certain standards and qualifications set forth by an association or accrediting organization. The organization that grants the accreditation usually requires site visits for the purpose of evaluating the institution initially and on an ongoing basis. Thus, programs in psychology will boast accreditation via the APA (American Psychological Association) while counseling programs can be accredited by CACREP, mentioned earlier. Important reminder: The term "accreditation" applies to programs, not individual counselors. Moreover, experts warn that accreditation is not without disadvantages. Disadvantages include that doing so is very costly for the institution; that faculty are busy teaching required courses and thus often don't have time to teach creative alternative courses; that the accreditation organization and not the school determines the curriculum; that faculty credentials are determined via accreditation guidelines, and this does not necessarily mean such individuals have the best teaching, clinical, or research skills; and that the program approval can be misleading inasmuch as the program could be accredited yet ineffective.   **(a)**

810. A social worker who has a client who is struggling with career and life-style issues would most likely refer the client to a counselor with _____ after his or her name.

    a.   NCC
    b.   NCCC
    c.   AAMFT
    d.   CRC

Now truthfully, all of the above-referenced helpers probably could be viable resources. The individual sporting the most appropriate credentials, however, would be the NCCC, or the National Certified Career Counselor. NCCC was NBCC's first specialty designation in 1985. As of 1990 there were over 900 NCCC's. NCC's who wish to snare this specialty need a graduate program with required coursework; two professional references who will assess career counseling skills; two years of at least 20 hours per week doing career counseling; and yes, still another exam! (Applicants will need to pass the National Career Counselor Examination [NCCE].) Exam content categories include Career Counseling/Consultation, Career Development Concepts/Theory and Special Populations, Career Information/Resources, Individual/Group Assessment, and Program Management and Implementation.   **(b)**

811. An executive director for a not-for-profit counseling agency who terminates his position to begin a private practice will discover that

    a.   NBCC ethics remain the same for private practitioners.
    b.   NBCC ethics for private practitioners are markedly different.
    c.   NBCC ethics simply do not mention private practice.
    d.   APA ethics will apply rather than those set via NBCC.

NBCC ethics are intended for private practitioners or those working in alternative settings. Private practice is covered in Section F of the Code of Ethics. Choice "d" would be correct only if the executive director was practicing as a psychologist. **(a)**

812. Privileged communication refers to the fact that anything said to a counselor by a client

    a.   can be revealed in a court of law.
    b.   can be revealed only if a counselor testifies in court.
    c.   is protected by laws in every state.
    d.   will not need to be divulged outside the counseling setting.

By definition "privileged communication" is a legal term that implies that a therapeutic interaction (verbal or written) will not be available for public inspection. A counselor/client relationship protected by privileged communication is one in which the client can choose not to have confidential information revealed during a legal proceeding (generally on the witness stand). Simply put—and this is a fine memory device—it is the "client's privilege" to reveal. In relation to choice "c," the law varies from state to state. In some states, one mental health provider will be covered by the law (e.g., a psychologist or psychiatrist), while another provider (often a counselor, social worker, or caseworker) will not be covered. **(d)**

813. In regard to state law and privileged communication, counselors must be aware that

    a.   privileged communication exists in every state in the union for LPC's.
    b.   laws are unclear and may vary from state to state.
    c.   there are no laws which govern this issue.
    d.   state psychology laws are applicable in this respect.

Privileged communication protects clients, not counselors. If a client decides to waive his or her right to privileged communication, then the counselor must reveal the information. Privileged communication legislation varies from state to state (so much for choices "a" and "c"). Check your state laws if you are taking an exam for state licensure. As of this time, most states do not have privileged communication for the licensed counselor/ client relationship. Privileged communication is not applicable in cases of child abuse, neglect, or exploitation; suicide or homicide threats; criminal intentions; clients in dire need of hospitalization; or in cases where a counselor is the victim of a malpractice lawsuit. As for choice "d," state psychology laws would not govern the behavior of licensed professional counselors. **(b)**

814. When counselors state that privileged communication is "qualified," they actually mean that

    a.   the counselor must have certification before privileged communication applies.
    b.   privileged communication applies only to doctoral level counselors.
    c.   exceptions may exist.
    d.   all of the above

See the answer to 813 for exceptions. In regard to choices "a" and "b," it is important to note that privileged communication is based on licensure status rather than one's graduate degree or certification credentials. **(c)**

815. You are a counselor in a state that does not legally support privileged communication. You refuse to testify in court. In this situation

    a.   ACA will back you for doing the ethical thing.
    b.   NBCC will back you if and only if you have attained NCC status.
    c.   you need not testify if your case was supervised by a licensed psychologist and/or psychiatrist.
    d.   you could be held in contempt of court.

Your client in this situation would not have the "privilege" to say no if you are asked to testify. **(d)**

816. An eleven-year-old child comes to your office with a black eye and tells you she can't remember how she received it. You should

    a.   merely discuss her feelings regarding the matter.
    b.   drop the matter as it could embarrass her.
    c.   refer her to a medical doctor of your choice.
    d.   call the child abuse/neglect hotline.

Counselors are mandated reporters for child abuse. It is legal and ethical to break confidentiality in such cases. Your state may have a legal penalty for failure to report child abuse, sexual abuse, neglect, or exploitation. Check your state laws. Generally, counselors report incidents via the state child abuse hotline. Some exams may refer to this area of concern as "protective services." The October, 1991 "Guidepost" quotes expert Ted Remley who suggested the following as **exceptions** to confidentiality.

1. Client is a danger to self or others.
2. Client requests a release of information.

3. A court orders a release of information.
4. The counselor is engaged in a systematic supervision process.
5. Clerical assistants who process client information and papers.
6. Legal and clinical consultation situations.
7. Client raises his or her mental health in a lawsuit
8. A third party is present in the room.
9. The client is below 18 years of age. (If a client is a minor, a parent or guardian can demand information disclosed that was revealed during a session.) **(d)**

817. During a counseling session a 42-year-old male client threatens suicide. You should

    a.   keep it a secret as the client is not a minor.
    b.   call the state child abuse/neglect hotline even though he is an adult.
    c.   call his wife and mention that a serious problem exists but be very careful not to discuss the issue of suicide since to do so would violate the client's confidentiality.
    d.   contact his wife and advise her of possible suicide precautions.

Most experts would agree with choice "d." Section B of NBCC's and ACA's Code Of Ethics, mentions that, "When a client's condition indicates that there is a clear and imminent danger to the client and others, the certified counselor must take reasonable personal action or inform responsible authorities . . . " This may seem a bit vague (i.e., specific words such as "suicide" and/or "homicide" are not mentioned). Indeed, ethics are often not nearly as specific as counselors would like them to be. **(d)**

818. A 39-year-old female secretary you are seeing in your assertiveness training group reveals that she is plotting to shoot her husband. Based on the *Tarasoff* case you should

a. warn the husband.
b. keep it confidential as an assertiveness training group is decidedly not the same as one-to-one counseling.
c. make a police report in the city in which the husband resides.
d. tell a supervisor, administrator, or board member if one exists, but do not contact her husband.

Tarasoff implies that a responsible helper will warn an intended victim. Another landmark case, the *Hedlund* case, suggests that therapists should warn others (i.e., third parties) who also may be in danger. *Tarasoff* is controversial and based on a California court decision that may or may not apply to your state. Again, I recommend checking your state's laws if your exam is for licensure status. Choice "d" also might be appropriate had the phrase "do not contact her husband," been eliminated. **(a)**

819. During a staff meeting a clinical director explains to you that from an ethical standpoint your primary duty is to the agency. Most experts in the field of counselor education would

a. agree with this position with very few reservations.
b. disagree inasmuch as professional ethics emphasize that your primary responsibility is to your clients.
c. disagree inasmuch as professional ethics emphasize that your primary responsibility is to ACA.
d. say that your profession comes first.

The answer is choice "b." Skeptical? Then please read NBCC's or ACA's Code Of Ethics. Believe me, you won't have to read very far! You have my promise. The second paragraph of the first section (i.e., Section A: General) states that if a dispute cannot be remedied so that institutional policy is conducive to "positive growth and development of clients, then terminating the affiliation should seriously be considered." The next time your well-meaning supervisor tells you the agency comes first hand him or her a copy of ACA or NBCC ethics.   **(b)**

820. One impetus for counselor licensing was that

   a.   ACSW wanted to restrict counselors.
   b.   politicians demanded that counselors be licensed.
   c.   psychology licensure bodies sought to restrict the practice of counselors.
   d.   insurance companies pushed strongly for it.

Many—if not most—counselors were not able to be licensed as psychologists since one popular requirement was that the graduate program had to be "primarily psychological in nature," which basically meant that persons who attended counseling programs were considered inappropriate. Licensing for counselors was needed as psychologists attained licensing (and had somewhat of a monopoly on nonmedical treatment services) in every state in the U.S.   **(c)**

821. A counselor who possesses a graduate degree wishes to become a licensed psychologist. Which statement most accurately depicts the current situation?

   a.   Any counselor can easily become a psychologist if he or she can pass the EPPP.
   b.   A counselor can become a licensed psychologist by taking three graduate credit hours in physiological psychology and then passing the EPPP.
   c.   In nearly every case individuals trained in counseling departments would not be allowed to sit for the EPPP and thus could not become licensed psychologists.
   d.   A counselor with a doctorate in counseling could be licensed as a counseling psychologist if he or she has a degree from a recognized department of counseling.

Choice "c" (the correct response) provides a good rationale why counselors needed a license to call their own. EPPP stands for Examination for Professional Practice in Psychology. The EPPP consists of 200 multiple choice items, and each item is reviewed by at least 40 licensed psychologists before it is selected for the exam. Roughly speaking, the EPPP is to psychologists, as the NCE is to counselors. Choice "d" would be incorrect in most cases as the applicant would still generally need a degree from a psychology rather than a counseling department. **(c)**

822. A woman who is in private practice mentions in her phone book advertisement that she is a licensed counseling psychologist. This generally means that

    a.   she has a doctorate from a counselor education program.
    b.   she has a graduate degree from a psychology department.
    c.   she has a degree from a CACREP program.
    d.   she has a degree in counseling but is trained in projective testing.

The trick to answering this question is to remember that the word "psychology" is a term that can only be used if the helper is a licensed psychologist . . . even if the person specializes in counseling. Hence, the degree would need to be from a program which is primarily psychological, a psychology rather than a counseling department (rendering choice "a" incorrect). For review purposes, pertaining to choice "c" you will recall that CACREP is the Council for Accreditation of Counseling and Related Educational Programs which is ACA's accrediting agency. CACREP, which set up shop in 1981, currently has 72 programs accredited. Fewer than 15% of all counselor preparation programs have CACREP accreditation. Critics charge that this is not enough. **(b)**

823. One major difference between the psychology versus the counseling movement seems to be that

    a.   the psychologists are working to eliminate practitioners with less than a doctorate, while the counselors are not.

    b.   counselors are working to give up tests for licensure.

    c.   psychology boards are made up primarily of psychiatrists.

    d.   in most states psychologists do not need to take an exam.

Counselors and social workers seem comfortable with master's level practitioners. In an early study in which ACES members were asked to comment on the minimum level of education necessary for licensure, over 45% of the respondents felt comfortable with master's level practitioners. A little over 41% insisted that a doctorate was necessary. **(a)**

824. APA is to psychologist as ACA is to

    a.   APGA.

    b.   certified clinical mental health counselor.

    c.   counselor.

    d.   NCC.

Here is a straightforward example of an analogy item. First, recall that the APA (in the context of this question) refers to the American Psychological Association, which is the major professional body for psychologists. ACA plays the same role for counselors. **(c)**

825. You have achieved the status of NCC. NBCC, nevertheless, feels you have violated professional ethics. NBCC can do any of the following except

a. revoke your state counseling license.
b. remove your name from the list of NCC's in the U.S.
c. revoke your NCC status.
d. note in their newsletter that your NCC status has been revoked.

Here is the key point: certification is not the same as licensing. Thus, a certified reality therapist cannot legally use the title counselor (assuming the state has licensing) unless he or she is licensed by the state. A certification is given to an individual via an organization which is not part of the state or federal government. A counseling license is granted by the state government. Nevertheless, you must (yes must) be certified to call yourself a certified counselor. You could, however, call yourself a professional counselor if you are not certified. A certification is a title mastered by living up to certain standards. Does the fact that choice "d" is true surprise you? It shouldn't! NBCC is very open and upfront about this fact and specifically states that certification violations (e.g., using the title NCCC when you have not fulfilled the requirements) may be published in NBCC "NewsNotes," which is the NBCC newsletter. Believe me, this is one situation where you certainly don't need the notoriety! And oh yes, I almost forgot; this is what makes this such a difficult question. Although a certification board cannot revoke your license for an ethics violation, they do indeed reserve the right to contact your state licensing board (or other certification boards, for that matter), and your state board may well decide to take your license. The certification organization also could deny you further certification and take legal action against you. Important exam reminder: Ethical guidelines drafted via your state licensing board may indeed be at odds with your national organization's standards (e.g., ACA, NASW). Take, for example, the issue of non-erotic touching. Most ethical guidelines do not view this strictly as an ethics violation, though some state licensing boards clearly do list it as an ethics violation. **(a)**

826. A counselor who is alcoholic and suffers from MPD (multiple personality disorder) and burnout could best be described as

    a.   a mesomorph.
    b.   an impaired practitioner.
    c.   a paraprofessional.
    d.   a counselor who is wise enough to use his own experiences to help others.

Impaired here means a deterioration in the ability to function as a counselor. The counselor described in this question definitely meets the criteria. Choice "a" is derived from an old theory of personality proposed by Sheldon, which suggested three basic temperaments based on one's physical build. The mesomorph or muscular type was said to be assertive, courageous, and willing to take risks. The ectomorph, characterized by a slender or frail build, was thought to be sensitive and inhibited. The endomorph, or soft rotund individual, was inclined to love food, comfort, and relaxation. Choice "c," paraprofessional, is used to describe a helper who does not possess the education and experience necessary to secure professional credentials.　　**(b)**

827. Counselor certification

    a.   is synonymous with licensure.
    b.   is synonymous with program certification.
    c.   recognizes that you have reached a given level of competence and thus are authorized to use a title.
    d.   is primarily a legal process.

If you marked anything other than choice "c," review the explanation given in answer 825.　　**(c)**

828. Accreditation

   a.   is when an association specifies that a program
        or school has met a set of standards for program
        approval.
   b.   is synonymous with certification in the
        counseling field.
   c.   is always conducted by a state agency.
   d.   is synonymous with licensing.

The exam you are taking could use the word "provisional
accreditation." This simply means that a program or
school has a given period of time to comply with the
accreditation's guidelines. CACREP's provisional approval
period is two years. Remember: Accreditation is for schools,
etc.; certification is for individuals. It can be noted that
choice "c" is incorrect by pointing out that CACREP
is not a state agency. To be sure, a government agency
could accredit a program (e.g., by a department of
education) . . . but if you read choice "c" correctly then
you noticed the word "always" . . . or did you?   **(a)**

829. Virginia was the first state to license counselors in 1976.
     The APGA (which is now ACA) division that was initially
     the most instrumental in pushing for licensing was the

   a.   American College Personnel Association.
   b.   American School Counselor Association.
   c.   Association for Specialists in Group Work.
   d.   American Counselor Education and Supervision.

Known as ACES, for short. The APGA set up a licensure
commission in 1975.   **(d)**

830. ACA has

   a.   33 divisions.
   b.   6 divisions-3 affiliates.
   c.   16 divisions-1 affiliate.
   d.   3 divisions.

Warning! Warning! This may not be the answer on the test you are taking! The idea of this or any other study guide is to emphasize the general "types" of questions you might see on an exam. The reason why choice "c" (the correct answer as of this writing) could be incorrect is that organizations are not static and often undergo changes. For example, the American College Personnel Association (ACPA) has disaffiliated from AACD, and AACD (now ACA) created a new division to serve the needs of college personnel. Such changes could ultimately have an impact on the number of divisions as well as membership numbers. ALWAYS REVIEW THE MAJOR NEWSLETTERS AND JOURNALS IN THE FIELD BEFORE TACKLING ANY COMPREHENSIVE EXAM! **(c)**

831. One possible negative aspect of counselor licensure is that

    a.   counselors would receive more third-party payments.
    b.   counselors might be accepted as providers by insurance companies.
    c.   counselors may not be as creative during their graduate work and simply take courses aimed at fulfilling the requirements to take the licensure exam.
    d.   it will take business away from psychologists.

Choices "a" and "b" are anything but negative, and in fact constitute two excellent reasons why counselors fought (and continue to fight) for licensure. Licensing generally adds prestige to a profession and can serve to protect the public. **(c)**

832. A client wants his records sent to a psychiatrist he is seeing. You should

    a.   advise against it based on current research.
    b.   refuse to do so based on ethical guidelines.
    c.   first have the client sign a release of information.
    d.   call the psychiatrist to discuss the case but send nothing.

Clients have a right to "privacy." Do not use a xerox or photocopy of the client's signature. **(c)**

833. You are a licensed professional counselor in one state but will soon relocate to another state. The new state informs you that they will grant you reciprocity or so-called "endorsement." You will thus

    a. simply need to take the LPC test in the new state.
    b. be permitted to practice in the new state based on your current credentials without taking another exam.
    c. need to take numerous graduate courses.
    d. not be allowed to practice until you serve an internship.

Reciprocity occurs when one state or organization accepts the license or credential of another state or organization. **(b)**

834. According to the Family Educational Rights and Privacy Act of 1974 (also known as the Buckley Amendment)

    a. a parent can see his or her daughter's middle school record.
    b. an eighteen-year-old college student can view his or her own educational record.
    c. a and b.
    d. a and b are both illegal.

Professional counselors should keep up-to-date records on each client. **(c)**

835. You are a school counselor who wishes to refer an orthopedically disabled student to a private therapist. In general, the best referral would be to

    a. a CRC.
    b. a NCCC.
    c. a licensed clinical psychologist.
    d. a licensed social worker.

CRC stands for Certified Rehabilitation Counselor. CRC's will need at least a master's in rehabilitation counseling, acceptable experience in the field, and a passing score on a 400-question multiple choice examination. **(a)**

836. A registry would be

    a.   a list of licensed psychologists in the state of Illinois.
    b.   a list of CRCs in the U.S.
    c.   a and b.
    d.   the registration process for counselor licensure in the state of Missouri.

A registry is always a list of providers. A person whose name is included in a state counseling registry can sometimes use the title "registered professional counselor" or RPC. As of this writing, two states, Kansas and North Carolina, use this approach in lieu of licensing. The difference between a state using LPC versus RPC is usually that in an LPC state only LPCs can use the designation of "counselor," while states which use RPC do not regulate the use of the word "counselor." (An RPC state would, however, regulate the title "registered professional counselor." Furthermore, such states do not regulate who can practice the activity of counseling. This practice is somewhat similar to the practice of certification.) **(c)**

837. Licensure

    a.   is the same as a registry.
    b.   is the same as certification.
    c.   is the process in which a government agency or division grants an individual permission to practice an occupation based on competency.
    d.   is defined as the act of passing a written LPC exam.

Again, a registry (choice "a") is a list of professionals who have met a given set of qualifications. Certification (choice "b") is not a legal process and therefore differs from licensing. Choice "d" is almost the correct answer, but falls short since some states have additional requirements such as an oral exam. **(c)**

838. A counselor involved in litigation might take advantage of

    a.   free insurance provided to LPCs in many states.
    b.   the ACA legal defense funds.
    c.   professional liability insurance.
    d.   b and c.

Put choice "a" in your hope chest. **(d)**

839. A counselor who sports NCC after her name

    a.   will need not concern herself with continuing education.
    b.   will need 3 graduate courses every 10 years.
    c.   will never receive credit for workshops but should attend for her own personal growth nevertheless.
    d.   will need a specified amount of continuing education contact hours before she can be recertified, or she will need to take the NCE again.

One hundred hours of professional development are needed during a five-year period. Recently, ACA has introduced "Home Study Programs" for convenience to help with NBCC or NACCMHC recertification. Announcements of these programs appear in "Guidepost." **(d)**

840. You find yourself sexually attracted to a client. This is known as

    a.   counter transference.
    b.   ambivalent transference.
    c.   negative transference.
    d.   positive transference.

A typical manifestation of counter transference would be romantic or sexual feelings toward a client. Counter transference is an indication of unresolved problems on the part of the helper. **(a)**

841. Your sexual attraction for the client is hindering the counseling process. You should

    a.   continue treatment but be honest and empathic with the client.

    b.   ignore your feelings; after all you are a professional.

    c.   explain this to the client and then refer the client to another provider.

    d.   continue to see the client but ignore psychosexual topics.

The word "hindering" is critical to answering the question correctly. If the counselor felt a sexual attraction which had "not" as yet hindered the treatment process, then personal therapy for the counselor would be the most desirable plan of action. Moreover, prior to the point where the counselor's attraction interfered with the treatment, most experts would advise against discussing the attraction with the client. **(c)**

842. An insurance company is least likely to defend you if

    a.   you are sexually involved with a client.

    b.   you violate confidentiality.

    c.   you do not have a client sign a release of information and send a record to another agency or provider.

    d.   you call a state child abuse hotline and a client takes legal action since the child was actually the victim of an accident.

Some states will revoke your license for sexual misconduct even if it occurs outside the session and even if the client has consented! In addition, your license may be revoked even if the client is not damaged or harmed by the experience.

The fact that a client seduced you is irrelevant even if it is true. Some insurance companies pay smaller settlements in cases of sexual harassment or misconduct. Let me share with you what my current professional liability insurance occurrence form states. It says: "NOTE: A smaller limit of liability applies to judgments or settlements when there are allegations of sexual misconduct." Hint: Check your state regulations regarding non-erotic touching; some states stipulate that behaviors such as hugging a client are unethical. **(a)**

843. Computers are now being used in various counseling settings. Counselors speak of Computer Assisted Counseling (CAC) and Computer Managed Counseling (CMC). An office that employs an IBM computer to schedule clients would be an example of

    a.   CMC.
    b.   CAC.
    c.   an ethical violation.
    d.   the misuse of computers, though the practice is ethical.

When a computer helps manage your practice (yes, just like a manager) then it is known as CMC. CMC would include tasks such as book keeping, client scheduling, printing billing statements, and compiling referral sources. CAC is like having a counseling "assistant" do the counseling for you. A computer software program that attempts to counsel clients is an example of CAC in action. CAC is controversial, and certainly some conservative counselors would like to see choice "c" as the correct answer, though it is not.   **(a)**

844. A college student who suffers from panic disorder types his symptoms and concerns onto a PC screen and then waits for the computer program to respond or question him further. The student engages in this practice for one 40-minute session per week. This is an example of

a. CAC.
b. CMC.
c. Computer Managed Counseling.
d. b and c.

Again, the computer "assists" in the actual practice of counseling, hence the term "Computer Assisted Counseling," a humanistic counselor's worst nightmare! **(a)**

845. As a professional counselor you develop a self-help software package for use by the general public. Ethics indicate that

a. the package must be designed to use with counseling.
b. the package must be designed to use with counseling and then modified for stand-alone usage.
c. the package must be initially designed for stand-alone usage as opposed to modifying a package requiring counselor support.
d. this is an unethical practice.

If you're scratching your head, then I'd strongly suggest you peruse Section B, paragraph 17 of NBCC ethics to see why item "c" is right on target. Ethics also dictate that the certified counselor must provide descriptions of appropriate and inappropriate applications, suggestions for using the software, statements regarding the intended outcomes, and how and when counseling services are beneficial. Lastly, the manual must delineate the counselor's qualifications, the process of development, validation data, and operating procedures. **(c)**

846. Which statement best describes the counseling profession's reaction to Computer Assisted Counseling and Computer Managed Counseling?

a. Counselors are very humanistic and seem to dislike CMC and CAC technology.

b. Counselors have welcomed both forms of computer technology with open arms.

c. CMC has been well received since it cuts down time on paperwork, scheduling, and record keeping, but there is a mixed reaction to CAC as some feel it depersonalizes counseling.

d. Counselors dislike CMC but praise CAC highly.

Work around any agency, school counseling office, or private practice and you'll surely hear counselors complaining about paperwork, ergo the enthusiasm over CMC procedures. CAC, nevertheless, seems a bit cold and depersonalizing in a field which emphasizes concepts like empathy and positive regard. Besides, when computers display warmth they tend to electronically shut down! **(c)**

847. You receive a call from a high ranking military intelligence officer as an ex-client of yours has applied for a very important, yet extremely stressful top-secret project. The officer needs to know your opinion of the client's stability and emphasizes how important your cooperation is to the success of this particular project. You should

a. cooperate immediately as counselors are mandated to help the armed services secure personality profiles.

b. absolutely refuse to reveal anything under any circumstances; otherwise it is a breach of confidentiality.

c. contact the officer's superior since he has no legal right to ask you for this information.

d. inform the officer that you will need to obtain your ex-client's permission before you can assist the military.

Forget the top-secret stuff . . . your client will still need to sign a release of information form giving his or her consent to give out any information. **(d)**

848. APA approved is to a Ph.D. counseling psychology program as CACREP approved is to

    a. a doctorate in counselor education and supervision.
    b. a master's in geriatric counseling.
    c. an Ed.D. in special education.
    d. a master's or doctorate in clinical psychology.

CACREP certifications include master's level programs in school counseling, master's level programs in student development in higher education, master's level counseling in community and agency settings, and the doctoral counselor education program noted above. Many jobs specify graduates from APA or CACREP programs. Small schools with outstanding programs often fail to qualify for CACREP accreditation since there must be a minimum of three full-time faculty members. APA Division 17 is "Counseling Psychology," and all members must hold a doctorate.   **(a)**

849. A 14-year-old male threatens to blow up his parents' garage because he has been grounded. You believe his threat is genuine. You should

    a. ask the child if he will sign a release of information so you can talk to his parents.
    b. not talk to the parents since this would weaken the bond of trust you have with the client.
    c. have the child sign a contract stating he will not blow up the garage but mention nothing to the parents.
    d. warn the parents that their property is in danger.

There is little evidence to suggest a right or a wrong answer to this question. Nevertheless, a case tried in the Supreme Court of Vermont suggested that a mental health agency was negligent for not warning parents that their son, who was in therapy, threatened to burn down their barn—which he did. So until further notice . . .   **(d)**

850. A 16-year-old girl threatens to kill herself and you fail to inform her parents. Your behavior as a counselor is best described as

    a.   an example of a dual relationship.
    b.   an example of informed consent.
    c.   an example of negligence, which is a failure to perform a duty.
    d.   multiple submission.

Here is a myriad of terms related to counseling ethics. A dual relationship (choice "a") occurs when a counselor has a relationship with the client in addition to being his or her counselor (e.g., a sexual relationship, or a business deal with the client). Ethics frown on this practice, claiming that it prevents professional objectivity. Informed consent, on the other hand, is an example of a desirable counselor behavior that can actually reduce the chances of a malpractice suit. Informed consent is roughly the opposite of mystifying the counseling process. The counselor "informs" the client what will take place so the client will have the necessary information to decide whether he or she wants to "consent" to the procedure. Multiple submission (choice "d")—a violation of ethics— transpires when a journal article is submitted to more than one journal at a time. Negligence (choice "c") is evident when a counselor "neglects" or fails to perform a required behavior. **(c)**

851. NBCC has developed a Code of Ethics to help counselors behave in a professional manner. The code is divided into six sections. The first section (i.e., Section A) warns against stereotyping and discrimination. All of the following would be examples of stereotyping and discrimination except

a. advising a Black client to avoid graduate school because you believe the Jensen research regarding Blacks and IQ scores.
b. advising a client to consider switching his college major based on your clinical judgment as well as the results from an extensive test battery.
c. advising a female client to avoid taking a management position because you feel women are generally nonassertive.
d. advising a female client to avoid taking a management position because you feel women managers are generally too aggressive.

Discrimination is the practice of not treating all clients in an equal manner especially due to religious, racial, ethnic, sexual, or cultural prejudice on the part of the therapist. Stereotyping occurs when a counselor views all persons of a given classification or group in a biased manner (e.g., all women are too nonassertive to hold management positions; or all therapists are crazy . . . I knew that one would get your attention even after pondering 851 questions!). **(b)**

852. Section A, which is the general section of NBCC's Code of Ethics, cautions counselors against sexual harassment defined as "deliberate or repeated comments, gestures, or physical contacts of a sexual nature." An example of an ethics violation in this respect would be

a. a female counselor who repeatedly tells a male client how sexy his hairy chest looks when he leaves his shirt unbuttoned.
b. a male counselor who smiles to reinforce a female client (who is overly critical of her looks) who has just said that she is beginning to accept her feminine qualities.
c. a female career counselor who tells a male client that she feels his gray flannel suit would be the most appropriate for a given job interview.
d. when a client who has been very depressed and neglecting her looks comes into the therapy session looking much better and the counselor comments, "You certainly look nice today."

A 1977 study by Holroyd and Brodsky of 1,000 Ph.D. licensed psychologists (500 females and 500 males) found that when erotic contact did occur it was usually between male therapists and female clients. And of those therapists who had intercourse with patients, 80% repeated the act. Of male therapists, 5.5% reported having intercourse with a patient while the female therapist rate was .6%. Most of the therapists in the study felt erotic contact is never beneficial to clients. Response "a" is illustrative of a sexually inappropriate comment on the part of a helper. Ethics warn against deliberate or repeated comments of a sexual nature. **(a)**

853. You feel that your supervisor's decision for you to place a client in the Wednesday night encounter group could be very dangerous to the client's mental health. After numerous meetings with the executive director and the board, you are warned that you must enroll the client in the group. Ethically, you

a. should enroll the client and do what your supervisor says.
b. seriously should consider terminating your affiliation with the agency.
c. should continue to work there but contact the local ACA chapter.
d. should let your liability insurance representative handle the dilemma.

Nobody said you were going to like this answer but here goes. ACA and NBCC ethics dictate that if your employer or agency policy is not conducive to "positive growth and development of clients, then terminating the affiliation should be seriously considered." The ethics stipulate that the counselor will make "concerted efforts" to remedy the situation before considering termination. The counselor in this question appears to have followed this recommendation. **(b)**

854. A colleague of yours who is not a certified counselor behaves in an unethical manner. The ethical thing for you to do is

    a.   ignore it; unfortunately you have no rights in this situation.
    b.   consult the school the person graduated from.
    c.   attempt to rectify the condition via institutional channels turning to NBCC procedures if this fails.
    d.   all of the above are considered ethical.

NBCC does not beat around the bush in regard to this critical issue. The certified counselor must take action to "attempt to rectify" unethical behavior of professional colleagues "whether certified or not." Read Section A: General, paragraph 3, of NBCC's Code of Ethics. **(c)**

855. A client asks you for classical psychoanalysis yet you have no training whatsoever in this area. If you agree to analyze the client, you are

    a.   violating the duty to warn.
    b.   still ethical if you possess LPC or NCC.
    c.   unethical as this is misrepresentation.
    d.   still ethical if and only if you have a doctorate.

Six doctorates and a wall covered with LPC and NCC credentials will not change the situation. The general section of NBCC's Code Of Ethics states in paragraph 8 that "certified counselors recognize their limitations and provide services or only use techniques for which they are qualified by training and/or experience." Paragraph 4 of the same section administers the coup de grace, explaining that "certified counselors neither claim nor imply professional qualifications which exceed those possessed." A counselor who had extensive training, say via an analytic institute, could perhaps provide this service ethically. Moreover, most psychologists and counselors would agree that it is ethical to withhold or summarize test results requested by another professional who does not have sufficient training to properly analyze or interpret the data. **(c)**

856. A client needs counseling but can afford only $5 per session. As a private practitioner you charge $75 per hour. You should

    a.   still charge the client $75 per hour, but let her pay you $5 per week indefinitely until she has actually paid your normal rate.

    b.   be firm and tell her the fee is $75 per hour regardless of her income.

    c.   immediately refer her to a state funded agency.

    d.   consider the client's financial status and the locality.

If she cannot afford your reduced rate, you should assist her to find a comparable service at an acceptable cost. NBCC ethics tell the story. In accordance with Section A: General, paragraph 6, the certified counselor is told to "consider the financial status of clients and the respective locality" when establishing fees. If the fee is inappropriate, you must assist the client "finding comparable services of acceptable cost." Incidentally, NBCC, ACA, APA, and NASW ethics do not require therapists to provide "pro bono" (i.e., free) services to clients, though APA ethics recommend the practice of working for little or no financial return. **(d)**

857. Dr. X recommends to his agency clients that he would rather counsel them in his private practice. Ethically speaking

    a.   Dr. X has every right to do this.

    b.   Dr. X is diverting agency clients to his practice and this is unethical.

    c.   NBCC takes no position on this practice.

    d.   NBCC encourages this method for private practitioners.

Certified counselors must not divert clients to private practice if these clients can receive the service at the agency or institution. IT IS IMPERATIVE THAT YOU STUDY ACA/NBCC OR THE CODE OF ETHICS THAT APPLIES TO YOUR SPECIALTY BEFORE TAKING YOUR EXAM. In this case the answer appears in Section A: General, paragraph 5 of the NBCC code.   **(b)**

858. Section B of NBCC Code of Ethics deals with the counseling relationship. Thus a counselor who uses a paradoxical strategy

    a. has committed a blatant ethics violation.
    b. does not need to explain the purpose of the paradox to the client.
    c. should explain the purpose of this technique to the client.
    d. must tape record the interview.

Paragraphs 8 and 9 specify that certified counselors will clearly inform clients of the purposes, goals, and techniques utilized. Some textbooks in the field may have inadvertently given counselors the false notion that it is best to mystify the counseling process. Paradoxical interventions are contraindicated in cases with homicidal and/or suicidal clients.   **(c)**

859. A counselor is counseling his secretary. This is an example of

    a. a dual relationship.
    b. a common situation which is not unethical.
    c. good clinical judgment in many instances.
    d. informed consent.

And what happens to the counselor's objectivity if his secretary is doing a poor job, steals from him, or needs to be fired? Section B: Counseling Relationship, paragraph 10 of the NBCC code warns that dual relationships could impair objectivity and a referral for services is indicated.

The practice of "bartering" for services is not deemed unethical at this time, though it is rumored that the respective ethics committees are examining this practice very carefully. Bartering occurs when a client exchanges a good or service for therapy (e.g., I'll paint your car if you provide me with six sessions of therapy). Many experts insist bartering should be delineated specifically as an unethical form of a dual relationship. **(a)**

860. NBCC ethics state that a counselor should _____ all clients for group counseling.

    a.   diagnose
    b.   test
    c.   screen
    d.   a and b

NBCC's Section B, paragraph 15 is very clear about this point. **(c)**

861. According to NBCC Section C, which discusses ethical considerations in Measurement and Evaluation, a counselor who gives the client a WISC-R

    a.   needs only a master's degree.
    b.   needs a doctorate.
    c.   must have an advanced graduate certificate or a doctorate.
    d.   must have specific training in this respect.

Paragraph 6 tells counselors that they should "perform only those functions for which they have received appropriate training." What is the rationale? Well, even if you have a room full of degrees on the wall, there are far too many assessment techniques to assume that each one was covered in your graduate program. In respect to this question, I am certain there are many counselors reading this book who have not received specific training in the administration of the WISC-R. If you imply that you have credentials that exceed those which you possess then you are guilty of an ethics violation known as "misrepresentation." See NBCC ethics, Section A, paragraph 4. **(d)**

862. Section D of the NBCC Code of Ethics deals with Research and Publication. According to this section, which of the following is not an ethical consideration?

    a.   Informing the client of risks and/or discomfort.
    b.   Informing the client that he or she can withdraw from a research study at any time.
    c.   Informing the client of the exact statistical test that will be utilized to analyze the data.
    d.   Giving the client a fair explanation of the procedure.

Paragraph 8 admonishes that you will make the data available to others who may wish to replicate the study, but it is likely your client is not one of those folks. And even if he or she is, advance notice of the statistical procedure could confound the results. Choices "a," "b," and "d" are all steps that need to be taken by any ethical researcher. **(c)**

863. You have just made a landmark discovery which you feel could literally change the entire field of counseling and thus you write an article which depicts your findings. The next step would be to

    a.   submit the article to no more than two journals simultaneously.
    b.   submit the article to every major APA and ACA journal published.
    c.   submit the journal to one publication at a time despite your conviction that the article must get published.
    d.   write NBCC and request permission for multiple submission privileges.

Here is a concept I mentioned earlier and Section D, paragraph 14 of the NBCC code sets the record straight: "certified counselors must not submit the same manuscript, or one essentially the same in content, for simultaneous publication consideration by two or more journals." **(c)**

864. NBCC and ACA both have a Section E which is concerned with ethics related to consulting. Consulting or consultation can best be defined as

    a.   a brand or paradigm of brief psychotherapy.

    b.   a brand or paradigm of long-term psychotherapy.

    c.   a systematic process based on classical conditioning.

    d.   a voluntary relationship between a professional helper and an individual, group or social unit in which the consultant helps define or solve problems related to clients, the client system, or work related issues.

One ethical consideration here is that the consulting relationship encourages growth and self-direction for the consultee. Paragraph 4 explains that the consultant should not become a decision maker for clients and/or create a dependent relationship. If choices "a," "b," and "c" are unclear, reread the questions and answers in this book in the Helping Relationship section. **(d)**

865. Section F of NBCC describes ethical issues related to private practice. Which of these situations is clearly an ethics violation.

    a.   A private practitioner who advertises in the Yellow Pages.

    b.   A private practitioner who advertises in a daily newspaper.

    c.   A counselor who terminates a professional relationship with a client as she feels it is no longer productive for her client.

    d.   An executive director of a private practice who has his name listed in a Yellow Pages advertisement despite the fact that he is out of the country and is engaged in a research project for the next two years.

HOPEFULLY I AM GETTING MY MESSAGE ACROSS HERE: EXPECT TO SEE A HOST OF QUESTIONS RELATED TO THE PRACTICAL APPLICATION OF ALL THE MAJOR AREAS OF COUNSELING—NOT JUST ETHICS—ON YOUR EXAM. The helping professions have become more liberal about advertising practices and thus, based on the information in items choices "a" and "b," you cannot say they are unethical. Paragraph 3 in this section states, however, that certified counselors in executive leadership roles should not allow their names to be used in professional notices at times when they are not performing counseling. **(d)**

866. Nosology refers to a system of classification. Name the nosological system(s) utilized by professional counselors who diagnose clients?

   a.   DSM-III-R.
   b.   ICD-9.
   c.   a and b.
   d.   The Rogerian classification system.

Did you mark choice "a"? Well give yourself an A- because that's not really a bad answer. In fact, it is not even an incorrect answer. The answer I wanted you to mark, nevertheless, was choice "c" since some third-party payers have begun asking for ICD (International Classification of Disease) codes (choice "b"). **(c)**

867. The DSM-III-R was created by the American Psychiatric Association. DSM-III-R stands for the *Diagnostic and Statistical Manual Three Revised*. ICD-9 refers to the *Manual of the International Statistical Classification of Diseases, Injuries, and Causes of Death* created by the World Health Organization (WHO). Which counselor would most likely be required to utilize one of these guides to diagnose a client?

a. A counselor who wishes to secure insurance payments.
b. A guidance counselor discussing a child with a teacher.
c. A multicultural counselor who is seeing a Black client.
d. A counselor leading a T-group.

Some experts (e.g., Jay Haley and Carl Rogers) have noted that the formal process of diagnosis is not necessarily a good thing. Giving the client a diagnosis may bias the counselor or cause the counselor to stereotype the individual. Diagnosis has been seen as dehumanizing, and a given diagnosis does not imply a given cure. Despite all the aforementioned difficulties, insurance companies ask for a diagnosis before paying for a service; this is a remnant of the so-called medical model. Remember: the DSM is produced by a medical organization, the American Psychiatric Association (yes unfortunately, there's another APA to commit to memory). **(a)**

868. Traditionally, _____ counseling has caused the most ethical concerns.

    a. behavioral
    b. person-centered
    c. humanistic
    d. reality therapy

The concern has been that behavior therapists can control, manipulate, and shape behavior. Is it ethical, for example, to use aversive conditioning such as electrical shocks, drugs, or paralysis to eliminate smoking, alcoholism, gambling, or homosexual tendencies? Some clients in token economy behavior modification systems have questioned the legality of using contingencies in the form of reinforcement to get them to talk, work, behave, dress, or interact in a certain way. **(a)**

869. Insurance payments are also called

    a.   mandated payments.
    b.   third-party payments.
    c.   optional payments.
    d.   psychometric payments.

Keep in mind that third-party payments do not always cover the entire counseling fee. An insurance policy, for example, could pay only 50% or 80%. Other third-party systems have a maximum fee for services which could conceivably be less than your normal rate. When a client pays for a portion of the service it is known as a "co-payment." **(b)**

870. The DSM-III-R uses a multiaxial classification system with five axes. Diagnostic codes have _____ digits.

    a.   five
    b.   four
    c.   nine (which correspond to the DOT)
    d.   twelve

The first DSM appeared on the mental health scene in 1952 and was updated as the DSM-II in 1958, and the DSM-III in 1980. The DSM draft completed in November of 1986 picked up the "R" which stands for "revised." A DSM-IV is being compiled at this time. This question introduces you to the word "axes." Each "axis" actually describes a different class of information. Thus, therapists refer to the DSM as a "multiaxial system of diagnosis." The first three axes constitute the "official diagnostic assessment," while the final two (i.e., axis IV and V) are used for research and special clinical settings to predict outcome and help in treatment planning. The axes include: Axis I—Clinical Syndromes and V Codes; Axis II—Developmental Disorders and Personality Disorders; Axis III—Physical Disorders and Conditions; Axis IV—Severity of Psychosocial Stressors; and Axis V—Global Assessment of Functioning, or GAF for short. The GAF is "global" in the sense that it rates psychological, social, and occupational functioning on a continuum of mental health/mental illness. The scale goes from 1 (persistent danger to the self or others) to 90 (minimal symptomatology or an absence of symptoms). Hence, the higher the rating, the higher the level of mental health. DSM instructions say that two GAF ratings should be given, one for the present level of functioning, and one for the highest level during the past year which endured for at least a few months. In children and adolescents, the second rating should include a school year month. Counselors need to be aware that third-party payment organizations sometimes require GAF ratings. All diagnostic codes, except the GAF rating, utilize five digits with a decimal point after the first three digits (e.g., 307.51 Bulimia nervosa or V62.30 Academic problem). An easy memory device might be that your hand has five digits (you know, as in fingers) and the DSM likewise has five digit codes and five axes. **(a)**

871. Identify the DSM-III-R code.

    a.   29622
    b.   29.622
    c.   296.22
    d.   2962.2

You would not need to know that this is the code for "major depression, single episode, moderate," to answer this question. In fact let me give you some friendly advice: Do not waste one second of your time memorizing the code numbers for diagnoses for either state licensing or NCC. The idea of these questions is to familiarize you with the format of the diagnostic process. Choice "c" is correct. As mentioned in the answer to the last question, the decimal point occurs after the third digit regardless of the diagnosis or lack of it. (Special note: I say lack of it since V71.09 stands for no diagnosis on Axis I, or it could mean no diagnosis on Axis II, while 799.90 is a diagnosis or condition deferred on Axis I or on Axis II.) **(c)**

872. As you are reading the DSM-III-R you see this code: 296.2X. In this case the X (i.e., the fifth digit) refers to

    a.   severity, and thus it will be replaced with a diagnostic number.
    b.   an adjustment disorder.
    c.   a developmental disorder.
    d.   physical disorders and conditions.

The fifth digit can also indicate a condition in a state of remission while a fifth digit of 0 means "unspecified." In this actual example the 296.2X indicates the condition of major depression, single episode. In the form of 296.20 the condition is "unspecified." Written 296.21 the condition is "mild." 296.22 is moderate, while 296.23 is "severe without psychotic features"; and finally 296.24 signifies the most serious state of "severe with psychotic features." 296.25 is "in partial remission" whereas 296.26 is "in full remission." This is an example of a mood disorder. For organic mental disorders and schizophrenia, the fifth digit code will take on a different meaning. Fifth digit codes for organic impairment include: 1 = with delirium (i.e., mental confusion); 2 = with delusions(a false belief unaltered by facts to the contrary); 3 = with depression; and 0 = uncomplicated. For schizophrenia 1 = subchronic; 2 = chronic; 3 = subchronic with acute exacerbation; 4 = chronic with acute exacerbation; 5 = remission; and 6 = unspecified. Also take note of the fact that the DSM routinely uses the abbreviation NOS, which means "not otherwise specified," while NEC ("not elsewhere classified") appears in the ICD. The DSM does not speculate about the causation of the condition. **(a)**

873. In the DSM the so-called V Codes refer to conditions which are not attributable to a mental condition. An example of a V Code would be

a. 6282.V
b. 62V.82
c. 628V2
d. V62.82

Although a V Code is not attributable to a mental condition, it is the focus of treatment such as adult antisocial behavior or an academic problem. Choice "d" is "uncomplicated bereavement." Please do not memorize this code. The salient feature to remember is that the "V" replaces the first digit in the five digit code. **(d)**

874. An example of a V Code diagnosis would be

a. Major Depression Single Episode Mild.
b. Borderline Personality.
c. Uncomplicated Bereavement.
d. Cocaine Dependence.

Certainly bereavement in response to a death of a loved one, for example, might not be attributed to any other "mental disorder" listed in the DSM. It might surprise you to discover that in addition to the aforementioned conditions, V Codes include marital problems, borderline intellectual functioning (an IQ of 71 to 84; 70 or below is considered retarded), malingering (which is avoiding life's work and/or duties by exaggerating or feigning physical symptoms or illness), parent-child problems, occupational problems, noncompliance with medical treatment, other interpersonal problems, and a phase of life or circumstances problem (such as enduring a divorce). In essence, these are what the average person might consider day-to-day problems rather than a psychiatric or psychological difficulty. This text is not intended to cover the DSM in depth. Read the DSM before sitting for your exam. **(c)**

875. Formal diagnosis, also known as nosology or taxonomy, is most closely related to the _____ model.

a. behavioral
b. medical
c. cognitive-behavioral
d. rational-emotive

The behaviorist, choice "a," is looking for an operational definition (remember I mentioned this term earlier?) of the problem. A DSM diagnosis such as 300.23 Social Phobia is vague and meaningless for the behaviorist. Instead, a diagnosis like "I cry whenever I have to give a presentation in my Counseling 502 class" is the type of specific information the behaviorist is interested in. Rational-emotive and other cognitive behavior therapists are generally more interested in the client's self-talk than in the DSM category. **(b)**

876. Which DSM-III-R diagnosis indicates the most serious pathology?

a. 296.21
b. 296.22
c. 296.23
d. 296.24

Review the answer to 872 unless you marked choice "d." **(d)**

877. The type of mental health service provided to the client is coded via _____ and is generally required for insurance payments.

a. the DSM-III-R (e.g., 296.22)
b. the ICD-9 (e.g., 311)
c. the AMA's Current Procedural Terminology (e.g., CPT 90844)
d. the Psychiatric Dictionary

If you want to accept insurance payments you will generally need to specify a CPT Code in addition to the DSM or ICD Code on your billing statement. The

CPT code will specify the exact nature of the treatment being utilized to help your client (e.g., psychotherapy, hypnosis, biofeedback, or group psychotherapy). A CPT Code also can specify the length of the service unit, such as "psychotherapy over 30 minutes." At the end of each session, a client seeking insurance or third-party benefits is given a statement which is sometimes called a "superbill." The superbill verifies the nature of the counselor/client interaction. At the very least, an acceptable superbill usually lists the client's name, the date, the DSM or ICD diagnosis, the CPT Code, and the provider's name and license. It is misrepresentation to list someone else as a direct service provider to secure third-party payments if you provided the service yourself. If an insurance company only reimburses a psychiatrist or a licensed clinical psychologist, then you are not allowed to put the psychologist's or psychiatrist's name on the superbill as if he or she were the service provider. The psychiatrist's or psychologist's name could, however, be clearly noted as a supervisor. This can help to secure insurance payments in some cases. Third-party providers can and have taken legal action against therapists for such misrepresentation. Moreover, therapists have been required to pay back funds received in this manner. My advice is to play it straight. Your bank account may not be quite as large, but I guarantee you'll sleep a lot better.   **(c)**

878. In 1983 APGA changed its name to the American Association for Counseling and Development, and in 1992 the name was changed again to American Counseling Association. The largest ACA Division is the

   a.   American School Counselor Association.
   b.   Association for Multicultural Counseling and Development.
   c.   Association for Marriage and Family Counselors.
   d.   Association for Humanistic Education and Development.

The ASCA has over 12,300 members. If the organization chooses to break away from ACA (as mentioned earlier) then AMHCA (American Mental Health Counselors Association) will be heir to the throne with approximately 11,400 members as of June, 1992.   **(a)**

879. Counseling clients by mail is

    a.   illegal.
    b.   unethical.
    c.   illegal and unethical.
    d.   questionable but has not been specifically addressed by ethical guidelines at this point in time.

This is the type of current events question you could expect on an exam, something that is novel and very controversial. Here the impetus comes from the October 25, 1990 issue of the "Guidepost" in a front page article entitled "Counseling By Mail?" The story depicts two New York private practitioners who have been interventionists via the mail for over five years using letters and cassette tapes. In the article, Larry Golden, the coauthor of *AACD's Ethical Standards Casebook*, questions the client's motivation in regard to this form of counseling as well as the dangers of the practice. Karen Pritchard, an AACD Ethics Committee chairperson, discusses her concerns regarding confidentiality. No conclusions as of yet, and the ethical codes have not taken a definitive stand on the matter. Stay tuned; this one is bound to raise a few eyebrows including whether counselors by mail are duly licensed professionals when the client resides in another state! Oh yes, I assure you this could get complicated.   **(d)**

880. An elementary school counselor is giving a child a standardized test. On several occasions the child says he does not understand what the counselor has said. The counselor should

a. refuse to repeat the question.
b. tell the child to answer the question nevertheless.
c. repeat the question, but talk more slowly.
d. ignore the child's verbalizations.

A word of caution is in order here. The counselor should always attempt to use the recommended wording. Changing the wording could alter the impact of the test question, possibly confounding the results. **(c)**

881. The most popular paradigm of mental health consultation has been proposed by

a. Satir and Minuchin.
b. Schein.
c. Caplan.
d. Bandura.

Mental health consultation occurs when a consultant works with a consultee regarding clients or administrative/ program issues. When the ultimate goal is to help a client, it is known as a "client-centered" consultation. When your licensing supervisor suggests a plan of action for a given client, then you as a consultee are the recipient of "client-centered" consultation (not to be confused with client-centered therapy). The exam you will take also may mention "consultee-centered" consultation. Here, the focus is on helping the consultee develop improved techniques or skills. Thus, when your licensing supervisor explains a better way for you to implement a hypnotic induction with one of your clients, then you are the recipient of "consultee-centered case consultation." A variation of this is the "consultee-centered administrative consultation" in which your supervisor or consultant's intention is to sharpen up your administrative skills (e.g., making you a better presenter at your agency board meeting). Finally, there is the "program-centered administrative consultation." As the name suggests, the emphasis here is on creating, designing, or evaluating the program in question. These four basic types of mental health consultation have been proposed by Caplan. Choice "a" identifies two well-known names in the family therapy movement, while Bandura (choice "d") is well-known for his work in modelling and vicarious learning by observation (sometimes known as "social learning theory"). In this approach, the consultant helps the consultee set up behavioral management programs for the clients. **(c)**

882. The doctor-patient consultation model relies on four distinct stages: entry, diagnosis, implementation, and evaluation. In order for the doctor-patient structure to work, the consultee (i.e., the person receiving the consultation) must accurately depict symptomatology, trust the consultant's diagnosis, and carry out the consultant's directives. This model is associated most closely with the work of

    a.   Caplan.
    b.   Freud.
    c.   Adler.
    d.   Schein.

Schein, who has written a book on consultation, uses the term "process consultation," which differs from other consultation models since the consultant and the consultee come to an agreement or a joint diagnosis about what needs to transpire. **(d)**

883. _____ is the leading cause of malpractice actions taken against counselors, therapists, and mental health providers.

    a.   Sexual misconduct
    b.   Dual relationships
    c.   Failure of the duty to warn
    d.   Inferior record keeping

It has been estimated that over 95% of those clients who were sexually involved with their therapists have been harmed, and that in about 1/3 of the cases, treatment literally ended as soon as sexual intimacy began. **(a)**

884. Advising clients of their rights and responsibilities is

    a.   the duty to warn.
    b.   a dual relationship.
    c.   known as informed consent.
    d.   generally not conducive to effective intervention.

The theory is simply that the client must have enough information to rationally give you permission to provide the service. In short, the client needs to be "informed" well enough to "consent" to the plan of action. Choice "a" means that confidentiality is thrown out the window and the counselor can warn those who are in danger. Choice "b," a dual relationship, occurs when a counselor is involved with a client in a nontherapeutic sense (e.g., dating a client). Ethics do not condone this practice.   **(c)**

885. You leave the country to take a vacation. Nobody is available to cover your caseload and your clients cannot reach you.

    a.   This is perfectly legal as well as ethical.
    b.   The relaxation will curb burnout, and thus this behavior is indeed recommended despite the apparent risk.
    c.   You could be sued for abandonment.
    d   It is the client's responsibility to find another counselor.

Whether it curbs burnout or not is irrelevant; the fact is that you (that's right you my friend, not the client as suggested in choice "d") need to find somebody to cover your caseload while you are on vacation or you take the chance that your client might see you in court!   **(c)**

886. Ethical dilemmas rarely have clear-cut answers. Thus when a complex ethical situation manifests itself, it is best to

a. consult only ethical codes and not colleagues.
b. consult with colleagues as well as ethical codes inasmuch as legal standards are very often based on the methods of fellow professionals in analogous situations.
c. consult ACA but not your colleagues.
d. consult your state licensing bureau but not your colleagues.

Legal standards and cases regarding malpractice suits are often decided by the behavior of your fellow professionals. If I were you, I'd check to make certain you're not the one soldier marching in the opposite direction! **(b)**

887. You have attempted to help a client for over two years with little or no success. You should

a. always refer the client to a board certified psychiatrist.
b. terminate the relationship and initiate an appropriate referral.
c. change therapeutic modalities and see the client for another six months.
d. change therapeutic modalities and see the client for at least another year.

NBCC's ethics Section B: Counseling Relationship, paragraph 11, suggests that when a certified counselor feels he or she is unable to help a potential or existing client, then the relationship should not be initiated, or the existing one should be terminated. In either case, the counselor is responsible for providing alternative referral sources to the client. **(b)**

888. Assume that you have decided to refer a client elsewhere because you were unable to help her. The client insists upon seeing you. NBCC ethics would dictate that

a. you must see her; your duty is to the client.
b. you must refer her to a medical practitioner.
c. you must ask her to consider hospitalization.
d. you are not obligated to continue the relationship.

Again, refer to Section B, paragraph 11 of the NBCC Code. **(d)**

889. Counseling is a relatively new profession. The first counselors in the U.S. were not called counselors. They were

a. psychoanalysts practicing short-term therapy.
b. behaviorists practicing short-term therapy.
c. deans and advisors employed after the Civil War in college settings to watch over young women.
d. humanistic psychologists.

For an excellent discussion of the early history of counseling read Chapter 2 in the book, *Counseling: A Professional Orientation* (1993), by Nicholas A. Vacc and Larry C. Loesch. The entire book is highly recommended as a resource in preparation for any major examination in counseling. **(c)**

890. Historically speaking, the first psychology laboratory was set up by

a. Frank Parsons who set up community centers to help individuals in search of work.
b. Sigmund Freud, the father of psychoanalysis.
c. Wilhelm Wundt in 1879 in Leipzig, Germany.
d. E.G. Williamson.

Wundt was convinced that psychology could be accepted as a science if consciousness could be measured. Wundt's school of thought is termed "structuralism" as his interest was in the "structure" of consciousness. German psychologists—and I'm certain you'll find this humorous in terms of our emphasis today on pragmatic strategies—were convinced that Wundt's theory was indeed pure science because it had no practical applications!!! Parsons, choice "a," has been called the "father of guidance." Some historians insist that the profession of counseling officially began when Parsons founded the Vocational Guidance Bureau of Boston and published the book *Choosing A Vocation* in 1909.   **(c)**

891. Counseling became popular after the 1931 publication of

   a.   *Workbook in Vocations* by Proctor, Benefield, and Wrenn.
   b.   *The Interpretation of Dreams* by Freud.
   c.   *Behaviorism* by John B. Watson.
   d.   *Counseling and Psychotherapy* by Rogers.

These are all landmark books in the field. Choice "a" is the correct answer as it set the stage for the popularization of the word "counseling." Prior to 1931, the word "guidance" was used for educational and vocational guidance. This work, as well as an earlier one by Proctor in 1925 entitled *Educational and Vocational Guidance*, began to conceptualize counseling as a psychological process. Choice "b" is considered Freud's most influential work, while choice "c" described the tenets of behaviorism, which was born in 1912. Watson's behaviorism asserted that the only subject matter for psychology was observable behavior. Choice "d" is the 1942 classic in which Rogers emphasized a theory of intervention in which the counselor was not an authoritarian figure such as in psychoanalysis, trait-factor, or directive schools of helping. Rogers was also known as one of the first theorists to employ audio recordings to improve practicum supervision.   **(a)**

892. PL94-142 (The Education Act for All Handicapped Children) states that

    a.   all children between 5 and 21 are assured free education.
    b.   handicapped persons are placed in the least restrictive environment (LRE).
    c.   an Individualized Education Plan (IEP) is developed for each child
    d.   all of the above.

This act was passed in 1975 after a congressional finding that the U.S. had over 8 million handicapped children. Over half were not receiving appropriate education while 1 million were excluded from public education. Enforcement relied on funding. That is to say, if a state did not meet the guidelines mentioned in choices "a," "b," and "c," funding was denied. Section 617 (c) of PL 94-142 (another stipulation for funding) gave individuals the right to read there own records and files if they were over 18, as well as the records of their children. **(d)**

893. The major trend that impacted upon the counseling movement in the 1980s

    a.   was reality therapy.
    b.   was behavior modification.
    c.   included an emphasis on professionalism, certification, and licensing.
    d.   was the group movement.

Credentialing helped counseling become a specific and separate profession such as psychology or psychiatry. Although group work is still very popular, it emerged as a driving force in the 1970s. **(c)**

894. APGA and APA had joint ethics for counselors and psychologists. This changed during the 1970s when

a. Psy.D. programs were introduced.
b. the APA did not wish to credential master's level counselors or psychologists.
c. psychologists were doing more testing.
d. joint ethics became illegal in the U.S.

Separate ethics were thus developed, which helped discern counseling from psychology as a profession. Psy.D., or so-called doctor of psychology programs (choice "a"), generally focus more on practitioner skills and less on research and experimental skills than Ph.D. programs in clinical psychology. **(b)**

895. The 1950s was the age of tremendous strides in

a. analysis.
b. developmental psychology.
c. behavior modification.
d. group work.

Piaget, Erikson, and Havinghurst were very influential. In addition, thanks primarily to the work of Carl R. Rogers, counseling rather than testing became the major task for professionals. **(b)**

896. The _____ movement began in the late 1960s.

a. testing
b. Rogerian
c. group
d. developmental psychology

Groups would remain popular in the 1970s. Some of the literature in the field refers to the 1960s and 1970s as the "decades of variation," in which we became "therapy of the month consumers"! Jerome Frank hypothesized at the time that the sudden flood of new therapies was due to the current upheaval in society. Gestalt, TA, Primal Scream Therapy, Encounter Groups, Marathon Groups, and yes, even Naked Encounter Groups became popular! **(c)**

897. In the 1960s Gilbert Wrenn's book, *The Counselor in a Changing World*, urged counselors to

    a.   use biofeedback.
    b.   rely more heavily on projective testing.
    c.   emphasize developmental concerns rather than merely focusing on crises and curing emotional illness.
    d.   stick to proven nondirective techniques.

This 1962 APGA publication was an attempt to steer counseling away from merely providing remedial services to students. **(c)**

898. One of the primary problems of counseling in the early 1960s was that it wrongly emphasized

    a.   social issues.
    b.   intrapsychic processes.
    c.   referrals to secure antidepressant medicinal.
    d.   career counseling.

This was not entirely a negative thing; nevertheless, social issues such as Vietnam, civil rights, and women's issues could have been emphasized to a greater degree. **(b)**

899. The significance of the 1958 National Defense Education Act was that it

    a.   provided financial aid for graduate education in counseling.
    b.   expanded school guidance services.
    c.   improved guidance for gifted children.
    d.   all of the above.

Many pilot programs developed as a result of the funding. Gradually, the funding found its way into helping counselors prepare to work with economically disadvantaged youth. Thus, the act eventually helped all types of young people secure better counseling and guidance services. Some exams may use the abbreviation NDEA when referring to this act. **(d)**

900. In terms of AIDS patients and the limits of confidentiality, it could be stated that

    a.   experts disagree on the matter, while NBCC ethics do not currently address the issue.

    b.   NBCC insists you ask the client to inform sexual partners.

    c   NBCC insists you contact sexual partners of the client.

    d.   NBCC insists you contact the state health department.

There are experts on both sides of the fence. Some feel that mandatory breaching of confidentiality is necessary to safeguard sexual partners, as well as society as a whole, and that some sharing with public health officials is necessary. Others wonder whether such a measure would exacerbate the situation and cause AIDS clients to forego counseling. ACA/NBCC ethical guidelines have not yet taken a stand. Hence, as of this writing no court has applied the *Tarasoff* "duty to warn" to third parties who come in contact with HIV-positive clients. **(a)**

GOOD LUCK!

CHAPTER 12

GRAPHICAL
REPRESENTATIONS

Having a graphical concept is often very beneficial when answering questions. In this chapter are presented several graphical representations including the following:

Bell-shaped curve and related statistical information (Figure 12.1)

Graphical representations other than bell-shaped curve (Figures 12.2, 12.3, and 12.4)

Skewed distributions (Figures 12.5 and 12.6)

Bar graph or histogram (Figures 12.7 and 12.8)

Scattergrams showing correlations (Figures 12.9, 12.10, and 12.11)

Holland's hexagon model (Figure 12.12)

Berne's transactional analysis (Figure 12.13)

The normal Gaussian bell-shaped curve is symmetrical, unimodal, and mesokurtic. Here, the curve is matched up with an array of popular standard scores (Figure 12.1).

The normal Gaussian bell-shaped curve is symmetrical, unimodal, and mesokurtic. Here, the curve is matched up with an array of popular standard scores (Figure 12.1).

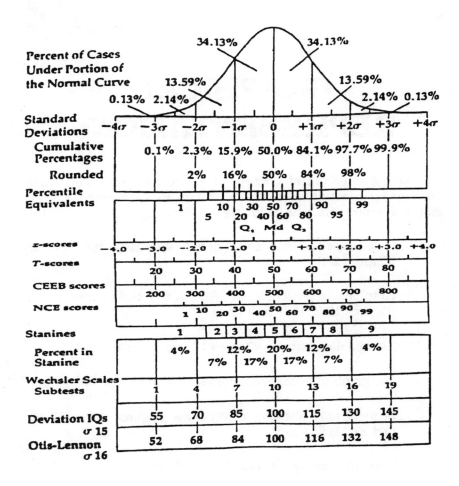

Figure 12.1 Bell-shaped curve and related statistical information.

Reprinted courtesy of Psychological Corporation from Test Service Notebook No. 148.

The so-called bimodal curve is characterized by two peaks (Figure 12.2). When a frequency polygon sports three or more peaks, it is known as multimodal.

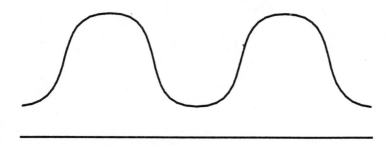

Figure 12.2. Bimodal curve.

Platykurtic distributions are flatter and more spread out than the normal curve. The number of persons scoring very high, very low, and in the average range would be similar (Figure 12.3).

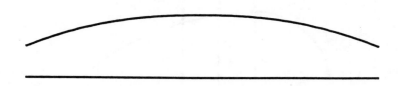

Figure 12.3. Flatter curve.

The leptokurtic distribution is taller, skinnier, and has a greater peak than the normal curve (Figure 12.4).

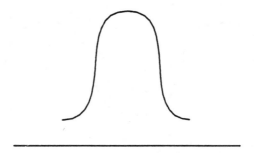

Figure 12.4. Leptokurtic distribution.

The positively skewed distribution has an abundance of low scores and is asymmetrical (Figure 12.5).

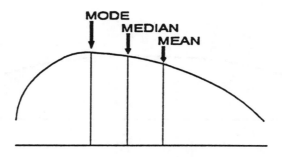

Figure 12.5. Positively skewed distribution.

The negatively skewed distribution reflects an abundance of high scores (Figure 12.6). The direction of the tail indicates whether the distribution is positively or negatively skewed.

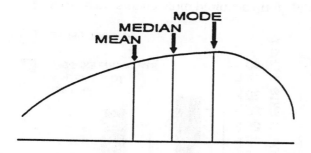

Figure 12.6. Negatively skewed distribution.

A bar graph, also called a histogram, can effectively represent data (Figure 12.7).

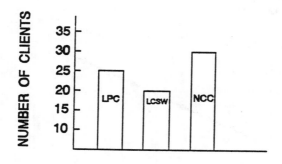

Figure 12.7. Bar graph or histogram.

In Figure 12.8, a double-barred histogram is utilized to compare two sets of scores. In this hypothetical example, LPCs and LCSWs in a control group are compared to an experimental group of professionals who received a seminar in marketing. The DV, which is plotted on the Y axis, would seem to indicate that the marketing strategies were helpful. Therapists in the experimental group acquired more clients each week.

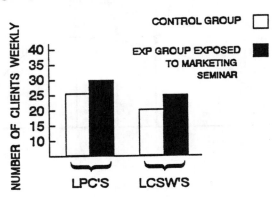

Figure 12.8. Double-barred histogram.

Scattergrams—also known as scatter plots or scatter diagrams—graphically depict the Pearson Product-Moment Correlation Coefficient. Representation of three scattergrams are presented in Figures 12.9, 12.10, and 12.11.

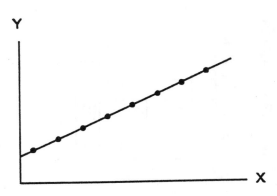

Figure 12.9. Scattergram of a perfect linear positive correlation.
r = +1.00

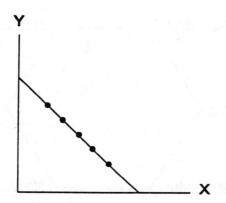

Figure 12.10. Scattergram of a perfect linear negative correlation. r = -1.00

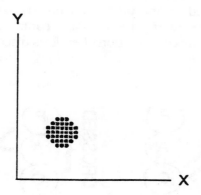

Figure 12.11. Scattergram showing a lack of relationship. r = 0.00

Career theorist John Holland proposes a hexagon model with six vocational personalities/work environments (Figure 12.12). Adjacent types are seen as consistent.

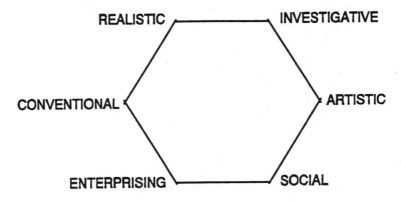

Figure 12.12. Holland's hexagon model.

Eric Berne's transactional analysis relies on three ego states: the Parent, the Child, and the Adult (Figure 12.13). When a message sent from a given ego state receives a predicted response, the transaction is said to be complementary. The complementary exchange is healthy. Contrast this with the crossed transaction, which occurs when a message is returned with an unexpected response. Crossed transactions abet emotional discord between the persons communicating. The person who initiated the conversation often feels discounted.

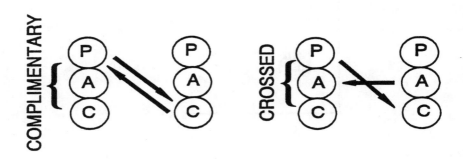

Figure 12.13. Schematic of Berne's transactional analysis.

CHAPTER 13

RESOURCES

In this chapter are listed resources frequently used by counselors. The first list is of statistical tests used in counseling research. Parametric and nonparametric tests are listed alphabetically. These explanations are in brief summary form. For a more complete explanation, please refer to a statistics book.

The second list consists of major psychoeducational diagnostic tools. These are listed alphabetically. The brief explanation is to help you know the kind of instrument, the age range (in most cases), and the general construct of each. The manual for the specific diagnostic tool and/or a comprehensive psychological testing text would be excellent references for more information.

Each professional group of mental health practitioners has a code of ethics. These codes are reviewed regularly and updated frequently. Therefore, each professional needs to keep abreast with the ethical codes applicable to him or her. The third list in this chapter provides the name and address of the source for each of eight codes.

STATISTICAL TESTS USED IN COUNSELING RESEARCH

Parametric Tests:

Analysis of Covariance (ANCOVA or ANACOVA). An extension of the ANOVA that controls the impact that one or more extraneous/unstudied variables (covariates) exert on the dependent variable.

Analysis of Variance (ANOVA). Also called a one-way analysis of variance, this test is used to determine whether two or more mean scores differ significantly from each other. The ANOVA examines a null hypothesis between two or more groups.

Factorial Analysis of Variance. Used to describe an ANOVA that is used to compare two or more independent variables. When two independent variables are utilized, the term "two-way ANOVA" is used; with three independent variables, the term "three-way ANOVA is used"; and so on.

Multivariate Analysis of Variance (MANOVA). Used to describe an ANOVA when a researcher examines more than one dependent variable.

Pearson Product-Moment Correlation (r). Used with interval and ratio data, this statistic examines the direction and magnitude of two variables. Correlation describes a relationship or association between variables. When relying on correlational research,variables are merely measured, not manipulated via the researcher.

Phi-Coefficient/Tetrachoric Correlation Coefficient. Used to assess correlation when both variables are dichotomous (i.e., binary or two-valued). Also known as a "fourfold-point correlation."

Point Bi-Serial/Bi-Serial Correlation. Used when one variable is continuous and the other is dichotomous (i.e., placed in two classes), for example correlating IQ with sex.

Scheffe's S Test/Newman-Keuls/Tukey's HSD/Duncan's New Multiple Range Test. Used after a researcher discovers a significant F ratio in an ANOVA to test the differences between specific group means or combinations of group means. Such measures are known as "a posteriori tests" or "post-hoc tests" for the ANOVA.

t-test. Used to ascertain whether two means or correlation coefficients differ significantly from each other. The t-test procedures can be employed for correlated/related/matched samples and for uncorrelated/independent/unmatched samples. The t-test is used also to determine whether a single sample or correlation coefficient differs significantly from a population mean.

Nonparametric Tests:

Chi-Square Test. Used to assess whether an obtained distribution is significantly different than an expected or theoretical distribution.

Kruskal-Wallis Test. Used as a nonparametric one-way analysis of variance. The Kruskal-Wallis statistic is called "H"; hence researchers sometimes refer to it as the "H-Test."

Mann-Whitney U-Test. Used to test whether a significant difference is present between two uncorrelated/unmatched means. Can be used in place of the t-test for uncorrelated/independent/unmatched means when parametric assumptions cannot be met. A "Whitney Extension" allows the test to be used with three samples.

Spearman Rank-Order Correlation (rho)/Kendall's tau. Used in place of the Pearson correlation coefficient when parametric assumptions can't be met (i.e., ordinal data are involved).

Wilcoxon Matched-Pairs/Signed-Ranks Test. Used to determine whether two correlated means are significantly different. Can be utilized in place of the related samples t-test when parametric assumptions cannot be met.

MAJOR PSYCHOEDUCATIONAL DIAGNOSTIC TOOLS

Contributed by Peggy Grotpeter, M.Ed., and
Arthur C. Myers, Ed.D.

Bayley Scales of Infant Development (Bayley). A test that provides a downward extension of the Stanford-Binet and measures early mental and psychomotor development of infants and young children. Test items measure responses to visual and auditory stimuli, manipulation, play with objects, and discrimination of sounds and shapes. The test is comprised of a Mental Scale, a Motor Scale, and an Infant Behavior Record.

Bender-Gestalt Test of Visual-Motor Integration (Bender). An expressive test consisting of nine stimulus cards that the person copies. It assesses visual perception and perceptual motor integration. It can be used also to detect the presence of underlying emotional difficulties and brain damage.

Beery Developmental Test of Visual-Motor Integration (Beery). A test consisting of 24 geometric shapes that the person reproduces. The test measures visual perception and eye/hand coordination.

California Psychological Inventory (CPI). A test intended for reasonably well-adjusted individuals that focuses on the assessment of personality characteristics that are important for social living and interaction. It has been used with ages 12 and older. Of the 480 test items, 178 are taken from the MMPI.

Career Decision Scale (CDS). This is a 19-item, self-reporting measure suitable for high-school and college-aged students. It can be used in both individual and group settings.

Children's Apperception Test (CAT). A downward extension of the TAT that is utilized with children ages 3 to 10. It consists of 10 picture cards depicting animals in various situations that a trained examiner uses to reveal dominant drives, emotions, sentiments, and personality characteristics.

Draw-A-Person Test (DAP). A norm referenced projective/ expressive test in which the person is asked to draw human figures. It is a nonverbal measure of intellectual ability and can be used as a projective measure of personality.

General Aptitude Test Battery (GATB). An aptitude test developed specifically for vocational counseling in schools and job placement settings. The test focuses on in-depth measurements of aptitude and skills that they relate to potential occupational success. The test is designed for use with students in grades 9 through 12, as well as with adults.

Guilford-Zimmerman Temperament Survey (GZTS). This inventory is designed to be used with normally functioning individuals. It was initially developed to assess Carl Jung's constructs of introversion and extroversion. It can be used in a variety of settings, but it has been used most frequently with the collegeaged population.

Halstead-Reitan Neuropsychology Battery. This test is used not only to diagnose neuropsychological dysfunction but to establish a baseline of function against which to measure future functioning. It consists of three batteries, one for children ages 5 to 8, one for children ages 9 to 14, and one for adults. Each battery includes a minimum of 14 separate tests which are scored as 26 variables.

Holtzman Inkblot Technique (HIT). Initially developed in an attempt to improve the reliability of the Rorschach Test. There are two parallel forms (A and B), each consisting of 45 inkblot cards. There are two practice blot cards that are identical for each test. The client is encouraged to give only one response for each card. Parallel forms allow for test-retest reliability.

House-Tree-Person (HTP). A projective/expressive drawing test that provides the examiner with information pertaining to intrapersonal, interpersonal, and environmental adjustment of the individual evaluated.

Kinetic Family Drawing (KFD). This instrument is a supplement to the DAP in which the person is asked to draw everyone in his/her family doing an activity. It is used as a projective measure of personality.

Kuder Occupational Interest Inventory (KOIS). An interest inventory that makes the assumption that a person will find satisfaction in an occupation where workers have similar interest patterns. This is a 100-triad inventory in which the respondent must choose between three activities, stating the one activity preferred the most and the activity preferred the least. It takes approximately 30 minutes to complete and must be scored by computer. Primarily suited to those in the tenth grade and beyond.

Leiter International Performance Scale (LIPS). A completely nonverbal measure of intelligence used with individuals from age 2 to adults. It is most often used to evaluate individuals who are deaf, nonverbal, non-English-speaking, culturally deprived, or have severe medical complications. The test consists of 54 sub-tests that increase in difficulty at each age level.

Minnesota Multiphasic Personality Inventory (MMPI and MMPI-2). A test that was designed to assess some major personality characteristics that affect personal and social adjustments. It contains 566 statements covering a range of subject matter including physical conditions, moral attitudes, and social attitudes. The test is individually administered and is suitable for persons 16 years of age who have had at least six successful years of schooling.

Myers-Briggs Type Indicator (MBTI). A widely used measure of personality disposition and preferences. It is based on Carl Jung's theory of perception and judgement. Four bipolar scales are used, resulting in 16 individual personality types, each of which are given a four-letter code used for interpreting personality type. It is suitable for use with upper elementary-aged children as well as adults.

Otis-Lennon School Ability Test (OLSAT). A group-administered multilevel mental ability battery designed for use in grades one through 12. The test's results are often used to predict success in school.

Peabody Individual Achievement Test (PIAT). This test is designed to measure the level of educational achievement in the areas of basic skills and knowledge. It does not require written responses and can be used with individuals in K (kindergarten) to adulthood.

Piers-Harris Children's Self Concept Scale. This is an 80-item scale that provides a self-descriptive scale entitled, "The Way I Feel About Myself." This test yields a self-concept score as well as six sub-scores.

Portage. A developmentally-sequenced, criterion-referenced checklist used as a measure with infants, children, and developmentally disabled individuals with functional age levels from birth to five years. It is used to measure skills in the cognitive, language, self-help, motor, and socialization areas.

Rorschach Inkblot Test. A projective test that utilizes ten 6 5/8 by 9 1/2 inch cards. Five of the cards are grey or black, while five are colored. The examinee is asked to describe what he or she sees or what the card brings to mind. The test is appropriate for ages three and beyond.

Rotter Incomplete Sentence Blanks (ISB). A semi-structured method of evaluating personality. The person is asked to complete 25 sentences for which the first word or words is/are provided. It is assumed the individual reflects his/her own wishes, desires, and fears.

Self-Directed Search (SDS). A self-administered career interest assessment that is available in several forms addressing the needs of a variety of clients, both students and professionals. It is a self-scoring instrument that can be completed and scored in approximately 35 to 45 minutes.

16 Personality Factor Questionnaire (16 PF). An 187-item, normal adult personality measure that can be administered to individuals age 16 and above.

Slosson Intelligence Test (SIT). A verbally administered measure of intelligence utilized to gain a quick estimate of intellectual ability. This test can be utilized from infancy to adulthood.

Stanford-Binet Intelligence scale (4th ed.). A test designed to measure cognitive ability as well as provide analysis of the pattern of an individual's cognitive development.

Stanford-Binet Intelligence Scale (form L-M). An age scale using standards of performance to measure intelligence regarded as general mental adaptability.

Strong-Campbell Interest Inventory (SCII). This career inventory is based on the career theory of John Holland and can be used with anyone who can comprehend the test items; that is, most people over 16. The SCII compares a person's interests with those of persons who have been in their occupation for at least three years and state that they enjoy their work. The test consists of 325 items and can be completed in approximately 35 minutes.

Test of Nonverbal Intelligence (TONI). A language-free measure of intelligence and reasoning. It consists of 50 abstract symbols in patterns with a variety of problem-solving tasks presented. The tasks increase in difficulty. The administration does not require reading, writing, listening, or speaking on the part of the individual evaluated.

Thematic Apperception Test (TAT). A projective test consisting of a pool of 30 picture cards (and one blank card) for which the individual is asked to make up emotions, sentiments, complexes, and conflicts of the individual's personality. Generally, a full TAT consists of 19 picture cards and the one blank card. If more than 10 cards are used, then it is appropriate to have a test sessions on different days. It is suitable for age 4 and older.

Vineland Adaptive Behavior Scale—Interview Edition. This is a survey form that assesses the individual's personal and social sufficiency. This instrument measures adaptive behavior from birth to adulthood.

Wechsler Adult Intelligence Scale-Revised (WAIS-R). A test comprised of verbal and nonverbal scales designed to measure intellectual functioning of adolescents and adults based on a capacity to understand and cope with the world.

Wechsler Intelligence Scale for Children-Revised (WISC-R/WISC-III). A test comprised of verbal and nonverbal scales designed to measure intellectual functioning of children based on capacity to understand and cope with the world. Appropriate for ages 6 to 16 1/2.

Wechsler Preschool and Primary Scale of Intelligence-Revised (WPPSI-R). A test comprised of verbal and nonverbal scales designed to measure intellectual functioning of young children based on capacity to understand and cope with the world. Appropriate for ages 4 to 6 1/2.

Wide Range Achievement Test - Revised (WRAT-R). An instrument used to measure progress in coding aspects of basic school subjects. It studies the sensorimotor skills involved in the learning process yielding a measure of simple and homogenous content. Often utilized for a quick estimate of academic achievement.

SOURCES FOR OBTAINING ETHICAL GUIDELINES

Counselors can secure "ACA Ethical Standards" from the American Counseling Association, 5999 Stevenson Avenue, Alexandria, Virginia 22304. Phone: (703) 823-9800

National Certified Counselors can secure the "NBCC Code of Ethics" from the National Board for Certified Counselors, 3-D Terrace Way, Greensboro, NC 27403. Phone: (919) 547-0607

Marriage and Family Therapists can secure the "AAMFT Code of Ethics" from the American Association for Marriage and Family Therapy, 1100 17th Street, NW, 10th floor, Washington, DC 200364601. Phone: (202) 452-0109

Psychologists can secure "Ethical Principles of Psychologists" from the American Psychological Association, 750 First Street, NE, Washington, DC 20002-4242. Phone: (202) 336-5500.

Social Workers can secure the "NASW Code of Ethics" from the National Association of Social Workers, 750 First Street, NE, Washington, DC 20002-4241. Phone: (202) 408-8600

Sociologists can secure the "Ethical Standards of Sociological Practitioners" from the Sociological Practice Association, RD 2, Box 141A, Chester, NY 10918

Psychiatrists can secure "Principles of Medical Ethics, with Annotations Especially Applicable to Psychiatry" from the American Psychiatric Association, 1400 K. Street, NW, Washington, DC 20005. Phone: (202) 682-6000

Psychoanalysts can secure the "Code of Ethics" from the American Psychoanalytic Association, 309 East 49th Street, New York, NY 10017.

INDEX

Numbers Refer to Question Numbers
Unless Otherwise Specified

A

AB or ABA design 92, 739
ABC theory of personality 341, 342
Abreaction 216
Abscissa 756
Absolutist thinking 343
Abused persons 152
Accommodation (Piaget) 92
Accreditation 809, 828
Accurate empathy 253
Achievement test 614, 677
Acquiescence 676
    period 263
Acquisition period 263
Action phase of counseling 391
Active therapy 285
Actuarial approach 511, 513
Adaptation 594
Adler, A. 15, 201, 229, 238, 242, 243, 244, 247, 248, 258, 259, 405
Adlerian 386
Adolescence 33
Adult ego state 356
Affective education group 413
Aggression 83, 108, 117, 119, 152
Agoraphobia 310
Ahistoric therapy 791
AIDS patients 900
Alloplastic 173, 174, 178
Allport, F.H. 183
Alpha coefficient 644
Alpha waves 297
Altruism 145
Ambivalence 451
American College Test (ACT) 628

American Counseling Association (ACA) 802, 824, 830, 878
American Counselor Education and Supervision (ACES) 829
American Group Psychotherapy Association 404
American Mental Health Counselors Association (AMHCA) 878
American Personnel and Guidance Association (APGA) 574, 829, 878
American Psychological Association (APA) 824, 848
American School Counselor Association (ASCA) 878
American Society for Group Psychotherapy and Psychodrama 404
Analysis
    multiple regression 794
    simple linear regression 794
Analysis of Convariance (ANCOVA or ANACOVA), 510, 727, 783
Analysis of Variance (ANOVA) 363, 727-729, 783, page 510
Analytic Psychology 201, 211, 386
Anchoring 367
Anima 73, 250
Animus 73, 250
Anna O. 214
Anxiety 78
Appraisal 601-700
Approach
    actuarial 511, 513
    developmental 515
    matching 511, 512
    trait-factor 511, 513
Approach-approach conflicts 189, 191

Aptitude test 666, 675, 677
Archetype 251, 252
Armed Services Vocational Aptitude Battery (ASVAB) 583, 584
Army Alpha and Beta 657
Asch, S. 198
Assertiveness training groups 418
Assimilation 92
Assimilation-contrast theory 158
Association for Measurement and Evaluation in Counseling and Development 673
Association for Non-White Concerns in Personnel and Guidance 109
Association for Specialists in Group Work (ASGW) 404
Associationism 52, 260
Attraction
    interpersonal 111, 118, 138
Authentic 366
Authoritarian 436
    leader 437
Authority figure 150
Autistic 60
Autocratic 437
Autoplastic 173, 174
Aversive conditioning 304
Avoidance-avoidance conflict 190, 476
Awfulization 344, 345
Axelrad, S. 515
Axis 870

B

Back-up reinforcer 293, 303
Backward conditioning 271
Balance theory 92, 120, 137
Bandler 367
Bandura, A. 108, 386, 392, 553, 570, 881
Bar graph 755, page 505
Barber, T.X. 185
Bartering 859
Baseline 244, 279
BASIC-ID 72
Bayley Scales of Infant Development (Bayley), page 512
Beck Depression Inventory (BDI) 352

Beck, A.T. 320, 352
Beery Developmental Test of Visual-Motor Integration (Beery) page 512
Behavior modification 278, 386
Behavioral contract 368
Behavioral rehearsal 306
Behaviorism 10, 179, 214, 260, 891
Behaviorist 2, 24, 40, 52, 555, 875
Bell-shaped curve 741, page 502
Bem, S. 69
Bender, L. 669
Bender-Gestalt Test of Visual-Motor Integration (Bender), page 512
Bender Visual Motor Gestalt Test 669
Benne, K. 411
Bergland 558
Berkowitz 119
Berne, E. 82, 106, 202, 203, 217, 354, 355, 364, 365, 386, page 508
Bias
    leniency/strictness 473
    test 668
Bibliotherapy 343, 346
Bimodal curve, page 503
Bimodal distribution 743, 759
Binet, A. 6, 643, 645, 649, 655
Biofeedback 280, 288, 293-295, 776
Birth order 258
Biserial correlation 733, page 510
Bivariate 736
Blanchard, K. 469
Blocking 451, 484
Bogardus 128
Bonding 25, 36, 59, 70
Bordin, E. 528, 529
Bowlby, J. 25, 31, 59, 70
Boys 37
Bradford, L. 411
Breuer, J. 201, 214, 216
Brewer, J.M. 501
Brill, A.A. 3, 512, 530, 531, 534
Buber 319
Buckley Amendment 698, 834
Buros, O.K. 664

C

California Psychological Inventory (CPI) page 512
California Test of Mental Abilities 656
Campbell, D.P. 576
Caplan, G. 392, 406, 881
Career
    counseling 506, 508
    development 501-600
    planning 503
    theory 511
Career Decision Scale (CDS), page 512
Carkhuff, R.R. 291, 314, 366, 399
Catastrophizing 344, 345
Catharsis 216
Cattell, J. 663
Cattell, R. 659
Centration 65
Cephalocaudal 43
Certification 825, 827, 893
Certified Clinical Mental Health Counselor (CCMHC) 802
Certified Rehabilitation Counselor (CRC) 803, 835
Chaining 277
Charged stimulus 271
Checklist 692
Chi-square 701, 727, 789
    Test, page 511
Child abuse 816
    ego state 357
    rearing 39
Children's Apperception Test (CAT), page 512
Civil Rights Act 510
Civil Rights Measurement 109
Clarification 484
Classical conditioning 262
Client-centered 285, 382, 387
    consultation 881
Close-ended question 312
Closed group 425-427
Cluster sample 793
Codependency 196
Co-facilitation 407
Cognitive
    behavioral 90

behavioral issues 377
consistency 92
dissonance 151, 257
dissonance theory 144, 148
restructuring 345, 348
theory 353
therapy 352, 353
Cohesiveness 459, 466, 480
Coleaders 439-443
Coleadership 407, 412
Collective unconscious 248
College Entrance Examination Board (CEEB) 767
Compensation 232
Compensatory effect 572, 573
Competence 395
Complementary transaction 358
Comprehensive model 490
Computer Assisted Career Guidance Systems (CACG) 571, 595
Computer Assisted Counseling (CAC) 843, 844, 846
Computer-assisted testing 689
Computer Managed Counseling (CMC) 843, 846
Conciliator 463
Concreteness 286
Concurrent validity 621, 628
Conditioned 263
Conditioned Reflex Therapy 247, 308, 462
Conditioned Stimulus (CS) 269, 271, 275
Conditioning
    aversive 304
    backward 271
    classical 262
    forward 271
    high order 293
    operant 264
    vivo aversive 304
Confidence 718, 719
Confidentiality 500, 806, 812-817, 847
Conflict of interest 472
Conflicts
    approach-approach 189, 191
    avoidance-avoidance 190
    unconscious 155
Conformity 30, 141, 198

Confounded 706
Confrontation 253
Congruence 388
Congruent 290
Connotation 165
Conscious mind 220
Consent
    informed 884
Conservation (Piaget) 7,8,9
Consonance 144
Constancy of objects 58
Construct validity 621, 624
Consultants 392
Consultation 392-393, 881, 882
    client-centered 881
    consultee-centered administrative
        881
    consultee-centered case 881
    models 393, 882
    process 882
    program-centered administrative
        881
Consultee-centered administrative
    consultation 881
Consultee-centered case
    consultation 881
Consultee-centered consultation 881
Content validity 621
Counterbalancing 791
Continuous reinforcement 298
Contract 179
    behavioral 368
Contracting 328, 361
Contrast effect 572
Control group 710
Control Theory 326, 333, 350
Convergent thinking 643
Convergent validity 627
Converting questions to statements
    368
Coopersmith, S. 39
Corey, G. 354, 440, 444, 479, 499
Corey, M.S. 440, 449
Correlated means 796
Correlation
    biserial 733
    Pearson r 740, pages 506, 510
    Spearman 727, page 511
Correlation coefficient 715, 732-736,
    740

Council for Accreditation of
    Counseling and Related
    Educational Programs
    (CACREP) 802, 822, 828, 848
Counseling
    action phase 391
    behavioral 868
    cross-cultural 101, 112, 163,
        179, 182
    directive 285
    existential 201, 316, 319, 323,
        324
    geriatric 139
    group 413
    intercultural 101
    multicultural 101, 103, 110, 163
    multicultural career 593
    nondirective 285, 382
    paradigm 285
    theories 301-400
Counselor in a Changing World, The
    897
Counselors, page 516
    cross-cultural 179
    multicultural 103
Counterbalancing 92
Counter transference 240, 257, 840
Covert 49, 302
Conyne R.K. 497
Criterion-related validity 621
Crites, J. 551
Cronbach, L.J. 644
Cross-cultural counseling 101
Cross-sectional study 788
Crossed transaction 358, 487
Cross validation 644
Cultural awareness 104
Culture 102, 121
    bound values 165
    different 161
    ecological 125
    ideal 105
    national 105, 125, 130
    real 105
    universal 126
Culture-epoch theory 104
Culture-fair test 658
Current Procedural Terminology 877
Cyclical test 616

D

Decision-making theory 552-558

Defense mechanisms 146, 221, 222-235

Denial 222, 229

Dependent variable (DV) 701, 707, 708, 758

Depressive neurosis 188

Deprivation (Harlow) 27, 31, 54, 60, 80

Descriptive statistics 715

Desensitization 49, 219, 309
    systematic 211

Design
    AB or ABA 92, 739
    matched 796
    multiple-baseline 739
    withdrawal 739

Development 42, 43, 85, 96
    boys 71
    girls 71
    moral 9, 13, 47
    theories 93

Developmental
    approaches 515
    career theorists 510, 515, 545, 556
    psychology 895
    stages (See stages)

Diachronic method 788

Diagnosis 116, 140, 142, 867, 875, 876

Diagnostic and Statistical Manual Third Edition Revised (DSM-III-R) 78, 116, 682, 866, 867, 870-877

Dichotomy 608

Dictionary of Occupational Titles (DOT) 371, 551-565

Differential Aptitude Test (DAT) 583, 584

Differential reinforcement of other behavior (DRO) 266

Difficulty index 606

Directional test 790

Directive 209, 287

DISCOVER 571, 595

Discriminant validity 627

Discrimination 510, 851

Descriptive research 778

Disonnance 120, 137

Displaced homemaker 590

Displacement 226

Distribution
    bimodal 743
    platykurtic 770
    skewed 748, 753, page 504

Distribution-free 796

Divergent thinking 643

Divorces 502

Dollard/Miller hypothesis 119

Double blind study 739

Down's syndrome 91

Draguns, J.G. 169

Drama 360

Draw-A-Person Test (DAP), page 513

Dream 212

Dreikurs, R. 247

Dual career family 504, 505, 509

Dual relationship 850, 859, 884

Duncan's New Multiple Range Test, page 511

Durkeim, E. 106

Duty to warn 807, 884

Dyer, W. 258

Dynamic 454

Dysthymia 188

E

Eclectic counselor 255

Eclecticism 168, 225, 256

Economic conditions 117

Ectomorph 826

Education Act for All Handicapped Children, The 892

Educational Resources Information Center (ERIC) 792

Educational Testing Service (ETS) 767

Effect
    compensatory 572, 572
    contract 572
    Halo 782
    Hawthorne 779-781
    placebo 779
    pygmation 791
    Rosenthal 781
    Rosenthal/experimental 791

Egan, G. 397
Ego 2, 205, 207, 208
    defense mechanisms 146, 221
    ideal 220
    identity 73
    psychologists 2
    state analysis 482
Egocentrism 12, 65
Eidetic imagery 241
Eigenwelt 321
Electra Complex 49, 204, 218
Electrocardiogram (EKG) 294
Electroencephalogram (EEG) 294, 297
Electromyogram (EMG) 294, 295
Elkind, D. 8
Ellis, A. 80, 119, 316, 320, 338, 339, 342, 343, 347, 349, 351, 386
Emic 169, 172
Empathy 162, 253, 291, 388, 398, 399
Experimental research 701
Empiricists 52, 53, 55
Empty chair technique 361, 365, 368, 378
Encounter group 417
Endomorph 826
Energizer 460
Epictetus 316, 340
Epigenetic 10
Epistemology 66
Equilibration 92, 97
Equivalent forms 618
Erickson, M.H. 3, 4, 249
Erikson, Erik 1, 3, 4, 15, 17, 18, 24, 68, 73, 77, 78, 477
Eriksonian stage 7, 26, 29, 35
Eros 32, 206, 240
Error
    cognitive dissonance 165
    connotative 165
    Type I 721, 722, 724, 726
    Type II 721, 723, 725, 726
Ertl, J. 659
Ethical Standards Casebook 879
Ethics 423, 448, 450, 500, 709, 805-808, 811, 817, 819, 825, 841, 844, 849-865, 868, 878-880, 885-888, 894, 900
Ethnic 128

Ethnocentrism 132-134
Ethology 64
Etic 169, 171
Evaluation 701-800
Examination for Professional Practice in Psychology (EPPP) 821
Existential group 418, 474
Existentialism 201, 260, 315-324
Experimental
    group 710
    hypothesis 714
    neurosis 274
Extinction 275
    burst 277
Extroversion 245

F

Face validity 625
Faction 466
Factor analysis 701
Factorial Analysis of Variance, 510
Factorial experiment 750
Failure identity 330
Family
    constellation 258
    dual career 504, 505, 509
    sculpturing 482
Family Educational Rights and Privacy Act of 1974 834
Fear of death 35
Feedback
    Galvanic skin response (GSR) 295
Festinger, L. 120, 144, 197
Field
    occupational 519
    theory 412
Fisher, R.A. 712
Fixation 61, 81
Fixed 299
    action pattern 94
    role therapy 306
Flight from reality 155
Flooding 310
Folkways 123
Follower 461, 462
Foot-in-the-door obedience 129
Forced choice test items 605

Formal operations 45
Formative process research 790
Forward conditioning 271
Frankl, V. 167, 249, 315, 316, 320, 322, 325, 386
Free association 209, 213
Free choice test 604, 605
Freedman and Fraser study 129
Frequency polygon 744
Freud, S. 4, 14, 24, 32, 48, 49, 68, 82, 96, 106, 107, 201, 202, 204-206, 212, 214-216, 218, 222, 236, 244, 281, 386, 891
    stages 1
    theory 2
Freudian
    psychosexual stages 50
    stages 38
    theory 2, 36
Fromm, E. 244
Frustration-aggression theory 119
F-statistic 727
F-test 790
Fugue state 19
Fulcrum analogy 208
F-value 730

G

Galton, F. 641, 642
Galvanic skin response (GSR) 776
    feedback 295
Games 360, 362
Garland, Jones, and Kolodny 478
Gatekeeper 460, 463
Gauss, K.F. 741
Gaussian curve 741
Gazda, G. 366, 413, 495
Gelatt Decision Model 556, 557
Gender
    bias 510, 588
    disorder 91
    differences 37, 71
General Aptitude Test Battery (GATB) 583, 584, 675, page 513
Generativity 77
Generic certification for counselors 803
Genetic disorders 91

Genuine 366
Genuineness 290, 397, 430
Gestalt 55, 179, 386
Gestalt Therapy 167, 320, 365, 369-381, 386
Ginsburg, S. 515
Ginzberg, E. 515, 545-547
Girls 37
Glasser, W. 66, 268, 325, 330-335, 337, 338, 347, 350, 386
Global Assessment of Functioning (GAF) 870
Global measures 498
Goal setting 455
Graduate Record Examination (GRE) 628, 767
Grinder 367
Group
    advantage 493, 494
    affective education 413
    assertiveness training 418
    behavioral 418
    closed 425-427
    cohesiveness 412, 424, 432, 459, 466, 477
    content 411, 415
    control 710
    counseling 413, 430, 860, 896
    dynamics 453, 473
    development 473
    encounter 417
    goals 455
    grid 497
    guidance 413
    heterogeneous 431
    intervention 497
    IQ test 657
    length of sessions 447
    limitation 492
    marathon 419
    norms 409, 451, 452
    open 425-429
    primary 406
    process 415, 433
    product 434
    psychological education 413
    research 489-491, 496, 498
    risks 448, 449
    roles 460-465
    secondary 406, 407

self-help 419
sensitivity 417
size 445, 446
stages 473-481
structural exercise 414
T-group 411, 417
tertiary 406, 408
therapy 403, 310, 413
unity 459
work advantages 493, 494
work grid 497
work limitations 492
Groups 401-500, 896
Guidance (Parsons) 112, 124
Guidance group 413
Guide for Occupational Exploration
(GOE) 569
Guidepost 804
Guilford, J.P. 643
*Guilford-Zimmerman Temperament
Survey* (GZTS), 675, page 513

H

Habituation 594
Haley, J. 4, 249
Halo Effect 782
*Halstead-Reitan
Neuropsychology Battery*, page 513
Harlow, H. 27, 31, 54, 60, 80
Harmonizer 463
Harper, R. 343
Harris, T. 359
Hartley, D. 260
Havinghurst 68
Hawthorne effect 778-781
Heavy work 578
Hedlund Case 818
Heinz story 14, 75
Helping relationships 201-300
Here and now 369
Heredity 44
Herma, J. 515
Hersey, P. 469
Heterogeneous group 431
Hexagon 581
Hexagon model, page 508
Hierarchy of needs 88, 98, 125, 247,
518, 523

High order conditioning 293
Higher probability behavior (HPB)
296
Histogram, pages 505, 506, 755
HIV-positive clients 900
Holland, J. 185, 371, 512, 532-544,
557, 576, 577, 581, page 508
Holtzman Inkblot Technique (HIT),
page 513
Holophrase 127
Homework 346
Homogeneity 431
Hoppock, R. 544
Horizontal
intervention 486
relationship 319
sampling 793
test 617
Horney, K. 244
Hot seat technique 453
House-Tree-Person (HTP), page 513
Human growth and development 1-
100
Humanistic psychology 383
Humanists 88
Hume, D. 260
Hunn, Zimpfer, Waltman, and
Williamson 444
Hypothesis
alternative 714
Hysteria 94

I

I-Thou relationship 319
Id 2, 4, 205, 207, 210, 221
Identification 226, 233
Identity
crisis 73
ego 73
Idiographic studies 737
Immediacy 408
Impaired
helper 807, 826
practitioner 826
professional 807
Implicit 409
Implosive therapy 310, 320
Imprinting 85, 86

Incremental validity 626
Independent variable (IV) 701, 704, 707-709, 711
Individual Psychology (Adler) 201, 229, 238, 386
Inductive reasoning 797
Infant studies
    Gibson 51
    Lorenz 86
Informed consent 449, 850, 884
Inhibited 275
Initial stage 473, 476
Insight 213, 222, 239
    learning 376
Instincts
    Freud 2, 63, 107
    Lorenz 86, 107
    McDougall 107
Insurance 838, 842, 867, 869
Instrumental learning 264
Intelligence
    fluid 642
    quotient (IQ) 640, 644, 647-653
    test 6, 695
Inter-rater reliability 683
Intercultural counseling 101
Interest inventory 670-672, 676
Intermittent reinforcement 298, 299
Internal
    consistency 644
    verbalizations 339, 350
International Classification of Disease (ICD) 331, 866, 867
Interpersonal leaders 486
Interposition 307
Interpretation 237, 286
Inter-rater/inter-observer 634
Inter-rater reliability 683
Interrogator 461
Interval 299, 300, 773, 775
    scale 775
Intervention
    horizontal 486
    vertical 486
Intrapersonal leadership 486
Intrapsychic 898
Introjection 225, 234
Introspection 199, 217
Introversion 245
In vivo treatment 302

Ipsative 609, 611, 789
Irradiation 272
Irrational thinking 347
Isolates 465
Item difficulty index 697, 700
I-thou 319
Ivey 398

J

Jacklin 71
Jacobson, E. 295
Janov, A. 320
Jennings, 482
Jensen, A. 114, 659
Job 527, 559, 579
    clubs 598
    factors 511
John Henry Effect 762
Johnson, V. 308
Jones and Seagall 180
Jones, M.C. 282
Jung, C.G. 14, 73, 201, 211, 240, 241, 245, 246, 250, 251, 386
Justification 144
Juxtapose 572
Juxtaposition 572

K

Karpman's Drama Triangle 360, 459
Kegan, R. 95
Kelly, G.A. 306
Kendall's Tau 727, page 511
Kinetic Family Drawing (KFD), page 514
Klinefelter's syndrome 91
Kolberg L. 13, 14, 16, 19, 20, 21, 22, 23, 46, 68, 82, 96
    stage 75, 84
Kohler, W. 239, 376
KR-20 or KR-21 formulas 644
Krumboltz, J. 528, 553, 554
Kruskal-Wallis Test, page 511
    ANOVA 727, 796
Kuder Occupational Interest Inventory (KOIS), 582, page 514
Kuder, G.F. 582

Kuder-Richardson coefficients of equivalence 644
Kurtosis 770

L

Labor market 594
Laissez-faire 436, 437
Language differences 165
Latent 32
Law of effect 261, 280
Law School Aptitude Test 675
Lazarus, A. 4, 72
Leaders
  autocratic 486
  interpersonal 486
  intrapersonal 486
Learned 214, 263
Leisure time 508, 509
Leiter International Performance Scale (LIPS), page 514
Length of group counseling sessions 447
Leniency/strictness bias 573
Leptokurtic 770, page 504
Level
  confidence 718, 719
  occupational 520
  probability 716-720
  significance 716, 718, 719, 731
Levine and Campbell 134
Levinson, D.J. 26, 76
Lewin, K. 189, 412, 436
Libido 204
Licensure 801, 808, 809, 820, 821, 829, 831, 837, 842, 893
Life script 363, 364
Life-skills model 495
Life-style 258, 501-600
  definition 575
Light work 578
Likert scale 800
Likert, R. 800
Limitation 232
Linking 484, 485
Lippitt, R. 411, 436
Listening skills 160
Litigation 838
Little Albert 214, 276, 281, 283

Little Hans 214
Lloyd Morgan's Canon 703
Locke, J. 52, 260
Loevinger, J. 68, 532
Logos 240
Logotherapists 323
Logotherapy 167, 249, 260, 315, 323, 325, 386
Longitudinal study 788
Lorenz, K. 64, 83, 86, 107, 108
Lorge-Thorndike 656
Low probability behavior (LPB) 296

M

Maccoby 71
Maintenance
  actions 469
  role 468, 469, 471
Mandalas 241
Manifest 32
Mann-Whitney U-Test 727, 796, page 511
Marathon group 419
Marital satisfaction 87
Marriage and family therapists, page 516
Marriage rates 87
Maslow, A. 68, 88, 89, 98, 247, 523
Masochistic personality 359
Masters, W. 308
Matched design 796
Matching approach 511, 512
Maultsby, M., Jr. 325, 351
May, R. 201, 320
McDougall, W. 106, 107, 185
Mean 742, 744-747
Measures of central tendency 742
Median 742, 744, 745, 749
Medical College Admission Test (MCAT) 675
Medical model 875
Medium work 578
Meichenbaum, D. 345, 353
Menninger Clinic 14
Mental health consultation 881
Mental Measurements Yearbook 664

Merrill-Palmer Scale of Mental Health Tests 653
Mesokurtic 756
Mesomorph 826
Metaneeds 88
Middle-age (Erikson) 35
Mid-life career change 591
Milgram, S. 186, 187
Mill, J. 260
Miller, N. 280
Mind
    conscious 220
    unconscious 220, 248
Minnesota Multiphasic Personality Inventory (MMPI and MMPI-2), 605, 660, page 514
Minnesota Occupational Rating Scales 516
Minnesota viewpoint 262, 511, 516
Mistrust 79
Mitchell 366
Mitwelt 321
Modal 742
    personality 135
Mode 742, 744, 745, 751
Modelling 881
Momentum of compliance 129
Morality (Kohlberg) 10, 13, 14, 16, 19-21, 46, 47, 75, 82, 84
Morality 16, 20, 21, 82
Moreno, J.L. 185, 372, 403, 410, 482
Mores 123
Morgan, C. 544
Morgan, L. 703
Multicultural career counseling 593
Multicultural counseling 101, 103, 110, 163
Multiculturalism 514
Multiple
    baseline design 739
    regression analysis 794
    submission 850
Multimodal therapy (Lazarus) 4
Multivariate 736
Multivariate Analysis of Variance (MANOVA), 728, page 510
Murray, H. 247, 544
Musturbation 343, 344

Myers-Briggs Type Indicator (MBTI) 246, 654, 664, page 514
Myths 139

N

National Association For Social Work (NASW) 404
National Board for Certified Counselors (NBCC) 802, 803, 825, page 518
National Certified Career Counselor (NCCC) 803, 810
National Certified Counselor (NCC) 802, 810, 825, 839, page 518
National Certified Gerontological Counselor (NCGC) 803
National Certified School Counselor (NCSC) 803
National Counselors Examination (NCE) 674, 784, 821
National Defense Education Act 899
National Training Laboratories (NTL) 411
National Vocational Guidance Association 574
Naturalistic observation 777
Nature vs. nuture 40
Needs
    hierarchy of 247, 518, 523
Negative reinforcement 267
Negative reinforcer 292
Negligence 850
Neo-behavioristic 386
Neo-Freudians 244
Neopsyche 356
Neurolinguistic Programming (NLP) 367
Neurotic depression 188
Neutral stimulus 271
Newman-Keuls, page 510
Nominal scale 773, 774
Nondirectional test 790
Nondirective 285, 705
Nondirective counseling 382
Nonparametric 789, 796
Nonparametric tests 727, 773, 796, page 511
Noogenic neurosis 323

Norm 409, 451, 452
  cultural 121, 122, 125
  statistical 122
Normal curve 741
Normal Curve Equivalent Scale 784
Normative 789
Normative test 609, 610
Nosology 78, 331, 417, 866, 875
Null hypothesis 713, 721

O

Obedience (Milgram) 186, 187
Object permanence 57
Objective test 602-604
Obsessive-compulsive disorders
  (OCD) 310
Occam's Razor 703-705
Occupational
  fields 519, 520
  levels 520, 521
  sex segregation 587
Occupational Outlook Handbook
  (OOH) 371, 560, 565, 566, 568
Oedipus complex 48, 49, 204,   218
O'Hara, R. 515, 552
O'Hara, R.P. 512
One-tailed test 790
Ontology 324
Open group 425-429
Open-ended questions 312
Operant conditioning 264, 265, 292
Operational definition 795
Ordinal scale 773, 774
Ordinate 756, 758
Organ inferiority (Adler) 229, 238
Organismic theorists 52, 55
Organ box therapy 308
Orientation, professional 801-900
Osgood's Congruity theory 192, 193
Otis-Lennon School Ability Test
  (OLSAT) 656, page 515
Outcome research 491
Overt 302

P

Paradigm 285
Paradoxical

intention 315
interventions 858
techniques 249
Parallel
  forms 618
  transaction 487
Parameter 716
Parametric tests 727, 773, 793, 796,
  page 510
Paraphrasing 209, 328
Parapraxis 219
Paraprofessional 826
Parent, Child, Adult (P-A-C) 355
Parenthood 87
Parenting styles 522
Parroting 287, 314
Parsimon 702-705
Parsons, F. 83, 112, 124, 501, 511,
  512, 514, 890
Partial reinforcement 299
Pattern fixed-action 94
Patterson, C.F. 512
Pavlov I., 262, 265, 269, 272, 274,
  292, 293
Peabody Individual Achievement Test
  (PIAT), page 515
Pearson Product-Moment Correlation
  (r), 727, 740, page 510
Pearson Product-Moment Correlation
  Coefficient, page 506
Pearson r 727, 740
Peeping Tom 461
Peer conformity 30
Percentile rank 610, 715
Percentile score 784
Perfection 210
Period
  critical 85
Perls, F. 167, 320, 365, 370, 375,
  386, 453
Permanency of objects 58
Person-centered 382, 384, 705
Person-centered therapy 153
Person-environment theory 518
Personal therapy 444
Personalism 177
Personality
  ABC theory of 341, 342
  anal retentive 99
  Berne 202, 203

Freud 201, 202, 205, 207
    masochistic 359
    modal 135
    Roe 518
    theory 534
Personology 247
Phenomonology 324
Phenylketonuria (PKU) 91
Phi-Coefficient 733, page 510
Phobia 78, 281, 282
Photographic memory 241
Piaget J. 3, 5, 6, 11, 23, 65, 66, 67, 90, 92, 96
    developmental theory 56
    stages 5, 45
    theory 5, 7
Pica 94
Piers-Harris Children's Self Concept Scale, page 515
Placebo effect 779
Platykurtic distribution 770, page 503
Pleasure 210
Pluralism 182
Point Bi-Serial, page 510
Popularity 135
Portage, page 514
Positive
    addiction (Glasser) 333, 335
    punishment 267
    reinforcement 266, 289
    reinforcer 292
Power test 612, 613
Preconscious mind 220
Predictive validity 621, 626, 628
Prejudice 195, 196
Premack principle 296
Prenatal 42
Primal Scream Therapy 320
Primary
    group 406
    reinforcement 302
Privacy 832
Privileged communication 806, 812, 817, 832, 347, 849, 850
Pro bono 856
Probability level 716-720
Process 434
    consultation 882
    focused 415

research 491
Prochaska, J.O. 391
Proctor, Benefield, and Wrenn 891
Professional
    credentialing 802
    orientation 801-900
Prognosis 115
Program-centered
    administrative consultation 881
Projection 230
    technique 368
Projective test 662, 665, 694
Proxemics 111
Psychiatrists, page 516
Psychoanalysis 386, page 516
Psychoanalytic 281
Psychodiagnosis 1
Psychodrama 372, 403
Psychodynamic therapy 215
Psychological education group 413
Psychological needs theory 539
sychologist licensure 809
Psychologists 801, 822, 823, page 518
Psychology
    analytic 386
    developmental 895
    humanistic 383
    individual 386
    of personal constructs 306
    third force 383
Psychometric 661
    data 517
Psychopharmacology 1
Psychosexual stages
    Freud 1, 32, 36, 48, 49, 50
Psychosocial stages
    Erikson 1
Psychotherapy group 413, 421
Psychotic 421
Punishment 268, 311
Pygmalion effect 791

Q

Q-Sort 614
Qualitative change 52, 55, 90
Quantitative change 52, 53, 55

Quartile 786
Quasi-experiment 701

R

Racism 196
Rackets 363
Random sampling 793
Range 744, 761, 763
Ratio 299, 300, 773, 776
Rational-Behavior Therapy (RBT) 325, 351
Rational-Emotive 386
    imagery 325, 350, 351
    psychotherapy 80
    Therapy (RET) 181, 315, 316, 320, 338-341, 350, 386, 529
Rationalization 147, 224, 227, 228
Raw score 754
Rayner, R. 214, 281
Reaction formation 222, 231
Reactive schizophrenia 460
Reality Therapy 268, 325-327, 330, 331, 338, 386
Recency effect 573
Reciprocity 833
Recognition items 607
Recommendations 116
Reentry woman 592
Reflexes 265
Reframing 367
Registered Professional Counselor 836
Registry 836, 837
Reich, W. 308
Reinforcement 261, 266, 288
    back-up 293, 303
    continuous 298
    intermittent 298
    negative 267, 292
    partial 299
    positive 266, 289, 292
    schedule 299, 300
    secondary 302
Reinforcers 266, 292, 293, 302, 303
Reinforcing stimulus 271
Relativism
    cultural 142
Release of information 847

Reliability 619, 620, 623, 629, 630-638, 681, 760
    alternate forms 631, 632
    coefficient 635-639
    equivalent forms 631, 632
    inter-rater 683
    split-half 631-633
    test-retest 631
Repeated-measures design 796
Representational thought 57
Repression 222, 223
Research 701-800
    descriptive 778
    experimental 701
    formative process 790
    outcome 491
    process 491
    summative 790
Resistance 159, 213, 235
Respondent
    behavior 265
    conditioning 292
Response burst 277
Respression 223
Restructuring
    cognitive 345, 348
Resume 596, 597
Retirement adjustment 139
Retroflection 373
Reversibility 11
Rhesus monkeys (Harlow) 27, 31, 54, 60
Risky shift phenomenon 416
Robber's Cave experiment 194
Roe, A. 52, 185, 518-528, 534, 543
    maintenance 468, 469, 471
    self-serving 468
Roethlisberger and Dickson 780
Rogerian theory 381-391
Rogers, C.R. 83, 153, 244, 285, 382-391, 891
Role conflict 472
Role reversal 467
Rolfing 326
Rorschach Inkblot Test 524, 667, 685, page 515
Rosenthal effect 781
Rosenthal/experimental effect 791
Rosenthal, R. 544
Ross 185

Rotter Incomplete Sentence Blanks (Rotter ISB) 667, page 515

S

Salter, A. 185, 308, 462
Sample
 chester 793
  horizontal 793
  random 793
  stratified 793
Sarnoff and Zimbardo 197
Scapegoat 460, 464, 465
Scapegoating 451
Scattergram 762, pages 506, 507
Schachter, S. 188, 197
Scheffe's S Test, page 511
Schein 392, 882
Schema 7, 97
Schizophrenia 460
Schlossberg and Pietrofesa 195
Schlossberg's theory 551, 599
Scholastic Aptitude Test (SAT) 628
Schreber, D.P., 214
Score
 percentile 784
 standard 647, 766
 standard age 650
 T-score 766, 768
 Z-score 766,768
Screening (group) 420-423
Script analysis 364
Sculpturing 482
Seating arrangement 432
Secondary group 406, 407
Secondary reinforcement 302
Sedentary 578
Seesaw analogy 208
Segregation 113
Self
 actualization 89
 concept 548-550
 destructive behavior 206
 disclosure 157
 efficacy theory 570
 exploration 444
 help group 419
 instructional therapy 353
 reports 684
 serving roles 468
 talk 339
Self-Directed Search (SDS) 577, 580, page 515
Seligman, M.E.P. 81
Semantic differential 165, 166
Senile psychosis 78
Sensate focus 308
Sensitivity group 417
Sensitization 309
Sensorimotor 56, 79
Separation stage 473, 475
Sex role stereotyping 195
Sexual
 attraction/misconduct 841, 842, 852, 883
 harassment 852
Shadow 252
Sheehy 76
Sheldon 826
Sherif, M. 194, 198
Sibling rivalry 72
Signed-Ranks Test, page 511
Significance
 level of 716, 731
 test of 715
Silence 329
Simon, T. 643, 649
Simple linear regression analysis 794
Single blind study 738
Skewed distribution 748, 752, 753, page 504
Skinner, B.F. 40, 64, 260, 261, 264, 265, 267, 292, 311, 386
Sleeper effect 184
Slosson Intelligence Test (SIT), page 516
Social
 connectedness 248
 distance scale (Bogardus) 128
 exchange theory 136
 facilitation 183
 influence 395, 399
 learning 108, 553
 psychology 184, 185, 194
 skills 135, 138
 workers, page 518
Social and Cultural
 Foundations 101-200
Society 131

Sociogram 459, 482, 762
Sociologists, page 518
Somatic characteristics 105
Sour grapes rationalization 227
Spearman Brown formula 681
Spearman, C. 642
Spearman correlation 727
Spearman Rank-Order Correlation (rho), page 511
Spearman rho 740
Specificity 286
Speed test 612
Spillover 572
Spiral test 615
Spitz, R. 27
Split-half reliability 631-633
Spontaneous recovery 275
Stages 473-481
    Erickson 3, 17, 26, 68, 74, 77-79
    Freud 3, 38, 61, 68, 79, 82, 100, 243
    genital 3
    group (See Group stages)
    initial 473
    Kegan 95
    Kohlberg 23, 46, 75, 84
    Piaget 5, 23, 45, 56, 58, 65-67, 73, 79
    separation 475
    Sullivan 17, 18
    theorists 41
    transition 473
    working 473
Stagnation 77
Stampfl, T.G. 310, 320
Standard
    age score 650
    deviation 693, 744, 764-769, 771, 785
    error of measurement 679, 680, 799
    score 647, 766
Standard Aptitude Test 767
Standard Industrial Classification Manual (SIC) 565
Standard Occupational Classification Manual (SOC) 565
Standardization 787
Stanford-Binet Intelligence

Scale 645, 647-651, 655, page 516
Stanine scores 772
State laws
    counselor licensure 808
    governance 809
Statistic 716
Statistical information, page 502
Statistical Package for the Social Sciences (SPSS) 792
Statistical regression 786
Steiner, C. 363
Stereotyping 851
Stern, W. 647
Stimulus
    charged 271
    conditional (CS) 269-271, 275
    discrimination 273
    generalization 272, 273, 283
    neutral 271
    reinforcing 271
    unconditional (UCS) 269-271, 275
Stogdill 436
Storyteller 464
Stranger anxiety (Gibson 51)
Stratified sampling 793
Stress inoculation 353
Strong Vocational Interest Inventory (SVII) 371
Strong, E.K., Jr. 576
Strong-Campbell Interest Inventory (SCII) 576, page 516
Strong, S. 395
Structural differences 512
Structural theory 534
Structuralism
    Piaget 90
    Wendt 890
Structured goup exercise 414, 418, 453, 456, 458
Study
    cross-sectional 788
    double blind 739
    longitudinal 788
    single blind 738
Subgroup 466
Subjective test 602, 603
Subjective units of distress scale (SUDS) 219, 301
Sublimation 222, 224, 225

Success identity 337
Sue and Sue 200
Suicide 33, 34, 106, 373, 817
Sullivan, H.S. 244
Summarization 253, 336, 483
Summative research 790
Super, D. 512, 515, 548
Superego 2, 82, 205, 207, 210, 221
Superiority 242
Suppression 223, 224
Survey 778
Sweet lemon rationalization 227, 228
Sychronic method 788
Symbolic schema 7
Symbolism 212
Sympathy 291, 313
Symptom substitution 254
Synthetic validity 626
System of Interactive Guidance and Information (SIGI) 571, 595
Systematic desensitization
    Lazarus 4
    Wolpe 211, 301, 305, 307

T

Talk therapy 326
Tannenbaum's Congruity theory 193
Tarasoff case 114, 807, 818
Tarasoff versus the Board of Regents of the Univ of CA 807
Task
    action (Hersey & Blanchard) 469
    roles 468, 471
Taxonomy 417, 875
Technique
    empty chair 361, 365, 368, 378
    goal setting 455
    hot seat 453
    projective 368
    psychodrama 403
Temperature trainer 294
Terman, L. 699
Tertiary group 406, 408
Test 601, 602
    See reliability
    See specific name of test
    See validity

    achievement 614
    aptitude 666
    battery 617
    bias 668
    computer-assisted 689
    culture-fair 658
    cyclical 616
    equivalent forms 618
    F-test 790
    format 602-605, 609
    forced choice 605
    free choice 604
    horizontal 617
    nonparametric 773, 796, page 511
    normative 610
    objective 602, 603
    one-tailed 790
    parallel forms 618
    parametric 773, 796, page 510
    power 612
    projective 662, 665, 694
    reliability 629-639
    retest reliability 631, 632
    significance 715
    speed 612
    spiral 615
Test of Nonverbal Intelligence (TONI), page 516
Test of significance 715
Test-retest reliability 631
Tetrachoric Correlation Coefficient, page 510
T-group 411, 417
Thanatos 206
Thematic Apperception Test (TAT) 247, 524, 667, page 516
Therapeutic
    cognitive restructuring 348
    resistance 159, 213, 235
    surrender 154-156, 160
Theorists
    developmental 40
    stage 41
Theory
    See Author's name
    ABC theory of personality 341, 342
    ahistoric 791
    assimilation-contrast 158

balance 137
career 511
cognitive 353
cognitive dissonance 144, 148, 151
Conditional Reflex 462
control 326, 333, 350
counseling 301-400
culture-epoch 104
decision-making 552
developmental 40, 42, 43, 93
developmental career 545
fixed 412
Freud 2
Freudian 36
frustration-aggression 119
Osgood's congruity 192, 193
person-centered 153, 382, 384-386, 705
person-environment 518
personal 444
personality 534
Piaget development 56
psycho 413, 421
psychological needs 539
Schlossberg's 599
self-efficacy 570
Social comparison 197
social exchange 136
structural 534
Tannenbaum's congruity 193
topographical 217, 284
Therapeutic surrender 154, 156
Therapy 143, 181
    active 285
    ahistoric 791
    behavior 278
    biblio 343, 346
    client-centered 382, 387
    cognitive 352, 353
    conditioned reflex 308
    fixed role 306
    Gestalt 167, 365, 369-381, 386
    group 403, 410, 413
    implicit 409
    Logo 167, 249, 260, 315, 325, 386
    Orgone box 308
    personal 444
    personal-centered 382, 384, 705

person-environment 518
primal scream 320
psychodynamic 215
Rational-Behavior 325, 351
Rational-Emotive 181, 316, 339, 386, 529
Reality 325-327, 330, 331, 338, 339, 386
Self-instructional 353
Third
    cultures 130
    force psychology (Maslow) 88, 383
    party payments 869
Thorndike, E. 261, 280
Thorne, F.C. 256
Tiedeman, D. 512, 515, 552
Timing of interpretation 286
Top dog 365, 378
Topographic hypothesis 284
Topographical theory (Freud) 202, 217, 284
Torrey, E.F. 395
Training group 417
Trait-factor 386, 512, 513
Trait-factor approach 262, 511-515, 517
Transaction
    complimentary 358
    crossed 358
    ulterior 364
Transactional Analysis (TA) (Berne) 106, 179, 202, 203, 354-365, 386, page 508
Transference 159, 204, 213, 240, 347
    ambivalent 176, 451
    counter 257
Transition stage 473
Trend 689, 690
Trend analysis 782
Trial and error learning 280
Truax 366, 399
Trust 156
Trust versus mistrust 79
T-score 766, 768
t-test 6, 715, 727, 730, 790, page 511
Tuckman and Jensen 474
Tukey's HSD, page 511

T-values 730
Two-tailed test 790
Type I error 721, 722, 724-726
Type II errors 226, 721, 723, 725, 726

U

Ulterior transaction 364
Umwelt 321
Unconditioned 263
    response 269
    stimulus (UCS) 269-271, 275
Unconscious 219-221, 236
    conflicts 155
    mind 220
Underdog 365, 378
Underemployment 567
Unfinished business 376
Universality (group) 435
Unstructured (group) 418, 457

V

Validity 619-621, 629, 630
    concurrent 621
    construct 621, 624
    content 621
    convergent 627
    criterion-related 621
    differntial 510
    discriminant 627
    face 625
    incremental 626
    predictive 621, 628
    synthetic 626
Values
    class bound 165
    dependent (DV) 701,707, 708, 758
    independent (IV) 701,707,708, 709
Variable 299, 704, 744, 764
Variance 639, 764
Verbal tracking 394
Vertical intervention 486
Vertical test 617
Very heavy work 578
Vicarious learning 881

Vineland Adaptive Behavior Scale— Interview Edition, page 517
Violence 62
Visual cliff (Gibson) 51
Vivo 49
    aversive conditioning 304
    treatment 302
Vocalization in infants 127
Vocational guidance 506, 514
Vocational Guidance Bureau of Boston 890
Vontress, C. 125

W

Wage discrimination 586
Watson, J. B. 10, 214, 276, 281, 282, 891
Wechsler Adult Intelligence Scale-Revised (WAIS-R), 651-655, 693, page 517
Wechsler Intelligence Scale for Children-Revised (WISC-R/WISC-III) 652, 653, page 517
Wechsler Pre-school and Primary Scale of Intelligence-Revised (WPPSI-R) 652, 654, page 517
Wechsler, D. 544, 651
Wertheimer, M. 376
White 436
Wide Range Achievement Test-Revised (WRAT-R) page 517
Wilcoxon Matched-Pairs, page 511
Wilcoxon signed-rank test 727, 796
Williams, R. 659
Williamson, E.G. 262, 386, 511, 512, 516
Withdrawal designs 739
Within subjects design 796
Wolpe, J. 80, 211, 301, 305
Women
    reentry 592
    workers 502, 507
Workbook in Vocations 891
Working stage 473
World Health Organization (WHO) 867
Wrenn, G. 891, 897
Wundt, W. 890

X

X axis 756, 756, 757

Y

Yalom, 444
Yalom, I. 185, 320, 414, 424, 444, 474, 480
Y axis 756, 758
Yerkes-Dodson Law 301

Z

Zeigarnik, B. 376
Zimbardo 119
Z-scores 766-768

ABOUT THE AUTHOR

Dr. Howard Rosenthal is the author of the popular *NBCC and State Counselor Examination,* 2nd edition, audio series as well as the innovative book, *Not with My Life I Don't: Preventing Your Suicide and That of Others* and the companion tapes, *Suicide Prevention for Young People* and *Suicide Prevention: Crash Course for Counselors and Therapists.*

He is listed in the *National Directory of Distinguished Providers for Counseling and Development, Who's Who Among Human Services Professionals,* and *Who's Who in the Midwest.* In 1987 he was the recipient of Missouri's Wayne B. McCellend Award, given by the Police Juvenile Association for his work in crisis intervention, and in 1988 he was inducted into the St. Louis Community College Hall of Fame for his accomplishments.

Dr. Rosenthal received his master's degree from the University of Missouri at St. Louis and his doctorate from St. Louis University. He is a licensed professional counselor, a national certified counselor, and a certified clinical mental health counselor. Over 75,000 people have heard his mental health lectures. He has been a consultant and a guest on numerous radio and television shows. He has appeared as the expert in videos and movies, and has been quoted frequently in magazine and newspaper articles.

He is currently a private practice therapist at the Midwest Stress Center in St. Charles, Missouri, and teaches courses at St. Louis Community College at Florissant Valley and Webster University. He lives in St. Louis with his wife Patricia who is Executive Director for "Kids in the Middle," one of the nation's foremost treatment centers for children of divorced families.